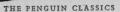

THE PENGUIN CLASSICS

FOUNDER EDITOR (1944–64): E. V. RIEU

PRESENT EDITORS:
Betty Radice and Robert Baldick

TITUS LIVIUS was born in 59 B.C. at Patavium (Padua) but later moved to Rome. He lived in an eventful age but little is known about his life, which seems to have been occupied exclusively in literary work. When he was aged about thirty he began to write his *History of Rome* consisting of 142 books of which thirty-five survive. He continued working on it for over forty years until his death in A.D. 17.

AUBREY DE SÉLINCOURT, scholar, translator and athlete, translated Livy's *The Early History of Rome* (Books I–V) and *The War with Hannibal* (Books XXI–XXX), *The Histories* of Herodotus and *The Life of Alexander the Great* by Arrian, all for the Penguin Classics. He was born in 1896 and educated at the Dragon School, Oxford, at Rugby, and University College, Oxford. A schoolmaster of genius for twenty-six years, he retired in 1947 to the Isle of Wight and devoted himself to writing. He also wrote for children, and his last book, a study of the civilized world in the fifth century B.C., was *The World of Herodotus*. Aubrey de Sélincourt, who was married, died in 1962.

ROBERT MAXWELL OGILVIE was educated at Rugby and Balliol College, Oxford. He was a fellow of Clare College, Cambridge, from 1955 to 1957 and of Balliol from 1951 to 1970. He is now headmaster of Tonbridge School. He is the author of a standard commentary on Livy Books I–V and, with the late Sir Ian Richmond, of a standard commentary on Tacitus's *Agricola*; in addition he has written books on Roman religion and on the influence of the classics on English life. His main interests are early Roman history and archaeology, and Roman Scotland.

LIVY

THE EARLY HISTORY
OF ROME

Books I–V of
*The History of Rome from its
Foundation*

TRANSLATED BY
AUBREY DE SÉLINCOURT
WITH AN INTRODUCTION BY
R. M. OGILVIE

PENGUIN BOOKS

Penguin Books Ltd, Harmondsworth, Middlesex, England
Penguin Books Inc., 7110 Ambassador Road, Baltimore, Maryland 21207, U.S.A.
Penguin Books Australia Ltd, Ringwood, Victoria, Australia

—

This translation first published 1960
Reprinted 1961, 1965, 1967, 1969
Reprinted with a new Introduction 1971
Reprinted 1973

—

—

Made and printed in Great Britain
by Hazell Watson & Viney Ltd,
Aylesbury, Bucks
Set in Monotype Bembo

CONTENTS

Dates have been added to the text at the top of each page. Those marked *c.* are historically reasonably accurate. Those given in brackets are purely conventional dates based on traditional Roman chronology.

References in the Introduction and at page-heads are to the Latin text of Livy.

INTRODUCTION

LIVY

LIVY (Titus Livius) was born at Padua in northern Italy in 59 B.C., or possibly 64 B.C.[1] We know little about his family background, except that Padua, a city famous for its moral rectitude, had suffered severely in the Civil Wars. Livy himself may have been prevented from going to the university in Greece, as most educated young Romans did, but he made a study of philosophy (according to the elder Seneca,[2] he wrote philosophical dialogues) and other traditional subjects. Nor does he seem to have aimed at a public career either at the bar or in politics; we have no record of his holding any office or engaging in public activity. Instead he devoted the course of a long life to writing his *History of Rome* which comprised 142 Books (35 are still extant) from the foundation of Rome down to 9 B.C. Most of his life was passed at Rome. His reputation brought him into contact with Augustus but there is little evidence of intimacy between the two men, except that about A.D. 8 he helped the young Claudius (the future Emperor) with his literary efforts.[3] Augustus, indeed, disapproved of Livy's outspoken treatment of the recent past (Tacitus says that he called him a Pompeian)[4] and a note in the summary of Book 121 states that that book (and presumably the remaining books which dealt with Augustus's principate) were not published until after the emperor's death in A.D. 14, for fear, we may assume, that they might give offence. Thus, although in touch with the seat of power, Livy retained an uninvolved independence. He was criticized by a contemporary, Pollio, for his 'Paduaness' (Patavinitas) – a provincial manner of speech.[5] It is notable that he is not referred to by any contemporary writer. He died at Padua, not Rome, in A.D. 17.

The first five books, which deal with the period from the foundation of Rome to the Gallic occupation in 386 B.C., were conceived and published as a whole. They have a unity of design and construction, with the Commission of Ten at the centre and Camillus' great speech, echoing the foundation of the city, at the end. The Preface is a preface

---

1. Jerome/Eusebius, *Chron. ad Ann. Abr.* 1958.   2. *Controversiae* X Praef. 2.
3. Suetonius, *Claudius* XLI. 1.   4. *Annals* IV. 34.   5. Quintilian I. 5.56.

to these five books and not to the complete work nor to the first book alone. Internal references, such as the closing of the Temple of Janus (I.19.3), suggest that Livy began his task in 29 B.C. and finished the five books by 27 B.C., but the version which we have is almost certainly a revised edition published in or after 24 B.C., because the excursus on Cossus (IV.20.5–11) with the reference to 'sacrilege' is an awkward addition which contradicts the narrative, and can only have been composed after Augustus had adopted the title of *Divi filius* 'son of god'. 29 B.C. is a plausible starting date. The Battle of Actium in 31 B.C. had brought an end to the Civil Wars. However uncertain the future might be, some security and stability had been restored to the world which might encourage a historian to take stock of the situation. It is no accident that the Greek historian Dionysius of Halicarnassus, who was to cover in his *History* the same ground as Livy, arrived in Rome in 30 B.C.

Livy, therefore, differed from the great majority of his predecessors in that he was not a public man: he did not turn to history as a recreation. For him it was life. We would not expect to find in him the crude political interpretations of history, discussed in the following section, which characterized the approach of earlier writers. Yet it would be a mistake to think of Livy's history as unconcerned with the problems of his generation. The difference between Livy and the others is that his philosophical detachment enabled him to see history in terms of human characters and representative individuals rather than of partisan politics. Livy accepted a tradition going back to Aristotle (especially in the *Rhetoric*) and to Thucydides which explained historical events by the characters of the persons involved. As Aristotle said, 'actions are signs of character'.[6] Because people are the sort of people that they are, they do the sort of things that they do, and the job of the historian is to relate what happens to the appropriate character. Equally, however, it follows that if similar characters occur in 500 B.C. and 20 B.C. their possessors will tend to act in a similar way, so that one can infer from what a man of a certain character did in 20 B.C. what a similar character must have done in 500 B.C. Human nature, Thucydides argued, is constant and hence predictable.[7] This philosophy helps to account for the readiness with which historians transferred events from the recent to the remote past (see below, p. 14) but Livy used it as the framework of his history. Instead of a barren list of unconnected events Livy constructs a series

6. *Rhetoric* 1367b.   7. I.22.4.

of moral episodes which are designed to bring out the character of the leading figures. Tullus Hostilius (I.22–31) is fierce (*ferox*) and the events of his reign are tailored to display that ferocity. In the same way Livy moulds the story of the Commission of Ten round the lust of Appius Claudius and the chastity of Verginia (III.36*ff*) or the stories of Veii and the Gauls round the piety of M. Furius Camillus. The last Tarquin was Proud and pride is the hall-mark of his reign.

This technique had a further advantage besides giving unity and shape to the narrative. It helped Livy to bring the tale alive. The climax of almost every moral episode is a short speech or dialogue uttered by the principal characters. It was a device used, for example, by Horace in his *Odes* to highlight the key moment of the story. But ancient literary criticism insisted that where an author composed a speech either in history or in oratory it should fit the character of the speaker. Thucydides was often criticized for the sameness of his speeches.[8] To achieve the right effect Livy deployed the whole range of the Latin language but the subtlety of his tones is inevitably lost in any translation, however good. Sometimes he sets out to recreate the great rhetorical effects of the orators of his youth, such as Cicero or Hortensius. When we read the speech of T. Quinctius (III.67–68), C. Canuleius (IV.3–5), Ap. Claudius (V.3–6) or Camillus (V.51–54) we can hear the thundering periods, the political clichés, the emotive vocabulary of the late Republic. For those men were statesmen and that is how statesmen speak. On other occasions he flavours brief utterances with colloquial, archaic or poetical language as the situation demands. The coarse impetuosity of Turnus Herdonius is caught in a single vulgar exclamation (I.50.9); Coriolanus's mother addresses him in tragic language with tragic thoughts (II.40.5). C. Laetorius speaks as a crude, blunt soldier (II.56.9). Horatius Cocles jumps into the Tiber with a thoroughly epic prayer (II.10.11). The list could be multiplied indefinitely and it is important to remember, while reading a translation, that to a Roman's ears each of Livy's characters would have sounded real because he was made to speak in a distinctive and fitting way.

Livy made history comprehensible by reducing it to familiar and recognizable characters, but the process was one which could not be divorced from his attitude to his own times and his vision of the future. In the Preface he asserts that the present state of Rome was the direct consequence of the failure in moral character of the Roman. 'I would

8. e.g. by Dionysius of Halicarnassus, *ad Pompeium* 3.20.

have [the reader] trace the process of our moral decline, to watch, first, the sinking of the foundations of morality as the old teaching was allowed to lapse, then the rapidly increasing disintegration, then the final collapse of the whole edifice, and the dark dawning of our modern day when we can neither endure our vices nor face the remedies needed to cure them.' It was a commonplace among Roman historians that things had got worse and worse; Sallust, for instance, blamed the destruction of Carthage and the capture of Greece for the start of the deterioration, because the one removed an enemy that had kept Rome on her toes, the other familiarized Rome with the enervating vices and luxuries of the Greek world.[9] You will find in the early books of Livy several pessimistic asides, e.g. (III.20.5): 'fortunately, however, in those days authority, both religious and secular, was still a guide to conduct, and there was as yet no sign of our modern scepticism which interprets solemn compacts, such as are embodied in an oath or a law, to suit its own convenience'.

Yet, on the other hand, there is also in Livy a sense of pride that Rome had now reached the zenith of her power and her achievement, and that all previous history was leading up to this glorious hour. Even in the Preface he speaks of Rome as 'the greatest nation in the world' and claims that her success has been such that she could legitimately claim to have a god (Mars) as her ancestor. So too Camillus's speech at the end of Book V is an inspiring panegyric of the rise of Rome and a promise of the still greater heights that lie ahead in the centuries to come. The culmination is in the present. 'Augustus Caesar brought peace to the world by land and sea' (I.19.3).

At first sight, then, there is a contradiction, an inner tension, in Livy's attitude to history and, in particular, to the place of his own generation. One can see exactly the same tension in Horace and Virgil between pessimism and optimism, between the evils of modern Rome and the dawning of a Golden Age. The resolution of this conflict lay, for Livy, in the education of character through the study of history, which, he says, 'is the best medicine for a sick mind; for in history you have a record of the infinite variety of human experience plainly set out for all to see; and in that record you can find for yourself and your country both examples and warnings; fine things to take as models, base things, rotten through and through, to avoid'. Livy's remedy – all will be well if people's characters improve – was his own; there is no question, as

9. e.g. *Catiline* 9.1–3; *Jugurtha* 41.2.

the facts of his relations with the emperor show, of his handing out some party line for Augustus. Nevertheless it is interesting that his diagnosis and solution correspond closely with that of other thinking Romans of his age. Virgil, who in the *Georgics* had stressed the harshness of nature and the deterioration of life, used the long pageant of Roman legend and history in the *Aeneid* to illustrate those qualities, especially *pietas*, that had made and could keep Rome great. Horace has the same message (*Odes* III.24, written about 27 B.C.): 'whoever shall work to put an end to impious slaughter and civic savagery, if he shall seek to be inscribed on statues as the patron of cities, let him be brave to rein in uncontrolled licentiousness. . . . What is the point of sad lamentations if sin is not pruned by punishment or of laws that are useless without morality.' Above all Augustus himself attempted by legislation and by propaganda to effect a change in Roman character. He introduced moral legislation in 28 B.C. (which he was forced by bitter opposition to withdraw) and undertook the restoration of 82 temples at Rome. At the same time he tried to popularize his ideals by giving them every publicity. In 27 B.C. he set up a golden shield in the Curia Julia commemorating his *virtus, clementia, iustitia,* and *pietas*. These and other virtues were constantly depicted throughout his reign on coins, public monuments and other objects that came to people's eyes.

There is, therefore, a real sense in which Livy's *History* was deeply rooted in the Augustan revival, despite stories that Livy's recitations from it at Rome were poorly attended. Its fame was immediate. There is a legend of a man who came all the way from Cadiz just to look at Livy.[10] And it quickly established itself as a classic, being accepted as such by Tacitus[11] and by the critic and rhetorician Quintilian.[12] It superseded previous histories so completely that only scattered fragments of them have survived. Its very size, however, deterred men from reading it all, so that at an early date abridgements of it were made. A senator, Mettius Pompusianus, had an anthology of speeches from Livy which earned him death at the hands of the Emperor Domitian,[13] and Martial refers in a poem to a 'pocket' Livy.[14] These abridgements, of which three survive in part or whole, meant that by later antiquity only the most readable and exciting books of the original were still in circulation. The great pagan senator, Q. Aurelius Symmachus, was

10. Pliny, *Letters* II.3.8.   11. Cf. e.g. *Agricola* 10.3.   12. e.g. X.1.101 *ff.*
13. Suetonius, *Domitian* 10.3.   14. *Epigrams* XIV.190.

responsible about A.D. 396 for a new edition of the first ten books, presumably because they evoked for him the finest spirit of classical Rome, and it is to this edition that we owe the survival of these books through the Dark Ages.

THE EVIDENCE

What sort of evidence did Livy have for the early history of Rome? It comes as something of a shock to discover that the first Roman to write about Rome's history, Q. Fabius Pictor (I.44.2), lived as late as 200 B.C., over three hundred years after the expulsion of the Kings. Pictor was followed by a succession of historians who covered the same ground, adding new information or offering new interpretations. Livy refers to some of them, such as L. Calpurnius Piso (I.55.9) who was consul in 133 B.C., C. Licinius Macer (IV.7.12) who was tribune of the *plebs* in 73 B.C., Valerius Antias (IV.23.1) and Q. Aelius Tubero (IV.23.1), probably the son of a friend of Cicero's. They all have certain features in common: they were, for the most part, statesmen who turned to the writing of history as a leisure pastime; they were not interested in historical research as such but were concerned to use history as a means of reflecting the issues and controversies of their own times. Pictor, for instance, who wrote in Greek during the troubled times of the Second Punic War, was concerned to display Rome as a city with a heroic past which could rival Athens and Sparta in its achievements and its civilization. Licinius Macer, who was a partisan of Marius, rewrote history to foreshadow the policies and events of the Marian regime. Although they were interested in antiquarian curiosities and made use of them to add originality to their work, as Licinius Macer discovered, and exploited some linen-rolls in the Temple of Juno Moneta giving the names of early magistrates (IV.7.12), they did not seriously investigate or question the credentials of the traditional version of Roman history which had become established by the time of Pictor. They took it on trust and embroidered it.

If, however, you examine in detail this traditional version as it is retold by Livy, you quickly discover that it is not a true record of the past. Many of the stories are not really Roman but Greek stories re-clothed in Roman dress. Even some of the most famous turn out on inspection not to be native memories. The twins, Romulus and Remus, sons of a god, exposed by the river, suckled by a wolf and discovered by a shepherd, are an adaptation of an old Near Eastern myth, found in Greece in the legend of Neleus and Pelias, sons of the god Poseidon exposed on the river Enipeus and suckled by a bitch and a mare (I.4.3*ff.*). The fatal quarrel between the twins culminating in Remus derisively vaulting Romulus's walls recalls similar Greek legends of Oeneus and Toxeus or Poimander and Leucippus (I.7.2). The treachery and fate of Tarpeia was a familiar Hellenistic motif (I.11.6*ff.*). Sometimes the debt is even more obvious. Two of the most notorious events of Tarquinius Superbus's reign are openly imitated from the Greek historian Herodotus – the lopping of the poppy-heads (I.54.6) was Thrasyboulus's message to Periander (Hdt. 5.92.6) and the infiltration of Gabii by Sextus Tarquinius (I.53.5) was suggested by Zopyrus's ruse against Babylon (Hdt.III.154). Sometimes events which were chronologically close in Greek and Roman history have become assimilated. The tyrants at Athens were expelled as a result of a love-affair in 510 B.C.; it is no accident that the Tarquins are similarly expelled about 510 B.C. as a result of a love-affair also. The heroic stand of the 300 Fabii at Cremera (II.50) in 479 B.C. echoes down to the smallest particular the fate of the Spartans at Thermopylae. Even Coriolanus (II.34*ff.*) acquires the deeds and character of Themistocles who, banished from Athens in 471 B.C., led his country's enemies against it. There is practically no extensive story from early Roman history which cannot be proved to be Greek in origin.

The Romans seem to have had no mythology of their own. They did not have the resources of oral epic or choral lyric by which the Greeks preserved and handed on the memories and myths of their pre-history. Nor were there substantial written records before the fourth century. At the beginning of his sixth book Livy writes that the majority of earlier records were destroyed in the fire which devastated much of Rome during the Gallic occupation in 386 B.C. This fire can be traced archaeologically and evidently destroyed many of the main buildings, such as the Royal Palace (Regia) in the Forum, where such records might have been kept. When, therefore, the Romans came to reconstruct their own history in the centuries before Pictor, they had to borrow heavily from Greek literature and legend.

They also re-used events from their own more recent history. It was one of the beliefs of the ancient world, first expressed by Thucydides, that human nature remains the same and, since men do the things that they do because they are the kind of people that they are, it was reasonable to expect that history would repeat itself in the past as well as in the future. Historians, familiar with the popular measures of the Gracchi, such as agrarian legislation and corn subsidies, assumed that similar tactics had been employed in earlier times. Hence they had no qualms about attributing these same measures to demagogic figures like Sp. Cassius (II.41) or Sp. Maelius (IV.13 *ff.*). If such a dangerous plot as the Catilinarian Conspiracy could occur in 63 B.C., there was every reason to suppose that many of its characteristic features would have occurred before, as in the plot by which Tarquinius Superbus gained the throne (I.47 *ff.*) or in the abortive coup by the sons of Brutus (II.3–5).

Yet the fact that most of the flesh and blood of Livy's narrative is fictitious should not lead one to doubt the bare bones. There were at least four ways by which authentic facts were transmitted to the fourth and third century when the Romans became interested in their own history.

In the first place, Rome's neighbours to the south included several Greek colonies. Cumae, for instance, was founded as early as *c.* 750 B.C. and enjoyed a flourishing civilization comparable with that of mainland Greece and far more advanced than that of Rome. Greek writers were interested in the fortunes of the remarkable little town on the Tiber. There were probably local histories of Cumae which included information about Rome, especially since the Tarquins took refuge there (II.21.5). But the writers of Greece proper also paid attention to Roman history. We know, for instance, that the historians Hecataeus of Miletus (*c.* 500 B.C.) and Hellanicus of Mytilene (*c.* 450 B.C.) made reference in their works to Rome, while a fragment of Aristotle survives to show that he had a detailed knowledge of the Gallic occupation in 386 B.C. A little later Timaeus of Sicily (*c.* 356–260 B.C.) gave a substantial account of Roman affairs in his *History*. The Etruscans, Rome's neighbours to the north (see p. 18), may also have had a historical literature but, if so, it has left no trace.

Secondly, there was a variety of contemporary documents which had lasted down to the first century B.C. The earliest surviving inscription, a religious law from the Roman forum, is at least as old as 500 B.C. but Roman historians cite several other inscriptions which no longer exist but which have every sign of being genuine. Dionysius of Halicarnassus, a Greek contemporary of Livy, refers to an archaic inscription concerning Servius Tullius' dedication of the Temple of Diana (I.45)[15].

15. IV.26.

Polybius, 150 years earlier, had seen a treaty between the Romans and the Carthaginians which he dated to 507 B.C.:[16] Polybius has been disbelieved but striking confirmation appeared in 1966, when parallel Punic and Etruscan texts, dating from about 500 B.C., were discovered on gold leaves in a temple at the little port of Pyrgi, a few miles north of Rome. The scholar Verrius Flaccus, also a contemporary of Livy, seems to have transcribed an inscription from Rome, giving a list of notables killed in a battle against the Volsci: this battle may well be connected with the wars of Coriolanus (II.35*ff.*). Livy himself mentions that the treaty made by Sp. Cassius with the Latins was preserved on a bronze column (II.33.9) and alludes to a monument, also described by Cicero (*Phil.* IX.4–5), commemorating the four Roman ambassadors executed by Lars Tolumnius, King of Veii (IV.17.6). Above all, the great code of Roman Law, the Twelve Tables, which contained a mass of information about the social, legal and political situation in the middle of the fifth century, was on public display and was memorized by generations of Roman school-children.

There were also records of a more regular kind. Every year from its foundation a special magistrate drove a nail into the wall of the Temple of Jupiter Optimus Maximus on the Capitol, probably as a means of averting plague. Later, enthusiasts came to count the nails, thereby establishing the date of the temple and so of the beginning of the Republic, if, as Polybius and Livy assert, the two events are connected – approximately 507 B.C. This practice is also known from the Etruscan town of Nortia but nail-fixing as a means of time-reckoning was common in Rome: Cicero speaks of an annual calendar with holes opposite each day, on which you marked the day by moving a peg into the appropriate hole, and fragments of such a calendar have actually been discovered.[17] The Roman religious year was complicated and its secrets were for a long time jealously guarded by a body of priests (*pontifices*). In order that the ordinary man might know which were holy days or special festivals and on what days he could conduct public or legal business, the *pontifices* annually erected a large whitened board outside the Royal Palace. On this they entered from time to time the events of special religious significance – the dates of festivals, the occurrence of untoward incidents (plagues, floods, eclipses, famines, triumphs, etc.), the census totals (I.44.2) and, probably, the names of the chief magistrates (praetors, as they were called at first; later, consuls) and

16. III.22.4–13.   17. *ad Atticum* V.14.1; *Notiz. Scavi* 4 (1928), 202*ff.*

priests. We do not know for certain what happened at the end of the year, but it seems likely that the principal items were transcribed into a book-roll to provide a body of precedents to help the *pontifices* with the maintenance of religion and that the board was then rewhitened for the following year. Despite Livy's assertion (how could he have known?) that most of what was in the Commentaries of the Pontifices perished in the fire of 386 B.C. (VI.1.2), it is clear that in fact much of it survived. The mass of petty detail which is recorded for the fifth century B.C. could not conceivably have been invented by imagination alone, and when a Pontifex Maximus, P. Mucius Scaevola, who had been consul in 133 B.C., made these records (called the *Annales Maximi*) generally available by publishing them, he seems to have included material going back to the Regal period.

Thirdly, the Romans were conservative in their institutions. It is notable, for instance, that the festivals which still ranked as major occasions in the religious year in the first century B.C., were those which had been established at least four hundred years earlier. Many of them, e.g. the Robigalia (concerned with blight), belonged to a primitive agricultural community and were quite inappropriate to a busy, commercial city; many of them had become quite unintelligible. But they were still maintained. So too the cumbersome electoral and legislative system devised by Servius Tullius (I.43) – the *comitia centuriata* – remained the same with elaborations and refinements in Cicero's day. A scholar studying the religious and constitutional arrangements of his own time could validly work back from them to a picture of Roman society in the first years of the Republic.

Finally we should not underestimate the strength of memory. It is easy to believe that individual families would hand down the traditions of their own past, how the Fabii defended Cremera (II.50), how the Claudii migrated to Rome (II.16.4), how the Papirii served religion or how the Quinctii had provided a saviour of the state in Cincinnatus (III.26). Equally there were events of national importance that would impress themselves on public consciousness, such as the unification with the Sabines (I.13.8), the foundation of Ostia (I.33.9), the expulsion of the kings (I.60) or the war with Veii (V.1*ff.*).

The job of the historian is to separate fiction from fact and, on the basis of the available facts and with the help of such tools as archaeology, to reconstruct the story. In the following section a brief attempt is made to outline the history of early Rome, so far as it can be recovered, and to show how far it is imbedded in Livy's romantic narrative.

THE HISTORY

Traditionally Rome was founded in 753 B.C. but even in antiquity there had been many variant dates proposed, ranging from 814 to 729 B.C., before Atticus and Varro established a conventional chronology. Apart from some short-lived Chalcolithic and Bronze Age settlements (perhaps corresponding to the legends about the Aborigines; see I.1.5), the first substantial habitation at Rome dates from the Iron Age. Unfortunately, the archaeologists still disagree radically about its date; Müller-Karpe would put it as early as the tenth century whereas Gjerstad favours a date around 800 B.C. What is clear, however, is that there were two separate and distinct settlements, one on the Palatine and one on the Esquiline, almost from the beginning. The burial customs and the pottery styles of the two settlements are quite different. It seems probable that the site of Rome, with easily defended hills, at a convenient crossing of the river Tiber and with good pasture, attracted two separate groups of graziers from the Alban and the Sabine mountains down to the lusher coastal plains. There is, therefore, substance in the legend of the foundation from Alba Longa (I.3.4) and of the fusion between the Romans and the Sabines (I.13).

Early Rome was primarily a pastoral community. Its inhabitants built their huts on the tops of the hills and during the daytime led out their flocks and herds into the surrounding country. The groundplans of some of these early huts (one of which, the *casa Romuli*, was preserved as a museum piece down to the Empire; see V.53.8) have been recovered and we can form an idea of what they looked like from urns, made in the shape of huts, in which the ashes of the dead were stored. The earliest inhabitants were a branch of the Italic people, an Indo-European tribe that had spread over Italy during the second half of the second millenium B.C.

The advance of Rome, however, was due to the expansion of her mysterious neighbours to the north, the Etruscans. Some time, perhaps in the tenth century, groups of migrants, probably from the Balkans, arrived by sea in North Italy. Some of them came up the Adriatic and settled in the Po Valley (e.g. at Spina and Bologna), others came round the bottom of Italy and settled on the west coast at Tarquinia and other places. Both groups share a distinctive custom of burying their dead in two-storied urns which is obviously related to the great Urnfield cultures of Roumania that flourished from about 1600 B.C. In Italy this culture, which absorbed the native population, is called Villanovan. The Villanovans were reinforced about 700 B.C. by a new wave of immigrants, probably displaced from Asia Minor by the troubled conditions of the Cimmerian invasions. The new arrivals brought with them many fertile ideas, including a taste for Greek and Phoenician artistic styles, new techniques for working metals, an aptitude for building proper cities rather than untidy villages, Near Eastern religious customs and, it seems, a sophisticated non-Indo-European language, preserved in numerous inscriptions but not yet fully understood, which we call Etruscan. This mixture of elements transformed the Villanovans into the Etruscans, from a simple, agricultural people into an urban nation of craftsmen and traders, with a network of cities that stretched from the Po to the Tiber. It is, also, against this background that we should understand the legends of Antenor and Aeneas – refugees from Troy in Asia Minor who settled in the Po Valley and Latium respectively. Aeneas was from very early times a favourite subject for Etruscan artists. The legend of his carrying his father Anchises out of Troy is frequently portrayed in the later sixth century by Etruscan statuette- and scarab-makers.

The Etruscans were enterprising and outward-looking. They sought markets for their metal-work (there are large deposits of iron and copper in Etruria and on Elba) and for their pottery, and in return imported luxury goods from Greece, Egypt and Phoenicia. It was, therefore, inevitable that they should open a land-route to the Greek cities of Campania and Southern Italy. The easiest routes lay a few miles up-stream from Rome where there are good crossings of the Tiber at Fidenae (near Veii) and Lucus Feroniae. The road then led southwards past Praeneste, between the Apennines and the Alban Hills, to join the line of the Via Latina and on to Campania. But the site of Rome had other attractions. It was the last point before the sea where the Tiber could conveniently be crossed and so it gave access for the Etruscans to the rich plains of Latium. More important, salt was an essential commodity in the life of the great Etruscan cities inland and it could only be obtained at the big salt-beds at the mouth of the Tiber. The salt-road, called by the Romans the Via Salaria, led from these salt-beds, through Rome and so up the Tiber to cities such as

Volsinii, Clusium and Perugia. Rome thus grew from an agricultural community into a major commercial entrepôt.

It is difficult to date the first infiltration of the Etruscans into Rome exactly. Livy gives a dramatic story of the migration of Lucumo, the grandson of an exiled Corinthian Demaratus, with his family from Tarquinia to Rome, where, taking the name of L. Tarquinius, he managed to seize the throne on the death of Ancus Marcius *c.* 625 B.C. (I.34.2). The story is largely Greek romance but some features of it are true. There is good evidence that Corinthian exiles settled in Etruria in this period, ousted by the policies of the tyrant Periander; it is equally likely that the Tarquin family had connections both with Tarquinia and with its neighbour Caere where they eventually took refuge (I.60.2) and where a remarkable tomb, containing fifth- to third-century inscriptions of the Tarcra family, was found in 1850; it is also clear that from about 625–600 B.C. Etruscan influences can be detected in Roman pottery and in such engineering works as the draining of the marsh where the Forum was later built. But it will not have been an adventurous *coup d'état*. Rather, small groups of Etruscans, from different cities, will have moved into Rome and set up their own communities until the population of Rome became thoroughly mixed and integrated one in which the superior skills and abilities of the Etruscans predominated. This can be shown by the fact that the names of a very large number of Roman families in the Republic are Etruscan in etymology, e.g. the Sempronii, the Licinii, the Minucii, the Volumnii, the Larcii, the Herminii, and so on.

The earliest government of Rome comprised a king with military, religious and political power, a council (senate) of elders (*patres*) drawn from the chiefs of the leading families, and a consultative assembly constituted on a federal basis from the various parishes (*curiae*), where the different ethnic units lived, and called the *comitia curiata*. When, however, between about 600 and 575 B.C. the Etruscan element obtained the upper hand a number of significant changes were made. The city was unified by creating a single, central market-place, the Forum, and locating there certain communal buildings such as the shrine of Vesta and the Royal Palace. The king was invested with distinctively Etruscan regalia, special clothes and a ceremonial chair (*sella curulis*) which survived as symbols of Roman magistrates (I.8.3). The primitive religion which had been concerned chiefly to secure the successful operations of natural processes developed into an anthropomorphic religion on the Greek pattern; many new religious practices, such as augury and divination, were introduced now. The emphasis turned from pastoral to arable farming. Above all the distinction between ethnic groups which had survived under the curiate system was dissolved by creating three tribes, Ramnes, Tities and Luceres (the names are Etruscan), which were not based on residence or ethnic origin. For the first time the inhabitants of Rome became one people: they were Roman citizens. Later Romans had some awareness of this, as one can see from Livy (e.g. I.45.3) but there was an irresistible tendency to attribute most of the characteristic political and religious institutions to the very first kings Romulus and Numa (I.7.21).

Once Rome had become a city, it became vulnerable and had to defend itself. Standing crops are easier to plunder than elusive cattle; fine buildings enriched with silver and terracotta offer a more tempting target than thatched huts. The earliest ditch defences of certain weak parts of the city may date from about 540 B.C. although the earliest earth-wall seems not to have been constructed before about 480 B.C. and the so-called Servian Wall belongs to the period after the Gallic occupation (I.44.3). We know nothing about the organization of the earliest Roman army but in the first phase of Etruscan influence at Rome it will have relied heavily upon a cavalry formed from the leading and wealthier elements in the city, supported by a loose array of more or less lightly armed infantry. These had been the tactics of earlier Greece and seem to have been standard in the contemporary Greek cities of Italy, such as Cumae, and in Etruria. The accounts given of the Battle of Lake Regillus (*c.* 496 B.C.; see II.19–20), although much embellished with Homeric touches, as Macaulay noted, show that this method of fighting was still prevalent at that date among the Latins; for the decisive role of the cavalry in the battle is proved by the dedication of a temple to Castor and Pollux, the patron deities of horsemanship, in the Roman forum (II.20.12). But in mainland Greece an epoch-making change had occurred. Argos, about 670 B.C. was the first state to adopt a new system which relied upon a solid phalanx of well-drilled, well-armed infantry. The fashion quickly caught on and by 600 B.C. most of the Greek cities relied on infantry (hoplites as they were called) rather than cavalry which remained select and aristocratic but less effective. The change reached Rome in the middle of the sixth century; there is plenty of evidence, from the armour found in tombs to sculptured reliefs, to show that Rome, in common with most Etruscan cities, adopted some form of hoplite tactics between 570 and 540 B.C.

The change had profound consequences. A hoplite army has to be recruited from the richer classes because the armour is comparatively expensive and the tactics require leisure for drill and practice. Recruitment, therefore, has to be on the basis of wealth. This involved a reorganization of the Roman citizen-body. By a constitution unanimously attributed to King Servius Tullius, whose traditional dates are 578–535 B.C., the adult male citizen population was assessed into two groups, one which possessed the minimum hoplite qualifications (*classis*) and the other which fell below that minimum (*infra classem*). The *classis* was subdivided into a number of centuries or bodies of 100, and supplied the manpower for the Roman legion. The qualifying amount is unknown. It must have been calculated in terms of property, cattle, goods, etc. since coinage was a very late arrival in Rome and *pecunia*, the Latin word for money, originally meant 'cattle' (cf. *pecus*). A further corollary was to make residence rather than birth the condition of citizenship so that many of the resident immigrants, who had previously been ineligible, could not be enrolled by the censors as citizens and hence as potential soldiers. Servius Tullius, therefore, replaced the three tribes by a tribal system based on residence, dividing the city into four and creating additional tribes to cover the country-districts. Such a system could be expanded as Rome's territory grew. The Roman historians were aware of these reforms although the document which Livy quotes, with the five classes, represents a much later elaboration of the Servian constitution (I.43).

Rome's new army gave her an advantage over her Latin neighbours. Indeed a policy of expansion seems to have been followed by Servius Tullius and his successor. Livy has glamorous tales about Rome heading a Latin alliance (I.45.3) and attacking cities as far away as Gabii, Ardea and Suessa Pometia. The tradition is often doubted but there may well be truth in it. The treaty with Carthage, recorded by Polybius (see above, p. 15), names several cities including Ardea as being in the Roman sphere of influence. Moreover the cult of Diana, established by Servius Tullius in the Aventine (see above p. 14) was directly modelled on the cult of Artemis at Ephesus. The latter was a federal cult, the centre of a league of Ionian Greek cities. We must assume that Servius Tullius intended his cult of Diana to serve the same purpose of marking Rome as the head of an alliance. By 510 B.C.

it can be argued that Rome had some sort of control over most of the Latin coast as far south as Tarracina (Anxur) and most of the left bank of the Tiber as far up-river as Caenina.

In 507 B.C. the form of government at Rome changed. The kings were expelled and replaced by a college of two annual magistrates, either immediately or after a short interval during which power was exercised by a single annually elected magistrate (the *praetor maximus*) assisted by subordinates. The date and cause of the change have been much discussed. The traditional Roman date, as implied by Livy's figures, was approximately 510 B.C. but this results from assimilation with the expulsion of the Pisistratids, the tyrants of Athens. It has for some time been fashionable on the Continent to down-date the expulsion of the Tarquins to the early or middle fifth century, because after about 475 B.C. there is archaeologically a marked decline in Etruscan influence at Rome and a falling-off of imports. There is little to commend this theory which rests on a mistaken assumption about the nature of the change. Whatever its cause, the expulsion of the Tarquins was not a revolt by the Latin population of Rome against the Etruscan immigrants. After the kings Rome remained as much an Etruscan city as before. Etruscan families still held prominent places; the dual magistracy is an Etruscan institution (*zilath*); the insignia of the consuls are entirely Etruscan in origin (*fasces*, for instance, have been found at Vetulonia); religion continued Etruscan in form and idea. For by 500 B.C. Rome had become an ethnically integrated city. Three things strongly support the traditional date. Roman annalists preserve a list of 'consuls' that stretches back to about 507 B.C. Many of the names in this list are of families which later disappeared entirely or were of little importance. It is difficult to see how such a list could have been forged in the fourth or third centuries. It must represent authentic names either extracted from the Board put up outside the Royal Palace (I.56.4) or compiled, separately, like the Linen Books, containing the names of magistrates, found by Licinius Macer in the Temple of Juno Moneta and covering the period from about 445 B.C. onwards (IV.7.12). Secondly, recent research has tended to confirm the authenticity of the Carthaginian treaty recorded by Polybius under 507 B.C. which names *praetors* (ὕπατοι) but not a king: the spheres of influence defined for both Carthage and Rome only fit this period and Carthaginian interest in the area has been confirmed by the Pyrgi inscriptions (see above p. 15). Thirdly, a date as late as 470 and 450 does not leave enough time for the political evolution of Rome which can be re-constructed during the fifth century.

If Livy's date, therefore, is approximately correct, it is less easy to establish the cause. The story in Livy is a melodrama (I.57–60) of a charming Hellenistic kind. Equally improbable, as we have seen above, is the theory that it was a revolt against the Etruscans as such. It may have been the result of foreign intervention. Lars Porsenna of Clusium certainly campaigned in Latium during the period 507/6–505, and the defeat of his army at Aricia (II.14.7) was probably recorded by the Greek historians of Cumae. Roman patriotism pretended that he failed to conquer Rome but the truth seems to have survived in a few sources despite the official version. Lars Porsenna *did* capture Rome and he may well have decided to set up a puppet government. This, however, pre-supposes that there was a body of people in Rome who were opposed to the Tarquins and the real reason for the change of government may, therefore, lie in political and social factors. The experience of Greek cities was that the introduction of a hoplite army heightened the political awareness of the richer classes. They had to provide the soldiers for the citizen-army and, in consequence, claimed an increasing say in how that army was to be used and how the state was to be run. The centuriate organization of Servius Tullius was primarily a military reform but it was also used as the basis for an electoral and legislative assembly – the *comitia centuriata* – which largely replaced the older curiate assembly. Just as in Argos, Corinth, Mytilene and elsewhere the tyrants were deposed in favour of some form of democracy during the sixth century B.C., so at Rome the kings had become an anachron-ism. This is true, whether the last Tarquin was as Proud as Livy paints him or whether he was a conscientious, patriotic and successful monarch.

At all events the start of the Republic coincided with troubled times for Rome and Latium. The hegemony which the Tarquins had built up collapsed in the face of Porsenna's invasions and revolts of the Latins. The picture of chaos and insecurity is confirmed by an episode at this time which was never incorporated into the Roman historical tradition. An Etruscan wall-painting from Vulci depicts a man called Mastarna rescuing a comrade Cneies Vibenna, while another shows the death of Cn. Tarchunies the Roman. This Etruscan tradition was known to the Emperor Claudius who refers to it in an extant speech.[18] It must have

18. *Inscriptiones Latinae Selectae* 212.

23

been a brief exploit by an Etruscan adventurer who seized Rome for a short while in the confusion following the expulsion of the Tarquins. Like the humiliating success of Porsenna it was hushed up by the late Roman historians. Another indication is the activity of the Sabines, a hill people to the north-east of Rome. They seem to have taken advantage of the prevailing conditions and moved down the left bank of the Tiber, plundering and capturing as they went. There are trustworthy notices of Roman encounters with the Sabines in the years following 505 B.C. (II.16 ff.). Moreover Livy records the settlement of the Claudii, a Sabine family, in a newly acquired stretch of territory across the Anio (II.16.5) and the creation of two new tribes in that area in 495 B.C. (II.21.7). Even if the specification of the Sabine settlers as Claudii is false (for the Claudii, although Sabine in origin, were probably established in Rome much earlier), the detail about the new settlements and tribes is undoubtedly historical and reflects contemporary upheavals and movements of population.

The climax came when Rome found herself threatened by a league of Latin states whom she had once dominated, led by Tusculum, Aricia and Lavinium. She took the offensive and defeated them in a decisive battle at Lake Regillus near Tusculum (II.19–20). This battle proved the superiority of hoplites over cavalry. It was commemorated by a shrine of Castor and Pollux which has been proved to have been built in the early fifth century. It restored Roman control of Latium and was followed up by a treaty, recorded on bronze (II.33.9), which recognized Rome's mastery and settled the pattern of Rome's expansionist methods for centuries to come. Livy's account of the following fifty years is almost monopolized by a series of petty and inconclusive wars with hill-people, the Aequi, the Volsci and the Hernici, who harassed Rome's frontiers and threatened to overrun the coastal plain of Latium. Its centre-piece is the legendary tragedy of Coriolanus, who led the Volsci to the gates of Rome. Such wars have left little mark archaeologically but we can detect the incursion of the Volsci by a number of archaic inscriptions in the Volscian language which have been found for instance at Tarracina and Velitrae. The pressure by the hill-people at this date fits the historical situation. So long as the Etruscans had a lively interest in the south, they maintained a strong communications corridor from Etruria through the Praeneste gap down to Campania, which effectively isolated the hill-people from Latium; but a series of crushing defeats, notably at Cumae in 474 B.C. at the hands of the

Syracusans, forced the Etruscans to withdraw to Etruria proper and allowed the Aequi and Volsci to encroach on Latium just as it allowed the Samnites to overrun Campania. Rome with the help of her Latin allies gradually stabilized the situation but it would have meant annual campaigns and a war of steady attrition. The constant military activity in the fifty years from 505 to 455 only helped to exacerbate the problems which were already arising in Rome itself.

The social and economic evolution which led to the kings being replaced by consuls had other and more serious consequences. It did not so much matter when ultimate authority rested with a king that the poorer classes had no voice and few rights because the rich were not that much better placed; but the centuriate organization gave a definite say to one body of citizens, perhaps 10,000 out of a probable adult male population of between 30,000 and 60,000, and denied it to the rest. The poor may not have been concerned to have any part in government, but in hard times they did need some safeguards against the law which, being unwritten, was interpreted and controlled by *pontifices* and magistrates and was ultimately made and supervised by the centuriate assembly. And times were hard. The constant warfare damaged agriculture; the collapse of Etruscan power affected trade. In addition there is ample evidence that Latium was hit by a series of plagues in the first part of the fifth century and manpower may have been further debilitated by the advent of malaria. One sign of this is the dedication of several temples, for the purpose of religion is to secure the goodwill of the gods in the operation of nature. Temples were built to Ceres, a corn-goddess, in 493 B.C., to Saturn, a blight-god in 496 B.C., Mercury, a god of trade, in 495 B.C., and Apollo, a god of healing, in 433 B.C. (there had been an earlier cult): the dates are mostly confirmed archaeologically. The clearest evidence is the steady decline of imported pottery from about 500 B.C. to 450 B.C. Debt thus became endemic, aggravated by the absence of money, for a farmer could not pay his debts in corn if he had no corn to pay. Rome had a particularly harsh procedure for debt (*nexum*) whereby a debtor, either voluntarily or compulsorily, transferred his body (his services) to his creditor in return for a loan. By becoming in effect a bondsman, he had no real means of earning the wherewithal to repay the debt. The procedure was incorporated in the Twelve Tables and is vividly described by Livy (II.23).

The depressed state of the poor classes, craftsman and peasant farmer alike, led to great bitterness at Rome. The poor felt that they were helpless at the hands of the powerful, even though Roman society was organized in such a way that many of the poor were under the moral protection (as *clientes*) of a patron whose duty was supposed to be to look after their interests in return for their support. In Livy this conflict, the Struggle of the Orders, as it has come to be called, is identified with a conflict between two social groups, the patricians and the plebians. The patricians originally were simply the descendants of the early *patres*, the heads of families who formed the senate. They enjoyed certain exclusive and important religious privileges: for instance, on the death in office of the magistrates, the residual power of the state devolved on them; certain offices, such as the Priesthood of Jupiter, were open only to them. They were the hereditary aristocracy. The distinguishing features of the plebeians have never been satisfactorily explained. They can hardly be identical with those who were too poor to qualify for the centuriate organization (*infra classem*), because in late history many of the great families that played a prominent role in the first decades of the Republic, such as the Cassii and the Verginii, were certainly not classified as patrician but as plebeian. Such families had presumably migrated to Rome later than the original selection of *patres* or the increase attributed to king Tarquinius Priscus. Yet the first watch-dogs of the poor were almost certainly called the tribunes of the *plebs*. The problem of the plebeians has not been solved – like 'Tory' it may have changed and evolved in meaning as so many political words do – and the distinction between patrician and plebeian is probably irrelevant to the understanding of the history of the first five books of Livy. What mattered was the gulf between the privileged and the underprivileged. In their search for remedies the plebeians turned naturally for inspiration to their Greek neighbours in the south, because they had more democratic institutions and a more developed system of public justice. It is significant that the cult of Ceres, which attracted the special devotion of the plebeians, was derived from Cumae.

The prime need was protection against oppression. The Roman historical tradition records that in 494 B.C. the *plebs* went on strike and elected two officers of their own body called tribunes. The number was increased to four in 471 B.C. The tribunes had no constitutional power. Their power stemmed from the resolution of their fellows to rally to their aid, using force if necessary. Any Roman, threatened with legal proceedings, conscription or other oppressive acts, could run to a tribune and invoke his protection. In the face of such defiance the rich could do little. The tribunate by itself was only a last resort for the desperate and did not go far towards healing the real ills of society. These required more radical treatment. The agitation continued until in 451 B.C. the government agreed to set up a Commission of Ten to draw up a code of laws (III.33.3). The commission has been greatly written up by the historians. The visit to Athens to study the law of Solon (III.32.1) and the melodramatic story of Verginia (III.44*ff*.) are doubtless later accretions, but the Twelve Tables were set up and their surviving contents fit them firmly in the middle of the fifth century. It is hard to know how far they merely codified existing laws and how far they instituted reforms. Greek influences suggest that the law-givers consulted the codes of neighbouring Greek states which should mean that they were prescribing as well as describing the laws. Changes, for instance, in the debt-law, in the summary jurisdiction of the magistrates and in the right of trial before the *comitia centuriata* seem clear. But the chief value of the Twelve Tables, together with the simultaneous publication of the religious calendar containing the dates of festivals, etc., was that it made justice open and equitable. It listed all the things that could and could not be done, down to petty regulations about wills and funeral expenses. It did not cure Rome's economic or political ills but it restored confidence within the community.

This confidence was soon to be tried. While the wars on Rome's southern frontiers still continued, necessitating an increase both in the Roman army and in the number of supreme commanders (the consular tribunes; IV.7.1), a new and much more dangerous threat had arisen to the north. Nine miles from Rome lay the rich and impressive city of Veii which spread over a tongue of land nearly seven miles in circumference. The site is a fine one and recent excavations, especially by the British School of Archaeology at Rome, have added greatly to our knowledge of it. Veii commanded the right bank of the Tiber, with a bridgehead on the left bank at the rocky citadel of Fidenae to guard the crossing, and from it a great network of roads spread out to all the other cities of south Etruria. It was in a real sense the gateway to Etruria. Veii's wealth went back to Villanovan times. It was based partly on farming, partly on its situation as a trading centre with access to the salt-beds on the coast, and partly on its manufacture of terracotta. Veian artists were commissioned to make the statues for the temple of Jupiter Optimus Maximus at Rome and some magnificent examples of their art have been discovered at Veii itself. But Rome and Veii were too close. They could not expand without coming into conflict. There had been earlier engagements, notably the Roman defeat at Cremera in 479 B.C., but the main struggle belongs to the second half of the century. Rome seems to have taken the initiative, but whether this represents a political victory for the plebeians against the nobles who may have had ties with the nobility of Veii is quite uncertain. In general Livy's account is plausible. The first objective was Fidenae, a perpetual pinprick in Rome's side (IV.22). The second was the reduction of Veii itself in 396 B.C. after a prolonged siege – ten years according to Livy but the length has been exaggerated to make a parallel with the Trojan War. The name given to the king of Veii in 438 B.C., Lars Tolumnius (IV.17.1), has been found on Veian inscriptions. The capture and destruction of the city is clearly proved by the excavations although its subsequent desolation was not as absolute as Livy makes out. One intriguing detail provides a good example of the relationship of fact to fiction in Roman historiography. Livy tells how Veii eventually fell because the Romans managed to tunnel into the citadel (V.21.8). One of the features of Veii is the large number of drainage tunnels (*cuniculi*) which the Veians cut in the soft volcanic rock. The purpose of such tunnels, which are widespread in south Etruria and which required a high degree of engineering skill, was to control the floods that follow torrential rain-storms and to prevent the top-soil being washed away. Whether the Romans used one of these tunnels to effect an entry into Veii or not, they impressed themselves on Roman memory.

It is at first sight surprising that the other Etruscan cities did not come to Veii's rescue but, although there was a league of Twelve Cities, it was a religious rather than a political league, and Etruscan cities, like Greek city-states, seem to have been very independent of one another. But there was also another reason. About 500 B.C. Celtic tribes began to penetrate northern Italy. Some of them settled in the Po Valley in the areas later called Cispadane and Transpadane Gaul where numerous Celtic tribes have been found. Others pressed down to the east coast into Picenum where tombs of about 490 B.C. have been found, or crossed the Apennines into Etruria. Their marauding activities in the latter half of the century would have distracted the attention of the other Etruscans. It was an army of such Celts that in 386 B.C. marched down the Tiber to inflict a staggering defeat on the Romans and to capture and burn Rome itself. The traces of that conflagration are found in every excavation in the Roman forum.

Book 5 ends on a triumphant note with Camillus's great speech attesting the grandeur of Rome and evoking the most loyal sentiments of patriotism (I.51.54). In fact Rome's power was shattered. It took fifty years to recover from the Gallic occupation.

BOOK ONE

Rome Under the Kings

T H E task of writing a history of our nation from Rome's earliest days fills me, I confess, with some misgiving, and even were I confident in the value of my work, I should hesitate to say so. I am aware that for historians to make extravagant claims is, and always has been, all too common: every writer on history tends to look down his nose at his less cultivated predecessors, happily persuaded that he will better them in point of style, or bring new facts to light. But however that may be, I shall find satisfaction in contributing – not, I hope, ignobly – to the labour of putting on record the story of the greatest nation in the world. Countless others have written on this theme and it may be that I shall pass unnoticed amongst them; if so, I must comfort myself with the greatness and splendour of my rivals, whose work will rob my own of recognition.

My task, moreover, is an immensely laborious one. I shall have to go back more than seven hundred years, and trace my story from its small beginnings up to these recent times when its ramifications are so vast that any adequate treatment is hardly possible. I am aware, too, that most readers will take less pleasure in my account of how Rome began and in her early history; they will wish to hurry on to more modern times and to read of the period, already a long one, in which the might of an imperial people is beginning to work its own ruin. My own feeling is different; I shall find antiquity a rewarding study, if only because, while I am absorbed in it, I shall be able to turn my eyes from the troubles which for so long have tormented the modern world, and to write without any of that over-anxious consideration which may well plague a writer on contemporary life, even if it does not lead him to conceal the truth.

Events before Rome was born or thought of have come to us in old tales with more of the charm of poetry than of a sound historical record, and such traditions I propose neither to affirm nor refute. There is no reason, I feel, to object when antiquity draws no hard line between the human and the supernatural: it adds dignity to the past, and, if any nation deserves the privilege of claiming a divine ancestry, that nation is our own; and so great is the glory won by the Roman people in their wars that, when they declare that Mars himself was their first parent and father of the man who founded their city, all the nations of the world might well allow the claim as readily as they accept Rome's imperial dominion.

These, however, are comparatively trivial matters and I set little store by them. I invite the reader's attention to the much more serious consideration of the kind of lives our ancestors lived, of who were the men, and what the means both in politics and war by which Rome's power was first acquired and subsequently expanded; I would then have him trace the process of our moral decline, to watch, first, the sinking of the foundations of morality as the old teaching was allowed to lapse, then the rapidly increasing disintegration, then the final collapse of the whole edifice, and the dark dawning of our modern day when we can neither endure our vices nor face the remedies needed to cure them. The study of history is the best medicine for a sick mind; for in history you have a record of the infinite variety of human experience plainly set out for all to see; and in that record you can find for yourself and your country both examples and warnings; fine things to take as models, base things, rotten through and through, to avoid.

I hope my passion for Rome's past has not impaired my judgement; for I do honestly believe that no country has ever been greater or purer than ours or richer in good citizens and noble deeds; none has been free for so many generations from the vices of avarice and luxury; nowhere have thrift and plain living been for so long held in such esteem. Indeed, poverty, with us, went hand in hand with contentment. Of late years wealth has made us greedy, and self-indulgence has brought us, through every form of sensual excess, to be, if I may so put it, in love with death both individual and collective.

But bitter comments of this sort are not likely to find favour, even when they have to be made. Let us have no more of them, at least at the beginning of our great story. On the contrary, I should prefer to borrow from the poets and begin with good omens and with prayers to all the host of heaven to grant a successful issue to the work which lies before me.

It is generally accepted that after the fall of Troy the Greeks kept up hostilities against all the Trojans except Aeneas and Antenor. These two men had worked consistently for peace and the restoration of Helen, and for that reason, added to certain personal connections of long standing, they were allowed to go unmolested. Each had various adventures:

Antenor joined forces with the Eneti, who had been driven out of Paphlagonia and, having lost their king, Pylaemenes, at Troy, wanted someone to lead them as well as somewhere to settle. He penetrated to the head of the Adriatic and expelled the Euganei, a tribe living between the Alps and the sea, and occupied that territory with a mixed population of Trojans and Eneti. The spot where they landed is called Troy and the neighbouring country the Trojan district. The combined peoples came to be known as Venetians.

Aeneas was forced into exile by similar troubles; he, however, was destined to lay the foundations of a greater future. He went first to Macedonia, then in his search for a new home sailed to Sicily, and from Sicily to the territory of Laurentum. This part of Italy too, like the spot where Antenor landed, is known as Troy. Aeneas's men in the course of their almost interminable wanderings had lost all they possessed except their ships and their swords; once on shore, they set about scouring the countryside for what they could find, and while thus engaged they were met by a force of armed natives who, under their king Latinus, came hurrying up from the town and the surrounding country to protect themselves from the invaders. There are two versions of what happened next: according to one, there was a fight in which Latinus was beaten; he then came to terms with Aeneas and cemented the alliance by giving him his daughter in marriage. According to the other, the battle was about to begin when Latinus, before the trumpets could sound the charge, came forward with his captains and invited the foreign leaders to a parley. He then asked Aeneas who his men were and where they had come from, why they had left their homes and what was their object in landing on Laurentian territory. He was told in reply that the men were Trojans, their leader Aeneas, the son of Anchises and Venus; that their native town had been burnt to the ground and now they were fugitives in search of some place where they could build a new town to settle in. Latinus, hearing their story, was so deeply impressed by the noble bearing of the strangers and by their leader's high courage either for peace or war, that he gave Aeneas his hand in pledge of friendship from that moment onward. A treaty was made; the two armies exchanged signs of mutual respect; Aeneas accepted the hospitality of Latinus, who gave him his daughter in marriage, thus further confirming the treaty of alliance by a private and domestic bond solemnly entered into in the presence of the Gods of his hearth.

The Trojans could no longer doubt that at last their travels were over and that they had found a permanent home. They began to build a settlement, which Aeneas named Lavinium after his wife Lavinia. A child was soon born of the marriage: a boy, who was given the name Ascanius.

The Trojans and the Latins were soon jointly involved in war. Turnus, prince of the Rutuli, to whom Latinus's daughter Lavinia had been pledged before Aeneas's arrival, angered by the insult of having to step down in favour of a stranger, attacked the combined forces of Aeneas and Latinus. Both sides suffered in the subsequent struggle: the Rutuli were defeated, but the victors lost their leader Latinus. Turnus and his people, in their anxiety for the future, then looked for help to Mezentius, king of the rich and powerful Etruscans, whose seat of government was at Caere, at that time a wealthy town. Mezentius needed little persuasion to join the Rutuli, as from the outset he had been far from pleased by the rise of the new settlement, and now felt that the Trojan power was growing much more rapidly than was safe for its neighbours. In this dangerous situation Aeneas conferred the native name of Latins upon his own people; the sharing of a common name as well as a common polity would, he felt, strengthen the bond between the two peoples. As a result of this step the original settlers were no less loyal to their king Aeneas than were the Trojans themselves. Trojans and Latins were rapidly becoming one people, and this gave Aeneas confidence to make an active move against the Etruscans, in spite of their great strength. Etruria, indeed, had at this time both by sea and land filled the whole length of Italy from the Alps to the Sicilian strait with the noise of her name; none the less Aeneas refused to act on the defensive and marched out to meet the enemy. The Latins were victorious, and for Aeneas the battle was the last of his labours in this world. He lies buried on the river Numicus. Was he man or god? However it be, men call him Jupiter Indiges – the local Jove.

Aeneas's son Ascanius was still too young for a position of authority; Lavinia, however, was a woman of great character, and acted as regent until Ascanius came of age and was able to assume power as the successor of his father and grandfather. There is some doubt – and no one can pretend to certainty on something so deeply buried in the mists of time – about who precisely this Ascanius was. Was it the one I have been discussing, or was it an elder brother, the son of Creusa, who was born before the sack of Troy and was with Aeneas in his escape from the burning city – the Iulus, in fact, whom the Julian family claim as their eponym? It is at any rate certain that Aeneas was his father, and – whatever the answer to the other question may be – it can be taken as a fact that he left Lavinium to found a new settlement. Lavinium was by then a populous and, for those days, a rich and flourishing town, and Ascanius left it in charge of his mother (or stepmother, if you will) and went off to found his new settlement on the Alban hills. This town, strung out as it was along a ridge, was named Alba Longa. Its foundation took place about thirty years after that of Lavinium; but the Latins had already grown so strong, especially since the defeat of the Etruscans, that neither Mezentius, the Etruscan king, nor any other neighbouring people dared to attack them, even when Aeneas died and the control of things passed temporarily into the hands of a woman, and Ascanius was still a child learning the elements of kingship. By the terms of the treaty between the Latins and Etruscans the river Albula (now the Tiber) became the boundary between the two territories.

Ascanius was succeeded by his son Silvius – 'born in the woods' – and he by his son Aeneas Silvius, whose heir was Latinus Silvius. By him several new settlements were made, and given the name of Old Latins. All the kings of Alba subsequently kept the cognomen Silvius. Next in succession to Latinius was Alba; then Atys, then Capys, then Capetus, then Tiberinus – who was drowned crossing the Albula and gave that river the name by which succeeding generations have always known it. Tiberinus was succeeded by Agrippa, Agrippa by his son Romulus Silvius, who was struck by lightning and bequeathed his power to Aventinus. Aventinus was buried on the hill, now a part of the city of Rome, and still bearing his name. Proca, the next king, had two sons, Numitor and Amulius, to the elder of whom, Numitor, he left the hereditary realm of the Silvian family; that, at least, was his intention, but respect for seniority was flouted, the father's will ignored and Amulius drove out his brother and seized the throne. One act of violence led to another; he proceeded to murder his brother's male children, and made his niece, Rhea Silvia, a Vestal, ostensibly to do her honour, but actually by condemning her to perpetual virginity to preclude the possibility of issue.

But (I must believe) it was already written in the book of fate that this great city of ours should arise, and the first steps be taken to the founding of the mightiest empire the world has known – next to God's. The Vestal Virgin was raped and gave birth to twin boys. Mars, she declared, was their father – perhaps she believed it, perhaps she was

Romulus & Remus

merely hoping by the pretence to palliate her guilt. Whatever the truth of the matter, neither gods nor men could save her or her babes from the savage hands of the king. The mother was bound and flung into prison; the boys, by the king's order, were condemned to be drowned in the river. Destiny, however, intervened; the Tiber had overflowed its banks ; because of the flooded ground it was impossible to get to the actual river, and the men entrusted to do the deed thought that the flood-water, sluggish though it was, would serve their purpose. Accordingly they made shift to carry out the king's orders by leaving the infants on the edge of the first flood-water they came to, at the spot where now stands the Ruminal fig-tree – said to have once been known as the fig-tree of Romulus. In those days the country thereabouts was all wild and uncultivated, and the story goes that when the basket in which the infants had been exposed was left high and dry by the receding water, a she-wolf, coming down from the neighbouring hills to quench her thirst, heard the children crying and made her way to where they were. She offered them her teats to suck and treated them with such gentleness that Faustulus, the king's herdsman, found her licking them with her tongue. Faustulus took them to his hut and gave them to his wife Larentia to nurse. Some think that the origin of this fable was the fact that Larentia was a common whore and was called Wolf by the shepherds.

Such, then, was the birth and upbringing of the twins. By the time they were grown boys, they employed themselves actively on the farm and with the flocks and began to go hunting in the woods; their strength grew with their resolution, until not content only with the chase they took to attacking robbers and sharing their stolen goods with their friends the shepherds. Other young fellows joined them, and they and the shepherds would fleet the time together, now in serious talk, now in jollity.

Even in that remote age the Palatine hill (which got its name from the Arcadian settlement Pallanteum) is supposed to have been the scene of the gay festival of the Lupercalia. The Arcadian Evander, who many years before held that region, is said to have instituted there the old Arcadian practice of holding an annual festival in honour of Lycean Pan (afterwards called Inuus by the Romans), in which young men ran about naked and disported themselves in various pranks and fooleries. The day of the festival was common knowledge, and on one occasion when it was in full swing some brigands, incensed at the loss of their

ill-gotten gains, laid a trap for Romulus and Remus. Romulus successfully defended himself, but Remus was caught and handed over to
Amulius. The brigands laid a complaint against their prisoner, the main
charge being that he and his brother were in the habit of raiding Numitor's land with an organized gang of ruffians and stealing
the cattle. Thereupon Remus was handed over for punishment to
Numitor. *brother of Amulius*

Now Faustulus had suspected all along that the boys he was bringing
up were of royal blood. He knew that two infants had been exposed by
the king's orders, and the rescue of his own two fitted perfectly in point
of time. Hitherto, however, he had been unwilling to declare what he
knew, until either a suitable opportunity occurred or circumstances
compelled him. Now the truth could no longer be concealed, so in his
alarm he told Romulus the whole story; Numitor, too, when he had
Remus in custody and was told that the brothers were twins, was set
thinking about his grandsons; the young men's age and character, so
different from the lowly born, confirmed his suspicions; and further
inquiries led him to the same conclusion, until he was on the point of
acknowledging Remus. The net was closing in, and Romulus acted. He
was not strong enough for open hostilities, so he instructed a number of
the herdsmen to meet at the king's house by different routes at a pre-
ordained time; this was done, and with the help of Remus, at the head
of another body of men, the king was surprised and killed. Before the
first blows were struck, Numitor gave it out that an enemy had broken
into the town and attacked the palace; he then drew off all the men of
military age to garrison the inner fortress, and, as soon as he saw
Romulus and Remus, their purpose accomplished, coming to congratulate him, he summoned a meeting of the people and laid the facts
before it: Amulius's crime against himself, the birth of his grandsons,
and the circumstances attending it, how they were brought up and
ultimately recognized, and, finally, the murder of the king for which
he himself assumed responsibility. The two brothers marched through
the crowd at the head of their men and saluted their grandfather as
king, and by a shout of unanimous consent his royal title was confirmed.

Romulus and Remus, after the control of Alba had passed to Numitor
in the way I have described, were suddenly seized by an urge to found
a new settlement on the spot where they had been left to drown as
infants and had been subsequently brought up. There was, in point of

fact, already an excess of population at Alba, what with the Albans themselves, the Latins, and the addition of the herdsmen: enough, indeed, to justify the hope that Alba and Lavinium would one day be small places compared with the proposed new settlement. Unhappily the brothers' plans for the future were marred by the same source which had divided their grandfather and Amulius – jealousy and ambition. A disgraceful quarrel arose from a matter in itself trivial. As the brothers were twins and all question of seniority was thereby precluded, they determined to ask the tutelary gods of the countryside to declare by augury which of them should govern the new town once it was founded, and give his name to it. For this purpose Romulus took the Palatine hill and Remus the Aventine as their respective stations from which to observe the auspices. Remus, the story goes, was the first to receive a sign – six vultures; and no sooner was this made known to the people than double the number of birds appeared to Romulus. The followers of each promptly saluted their master as king, one side basing its claim upon priority, the other upon number. Angry words ensued, followed all too soon by blows, and in the course of the affray Remus was killed. There is another story, a commoner one, according to which Remus, by way of jeering at his brother, jumped over the half-built walls of the new settlement, whereupon Romulus killed him in a fit of rage, adding the threat, 'So perish whoever else shall overleap my battlements.'

This, then, was how Romulus obtained the sole power. The newly built city was called by its founder's name. ~ *became Roma* ~

Romulus's first act was to fortify the Palatine, the scene of his own upbringing. He offered sacrifice to the gods, using the Alban forms except in the case of Hercules, where he followed the Greek ritual as instituted by Evander. According to the old tale, Hercules after killing Geryon came into these parts driving his oxen. The oxen were exceedingly beautiful, and close to the Tiber, at the spot where he had swum across with them, he came upon a grassy meadow; here, weary with walking, he lay down to rest and allowed the beasts to refresh themselves with the rich pasture. Being drowsy with food and drink he fell asleep, and, while he slept, a shepherd of that region, a fierce giant named Cacus, saw the oxen and was instantly taken by their beauty. Purposing to steal them, he was aware that, if he drove them in the ordinary way into his cave, their tracks could not fail to guide their master thither as soon as he began his search; so choosing the finest from the herd he dragged them backwards by their tails and hid them in his cavern. Hercules awoke at dawn, and casting his eye over the herd noticed that some of the animals were missing. He went at once to the nearest cave on the chance that there were tracks leading into it, but found that they all led outwards, apparently to nowhere. It was very odd; so full of vague misgivings he started driving the remainder of his herd away from this eerie spot. Some of the beasts, naturally enough, missed their companions and began to low, and there came an answering low from the cave. Hercules turned. He walked towards the cave, and Cacus, when he saw him coming, tried to keep him off. But all in vain; Hercules struck him with his club, and the robber, vainly calling upon his friends for help, fell dead.

In those days Evander held sway over that part of the country. He was an exile from the Peloponnese and his position depended less upon sovereign power than upon personal influence; he was revered for his invention of letters – a strange and wonderful thing to the rude uncultivated men amongst whom he dwelt – and, still more, on account of his mother Carmenta, who was supposed to be divine and before the coming of the Sibyl into Italy had been revered by the people of those parts as a prophetess.

On the occasion of which I am writing Evander could not but observe the shepherds who were excitedly mobbing the unknown killer. He joined them, and upon being informed of the crime and its cause, directed his gaze upon the stranger. Seeing him to be of more than human stature and of a preternatural dignity of bearing, he asked him who he was, and, hearing his name and parentage and country, cried: 'Hercules, son of Jupiter, I bid you welcome. You are the subject of my mother's prophecy; for she, a true prophet, declared that you would increase the number of the Gods, and that here an altar would be dedicated to you, and the nation destined to be the mightiest in the world would one day name it Greatest of Altars and serve it with your own proper rites.'

Hercules gave him his hand and replied that he accepted the inspired words and would himself assist the course of destiny by building and consecrating an altar. A splendid beast was chosen from the herd, and on the new altar sacrifice, for the first time, was offered to Hercules; the rite itself, and the subsequent feast, being administered by members of the two most distinguished local families, the Potitii and Pinarii.

It so happened that the Pinarii were late for the feast. The Potitii were there in time, and were served in consequence with the entrails of the victim; the Pinarii came in only for the remainder. From this circumstance the custom became established that no member of the Pinarian family, throughout its history, was ever served with his portion of entrails at a sacrifice to Hercules. The Potitii were taught by Evander, and furnished the priests of this cult for many generations, until the solemn duty they had so long performed was delegated to public slaves and the family became extinct. This was the only foreign religious rite adopted by Romulus; by so doing he showed, even then, his respect for that immortality which is the prize of valour. His own destiny was already leading him to the same reward.

Having performed with proper ceremony his religious duties, he summoned his subjects and gave them laws, without which the creation of a unified body politic would not have been possible. In his view the rabble over whom he ruled could be induced to respect the law only if he himself adopted certain visible signs of power; he proceeded, therefore, to increase the dignity and impressiveness of his position by various devices, of which the most important was the creation of the twelve lictors to attend his person. Some have fancied that he made the lictors twelve in number because the vultures, in the augury, had been twelve; personally, however, I incline to follow the opinion which finds for this an Etruscan origin. We know that the State Chair – the 'curule' chair – and the purple-bordered toga came to us from Etruria; and it is probable that the idea of attendants, as well as, in this case, of their number, came across the border from Etruria too. The number twelve was due to the fact that the twelve Etruscan communities united to elect a king, and each contributed one lictor.

Meanwhile Rome was growing. More and more ground was coming within the circuit of its walls. Indeed, the rapid expansion of the enclosed area was out of proportion to the actual population, and evidently indicated an eye to the future. In antiquity the founder of a new settlement, in order to increase its population, would as a matter of course shark up a lot of homeless and destitute folk and pretend that they were 'born of earth' to be his progeny; Romulus now followed a similar course: to help fill his big new town, he threw open, in the ground – now enclosed – between the two copses as you go up the Capitoline hill, a place of asylum for fugitives. Hither fled for refuge all the rag-tag-and-bobtail from the neighbouring peoples: some free, some slaves, and all of them wanting nothing but a fresh start.

That mob was the first real addition to the City's strength, the first step to her future greatness.

Having now adequate numbers, Romulus proceeded to temper strength with policy and turned his attention to social organization. He created a hundred senators – fixing that number either because it was enough for his purpose, or because there were no more than a hundred who were in a position to be made 'Fathers', as they were called, or Heads of Clans. The title of 'fathers' (*patres*) undoubtedly was derived from their rank, and their descendants were called 'patricians'.

Rome was now strong enough to challenge any of her neighbours; but, great though she was, her greatness seemed likely to last only for a single generation. There were not enough women, and that, added to the fact that there was no intermarriage with neighbouring communities, ruled out any hope of maintaining the level of population. Romulus accordingly, on the advice of his senators, sent representatives to the various peoples across his borders to negotiate alliances and the right of intermarriage for the newly established state. The envoys were instructed to point out that cities, like everything else, have to begin small; in course of time, helped by their own worth and the favour of heaven, some, at least, grow rich and famous, and of these Rome would assuredly be one: Gods had blessed her birth, and the valour of her people would not fail in the days to come. The Romans were men, as they were; why, then, be reluctant to intermarry with them?

Romulus's overtures were nowhere favourably received; it was clear that everyone despised the new community, and at the same time feared, both for themselves and for posterity, the growth of this new power in their midst. More often than not his envoys were dismissed with the question of whether Rome had thrown open her doors to female, as well as to male, runaways and vagabonds, as that would evidently be the most suitable way for Romans to get wives. The young Romans naturally resented this jibe, and a clash seemed inevitable. Romulus, seeing it must come, set the scene for it with elaborate care. Deliberately hiding his resentment, he prepared to celebrate the Consualia, a solemn festival in honour of Neptune, patron of the horse, and sent notice of his intention all over the neighbouring countryside. The better to advertise it, his people lavished upon their preparations for the spectacle all the resources – such as they were in those days – at their command. On the appointed day crowds flocked to Rome, partly, no doubt, out of sheer curiosity to see the new town. The majority were from the neighbouring settlements of Caenina, Crustumium, and Antemnae, but all the Sabines were there too, with their wives and children. Many houses offered hospitable entertainment to the visitors; they were invited to inspect the fortifications, layout, and numerous buildings of the town, and expressed their surprise at the rapidity of its growth. Then the great moment came; the show began, and nobody had eyes or thoughts for anything else. This was the Romans' opportunity: at a given signal all the able-bodied men burst through the crowd and seized the young women. Most of the girls were the prize of whoever got hold of them first, but a few conspicuously handsome ones had been previously marked down for leading senators, and these were brought to their houses by special gangs. There was one young woman of much greater beauty than the rest; and the story goes that she was seized by a party of men belonging to the household of someone called Thalassius, and in reply to the many questions about whose house they were taking her to, they, to prevent anyone else laying hands upon her, kept shouting, 'Thalassius, Thalassius!' This was the origin of the use of this word at weddings.

By this act of violence the fun of the festival broke up in panic. The girls' unfortunate parents made good their escape, not without bitter comments on the treachery of their hosts and heartfelt prayers to the God to whose festival they had come in all good faith in the solemnity of the occasion, only to be grossly deceived. The young women were no less indignant and as full of foreboding for the future.

Romulus, however, reassured them. Going from one to another he declared that their own parents were really to blame, in that they had been too proud to allow intermarriage with their neighbours; nevertheless, they need not fear; as married women they would share all the fortunes of Rome, all the privileges of the community, and they would be bound to their husbands by the dearest bond of all, their children. He urged them to forget their wrath and give their hearts to those to whom chance had given their bodies. Often, he said, a sense of injury yields in the end to affection, and their husbands would treat them all the more kindly in that they would try, each one of them, not only to fulfil their own part of the bargain but also to make up to their wives for the homes and parents they had lost. The men, too, played their part: they spoke honeyed words and vowed that it was passionate love which had prompted their offence. No plea can better touch a woman's heart.

The women in course of time lost their resentment; but no sooner had they learned to accept their lot than their parents began to stir up trouble in earnest. To excite sympathy they went about dressed in mourning and pouring out their grief in tears and lamentations. Not content with confining these demonstrations within the walls of their own towns, they marched in mass to the house of Titus Tatius the Sabine king, the greatest name in that part of the country. Official embassies, too, from various settlements, waited upon him.

It seemed to the people of Caenina, Crustumium, and Antemnae, who had been involved in the trouble, that Tatius and the Sabines were unduly dilatory, so the three communities resolved to take action on their own. Of the three, however, Crustumium and Antemnae proved too slow to satisfy the impatient wrath of their partner, with the result that the men of Caenina invaded Roman territory without any support. Scattered groups of them were doing what damage they could, when Romulus, at the head of his troops, appeared upon the scene. A few blows were enough and defeat soon taught them that angry men must also be strong, if they would achieve their purpose. The Romans pursued the routed enemy; Romulus himself cut down their prince and stripped him of his arms, then, their leader dead, took the town at the first assault. The victorious army returned, and Romulus proceeded to dispose of the spoils. Magnificent in action, he was no less eager for popular recognition and applause; he took the armour which he had stripped from the body of the enemy commander, fixed it on a frame made for the purpose, and carried it in his own hands up to the Capitol, where, by an oak which the shepherds regarded as a sacred tree, he laid it down as an offering to Jupiter. At the same time he determined on the site of a plot of ground to be consecrated to the God, and uttered this prayer: 'Jupiter Feretrius (such was the new title he bestowed), to you I bring these spoils of victory, a king's armour taken by a king; and within the bounds already clear to my mind's eye I dedicate to you a holy precinct where, in days to come, following my example, other men shall lay the "spoils of honour", stripped from the bodies of commanders or kings killed by their own hands.' Such was the origin of the first temple consecrated in Rome. The gods ordained that Romulus, when he declared that others should bring their spoils thither, should not speak in vain; it was their pleasure, too, that the glory of that offering should not be cheapened by too frequent occurrence. The distinction of winning the 'spoils of honour' has been rare indeed: in the countless battles of succeeding years it has been won on two occasions only.

These proceedings on the Capitol had temporarily drawn the Romans from their farms, and a force from Antemnae took the opportunity of making a raid. Once again Roman troops pounced. The scattered groups of raiders were taken by surprise; a single charge sufficed to put them to flight, their town was taken, and Romulus had a double victory to his credit. His wife Hersilia had long been pestered by the young women who had been carried off at the festival, so she took this opportunity, when he was congratulating himself on his success, to ask him to pardon the girls' parents and allow them to come and live in Rome. It would, she urged, form a strong and valuable bond of union. The request was readily granted.

Romulus's next move was against the men of Crustumium, who were on the march against him; but the defeat of their neighbours had already undermined their confidence, and they were even more easily broken up. Settlers were sent out both to Antemnae and Crustumium, the fertility of the soil in the latter attracting the greater number of volunteers. On the other hand a number of people, chiefly parents or relatives of the captured women, moved from Crustumium to Rome.

The last to attack Rome were the Sabines, and the ensuing struggle was far more serious than the previous ones. The enemy gave no notice of their intentions and acted upon no hasty impulse of revenge or cupidity. Their plans were carefully laid, and backed by treachery. Spurius Tarpeius, the commander of the Roman citadel, had a daughter, a young girl, who, when she had gone outside the walls to fetch water for a sacrifice, was bribed by Tatius, the king of the Sabines, to admit a party of his soldiers into the fortress. Once inside, the men crushed her to death under their shields, to make it look as if they had taken the place by storm – or, it may be, to show by harsh example that there must be no trusting a traitor. There is also a story that this girl had demanded as the price of her services 'What they had on their shield-arms'. Now the Sabines in those days used to wear on their left arms heavy gold bracelets and fine jewelled rings – so they kept their bargain: paying, however, not, as the girl hoped, with golden bracelets, but with their shields. Some say that after bargaining for what they 'had on their left arms' she did actually demand their shields, and, being proved a traitor, was killed, as it were, by the very coin that paid her.

Sabines
or Romulus
& Romans

The Sabines were now in possession of the citadel. Next day the Roman troops occupied all the ground between the Palatine and Capitoline hills and there waited till they could tolerate the situation no longer. Fiercely determined to recover the citadel, they pressed forward to the attack. This was the signal for the enemy to move down to meet them. The first blows were struck by the rival champions Mettius Curtius, the Sabine, and Hostius Hostilius of Rome. The Romans were in the worse position, but they were kept going for a time by the great gallantry of Hostius; when he fell, their resistance at once collapsed and they retreated in disorder to the Palatine Old Gate. Romulus himself was swept along by the fugitive rabble, but, as he rode, he waved his sword above his head and shouted, 'Hear me, O Jupiter! At the bidding of your eagles I laid the foundations of Rome here on the Palatine. Our fortress is in Sabine hands, basely betrayed – thence are they coming sword in hand across the valley against us. Father of Gods and men, suffer them not to set foot on the spot where now we stand. Banish fear from Roman hearts and stop their shameful retreat. I vow a temple here – to you, O Jupiter, Stayer of Flight – that men may remember hereafter that Rome in her trouble was saved by your help.' It was almost as if he felt that his prayer was granted: a moment later, 'Turn on them, Romans,' he cried, 'and fight once more. Jupiter himself commands it.' The Romans obeyed what they believed to be the voice from heaven. They rallied, and Romulus thrust his way forward to the van.

Mettius Curtius had led the Sabine advance down the slope from the citadel. He had driven the Roman troops back in disorder over the ground today occupied by the Forum, and nearly reached the gate of the Palatine. 'Comrades,' he cried, 'we have beaten our treacherous hosts – our feeble foes. They know now that catching girls is a different matter from fighting against men!' The boast had hardly left his lips when Romulus, with a handful of his best and most courageous troops, was on him. The fact that Mettius was mounted proved a disadvantage to him; he turned and galloped off, the Romans in pursuit, and this bold stroke on the part of their leader inspired the Roman troops elsewhere on the field to make a fresh effort and to rout their opponents.

The yells of the pursuers so scared Mettius's horse that he took the bit between his teeth and plunged with his rider into the swamps. The Sabines were aghast; the imminent threat to their champion for the moment diverted them from the work in hand, and they tried to help him by shouting advice and signalling, until at last by a supreme effort he struggled out to safety. The battle was then renewed in the valley between the two hills, and this time the Romans had the best of it.

This was the moment when the Sabine women, the original cause of the quarrel, played their decisive part. The dreadful situation in which they found themselves banished their natural timidity and gave them courage to intervene. With loosened hair and rent garments they braved the flying spears and thrust their way in a body between the embattled armies. They parted the angry combatants; they besought their fathers on the one side, their husbands on the other, to spare themselves the curse of shedding kindred blood. 'We are mothers now,' they cried; 'our children are your sons – your grandsons: do not put on them the stain of parricide. If our marriage – if the relationship between you – is hateful to you, turn your anger against *us*. *We* are the cause of strife; on our account our husbands and fathers lie wounded or dead, and we would rather die ourselves than live on either widowed or orphaned.' The effect of the appeal was immediate and profound. Silence fell and not a man moved. A moment later the rival captains stepped forward to conclude a peace. Indeed, they went further: the two states were united under a single government, with Rome as the seat of power. Thus the population of Rome was doubled, and the Romans, as a gesture to the Sabines, called themselves Quirites, after the Sabine town of Cures. In memory of the battle the stretch of shallow water where Curtius and his horse first struggled from the deep swamps into safety, was named Curtius's Lake.

This happy and unlooked-for end to a bitter war strengthened the bond between the Sabine women and their parents and husbands. Romulus moreover marked his own special awareness of this deepened feeling by giving the women's names to the thirty wards into which he then divided the population. No doubt there were more than thirty of the women; but it is not known on what principle they were selected to give their names – whether it was by lot, or age, or their own or their husbands' rank. At the same time three centuries of knights were created, the Ramnenses named after Romulus, the Titienses after Tatius, and the Luceres, the origin of whose name is uncertain. As a result of these measures the joint rule of the two kings was brought into harmony.

Some years later the kinsmen of Tatius offered violence to some Laurentian envoys. The Laurentian people claimed redress under what passed in those days for international law, and Tatius allowed the ties

of blood to influence his decision. The result of this was that he drew
their revenge upon himself: he was murdered in a riot at Lavinium,
whither he had gone to celebrate the annual sacrifice. Romulus is said
to have felt less distress at his death than was strictly proper: possibly the
joint reign was not, in fact, entirely harmonious; possibly he felt that
Tatius deserved what he got. But whatever the reason, he refused to go
to war, and, to wipe out the double stain of Tatius's murder and the
insult to the envoys, renewed the pact between Rome and Lavinium.

Thus there was peace with Lavinium, as welcome as it was unexpected; all the same, Rome was at once involved in hostilities with an
enemy almost at the city gates. This time it was the men of Fidenae,
who, in alarm at the rapid growth of a rival on their very doorstep,
decided to take the offensive and to nip its power in the bud. They dispatched a force to devastate the country between the two towns; then,
turning left (the other way was barred by the river), carried on their
work amongst the farms. The men working on the farms fled in
sudden alarm and confusion to the protection of the town, and the
arrival of this mob brought the first news of the raid. Romulus acted
promptly. With the enemy so close delay was dangerous. He marched
out at the head of his troops and took up a position about a mile from
Fidenae, where he left a small holding force. Of his main body he
ordered a part to lie in ambush where dense undergrowth afforded
cover, while with the rest, the greater number, and all his mounted
troops he challenged the enemy with a feint attack, riding with his
cavalry right up to the gates of Fidenae. The ruse succeeded; the enemy
were drawn, and the cavalry skirmish lent an air of genuineness to the
subsequent Roman withdrawal of their mounted troops, which deliberately broke discipline as if undecided whether to fight or run.
Then, when the Roman foot also began to give way, the deluded enemy
came pouring *en masse* from behind their defences, flung themselves
with blind fury upon their retreating enemy, and were led straight into
the ambush. Their flanks were promptly attacked by the Roman troops
there concealed. At the same moment the standards of the holding
force left behind by Romulus were seen to be advancing, and these
combined threats proved too much for the Fidenates, who began a
hurried retreat before Romulus and his mounted men even had time
to wheel to the attack. A moment before, the Fidenates had been following up a feigned withdrawal; now, in good earnest and far greater
disorder, they were themselves on the run for the protection of their

own walls. But they were not destined to escape: the Romans in hot pursuit burst into the town close on their heels, before the gates could be shut against them.

The war fever soon spread to Veii, which, like Fidenae, was an Etruscan town. It was also a close neighbour of Rome, and the danger of such propinquity in the event of Rome proving hostile to all her neighbouring communities was a further exacerbation. Accordingly she sent a raiding force into Roman territory. It was not an organized movement; the raiders took up no regular position, but simply picked up what they could from the countryside and returned without waiting for countermeasures from Rome. The Romans, however, on finding them still in their territory, crossed the Tiber fully prepared for a decisive struggle, and assumed a position with a view to an assault upon the town. At the news of their approach the Veientes took the field, to fight it out in the open rather than be shut up within their walls and forced to stand a siege. In the fight which ensued Romulus used no strategy; the sheer power of his veteran troops sufficed for victory, and he pursued the retreating enemy to the walls of Veii. The town itself was strongly fortified and well sited for defence; Romulus, accordingly, made no attempt to take it, but contented himself on the return march with wasting the cultivated land, more by way of revenge than for what he could take from it. The loss the Veientes suffered from the devastation did as much as their defeat in the field to secure their submission and they sent envoys to Rome to treat for peace. They were mulcted of a part of their territory and granted a truce for a hundred years.

Such is the story of Rome's military and political achievements during the reign of Romulus. All of them chime well enough with the belief in his divine birth and the divinity ascribed to him after his death. One need but recall the vigour he displayed in recovering his ancestral throne; his wisdom in founding Rome and bringing her to strength by the arts of both war and peace. It was to him and no one else that she owed the power which enabled her to enjoy untroubled tranquillity for the next forty years.

Great though Romulus was, he was better loved by the commons than by the senate, and best of all by the army. He maintained, in peace as well as in war, a personal armed guard of three hundred men, whom he called Celeres – 'the Swift'.

Such, then, were the deeds of Romulus, and they will never grow old. One day while he was reviewing his troops on the Campus Martius near the marsh of Capra, a storm burst, with violent thunder. A cloud enveloped him, so thick that it hid him from the eyes of everyone present; and from that moment he was never seen again upon earth.

The troops, who had been alarmed by the sudden storm, soon recovered when it passed over and the sun came out again. Then they saw that the throne was empty, and, ready though they were to believe the senators, who had been standing at the king's side and now declared that he had been carried up on high by a whirlwind, they none the less felt like children bereft of a father and for a long time stood in sorrowful silence. Then a few voices began to proclaim Romulus's divinity; the cry was taken up, and at last every man present hailed him as a god and son of a god, and prayed to him to be for ever gracious and to protect his children. However, even on this great occasion there were, I believe, a few dissentients who secretly maintained that the king had been torn to pieces by the senators. At all events the story got about, though in veiled terms; but it was not important, as awe, and admiration for Romulus's greatness, set the seal upon the other version of his end, which was, moreover, given further credit by the timely action of a certain Julius Proculus, a man, we are told, honoured for his wise counsel on weighty matters. The loss of the king had left the people in an uneasy mood and suspicious of the senators, and Proculus, aware of the prevalent temper, conceived the shrewd idea of addressing the Assembly. 'Romulus,' he declared, 'the father of our City, descended from heaven at dawn this morning and appeared to me. In awe and reverence I stood before him, praying for permission to look upon his face without sin. "Go," he said, "and tell the Romans that by heaven's will my Rome shall be capital of the world. Let them learn to be soldiers. Let them know, and teach their children, that no power on earth can stand against Roman arms." Having spoken these words, he was taken up again into the sky.'

Proculus's story had a most remarkable effect; the army and commons, cruelly distressed at the loss of their king, were much comforted once they were assured of his immortality.

The senators were soon quarrelling over the succession to the throne. It was a rivalry of factions, not of individuals, for Rome was still too young to have produced any men of outstanding eminence. The Sabine element wanted a king of Sabine blood; for there had not been one since the death of Tatius and they were afraid that in consequence, and in spite of their equal political rights, they might lose their title to the sovereignty; the Roman element regarded the prospect of a foreigner on the throne with abhorrence. Despite their differences, however, both parties were united in their desire for a king, neither having yet tasted the sweets of liberty. It was obvious, meanwhile, that many of the neighbouring communities were far from friendly; Rome was without a ruler and her army without a commander, and the senators could not but see in this combination of circumstances a danger of attack. Some form of government there must be; this much was agreed, and, as neither party would yield, the hundred senators determined to exercise a joint control. They divided their number into ten decuries, with one man from each as president; these ten performed the functions of government, though only one carried its insignia and was attended by lictors. His period of power was limited to five days, and it passed to each senator in rotation. The monarchy was in abeyance for a year, and the period of its abeyance was known as the '*interregnum*', a term still in use.

The populace disliked this turn of events, and complained that it brought them a hundred masters instead of one, an even worse slavery than before. The senators, seeing that the commons were unlikely to continue to submit to any authority other than that of a king, elected, moreover, by themselves, decided to take the initiative by offering what in any case they were sure to lose. Accordingly they recovered the favour of the populace by granting them supreme power, but on condition that their election of a king should be valid only if it were ratified by themselves – thus keeping, in effect, as much power as they gave. The same right is exercised in political affairs today, though it has now become a mere empty form; before the commons vote, the senate ratifies the result, whatever it may be.

The interrex, on the occasion of which I am speaking, called an assembly of the people. 'Men of Rome,' he said, 'may luck and every blessing attend us. Choose your king, for such is the senators' decision. If the man you choose is a worthy successor to Romulus, the senators will ratify your choice.' The commons were delighted; determined to show no less generosity than their masters, they passed a resolution that the election should be decided by a decree of the senate.

Numa Pompilius had a great reputation at this time for justice and piety. He lived in the Sabine town of Cures, and was, by the standards of antiquity, deeply learned in all the laws of God and man. It has been said that he owed his learning to Pythagoras of Samos; but this is a mere shot in the dark, and is obviously untrue as it was not till a hundred years later, in the reign of Servius Tullius, that Pythagoras is known to have settled in Southern Italy in the neighbourhood of Metapontum, Heraclea, and Croton, where he formed groups of young men eager to study his philosophy. But even if the dates fitted, how could Pythagoras's fame have reached the Sabines all the way from the south? What mutually intelligible language could he have used to awaken amongst them the desire for learning? Under whose protection could a man have travelled alone through so many peoples all differing in language and manner of life? No; my own belief is, on the contrary, that Numa's noble qualities were all his own; it was not foreign learning that made him what he was, but the harsh, austere discipline of the ancient Sabines, most incorruptible of men.

Numa's name was put forward as successor to the throne, and the senate naturally felt that a Sabine king would unduly increase the influence of the Sabine element in the community; nevertheless, nobody ventured to put forward as a rival candidate either himself or another of his faction, or, indeed, any man at all, either senator or citizen, with the result that there was a unanimous decision to offer Numa the crown. He was therefore summoned to the city, and there expressed the wish that the gods should be consulted on his behalf, as in the case of Romulus who at the founding of Rome had assumed power only after the omens had been duly observed. An augur, whose service on the occasion was afterwards recognized by the grant of a permanent state priesthood, escorted Numa to the citadel, where he took his seat on a stone with his face to the south; the augur with veiled head sat on his left, holding in his right hand the smooth, crook-handled staff called the *lituus*. Gazing out over the city and the country beyond, he uttered a prayer, and marking with a glance the space of sky from east to west and declaring the southward section to be 'right' and the northward section 'left' he took an imaginary point full in front of him and as far away as his eyes could reach, transferred the staff to his left hand, placed his right upon Numa's head and spoke these solemn words: 'Father Jupiter, if it is Heaven's will that this man, Numa Pompilius, whose head I touch, should reign in the city of Rome, make clear to us sure signs within those limits I have determined.' Then he named precisely the nature of the signs he hoped would be sent. Sent they were; and Numa, duly proclaimed king, went down from the hill where the auspices were taken.

Rome under Numa

Janus

Rome had originally been founded by force of arms; the new king now prepared to give the community a second beginning, this time on the solid basis of law and religious observance. These lessons, however, could never be learned while his people were constantly fighting; war, he well knew, was no civilizing influence, and the proud spirit of his people could be tamed only if they learned to lay aside their swords. Accordingly, at the foot of the Argiletum he built the temple of Janus, to serve as a visible sign of the alternations of peace and war: open, it was to signify that the city was in arms; closed, that war against all neighbouring peoples had been brought to a successful conclusion. Since Numa's reign the temple has twice been closed: once in the consulship of Manlius at the end of the first war with Carthage and again on the occasion (which we ourselves were allowed by heaven to witness) when after the battle of Actium Augustus Caesar brought peace to the world by land and sea. Numa himself closed it after first securing the goodwill of all the neighbouring communities by treaties of alliance.

Rome was now at peace; there was no immediate prospect of attack from outside and the tight rein of constant military discipline was relaxed. In these novel circumstances there was an obvious danger of a general relaxation of the nation's moral fibre, so to prevent its occurrence Numa decided upon a step which he felt would prove more effective than anything else with a mob as rough and ignorant as the Romans were in those days. This was to inspire them with the fear of the gods. Such a sentiment was unlikely to touch them unless he first prepared them by inventing some sort of marvellous tale; he pretended, therefore, that he was in the habit of meeting the goddess Egeria by night, and that it was her authority which guided him in the establishment of such rites as were most acceptable to the gods and in the appointment of priests to serve each particular duty.

His first act was to divide the year into twelve lunar months; and because twelve lunar months come a few days short of the full solar year, he inserted intercalary months, so that every twenty years the cycle should be completed, the days coming round again to correspond with the position of the sun from which they had started. Secondly, he fixed what came to be known as 'lawful' and 'unlawful' days – days, that is, when public business might, or might not, be transacted – as he foresaw that it would be convenient to have certain specified times when no measures should be brought before the people. Next he turned

his attention to the appointment of priests; most of the religious ceremonies, especially those which are now in the hands of the Flamen
Dialis, or priest of Jupiter, he was in the habit of presiding over himself,
but he foresaw that in a martial community like Rome future kings
were likely to resemble Romulus rather than himself and to be often,
in consequence, away from home on active service, and for that reason
appointed a Priest of Jupiter on a permanent basis, marking the importance of the office by the grant of special robes and the use of the royal
curule chair. This step ensured that the religious duties attached to the
royal office should never be allowed to lapse. At the same time two
other priesthoods, to Mars and Quirinus, were created.

He further appointed virgin priestesses for the service of Vesta, a cult
which originated in Alba and was therefore not foreign to Numa who
brought it to Rome. The priestesses were paid out of public funds to
enable them to devote their whole time to the temple service, and were
invested with special sanctity by the imposition of various observances
of which the chief was virginity. The twelve Salii, or Leaping Priests,
in the service of Mars Gradivus, were also introduced by Numa; they
were given the uniform of an embroidered tunic and bronze breast-
plate, and their special duty was to carry the *ancilia*, or sacred shields,
one of which was fabled to have fallen from heaven, as they moved
through the city chanting their hymns to the triple beat of their ritual
dance.

Numa's next act was to appoint as pontifex the senator Numa Marcius, son of Marcus. He gave him full written instructions for all religious observances, specifying for the various sacrifices the place, the
time, and the nature of the victim, and how money was to be raised
to meet the cost. He also gave the pontifex the right of decision in all
other matters connected with both public and private observances, so
that ordinary people might have someone to consult if they needed
advice, and to prevent the confusion which might result from neglect
of natural religious rites or the adoption of foreign ones. It was the
further duty of the pontifex to teach the proper forms for the burial of
the dead and the propitiation of the spirits of the departed, and to
establish what portents manifested by lightning or other visible signs
were to be recognized and acted upon. To elicit information on this
subject from a divine source, Numa consecrated on the Aventine an
altar to Jupiter Elicius, whom he consulted by augury as to what signs
from heaven it should be proper to regard.

By these means the whole population of Rome was given a great many new things to think about and attend to, with the result that everybody was diverted from military preoccupations. They now had serious matters to consider; and believing, as they now did, that the heavenly powers took part in human affairs, they became so much absorbed in the cultivation of religion and so deeply imbued with the sense of their religious duties, that the sanctity of an oath had more power to control their lives than the fear of punishment for law-breaking. Men of all classes took Numa as their unique example and modelled themselves upon him, until the effect of this change of heart was felt even beyond the borders of Roman territory. Once Rome's neighbours had considered her not so much as a city as an armed camp in their midst threatening the general peace; now they came to revere her so profoundly as a community dedicated wholly to worship, that the mere thought of offering her violence seemed to them like sacrilege.

There was a certain little copse watered summer and winter by a stream of which the spring was in a dark grotto. Numa often visited the copse alone, to meet (as he put it) the goddess Egeria; he accordingly declared it sacred to the Muses, as the spot where they met to converse with his wife. He instituted an annual ceremony dedicated to Troth-keeping, with priests whose duty was to drive in a covered wagon drawn by a pair of horses to the place of celebration and there perform their rites with hands swathed to the fingers, signifying that troth must be religiously preserved and that she dwelt inviolable in a man's right hand. Many other rites owe their inception to Numa, together with various places, known by the priests as *Argei*, dedicated to their performance. But the grandest achievement of his reign was, that throughout its course, he remained the jealous guardian of peace even more than of power. Thus two successive kings each, though in opposite ways, added strength to the growing city: Romulus by war, Numa by peace. Romulus reigned thirty-seven years, Numa forty-three. When Numa died, Rome by the twin disciplines of peace and war was as eminent for self-mastery as for military power.

A second *interregnum* followed Numa's death; then, by the vote of the people, ratified by the senate, Tullus Hostilius, grandson of the Hostilius who fought the fine action on the lower slopes of the Palatine against the Sabines, was elected to succeed him. He proved a very different man from his predecessor; indeed, in his lust for action he surpassed Romulus himself, driven, as he was, along the path of adventure by his grandfather's fame and the strength of his own young manhood. In his view, Rome had been allowed to lapse into senility, and his one object was to find cause for renewed military adventure.

It so happened that a series of reciprocal cattle-raids was going on across the borders of Roman and Alban territory (ruled at that time by Gaius Cluilius). From both states envoys were sent almost simultaneously to negotiate the recovery of the stolen property. The Roman party had orders to carry out their instructions immediately they arrived; their demand would certainly be refused, and the refusal would allow Tullus to declare war with a good conscience. The envoys from Alba were less prompt in coming to business; welcomed by Tullus with every mark of gracious hospitality, they attended the state banquet as if nothing were amiss, while the Roman envoys had already made their demand for restitution and replied to Cluilius's refusal by a declaration of war, to take effect in thirty days. They then returned to Rome and made their report, whereupon Tullus asked the envoys from Alba to state the object of their mission. Not knowing what had happened they replied, not without embarrassment, that the last thing they wanted was to say anything disagreeable to their host; but orders were orders, and it was their duty to declare that they had come to demand restitution of stolen property, and to declare war in the event of a refusal.

'Tell your king,' Tullus answered 'that the king of Rome calls the gods to witness which of our two peoples was the first to refuse the demand for redress. Our prayer is that the guilty nation may suffer all the misery of the coming war.'

Tullus's words were duly reported in Alba, and preparations on a grand scale were put in hand by both peoples for a struggle which was to all intents and purposes a civil war. Romans and Albans were both of Trojan stock; Lavinium had been settled by men from Troy, Alba by men from Lavinium, and the Romans sprang from the line of the Alban kings. War between them would be like father against son. Luckily, however, what actually happened made the struggle less grievous than it might have been. No full-scale battle was fought; one only of the two cities was demolished, and the two peoples ended by amalgamating.

The Albans were first in the field and with a large force took up an entrenched position within Roman territory and not more than five

Albans
vs
Rome

miles from the town. The name 'Cluilius's Trench' stuck to the spot
for some centuries afterwards, until the actual digging disappeared and
the name fell into abeyance. It so happened that Cluilius died while his
men were holding this position, and the supreme command was given
by the Albans to Mettius Fufetius. Cluilius's death acted like a tonic
upon Tullus; the powers of heaven, he declared, had begun their vengeance on the wicked war-makers. Their king had been the first to
suffer; soon the wrath of God would be felt by every man and woman
in Alba. With the boast still on his lips, he advanced under cover of
darkness past the enemy's position into Alban territory. The move
roused Mettius to action; leaving his entrenchments he made straight
for the Roman army, sending in advance a spokesman with orders to
propose to Tullus that a conference should be held before engaging;
for he was confident, should Tullus agree to meet him, that he could
make a suggestion which would prove of equal value to both parties.
Tullus did not reject the proposal; nevertheless, in case the conference
should prove abortive, he took the precaution of setting his troops in
order of battle. The Albans followed suit, and Tullus and Mettius,
attended by a few high officers, stepped forward to meet each other
between the marshalled armies.

Mettius was the first to speak. 'Our king Cluilius,' he said, 'told me,
if I remember, that we were about to fight over a matter of brigandage
and the refusal to restore stolen property in accordance with our treaty;
and I have no doubt that you, Tullus, are prepared to retort in similar
terms. So be it. If, however, we let specious arguments go and tell
each other the truth, we should admit that our two nations, close
neighbours and blood relations as we are, have a deeper reason for
going to war: I mean, ambition and the love of power. Whether
rightly or wrongly I will not venture to say, for that is a question
decided, no doubt, by him who undertook to wage this war. As for me,
I am only the man the Albans chose to conduct it. But what I would
suggest to you, Tullus, is this: you know the strength of the Etruscans
who threaten to encircle us, and you know it even better than we, as
you are closer to them. They are strong on land, and at sea very strong
indeed. Do not forget, when you give the signal for battle, that they
will be watching us, ready, when we have worn each other out, to
attack us both, victor and vanquished alike. Surely, therefore, unless
both our countries are condemned to perdition, we should be able to
find a better solution. The assurance of liberty is not, it seems, enough

for us, and we are about to gamble for empire or slavery; nevertheless, can we not find some means of deciding the issue between us which, however the fight may go, will at least avoid crippling losses either to you or to ourselves?'

Tullus was not displeased by the proposal, though he was confident of victory and enjoyed a fight as much as any man. Ways and means were therefore considered; a plan was adopted, and a fortunate circumstance provided the means of carrying it out. In each army there were three brothers – triplets – all equally young and active, belonging to the families of the Horatii and Curiatii. That these were their names has never been in doubt, and the story is one of the great stories of ancient times; yet in spite of its celebrity historians have disagreed about which name belonged to which set of brothers. The majority, I find, say that the Horatii were Roman, and I am willing to follow their lead.

To these young men the two rival commanders made their proposal, that they should fight, three against three, as the champions of their countries, the victorious to have dominion over the vanquished: the proposal was accepted; the time and place for the contest were arranged and a solemn agreement entered into by the Romans and Albans to the effect that whichever of the two peoples should prove victorious through the prowess of its champions should be undisputed master of the other. The terms of treaties of course vary according to circumstance, but the form remains constant; on the present occasion, that of the oldest treaty on record, the procedure, we read, was as follows: the 'fetial' (priest) approached Tullus, the king. 'My lord,' he asked, 'do you bid me make this compact with the representative of the Alban people?'

'I do.'

'Then I demand of you, my lord, the holy herb.'

'Go and pluck it untainted.'

The priest brought from the sacred enclosure a fresh green plant, and said: 'My lord, do you grant me, with my emblems and companions, the king's sanction to speak for the people of Rome?'

'I grant it,' the king replied, 'without prejudice to myself and the people of Rome.'

The priest was Marcus Valerius, and he appointed Spurius Fusius, touching his head and hair with the ceremonial leaves, as *pater patratus*, or 'spokesman', whose duty is to pronounce the oath and thus to solemnize the compact. This he does in a long metrical formula, which is not worth the trouble of quoting here. Finally, the terms of the treaty having been read out, 'Hear me, Jupiter,' Fusius cried; 'hear me, Alba, and you who speak on her behalf: from the terms of this compact, as they have been publicly and openly read from these tablets today and clearly understood by us assembled here, the Roman people will never be the first to depart. Should they do so treacherously, and by public consent, then, great Jove, I pray that thou mayst strike them even as I strike this pig, and the more fiercely in that thy power and might are greater than mine.' He then dispatched the pig with a flint knife. The Albans, on their side, took a similar oath according to their own formula, and the treaty was made.

The six champions now made ready for battle. As they stepped forward into the lists between the two armies their hearts were high, and ringing in their ears were the voices of friends, bidding them remember that their parents, their country, and their country's gods, their fellow-soldiers and all they loved at home, would be watching their prowess and that all eyes were on their swords. The rival armies were still in position; danger there was none, but every man present was tense with anxiety. The stakes were high; upon the luck or valour of three men hung empire or slavery. In an agony of suspense the onlookers prepared for the spectacle.

The trumpet blared. The brothers drew their swords, and with all the pride of embattled armies advanced to the combat. Careless of death and danger, each thought only of his country's fate, of the grim choice between lordship and ignominy, which they themselves, and they only, were about to decide. They met. At the flash of steel and the clang of shield on shield a thrill ran through the massed spectators, breathless and speechless while as yet neither side had the advantage. Soon the combatants were locked in a deadly grapple; bodies writhed and twisted, the leaping blades parried and thrust, and blood began to flow. Alba's three champions were wounded; a Roman fell, then another, stretched across his body and both at the point of death. A cheer burst from the Alban army, as the two Romans went down, while from their adversaries all hope was gone; life seemed to drain from them, as they contemplated the dreadful predicament of their one survivor, surrounded by the three Curiatii.

The young man, though alone, was unhurt. No match for his three opponents together, he was yet confident of his ability to face them singly, and, with this purpose in mind, he took to his heels, sure that they would be after him with such speed as their wounds allowed. Not far from the scene of the first fight he looked back. His three enemies were coming, strung out one behind the other, the foremost almost upon him. He turned and attacked him furiously. A cry rose from the Alban army: 'Your brother! Save him!' But it was too late Horatius had already killed his man and, flushed with triumph, was looking for his next victim. The Romans' cheer for their young soldier was like the roar of the crowd at the race when luck turns defeat into victory. Horatius pressed on to make an end. He killed his second man before the last, near though he was, could come to his aid.

Now it was one against one; but the two antagonists were far from equally matched in all else that makes for victory. Horatius was unhurt, and elated by his double success; his opponent, exhausted by running and loss of blood, could hardly drag himself along; his brothers had been killed before his eyes; he was a beaten man facing a victorious enemy. What followed cannot be called a fight. 'I have killed two already,' the Roman cried, 'to avenge my brothers' ghosts. I offer the last to settle our quarrel, that Rome may be mistress of Alba.' With these proud words he plunged his sword with a downward stroke into the throat of his enemy, now too weak to sustain his shield, and then stripped him where he lay.

The cheering ranks of the Roman army, whose joy was the keener by the narrow escape from disaster, welcomed back their champion. The two sides then buried their dead, a common task but performed with very different feelings by victors and vanquished. Alba was subject now to her Roman mistress. The graves are still to be seen at the place where each man fell: those of the two Romans together, in the direction of Alba; those of the three Albans nearer Rome and at some distance from each other.

Before the troops left their stations, Mettius asked Tullus what, by the terms of the agreement, he now required him to do, and Tullus instructed him to keep his men under arms as they would be a useful reinforcement if Rome should find herself at war with Veii. — *Etruscan*

At the head of the Roman army on its return to the city marched Horatius, carrying his triple spoils, and it so happened that outside the Capena gate he met his sister, a young girl who had been betrothed to one of the Curiatii. Slung across her brother's shoulders was a cloak, and she recognized it as the cloak she had made with her own hands for her lover. The sight overcame her: she loosed her hair and, in a voice

choked with tears, called her dead lover's name. That his sister should
dare to grieve at the very moment of his own triumph and in the
midst of national rejoicing filled Horatius with such uncontrollable
rage that he drew his sword and stabbed her to the heart. 'Take your
girl's love,' he shouted, 'and give it to your lover in hell. What is Rome
to such as you, or your brothers, living or dead? So perish all Roman
women who mourn for an enemy!'

There were none who did not feel the horror of this deed. Horatius,
in spite of the great service he had just rendered to his country, was
arrested and brought for trial before the king. Tullus shrank from the
responsibility of passing the death sentence, which must, in the circumstances, have proved unpopular, so he summoned a mass meeting and informed the populace of his intention to appoint the special
officers known as *duumvirs*, to convict Horatius of treason according
to the regular law. The wording of the law was solemn and awe-
inspiring: 'Let the duumvirs', it ran, 'pass judgement for treason. If
the prisoner should appeal, let the appeal be weighed. If the conviction
is maintained, let the officer of the law veil the prisoner's head, hang
him with a rope on a barren tree, and scourge his body within or
without the city walls.' The duumvirs were duly appointed, and, on
the supposition that by the letter of the law they were bound to convict even an innocent man, one of them addressed the prisoner with
the words: 'Publius Horatius, I find you guilty of treason. Lictor, bind
his arms.' The lictor stepped forward and was about to pinion him
when Tullus intervened. Tullus was anxious to temper the severity
of the law and urged the prisoner to appeal. Horatius did so, and his
appeal was submitted to the judgement of the people. In the course of
the hearing the decisive factor was the statement of Horatius's father,
to the effect that his daughter deserved her death. Had it been otherwise, he declared, he would have exercised his right to punish his son
himself. He then appealed to the people to remember the fine family
of children he so recently possessed, and begged them not to leave
him wholly bereft. 'Men of Rome,' he cried, embracing his son and
pointing to the spoils of war set up in the place now known as the
'Horatian Spears', 'have you the heart to see this young soldier, fresh
from the joy and pride of victory, bound and beaten and tortured and
forced to bend his neck under the yoke? Even the men of Alba might
shudder at a sight so shameful. Do your work, lictor! Bind the hands
whose sword but yesterday gave Rome dominion! Blindfold our lib-

erator's eyes – hang him on the barren tree – scourge him within the walls, yes, in sight of the spears he took from the dead hands of his enemies or outside, if you will, amongst the tombs where those same enemies lie! For wherever you take him, the visible reminder of his noble service will surely save him from so foul a punishment.'

The young man's courage, in the face of this peril as of all others, no less than his father's moving appeal, had its due effect. Though he was guilty in law, popular admiration of his quality obtained his acquittal. It was felt none the less that something, at any rate, should be done to mitigate the stain of so notorious a murder, so the father was bidden to perform, at the public cost, certain ceremonies which would expiate the crime. These ceremonies, which were duly gone through, became from that day traditional in the Horatian family. After their performance a piece of timber was slung across the roadway and the young Horatius was made to pass beneath it with covered head, as under the 'yoke' of submission. The timber is still to be seen – replaced from time to time at the state's expense – and is known as the Sister's Beam. The tomb of the murdered girl was built of hewn stone and stands on the spot where she was struck down.

Peace with Alba was not of long duration. Mettius, a man of weak character, was unable to deal with the resentment of his people at what they felt to have been the folly of entrusting the nation's future to three men. The policy, in itself a good one, had failed, and, in the hope of regaining his popularity, Mettius now had recourse to dubious methods. In war he had wanted peace; now, in peace, he wanted war. Accordingly, as he knew his people, despite their courage, had little military strength, he proceeded to tamper with the neighbouring tribes; these he urged to declare war openly on Rome, intending that his own people, nominally Rome's allies, should in due course betray her.

The people of Fidenae, a colony of Rome, were induced in concert with Veii to declare war by a promise that Alba would join them. Tullus, at the secession of Fidenae, sent an order to Mettius to join him with his troops, and promptly took the field. Crossing the Anio, he halted at the confluence of the rivers; somewhere between him and Fidenae the Veientian troops had crossed the Tiber, and formed the right wing resting on the river, while the men of Fidenae formed the left, nearer the hills. Tullus stationed his own troops so as to confront the Veientians, and sent the Alban contingent to deal with the Fidenates. Mettius, however, the Alban commander, proved as much coward as traitor: not daring either to stand his ground or openly to desert, he began a cautious withdrawal to the hills. At what he thought to be a sufficient distance he brought up his whole force and deployed it, simply as a ruse for gaining time, until events should make up his mind for him; for his intention was to join the victors.

The Roman troops who had been in touch with the Albans and now found their flank exposed were at a loss to account for their withdrawal; then a messenger galloped up to the king with the report that the Alban army was deserting. It was a critical situation: Tullus (having vowed to create twelve Salian priests and to dedicate shrines to Pallor and Panic) promptly ordered the messenger back into the line. He spoke at the top of his voice so that everything he said might be heard by the enemy, and added that there was no need for alarm as the Albans were obeying his own orders to envelope the Fidenates and attack their unprotected rear. At the same time he ordered the cavalry to raise their spears vertically to form a screen which prevented most of the Roman infantry from seeing the Albans moving off; those who did see them were encouraged by what Tullus had said to fight with greater vigour. It was now the enemy's turn to be alarmed; Tullus's loud assertion had been audible enough, and most of the Fidenates understood Latin as emigrants from Rome had settled amongst them in the past. They accordingly beat a retreat, to obviate the danger of being cut off from home by a sudden descent of the Albans from the hills. Tullus attacked, made short work of the Fidenates on the wing, and then turned with increased fury on the Veientians, who were already shaken by their friends' discomfiture. Their resistance broke and they fled in disorder to the river in their rear. Checked by the river in their efforts to escape, some threw away their arms and plunged blindly into the water while others were caught and killed on the bank before they could make up their minds whether to fight or flee. It was the bloodiest battle that Rome had yet fought.

After the action the Alban troops, who had taken no part whatever in it, marched down from the hills. Mettius congratulated Tullus on his success; Tullus made a courteous reply. He expressed the hope that their luck would hold, and gave orders that the Roman and Alban troops should bivouac together for the night, as on the following day he proposed to offer a lustral sacrifice. At dawn next morning all was ready and he issued to both armies the customary order to assemble. The Albans, who formed the outer lines of the camp, were the first to be summoned by the criers, and took their stand immediately in front of the king, the better to enjoy the novel experience of hearing him address his troops. The Romans had already received instructions to parade armed, and were drawn up around the Albans, the centurions having been cautioned to obey all orders promptly. Tullus then spoke: 'My men,' he said, 'if ever in any war you have had cause to be thankful to God's mercy and your own valour, it was in yesterday's action. You were fighting yesterday not against your enemy only; you had a worse and more dangerous foe – the treachery of your friends. I want you now to know the truth: when the Albans withdrew to the hills, it was by no order of mine. When you heard me say that I had given that order, it was a deliberate falsehood, for I did not wish you to know of your allies' desertion lest you should lose heart, and at the same time I was confident that fear of being surrounded would break the resistance of the enemy. Now the guilt of desertion does not rest upon the Alban troops as a whole: the men merely followed their commander, as you would have done yourselves had I required to shift our position. No: Mettius is the guilty man; Mettius led the movement from the field; Mettius by his machinations started this war; Mettius is the treaty-breaker. I now propose to make such an example of him that nobody will ever be likely to commit such crimes again.'

Armed centurions stepped forward to guard the culprit, and Tullus proceeded: 'My purpose, men of Alba – and I pray that it may bring happiness and prosperity to us all – is to transfer to Rome the entire population of your city. Your commons shall have Roman citizenship, your nobles the right to be elected senators. We shall be one city, one commonwealth. Long ago the Alban people split into two; let them now be reunited.'

The Alban troops were unarmed and surrounded by armed men; one sentiment, at least, was shared by all of them when they heard these words, and that was fear. Not a man spoke. Tullus turned to Mettius.

'Mettius Fufetius,' he said, 'were you capable of learning loyally to abide by your word, I should have let you live, I should have taught you myself. But you are not capable; no medicine can cure your mind's disease. So be it: your punishment may teach mankind to hold sacred the honour you have besmirched. Yesterday you could not decide between Fidenae and Rome: doubtless it was a painful division of mind – but today the division of your body will be more painful still.'

Two chariots were brought up, each drawn by four horses. Mettius was tied, spread-eagled, to both of them. At a touch of the whip the two teams sprang forward in opposite directions, carrying with them the fragments of the mangled body still held by the ropes. All eyes were averted from the disgusting spectacle – never, in all our history, repeated. That was the first and last time that fellow-countrymen of ours inflicted a punishment so utterly without regard to the laws of humanity. Save for that one instance we can fairly claim to have been content with more humane forms of punishment than any other nation.

Meanwhile mounted troops had been sent to Alba to deal with the transference of the population, and a force of infantry followed charged with the task of pulling down the buildings of the town. There was no panic when the soldiers marched in; none of the wild confusion of a captured town when a victorious army, forcing its way through smashed gates and over the rubble of battered walls, spreads with yells of triumph through every street and alley dealing universal destruction with fire and sword; none of the horror of a citadel falling to the final assault. On the contrary, there was silence – the silence of despair and the grief which could not speak. All hearts were numbed, all minds bewildered; looking at their possessions, the unhappy people could not decide what to take or what to leave; again and again they asked each other's advice, now standing distraught before their doors, now wandering aimlessly through the familiar rooms which they would never see again.

Soon the Roman cavalrymen shouted their orders. It was time to leave, and the harsh command could not be disobeyed. On the outskirts of the town was heard the crash of falling masonry; in this direction and that clouds of rising dust darkened the sky. Alba's hour had come. People hurriedly snatched up what they could of their poor possessions, and the melancholy exodus began; the houses where they had been born and reared, the gods of their hearth, all they held sacred, were left behind for ever. The roads were packed with refugees in an unbroken line; pity at the sight of others as wretched as themselves renewed their tears; women – and men too – sobbed aloud as they passed the august temples where armed soldiers stood on guard, for it seemed they were leaving even their gods in captivity.

As soon as the inhabitants of the town had left, every building, public and private, was levelled to the ground. In a single hour the work of four hundred years lay in utter ruin. Only the temples, by Tullus's order, were left standing.

A result of the fall of Alba was an increase in the size of Rome. The population was doubled. The Caelian Hill was taken into the city boundaries; and to encourage building that quarter Tullus chose it as the site of a new palace, which became from that time forward his official residence. The number of families of senatorial rank was increased by the admission of some of the Alban nobility, such as the Tullii, Servilii, Quinctii, Geganii, Curiatii, and Cloelii. For the order thus enlarged Tullus built, for their solemn deliberations, the Senate House which till a generation ago was known as the Curia Hostilia. Finally, ten squadrons of Alban Knights were formed, the old infantry battalions recruited from the same source, and fresh battalions enlisted. Thus all three orders in the commonwealth received an addition to their strength from the newcomers.

Tullus soon felt strong enough to declare war on the Sabines, who at that period were the most populous and powerful nation in Italy, the Etruscans excepted. There were grievances on both sides, and neither had succeeded in getting redress. Tullus had lodged frequent complaints of the seizure in a crowded market, at the shrine of Feronia, of Roman citizens who had gone to do business there; the Sabines retorted that the Romans were the first offenders, in that they had arrested and detained in Rome Sabine refugees who had sought sanctuary.

The Sabines had not forgotten that a part of their manpower had been transferred to Rome long ago by Tatius, and they were well aware of the recent addition to Roman strength which had followed her defeat of Alba. They began, in consequence, to look round for external aid. Across the border lay Etruria, and the nearest Etruscan town was Veii. In Veii war had left certain smouldering resentments, always a rich soil for revolt, and a number of men volunteered to serve; a few paupers and vagabonds were also persuaded by the prospect of pay. But no regular assistance of any kind was forthcoming, and the government at Veii held firmly to the truce made long before with Romulus.

On both sides preparations for war were now in full swing, and it was becoming plain that the advantage would lie with whoever made the first move. It was Tullus who struck. He invaded Sabine territory, and a bloody battle was fought at a place called Mantrap Wood. The engagement ended in a Roman victory, due, more than to anything else, to the strength of their recently augmented cavalry, whose rapid charge flung the Sabines into such disorder that they were unable without severe losses either to reorganize or to extricate themselves by a withdrawal.

Just at the moment when, after the defeat of the Sabines, Tullus and Rome were more prosperous and respected than ever before, a disturbing thing happened: a shower of stones (or so it was reported to the king and Senate) had fallen on the Alban Mount. A party was sent to investigate this improbable story, which turned out to be true; for before the very eyes of the investigators stones in large numbers fell from the sky and lay on the ground like drifted hail. At the same time a great voice seemed to issue from the grove on the top of the hill, bidding the Albans return to the religion of their fathers which they had allowed to fall into abeyance as if the gods of Alba had been left alone in their abandoned shrines, while their people turned faithlessly to the deities of Rome or forgot religion altogether in anger at their fate. These strange events affected the Romans too: by the advice of their soothsayers – or perhaps even as a direct result of the mysterious voice from the hill-top – they decreed a nine-day public holiday for religious observance, and it was agreed that a similar festival should be held regularly in future should the phenomenon be repeated.

Not long afterwards there was an outbreak of the plague. The king's heart was always set upon war, and for a time he allowed no respite from military service in spite of the obvious reluctance of his subjects in their present unhappy circumstances. Moreover, he professed to believe that men of military age would keep healthier under arms than idling at home. However he finally fell ill himself, and protracted sickness caused him to change his mind. With the loss of his physical strength his proud spirit was so broken that he seemed to become another man: he who had once thought preoccupation with religion utterly unworthy of a king, suddenly found himself wide open as it were to the influence of every sort of superstition, great or small, and doing his best to inspire his subjects with a similar sense of the presence and power of the supernatural. Everyone in Rome was soon agreed that a return to the state of things under Numa was now their only resource, and that the only way of getting rid of the plague was to pray to heaven for pardon and peace. The story goes that Tullus found in the commentaries of Numa, which he was turning over one day, a reference to certain secret rites in honour of Jupiter Elicius. He performed these rites, unknown to anybody. Apparently, however, his procedure was incorrect, for not only was he denied any divine manifestation, but cruelly punished for his error. Jupiter was angry; the palace was struck by lightning, and Tullus perished in the flames. He had won great glory as a soldier, and reigned thirty-two years.

In accordance with long-standing custom, power, on the death of Tullus, reverted to the senate, who named an *interrex*. At the subsequent election the people's choice, ratified by the senate, fell upon Ancus Marcius, the grandson on the mother's side of Numa Pompilius. Ancus was deeply conscious of his grandfather's noble record, and well aware that the splendid achievements of his predecessor Tullus had fallen seriously short in one respect: the neglect or misconduct of religious observances. In the belief, therefore, that nothing was more important than the restoration of the national religion in the form established by Numa, he instructed the pontifex to copy out from his commentaries the details of all the various ceremonies and to display the document in public. To the war-weary Romans the prospect of peace seemed assured, and both they and their neighbours began to hope that the new king was to prove a second Numa. This was the Latins' opportunity. There had been a treaty between Rome and Latium in Tullus's reign, but now the Latins felt that they might in the changed circumstances be a match for their old enemy. Accordingly they raided Roman territory, and to the subsequent demand for restitution returned a haughty answer, convinced that Ancus was no soldier and would play the king only amongst his shrines and altars. However, there was more than one side to Ancus's character; he had in him something of Numa and something of Romulus too. He well understood the value of a policy of peace when Rome was young and her people still somewhat wild; but at the same time he knew that he could not himself enjoy without injury the tranquillity which, in Numa's reign, had brought such benefits. Hostile peoples were already beginning to prick him to see how much he would stand, and the result was not to his credit. Times were difficult, and called for a Tullus rather than a Numa. In one respect, however, Ancus did follow Numa's lead, though with a difference. Numa had established religious observances in time of peace; Ancus provided war with an equivalent solemn ceremonial of its own. It was not enough, he thought, that wars should be fought; he believed that they should also be formally declared, and for this purpose he adopted from the ancient tribe of the Aequicolae the legal formalities (now in the hands of the fetials) by which a state

demands redress for a hostile act. The procedure was as follows: when
the envoy arrives at the frontier of the state from which satisfaction is
sought, he covers his head with a woollen cap and says: 'Hear me,
Jupiter! Hear me, land of So-and-so! Hear me, O righteousness! I am
the accredited spokesman of the Roman people. I come as their envoy
in the name of justice and religion, and ask credence for my words.'
The particular demands follow and the envoy, calling Jupiter to witness, proceeds: 'If my demand for the restitution of those men, or
those goods, be contrary to religion and justice, then never let me be a
citizen of my country.' The formula, with only minor changes, is
repeated when the envoy crosses the frontier, to the first man he subsequently meets, when he passes through the gate of the town, and
when he enters the public square. If his demand is refused, after thirty-
three days (the statutory number) war is declared in the following
form: 'Hear, Jupiter; hear, Janus Quirinus; hear, all ye gods in heaven,
on earth, and under the earth: I call you to witness that the people of
So-and-so are unjust and refuse reparation. But concerning these things
we will consult the elders of our country, how we may obtain our due.'
The envoy then returns to Rome for consultation. The formula in
which the king asked the opinion of the elders was approximately this:
'Of the goods, or suits, or causes, concerning which the representative
of the Roman people has made demands of the representative of the
Ancient Latins, and of the people of the Ancient Latins, which goods
or suits or causes they have failed to restore, or settle, or satisfy,
all of them requiring restoration or settlement or satisfaction: speak,
what think you?' The person thus first addressed replied: 'I hold that
those things be sought by means of just and righteous war. Thus I give
my vote and my consent.' The same question was put to the others in
rotation, and if a majority voted in favour, war was agreed upon. The
fetial thereupon proceeded to the enemy frontier carrying a spear with
a head either of iron or hardened wood, and in the presence of not less
than three men of military age made the following proclamation:
'Whereas the peoples of the Ancient Latins and the men of Priscus
Latinus have committed acts and offences against the Roman people, and
whereas the Roman people have commanded that there be war with
the Ancient Latins, and the Senate of the Roman people has ordained,
consented, and voted that there be war with the Ancient Latins: I
therefore and the Roman people hereby declare and make war on
the peoples of the Ancient Latins and the men of the Ancient Latins.'

The formal declaration made, the spear was thrown across the frontier. It was in this form that redress was demanded of the Latins on the occasion of which we are speaking and war declared. The same formal procedure was adopted by subsequent generations.

Religious matters were now left by Ancus in the hands of the various orders of priests while he himself raised fresh troops and marched to the Latin town of Politorium, which he took by assault. The inhabitants he transferred bodily to Rome; former kings had increased the size of Rome by the absorption of conquered peoples; so the policy was not without precedent. The Palatine hill was where the Romans first settled; on one side of it were the Capitol and Citadel, subsequently occupied by the Sabines, and on the other lay the Caelian hill, occupied by the Albans; the Aventine was assigned to the newcomers, and they were joined soon after by others from the captured towns of Tellenae and Ficana.

Politorium, denuded of its people, was later reoccupied, and again attacked by Rome. This time, to prevent it from becoming a regular place of refuge for their enemies, the Romans saw fit to raze it to the ground. The war dragged on, until at last all the Latin troops were forced back from Medullia; the town was well fortified and strongly garrisoned; from a position outside the fortifications the Latins on several occasions came to close grips with the Romans, and a number of engagements were fought without decisive results. Finally, however, Ancus, by an all-out effort, was successful in a pitched battle. He took the town and returned to Rome with an immense quantity of plunder. Once again, thousands more Latins were given Roman citizenship and made to settle in the quarter where the Altar of Murcia stands, thus connecting the Aventine hill with the Palatine. The Janiculum, too, was brought within the compass of the city, not because the additional area was needed but as a precaution against its use as a stronghold by some hostile power. It was decided not only to fortify it but also to facilitate communication with the rest of Rome by building a pile bridge (the first ever to be constructed) across the Tiber. It was Ancus, too, who considerably strengthened the defences on the more accessible side of the city by the construction of the so-called Quirites' Trench.

One result of these enormous additions to the population was an increase in certain criminal activities, the dividing line between right and wrong becoming somewhat blurred. To meet this unhappy state of affairs and to discourage the further growth of lawlessness, the Prison was built in the centre of the city, just above the Forum. Beyond the city boundaries Roman territory was also enlarged during Ancus's reign; the Maesian Forest was taken from the Veientes, thus extending Roman dominion to the sea; Ostia was founded at the mouth of the Tiber; salt-works were constructed in its neighbourhood; and to mark a period of successful military adventure important additions were made to the temple of Jupiter Feretrius.

In the course of this reign a man named Lucumo left Tarquinii where he was born and came to settle in Rome. He was ambitious and wealthy and hoped to rise to a position of eminence there, such as his native town was never likely to afford him; for though born at Tarquinii he was by blood an alien, being the son of Demaratus of Corinth. Demaratus had been forced by political troubles to leave his country, and happened to settle in Tarquinii, where he married and had two sons, Lucumo and Arruns. Lucumo survived his father and inherited all his property; Arruns predeceased him, leaving his wife pregnant. Demaratus was unaware that his daughter-in-law was about to have a child, so when shortly afterwards he himself died too, he had made no provision in his will for his grandson. The child, thus deprived of his inheritance, was named Egerius – the Needy One. Lucumo, on the contrary, the sole heir of his father's property, became in time as proud as he was wealthy, and his self-confidence was further increased by his marriage to Tanaquil, an aristocratic young woman who was not of a sort to put up with humbler circumstances in her married life than those she had been previously accustomed to. The Etruscans of Tarquinii despised Lucumo as the son of foreign refugees, and to Tanaquil the indignity of his position soon became intolerable; wholly bent upon seeing her husband enjoy the respect he deserved, she smothered all feelings of natural affection for her native town and determined to abandon it for ever. For the purpose she had in mind she decided that the most suitable place was Rome: Rome was a young and rising community; there would be opportunities for an active and courageous man in a place where all advancement came swiftly and depended upon ability. After all, King Tatius had been a foreigner – a Sabine; Numa had been called to the throne from his native Cures; Ancus had had a Sabine mother and no ancestor of noble blood with the single exception of Numa. Tanaquil had no difficulty in persuading her husband: he was already set upon improving his position, and the prospect of leaving Tarquinii – the birthplace of his mother only – caused him no distress. So they packed their belongings and left for Rome.

The pair had reached Janiculum and were sitting together in their carriage, when an eagle dropped gently down and snatched off the cap which Lucumo was wearing. Up went the bird with a great clangour of wings until, a minute later, it swooped down again and, as if it had been sent by heaven for that very purpose, neatly replaced the cap on Lucumo's head, and then vanished into the blue. Tanaquil like most Etruscans was well skilled in celestial prodigies, and joyfully accepted the omen. Flinging her arms round her husband's neck, she told him that no fortune was too high to hope for. 'Only consider,' she cried, 'from what quarter of the sky the eagle came, what god sent it as his messenger! Did it not declare its message by coming to your *head* – the highest part of you? Did it not take the crown, as it were, from a human head, only to restore it by heaven's approval, where it belongs?' Thus dreaming upon future greatness, Lucumo and Tanaquil drove on into Rome, where they bought a house, and Lucumo took the name of Lucius Tarquinius Priscus.

In Rome Lucumo soon began to attract attention as a wealthy stranger, and wasted no opportunity of advancing himself. Hospitable, free with his money, and always ready with a kindly word, he made friends rapidly, and it was not long before his reputation got as far as the palace. Once known to the king, he was quick to improve the acquaintance, serving him with such liberality and adroitness that he was soon admitted into intimacy and consulted upon every matter of private interest or national importance, both in peace and war, until he became indispensable and was even named in the king's will as guardian of his children.

Ancus reigned twenty-four years. His fame as both soldier and administrator was unsurpassed by any previous occupant of the throne. His sons were on the verge of manhood, and for this reason Tarquin (as we shall now call Lucumo) was anxious that the election of a successor to the throne should be held at the earliest possible moment. A date was announced, and a few days before it Tarquin sent the two boys out of town on a hunting expedition. He is said to have been the first to canvass personally for votes, and to have delivered a public speech designed to win popular support. It was not without precedent, he declared, that he, a foreigner, aspired to the throne: were he the first to do so, there might well be suprise, or even anger; but he was not the first, but the third. Tatius had been not a foreigner only, but an enemy; and Numa was actually asked to accept the crown when he showed no signs of wanting it and knew nothing of Rome. 'Whereas I,' Tarquin continued, 'so soon as ever I was master of my fortunes, settled amongst you here with my wife and all my property, and here in Rome I have spent more years of active public life than in the town where I was born. The laws of Rome, the religion of Rome I have learned in peace and war from no negligible teacher – King Ancus himself. I have vied with all men in my defence and duty to the king, and not the king himself has surpassed me in generosity to others.'

Tarquin's claims were not unjustified and he secured the popular vote by an overwhelming majority. In most ways he was a man of outstanding character and ability; nevertheless after his accession he employed the same sort of means of assuring his position as he had employed to gain it. He was always something of a schemer, and it was as much to strengthen his own hold upon the throne as to increase the political influence of the Senate that he now added to that body a hundred new members, subsequently known as representing the 'lesser families'; owing their promotion to the king, these new members naturally constituted a party of 'king's men', supporting him in everything.

Tarquin's first campaign was against the Latins. He captured Apiolae, and returned to Rome with more plunder than what report had led people to expect, he celebrated public games on a scale more elaborate and opulent than any of his predecessors. It was on this occasion that our Circus Maximus was originally planned. On the ground marked out for it special places were assigned to Senators and knights to erect their stands in – or 'decks' as they were called. These stands were supported on props and raised twelve feet from the ground. Horses and boxers, mostly from Etruria, provided the entertainment. From then onward the games became an annual institution, and were called the Roman, or Greek, games. Tarquin also made grants of land round the Forum to be used as private building sites, and built shops and porticoes. His project of enclosing the whole city in a stone wall was, however, interrupted by a clash with the Sabines. The trouble began so unexpectedly that the enemy was across the Anio before Roman troops could make any move to stop him, and there were some moments of acute anxiety. For a while the fighting was in-decisive, with heavy losses on both sides; then the Sabines withdrew, giving Rome a breathing space in which to make fresh preparations. Tarquin seized his chance, and determined to make good what he felt to be the chief weakness of the Roman army, the inadequate number of mounted troops. For this purpose he proposed to reinforce the Ramnes, Titienses, and Luceres, the centuries originally enrolled by Romulus, with additional formations, to be distinguished by his own name. Now Romulus, before acting in this matter, had obtained the sanction of the auguries; and in consequence of this a certain dis-tinguished augur, named Attius Navius, declared that no change or innovation could possibly be made until the birds had given their con-sent. Tarquin was very angry. 'Ho ho!' he cried with a contemptuous laugh; 'then I would ask you, holy sir, to declare by your gift of prophecy if what I am thinking of at this moment, can be done.' His object, the story goes, was to ridicule the whole business of omens; but Navius was unperturbed. He took the auspices, and replied that the thought in the king's mind would, indeed, be realized. 'Very well,' said Tarquin; 'I was thinking that you would cut a whetstone in half with a razor. Get them, and do what those birds of yours declare can be done.' Believe it or not: without a moment's delay Navius did it. A statue of Navius, with the head covered, once stood on the spot where this occurred – on the steps of the Senate House, on the left-hand side. The whetstone too is supposed to have been preserved here, to remind posterity of the miracle. But whatever we may think of this story, the fact remains that the importance attached to augury and the augural priesthood increased to such an extent that to take the auspices was henceforward an essential preliminary to any serious undertaking in peace or in war: not only army parades or popular assemblies, but matters of vital concern to the commonwealth were postponed, if the birds refused their assent. Tarquin, on this occasion, made no change in the organization of the centuries of knights, but contented himself with doubling their number, so that the original three centuries now contained 1800 men. The recruits were known as 'posterior', or 'secondary', knights of the three centuries – Ramnes, Tities, and Luceres. We speak of the 'six centuries' today because of the doubling of the numbers they originally comprised.

Hostilities with the Sabines were now resumed. The striking-power of Rome had been increased by the expansion of the cavalry, but in what followed it was strategy that played the decisive part. A stack of dry timber which had been lying on the bank of the Anio was set alight and the blazing logs thrown into the water. A good wind kept them burning, and many were carried down by the stream and became lodged amongst the piles of the bridge, which they set on fire. This was alarming enough for the Sabines while they were fighting, but worse when their resistance broke; for the burning bridge prevented their retreat, and large numbers of them escaped the enemy only to perish in the river. Their equipment floated down the Tiber to Rome, where it was recognized for what it was and brought the news of victory almost before a messenger could get through. Reports of the engagement say that particular distinction was won by the Roman cavalry; they were posted on the wings, and at a critical moment when the infantry in the centre was being forced back, saved the day by a simultaneous charge on both the enemy flanks. Such was the vigour of their assault, that the Sabines were not only checked in their triumphant advance, but compelled to retreat in confusion.

A part of the routed army tried to reach the hills; a few men got there, but most of the fugitives, as I have said, were driven by the Roman cavalry into the river. Tarquin decided to press his advantage; having dispatched the plunder and prisoners to Rome, and made, as an offering to the god Vulcan, a huge bonfire of captured equipment, he moved forward into Sabine territory. The unfortunate Sabines had no time to think of how best to meet this second threat. Beaten once, they had little hope of success in a further battle; nevertheless they took the field with such forces as they could scrape together, and the inevitable result was another defeat. This time, all was up with them, and they sued for peace. Collatia and the territory south and west of it were taken from them, and Egerius, the king's nephew, was left to garrison the town. I have read that the formal procedure at the surrender of Collatia was as follows: the king asked: 'Are you the accredited representatives of Collatia, sent to surrender yourselves and the people of Collatia?'

'We are.'

'Are the people of Collatia free to make their own decisions?'

'Yes.'

'Do you surrender yourselves and the people of Collatia, together with the town, lands, water, boundary-stones, shrines, utensils, and all you possess for the service of your gods and of yourselves, into my hands and the hands of the Roman people?'

'We do.'

'I receive the surrender.'

The war over, Tarquin made his triumphal entry into Rome. His final campaign was against the Ancient Latins. No major battle was fought, and large forces were never engaged. The issue was decided piecemeal. One town after another was attacked and taken: Corniculum, Ficulea, Cameria, Crustumerium, Ameriola, Medullia, Nomentum – all of them settlements either of the Ancient Latins or of peoples who had joined their cause. Tarquin's success was complete, and peace was made.

However, it was peace with a difference; for the king set his people with such enthusiasm to various civic undertakings that they had even less leisure than they had had during the wars. The building of the stone wall, interrupted by the Sabine war, for the protection of those parts of Rome which were as yet unfortified, was resumed; the low-lying areas of the town around the Forum, and the valleys between the hills, where flood-water usually collected, were drained by sewers leading down into the Tiber; and, finally, the foundations of the temple of Jupiter on the Capitol were laid. Tarquin had bound himself, during the Sabine war, by a solemn vow to build this temple: one cannot but feel that in some way he already foresaw the future splendour of that famous place.

In the palace about this time there occurred a very odd thing, which was to have remarkable consequences. A little boy named Servius Tullius was lying asleep, when his head burst into flames. Many people saw it happen. The noise and excitement caused by such an extraordinary event came to the ears of the king and queen, and brought them hurrying to the spot. A servant ran for water and was about to throw it on the flames, when the queen stopped him, declaring, so soon as she could make herself heard, that the child must on no account be disturbed, but allowed to sleep till he awoke of his own accord. A few minutes later he opened his eyes, and the fire went out.

Tanaquil took her husband aside, where they could not be overheard. 'Listen,' she said; 'this child we are bringing up as if he were no better than a beggar – believe me, he will one day prove a light in our darkness, a prop to our house in the day of its affliction. We must see that he is taught and tended from now onward with every care,

77

as one through whom will come great glory to our family and to Rome.'

The story goes that from that instant the child was treated like a prince of the blood and received a prince's education. It was the will of heaven, and all went well: he grew in time to be a man of truly royal nature, and when Tarquin was looking for a son-in-law, he could find no one in Rome comparable in any way to young Servius; so to Servius he betrothed his daughter.

However we may try to account for this singular honour, the fact of it does, at least, make it impossible to believe that either Servius or his mother was ever a slave. There is another and, to me, more credible account of the matter, namely that a Servius Tullius was prince of Corniculum and was killed when the town was taken; his wife, who was pregnant at the time of his death, was recognized amongst the other prisoners, and the queen at Rome, as a tribute to her rank, spared her the shame of slavery and allowed her to live in the palace, where she gave birth to her son. This generous act led to a friendship between the two women, and the little boy, growing up from infancy in the palace, soon made himself beloved and was generally recognized as a person of importance. The story that he was the child of a slave-woman sprang merely from the fact that his unfortunate mother had been a prisoner of war.

The respect in which young Servius Tullius was held not only by the king but by all ranks of Roman society grew rapidly, until he became one of the most distinguished people in the state. About the thirty-eighth year of Tarquin's reign trouble began. The two sons of Tarquin's predecessor Ancus had always bitterly resented the trickery by which Tarquin had got them out of the country, when he was their guardian, and robbed them of their rights; it was bad enough in their view, that a mere immigrant, not even of native Italian blood should be king of Rome, but the future prospect was more intolerable still. For now, it seemed, even after Tarquin's death, the throne, instead of reverting to them, its rightful heirs, was to sink into the hands of slaves – an abyss indeed. Servius, the slave-woman's son, was to possess the power which a hundred years before had been enjoyed by Romulus – Romulus, the son of a god and himself divine. If foreigners and slaves could rule in Rome while sons of Ancus still lived, it would be not only an insult to the blood royal but a disgrace to the Roman name. The violence of their resentment suggested a desperate remedy: only the sword could save Rome from her shame.

Tarquin himself, not Servius, was their intended victim, and that for good reason: first, because the king, if he survived, would have more power to avenge the murder than a subject would have; secondly because, if Servius were killed, the king would certainly choose some other son-in-law, who would ultimately inherit the throne. They laid their plans accordingly to murder the king, and picked two country fellows, both desperate characters, to do the deed.

These men – they were shepherds – armed with the rough, country tools they were accustomed to use, presented themselves at the entrance-court of the palace, where they started brawling, or pretending to brawl, and raised such a racket that all the attendants came crowding round them to see what the matter was. One after the other the two ruffians appealed to the king at the top of their voices, until their shouts penetrated to the inner rooms and they were summoned into the king's presence. For a while they tried to shout each other down, until the king's lictor had had enough of it; he managed to stop them and told them to say what they had to say one at a time. Then the first, according to plan, started to put his case, and while the king was listening to him, the other, from behind, split his skull with an axe. Leaving the weapon in the wound, both men then made a dash for the door.

Hardly had the dying Tarquin been lifted by his attendants before the fugitives were caught by the lictors. There was an uproar; excited crowds gathered, eager to know what the trouble was. Tanaquil ordered the palace gates to be closed; then, getting rid of all who might observe what she was about, she began to prepare remedies for the wound, as if there were still hope of saving the king's life, at the same time taking certain other precautions in case her plan should fail. A few minutes later she sent for Servius. Seizing his hand, she directed his gaze to the king, now at the point of death, and begged him not to leave the murder unavenged or allow herself to be a creature of contempt in the eyes of those who hated her. 'Servius,' she cried, 'the throne is yours, if you are a man. It shall never be theirs who have done this deed of blood. Rise to your true stature; follow the gods who long ago by the circlet of heavenly fire declared that your head should wear the crown. Let the memory of those flames, assuredly divine, rouse you to act. Now is the time – now you must awake indeed. The king and I were foreigners, yet the throne was ours. Forget your origins, and remember only what you are – your manhood. What? The sudden shock has numbed your wits? What matter? – do as I bid you, and all will be well.'

Meanwhile the noise and excitement in the street were getting out of hand. The queen hurried to an upper room of the palace (which was near the temple of Jupiter Stator) and flinging open a window which looked out on the New Street, began to address the crowd. She urged them to be calm: the king, she declared, had been stunned by a blow – it was a surface-wound only. Already he had recovered consciousness; the wound had been cleaned and examined, and there was every reason for confidence. Without any doubt they would soon see him again for themselves. Meanwhile, she begged them to give their loyal obedience to Servius, who would see justice done and in all other ways deputize for the king.

Servius now began to appear in public wearing the white and purple robe of royalty and preceded by lictors; he sat on the king's seat of justice listening to suits, some of which he settled out of hand, while others he pretended that he would refer to the king. Thus for a number of days he concealed Tarquin's death, and by making it appear to the public that he was acting merely as the king's deputy, continued in fact, to strengthen his own position. Ancus's sons, on the arrest of their hired assassins and the report that Tarquin was alive and Servius in an almost impregnable position, retired to Suessia Pometia, where they lived in voluntary exile.

Servius then proceeded to personal as well as public measures to strengthen his hold upon the throne. It was not unlikely that Tarquin's sons, Lucius and Arruns, would resent his authority just as Ancus's sons had resented Tarquin's; so to obviate this danger, he married his two daughters to the young princes. But alas! fate is omnipotent and men are powerless to turn it aside. Nothing Servius could do prevented jealousy of his power from growing, even amongst members of his own household, to such a pitch that the palace was soon a hot-bed of intrigue and treachery.

A fresh upheaval was, however, most opportunely prevented by a war with Veii, the period of truce having expired, and other Etruscan communities. Servius proved a very able and successful commander; his victory over exceedingly powerful enemy forces was complete, and on his return to Rome there was no reason to doubt the loyalty of any section of society. His position was assured.

It was at this time that he undertook what was by far his most important service to the community; comparable, though in a different sphere, with the work of Numa. Numa had concerned himself with the proper establishment of religion; the political reputation of Servius rests upon his organization of society according to a fixed scale of rank and fortune. He originated the census, a measure of the highest utility to a state destined, as Rome was, to future pre-eminence; for by means of it public service, in peace as well as in war, could thenceforward be regularly organized on the basis of property; every man's contribution could be in proportion to his means. The population was divided into classes and 'centuries' according to a scale based on the census, and suitable for both peace and war. The scale was as follows:

1. Of those whose property was rated at a capital value of 100,000 *asses*[1] or more, 80 centuries were formed, 40 of 'seniors' and 40 of 'juniors'. This whole group was known as the *First Class*. The seniors were for civil defence, the juniors for service in the field. All were required to equip themselves with helmet, round shield, greaves, and breast-plate. The defensive armour was of bronze. Their weapons of offence were the sword and spear. To this class were attached two centuries of engineers, whose duty was the construction and maintenance of the siege-engines on active service. They were unarmed.

2. The *Second Class* comprised those whose property was rated between 100,000 and 75,000. From these 20 centuries – senior and junior – were formed, and required to provide the same equipment as Class I, save that the breast-plate was omitted and the long substituted for the round shield.

3. The *Third Class*. Property rating, 50,000. Same number of centuries, senior and junior as before. Same equipment, but with omission of the greaves.

4. The *Fourth Class*. Rating 25,000. Same number of centuries. Equipment: spear and javelin only.

5. The *Fifth Class*. Rating 11,000. This class comprised 30, not 20, centuries. Equipment: slings and stones. Rates with them were the buglers and trumpeters – two centuries.

6. Those assessed under 11,000 – the remainder of the population – were formed into a single century, exempt from military service.

1. The value of the *as* in the time of Servius cannot be precisely estimated. It is usually taken as rather less than 1d. of English money. Doubtless its purchasing power was much greater. (A. de S.)

These first five classes provided for the equipment of the infantry, graded according to property. There remained the reorganization of the cavalry, or 'knights'. Twelve centuries were enrolled, consisting of the most prominent and wealthy citizens. Six other centuries were also formed (Romulus had formed three) and called by the old names which had long been consecrated to their use. Each century had a grant from the treasury of 10,000 *asses* for the purchase of horses, with a further grant, levied on rich widows, of 2,000 a year for their feeding and maintenance.

The poor were thus exempted from contributions, and all financial burdens were shifted on to the shoulders of the rich. The latter were then compensated by political privilege: manhood suffrage with equal rights for all, which had obtained ever since the days of Romulus, was abolished, and replaced by a sliding scale. This had the effect of giving every man nominally a vote, while leaving all power actually in the hands of the Knights and the First Class. The procedure, when a vote was required, was to call first upon the Knights, then upon the eighty centuries of the First Class. In the rare case of disagreement, the *Second Class* was then asked to vote; that, in general, proved sufficient, and it was hardly ever necessary to go further – certainly not as far as the lowest orders.

The fact that the present organization, as it exists since the increase in the number of the tribes to thirty-five and the doubling of their members by the junior and senior centuries, does not correspond to the total established by Servius Tullius, need cause no surprise. Servius divided the city, taking in the built-over hills, into four regions, which he named 'tribes' – a word derived, I suppose, from 'tribute'; for it was also planned by Servius to have the 'contribution' of each citizen fairly apportioned on the basis of the census. These tribes bore no relation to the number or distribution of the centuries.

To expedite the completion of the census, a law was passed punishing with imprisonment or death all who failed to register. Thereupon the king issued a proclamation that all Roman citizens of all classes should present themselves, by centuries, in the Campus Martius at daybreak. There, with the sacrifice of a pig, a sheep, and an ox, the act of lustral purification was performed, the ceremony being termed the 'lustral close', as the final act of the whole business of the census. On that first occasion 80,000 names are said to have been registered; according to Fabius Pictor, our oldest authority, that was the number of men capable of bearing arms.

The population of Rome was by now so great that Servius decided to extend the city boundaries. He took in, accordingly, two more hills, the Quirinal and the Viminal, and subsequently added to the area of the Esquiline, which he made fashionable by residing in that quarter himself. The city defences he strengthened by constructing trenches, earthworks, and a wall. This involved extending the 'pomerium' – a term which needs some comment. By derivation the word is taken to mean the strip of ground 'behind the wall'; more properly, however, it signifies the strip on *both* sides of the wall: this ground the ancient Etruscans used to consecrate with augural ceremonies when a new town was to be founded. It was a narrow strip, precisely defined in width and following the course which the town wall would follow when it was built; its purpose was to keep the walls, on their inner side, clear of all buildings (which nowadays are, as a rule, actually joined to them), and at the same time to leave, on the outer side of the walls, an area unpolluted by the use of man. The whole strip, then, which it was felt to be impious to build over, on the one side, or to cultivate on the other, was called 'pomerium' by the Romans – just as much because the walls were *behind it*, as because it was *behind the walls*. Whenever, with the growth of the city, it was proposed to increase the area enclosed within the walls, this strip of consecrated ground was pushed outward accordingly.

Rome was now in a highly flourishing condition. The size of the city had been increased; internal affairs were satisfactorily settled to meet all demands both in peace and war. In these circumstances the king devised a project which he hoped would serve the double purpose of adding something to the architectural splendour of the city, and of extending her influence without the perpetual recourse to arms. By the time of which we are speaking, the temple of Diana in Ephesus was already famous, and report had it that the building had been erected as a joint enterprise of the Asian communities. Servius deliberately cultivated personal friendship with the Latin nobles and good public relations with their country, and then began, whenever opportunity offered, to praise in their presence, in glowing terms, the harmony of feeling and unity of worship amongst the townships of Asia, until, by continually harping upon the same theme, he at last carried his point, and a temple of Diana was built in Rome by the Latin peoples in association with the Romans. This was an admission that the long struggle for supremacy was over: Rome, by common consent, was the capital city. The Latins indeed had been defeated so often in this struggle that they had apparently ceased to concern themselves with it; there was, however, one man – a Sabine – who saw, or thought he saw, a chance of recovering power without involving his country in war. On one of the farms in the Sabine country there was a heifer of astonishing size and beauty, a truly marvellous creature remembered for many subsequent generations by its horns, which were hung in the vestibule of the temple of Diana. It had acquired, very properly, a certain numinous value, as if it were hardly of this earth and prophecies were made to the effect that imperial power would belong to the nation whose citizens offered it in sacrifice to Diana. This prediction came to the knowledge of the temple priest.

Now the Sabine I was speaking of, on the first suitable opportunity, drove the heifer to Diana's temple in Rome and led her to the altar. The Roman priest in attendance regarded with admiration the great beast of which he had heard so much – and, at the same time, he had not forgotten the prophecy.

'Stranger,' he said, 'what can you be thinking of? Surely you do not mean to sacrifice to Diana without first performing the act of purification? You must bathe yourself, before the ceremony, in a living stream. Down there in the valley the Tiber flows.'

The stranger was a religious man, and the warning went home. Unwilling to omit any part of the proper ritual, lest the event should fail to correspond with the prophecy, he hurried down to the river. During his absence the Roman priest sacrificed the heifer himself. All Rome, including the king, was delighted.

There was no doubt that by this time Servius had a definite prescriptive right to the throne. None the less he determined still further to strengthen his position. Young Tarquin was spreading malignant gossip about his never having received the popular vote, and Servius was well aware of what he was saying. Accordingly, to conciliate the goodwill of the commons, he first distributed land captured in war amongst private holders, and then took the bold step of demanding the people's vote upon his title to the throne. He was declared king by an overwhelming and unprecedented majority.

Tarquin was undismayed by Servius's success: indeed, his hopes of gaining the throne burned more hotly than before. One reason for this was that he knew that the distribution of land had been disapproved by the Senate, a fact which would enable him to vilify

Servius and increase his own influence in that body; another was his own character, for he was by nature ambitious, and his wife, Tullia, was not of the sort to let his ambition sleep. In ancient Greece more than one royal house was guilty of crime which became the stuff of tragedy: now Rome was to follow the same path – but not in vain; for that very guilt was to hasten the coming of liberty and the hatred of kings, and to ensure that the throne it won should never again be occupied.

Tarquin – or Lucius Tarquinius, son or grandson (more probably the former) of Tarquinius Priscus – had a brother called Arruns, a mild-mannered young man. The two brothers, as I mentioned before, had married Servius's daughters, both of them named Tullia but in character diametrically opposed to each other. By what I cannot but feel was the luck of Rome, it so happened that the two fiercely ambitious ones, Tarquin and the younger Tullia, did not, in the first instance, become man and wife; for Rome was thereby granted a period of reprieve; Servius's reign lasted a few years longer, and Roman civilization was able to advance.

The younger Tullia was bitterly humiliated by the weakness of her husband Arruns, and fiercely resented his lack of ambition and fire. It was to Tarquin that the whole passion of her nature turned; Tarquin was her hero, Tarquin her ideal of a true man and a true prince. Her sister she despised for failing to support with a woman's courage the husband she did not deserve. There is a magnetic power in evil; like draws towards like, and so it was with Tarquin and the younger Tullia.

It was the woman who took the first step along the road of crime. Whispers passed between her and her sister's husband; their secret meetings grew more frequent, their talk less guarded. Soon she was pouring into his ears the frankest abuse of her sister and Arruns, while Tarquin, though one was his brother and the other his brother's wife, let her talk on. 'You and I,' she said, 'would have been better single than bound in a marriage so incongruous and absurd, where each of us is forced by a cowardly partner to fritter our lives away in hopeless inactivity. Ah! if God had but given me the husband I deserve, I should soon see in my own house that royalty which I now see in my father's!'

The bold words struck an answering fire. Two deaths soon followed, one close upon the other, and Tarquin found himself a widower, Tullia a widow. The guilty pair were then married – the king not preventing, but hardly approving, the match.

From that day onward Servius, now an old man, lived in ever increasing danger. His wicked daughter soon found that one crime must lead to another; lest the two murders should prove to have been committed in vain, she gave her husband no rest by day or night. 'Did I want a man,' she urged, 'simply that I might call him husband, simply to endure slavery with him in silence? No! I wanted a man who knew he was worthy of a crown, who remembered that his father was a king, who would sooner reign now than languish in hope. If you are indeed the man I think I married, I salute you as my husband and my king; if not, it had been better for me to stay as I was than to marry not a criminal only but a coward. Come! Do your work! You are no stranger, as your father was, from Corinth or Tarquinii. No need for you to struggle for a foreign throne: it is yours already; the guardian gods of your hearth and home proclaim you king! Your father's bust, his palace, his royal seat, his name and yours – in these is your title. You dare not? Then why continue to play the cheat? Why let men look on you as a prince? It were better to slink back to Tarquinii or Corinth – like your brother, not your father; – better to be humble again, as your ancestors were humble long ago.'

His wife's taunts pricked young Tarquin to action. To Tullia the thought of Tanaquil's success was torture. She was determined to emulate it: if Tanaquil, a foreigner, had had influence enough twice in succession to confer the crown – first on her husband, then on her son-in-law – it was intolerable to feel that she herself, a princess of the blood, should count for nothing in the making, or unmaking, of kings. Tarquin could not stand against her maniacal ambition. Soon he was about his business: in and out of the houses of patrician families – the 'lesser' families especially – he began to solicit their support; he reminded them of the favours his father had done them, and urged them to show their gratitude; to the younger men he offered money as a bait; he vilified Servius, and promised heaven on earth, should he succeed. Support for him increased; everywhere his influence grew, until at last, when he judged the moment had come, he forced his way with an armed guard into the Forum. It was like a bolt from the blue. But worse was to come: taking his seat on the king's chair in front of the Senate House, he ordered a crier to summon the senators to appear before King Tarquin. They came immediately – some by prearrangement, others because they dared not keep away, for fear of the consequences. All were profoundly shaken by the sudden and extraordinary turn of events, and convinced that Servius was doomed.

Before the assembled senators Tarquin proceeded to blacken the king's name and pour contempt upon his origin: he was a slave and the son of a slave; after his father's shameful death he had usurped the throne. The customary *interregnum* had been ignored; no election had been held; not the people's vote, duly ratified by the Senate, but a woman's gift had put the sceptre in his hands. Base-born himself, and basely crowned, he had made friends with the riff-raff of the gutter where he belonged; hating the nobility to which he could not aspire, he had robbed the rich of their property and given it to vagabonds. All the burdens once shared by the community at large he had laid upon the shoulders of the wealthy and distinguished; the sole object of the census had been to make rich men's fortunes known and therefore envied – when it was not to plunder them for presents to the poor.

While Tarquin was still speaking, a report got through to Servius, who in anger and alarm at once hurried to the scene. Standing in the forecourt of the Curia, he loudly interrupted the speaker.

'Tarquin,' he cried, 'what is the meaning of this? How have you dared, while I live, to summon the Senate and to sit in my chair?'

'The chair is my father's,' was the insolent reply. 'A king's son is a better heir to the throne than a slave. We have let you mock and insult your masters long enough.'

Confusion followed. Some roared for Tarquin, some for Servius. The mob rushed the Senate House; a struggle was imminent, and it was clear that possession of the throne would depend upon the issue.

Tarquin had gone too far to turn back, and it was now all or nothing for him. Young and vigorous as he was, he seized the aged Servius, carried him bodily from the House and flung him down the steps into the street. Then he returned to quell the senators. The king's servants and retinue fled. While he himself was making his way, half-stunned and unattended, to the palace, he was caught and killed by Tarquin's assassins. It is thought that the deed was done at Tullia's suggestion: and such a crime was not, at least, inconsistent with her character. All agree that she drove into the Forum in an open carriage in a most brazen manner, and, calling her husband from the Senate House, was the first to hail him as King. Tarquin told her to go home, as the crowd might be dangerous; so she started off, and at the top of Cyprus street, where the shrine of Diana stood until recently, her driver was turning to the right to climb the Urbian hill on the way to the Esquiline, when he pulled up short in sudden terror and pointed to Servius's body lying mutilated on the road. There followed an act of bestial inhumanity – history preserves the memory of it in the name of the street, the Street of Crime. The story goes that the crazed woman, driven to frenzy by the avenging ghosts of her sister and husband, drove the carriage over her father's body. Blood from the corpse stained her clothes and spattered the carriage, so that a grim relic of the murdered man was brought by those gory wheels to the house where she and her husband lived. The guardian gods of that house did not forget; they were to see to it, in their anger at the bad beginning of the reign, that as bad an end should follow.

The reign of Servius Tullius lasted forty-four years. It was a good reign, and even the best and most moderate successor would not easily have emulated it. One of its most notable marks was the fact that with Servius true kingship came to an end; never again was a Roman king to rule in accordance with humanity and justice. Nevertheless, however mild and moderate his rule he intended, according to some writers, to abdicate in favour of a republican government, simply because he disapproved in principle of monarchy; but treachery within his family circle prevented him from carrying his purpose into effect.

Now began the reign of Tarquinius Superbus – Tarquin the Proud. His conduct merited the name. In spite of the ties of kin, he refused Servius the rite of burial, saying, in brutal jest, that Romulus's body had not been buried either. He executed the leading senators who he thought had supported Servius. Well aware that his treachery and violence might form a precedent to his own disadvantage, he employed a bodyguard. His anxiety was justified; for he had usurped by force the throne to which he had no title whatever: the people had not elected him, the Senate had not sanctioned his accession. Without hope of his subjects' affection, he could rule only by fear; and to make himself feared as widely as possible he began the practice of trying capital causes without consultation and by his own sole authority. He was thus enabled to punish with death, exile, or confiscation of property not only such men as he happened to suspect or dislike, but also innocent people from whose conviction he had nothing to gain

but their money. Those of senatorial rank were the worst sufferers
from this procedure; their numbers were reduced, and no new ap-
pointments made, in the hope, no doubt, that sheer numerical weakness might bring the order into contempt, and the surviving members
be readier to acquiesce in political impotence. Tarquin was the first
king to break the established tradition of consulting the Senate on all
matters of public business, and to govern by the mere authority of
himself and his household. In questions of war and peace he was his
own sole master; he made and unmade treaties and alliances with
whom he pleased without any reference whatever either to the commons or to the Senate. He made particular efforts to win the friendship
of the Latins, in the hope that any power or influence he could obtain
abroad might give him greater security at home. With this in view
he went beyond mere official friendly relations with the Latin nobility,
and married his daughter to Octavius Mamilius of Tusculum, by far
the most distinguished bearer of the Latin name, and descended, we
are told, from Ulysses and the goddess Circe. By this marriage he
attached to his interest Mamilius's numerous relatives and friends.

His influence with the leaders of Latin society was soon very great,
and this gave him confidence for his next move. Declaring that he
had certain matters of common interest to discuss, he summoned them
to a conference at the Grove of Ferentina. On the appointed day a
great number of them assembled at dawn. Tarquin was late: he did,
indeed, put in an appearance on the right day, but not much before
sunset. All day, while the Latins were waiting for him, various subjects were discussed, and a certain Turnus Herdonius, of Aricia, had a
deal to say in disparagment of the absent Tarquin.

'No wonder,' his arguments ran, 'that Rome has called Tarquin the
Proud!' (The name was already current, though as yet none dared
more than to whisper it.) 'It could hardly be better justified than by
his present behaviour, which is a deliberate insult to our country. We,
the heads of the chief families of Latium, have been made to travel
many miles to attend this meeting – and he who convened us does not
even take the trouble to be present. Why – it's as plain as a pikestaff:
he wants to see how much we will put up with, and then, if he finds
us submissive enough, he will stamp on us. A blind man could see he
covets the sovereignty of Latium. If his own people were right to entrust him with power – if indeed it *was* entrusted, and not stolen,
rather, by a murderous thief – then we, you may say, should do no

less. Even so, I would remind you that he is a foreigner. But what are the facts? His own people are sick of him; they are weary of the continual slitting of throats, exiles, confiscations that are going on in Rome. And, if that is true of Rome, could we in Latium expect anything better? Take my advice, and go home – all of you. Do not trouble to keep your appointment here any more than *he* has.'

Turnus, who had acquired some influence in Latium as an inveterate trouble-maker, was in the full flow of his eloquence, when Tarquin's unexpected arrival cut him short. The audience turned their backs on the orator to pay their respects to the king. There was silence, and Tarquin, advised to give some reason for being so late, said that he had been asked to settle a dispute between a father and son and that hoping to reconcile them he had been unavoidably delayed. 'And as that little business,' he added, 'has left us no more time today I will wait till tomorrow to deal with the matters I proposed to discuss.'

The excuse was not good enough for the angry Turnus. 'No dispute,' he is said to have replied, 'is more quickly settled than one between father and son: all one need say is, "obey your father – or take the consequences".'

With this parting shot Turnus took himself off.

Tarquin was more disturbed by this incident than he himself allowed to appear, and promptly considered ways and means of getting rid of Turnus. It would be politic, he felt, to make the Latins as much afraid of him as the Romans were. He was not as yet in a position openly to order his execution, so he decided to attain his object by having him convicted on a trumped-up charge. For this purpose he managed to persuade certain political enemies of Turnus to bribe one of his slaves to allow a large number of weapons to be smuggled into his lodging. It was done within the course of the night; and very early on the following morning Tarquin sent for certain distinguished members of the Latin nobility and pretended to have received alarming news, adding that his late arrival on the previous day had turned out to be a piece of extraordinary good luck, and had saved them all. 'Turnus', he went on, 'is, I am told, planning to assassinate me and the leading men in all the towns of Latium. His aim is the monarchy. He would have acted yesterday at the conference, had it not been for the absence of his chief victim – myself. He was obliged to wait, and his consequent disappointment was the reason for the bitter language he used against me. I am convinced, if the information I have is true, that when we assemble at dawn tomorrow he will be there to attack us. He will be well armed and strongly supported, for a great many weapons have, I learn, been conveyed to his inn. The truth or false-hood of this can be proved in a moment: come with me to his rooms, and we can see for ourselves.'

Several things contributed to make the story plausible: the reckless plot was typical of Turnus; then there was his speech at the conference, and, lastly, Tarquin's late arrival, which seemed a reasonable explana-tion of the postponement of the massacre. Consequently they were all predisposed to believe it, though they still needed the evidence of the weapons before accepting the other charges.

When they reached the inn, Turnus was still asleep. He was awakened and surrounded by guards. Some loyal slaves who offered resistance were seized. Weapons were found hidden in every corner of the building. Further proof was not needed, and Turnus was ar-rested.

Amid great excitement the Latins were immediately called upon to meet. The weapons found in the inn were produced as evidence, and so strong was the feeling against Turnus that he was convicted out of hand, without even the chance of defending himself. He was bound underneath a hurdle weighted with stones and flung into the water – a form of punishment which was a new invention of Tarquin's.

After the execution the Latins were again summoned to Tarquin's presence. 'Gentlemen,' he said, 'I congratulate you. Turnus was a traitor; he was caught in the act, and you have given him his just reward.

'Now I would remind you that an ancient treaty between Rome and Latium is still in existence, and that I could act upon it if I so wished. By that treaty the whole Alban community, together with all settlements founded by the Alban people, were brought by Tullus under the dominion of Rome. You Latins are of Alban descent and therefore bound by the terms of that treaty. However, it is my belief that everybody's interest would be better served if the old treaty were brought up to date in such a way as to allow the peoples of Latium to share the prosperity of Rome, instead of being forced to dread a re-petition of the miseries – the destruction of towns, the devastation of the countryside – which they suffered during the reigns of Ancus and my father.'

The Latins were quick to see the force of this, in spite of the fact that the treaty was more favourable to the Roman interest than to their own. Moreover it was obvious that the most influential amongst them took Tarquin's view of the matter – not to mention that the recent fate of Turnus was evidence of what would happen to anyone who ventured to oppose him. The treaty was accordingly revised, and a proclamation was issued to the effect that the Latins of military age should present themselves, fully armed, on a day fixed for the purpose at the Grove of Ferentina. In accordance with the edict men from all the Latin communities duly assembled. Tarquin then proceeded to take certain precautions: seeing it was inadvisable to allow them independent command, with their own general officers and their own standards, he reorganized the army units, so that each company should consist of Roman and Latin troops in equal numbers, under the command of a Roman centurion.

However lawless and tyrannical Tarquin may have been as monarch in his own country, as a war leader he did fine work. Indeed, his fame as a soldier might have equalled that of his predecessors, had not his degeneracy in other things obscured its lustre. It was Tarquin who began the long, two-hundred years of war with the Volscians. From them he took by storm the town of Suessa Pometia, where the sale of captured material realized forty talents of silver. This sum he allocated to the building of the Temple of Jupiter, which he had conceived on a magnificent scale, worthy of the king of gods and men, of the might of Rome, and of the majesty of the place where it was to stand. He was next engaged in hostilities with the neighbouring town of Gabii. This time, progress was slower than he expected: his assault proved abortive; the subsequent siege operations failed, and he was forced to retire; so he finally had recourse to the un-Roman, and disgraceful, method of deceit and treachery.

Pretending to have abandoned hostilities in order to devote himself to laying the foundations of the temple of Jupiter and to various other improvements in the city, he arranged for Sextus, the youngest of his three sons, to go to Gabii in the assumed character of a fugitive from the intolerable cruelty of his father. On his arrival in the town Sextus began to pour out his complaints: Tarquin, he declared, had ceased to persecute strangers and was now turning his lust for dominion against his own family; he had too many children, and was heartily sick of them; his one desire was to leave no descendants, no heir to his throne, and before long was likely to repeat in his own home what he had already done in the Senate, and leave it a desert and a solitude. 'I myself,' he continued, 'escaped with my life through the bristling weapons of my father's guard; and I knew that nowhere but in the homes of the tyrant's enemies should I be able to find safety. Make no mistake: the suspension of hostilities is a feint only; war still awaits you, and as soon as he thinks fit Tarquin will attack you unawares. You have no room in Gabii for suppliants? Very well then; I will try my luck through the whole of Latium; I will visit in turn Volscians, Aequians, Hernicans – seeking and seeking until I find some friend who knows how to protect a son from a father's impious savagery. Who knows but I may find, too, some spark of true manhood, some readiness to take up arms against the proudest of kings and the most insolent of peoples?'

The men of Gabii gave Sextus a friendly welcome, knowing as they did, that any show of indifference would provoke him to leave the town at once. In their view, they declared, there was no cause for surprise that Tarquin should be treating his children as brutally as he had treated first the Romans and then his allies – brutality was his nature, and for lack of other objects he would end by exercising it against himself. For their part, they were glad Sextus had come, and it would not be long before, with him to help them, the scene of battle would shift from the gates of Gabii to the walls of Rome.

Sextus was soon admitted to the councils of state, where he made it his business to express agreement on all matters of local politics which the men of Gabii might be expected to understand better than himself. On one issue, however – war with Rome – he took the lead. The advisability of this he urged repeatedly, pointing out that he was specially competent to do so because of his knowledge of the resources of both parties, and of his certainty that Tarquin, whose arrogance even his own children found insufferable, had brought upon himself the hatred of all his subjects.

Sextus's words gradually took effect, and the leading men in Gabii were soon in favour of reopening hostilities. Sextus himself meanwhile with small bodies of picked troops began a series of raids on Roman territory; everything he said or did was so nicely calculated to deceive, that confidence in him grew and grew, until he was finally appointed commander of the armed forces. War was declared; minor engagements took place, nearly always to the advantage of Gabii. Of what was really happening nobody had the smallest suspicion, and the

result of these apparent successes was that everyone in Gabii, from the
highest to the lowest, was soon convinced that Sextus had been sent
from heaven to lead them to victory. The common soldiers, too,
finding him ready to share their dangers and hardships, and generous
in distributing plunder, came to love him with such devotion that his
influence in Gabii was as great as his father's was in Rome.

At last he was able to feel that he had the town, as it were, in his
pocket, and was ready for anything. Accordingly he sent a con-
fidential messenger to Rome, to ask his father what step he should
next take, his power in Gabii being, by God's grace, by this time
absolute. Tarquin, I suppose, was not sure of the messenger's good
faith: in any case, he said not a word in reply to his question, but with
a thoughtful air went out into the garden. The man followed him, and
Tarquin, strolling up and down in silence, began knocking off poppy-
heads with his stick. The messenger at last wearied of putting his question and waiting for the reply, so he returned to Gabii supposing his
mission to have failed. He told Sextus what he had said and what he
had seen his father do: the king, he declared, whether from anger, or
hatred, or natural arrogance, had not uttered a single word. Sextus
realized that though his father had not spoken, he had, by his action,
indirectly expressed his meaning clearly enough; so he proceeded at
once to act upon his murderous instructions. All the influential men
in Gabii were got rid of – some being brought to public trial, others
executed for no better reason than that they were generally disliked.
Many were openly put to death; some, against whom any charge
would be inconvenient to attempt to prove, were secretly assassinated.
A few were either allowed, or forced, to leave the country, and their
property was confiscated as in the case of those who had been executed. The confiscations enriched the more fortunate – those, namely,
to whom Sextus chose to be generous – with the result that in the
sweetness of personal gain public calamity was forgotten, until at long
last the whole community, such as it now remained, with none to
advise or help it, passed without a struggle into Tarquin's hands.

Tarquin's next move was to make peace with the Aequians and to
renew his treaty with Etruria. This done, he turned his attention to
home affairs. His first concern was the temple of Jupiter on the
Capitoline, which he hoped to leave as a memorial of the royal house
of the Tarquins – of the father who had made the vow, and of the son
who had fulfilled it. It was his wish that the whole area where the

temple was to stand should be sacred to no god but Jupiter, so in order to clear it of other religious associations he proposed to 'exaugurate', or secularize, a number of places of worship, some containing sacred buildings, others an altar only, which had been originally vowed by King Tatius at the crisis of his battle with Romulus, and subsequently consecrated with the proper ceremonies. The new work was hardly begun, when, we are told, heaven itself was moved to give a sign of the future greatness of Rome's dominion: for when the auguries were taken, the birds allowed the secularization of all the places of worship except the shrine of Terminus. The fact that of all the gods Terminus alone was not moved from his place or called to leave the ground which was consecrated to his worship, was taken to portend the stability and permanence of everything Roman. Hard upon this happy augury came another strange event, which seemed to foretell the grandeur of our empire: a man's head with the features intact was discovered by the workmen who were digging the foundations of the temple. This meant without any doubt that on this spot would stand the imperial citadel of the capital city of the world. Nothing could be plainer – and such was the interpretation put upon the discovery not only by the Roman soothsayers but also by those who were specially brought from Etruria for consultation.

In view of all this, Tarquin became more extravagant in his ideas – so much so that the money raised from the sale of material captured at Pometia, which was intended to carry the building up to the roof, hardly covered the cost of the foundations. This inclines me to accept the statement of Fabius – who is, moreover, the older authority – that the money was not more than forty talents, rather than the statement of Piso, who writes that 40,000 pounds' weight of silver was put aside for this work. A huge sum like that could hardly be expected from material taken from a single town in those days, and it would be more than enough for the foundations of any of the most splendid buildings even of the present time.

Tarquin's chief interest was now the completion of the temple. Builders and engineers were brought in from all over Etruria, and the project involved the use not only of public funds but also of a large number of labourers from the poorer classes. The work was hard in itself, and came as an addition to their regular military duties; but it was an honourable burden with a solemn and religious significance, and they were not, on the whole, unwilling to bear it; but it was a very different matter when they were put on to other tasks less spectacular but more laborious still, such as the construction of the tiers of seats in the Circus and the excavation of the Cloaca Maxima, or Great Sewer, designed to carry off the sewage of the entire city by an underground pipe-line. The magnitude of both these projects could hardly be equalled by any work even of modern times. It was Tarquin's view that an idle proletariat was a burden on the state, so in addition to the major works I have mentioned he made use of some of the surplus population by sending settlers out to Signia and Circeii. This had the further advantages of increasing the extent of Roman territory and of providing points of resistance against future attack either by land or sea.

About this time an alarming and ominous event occurred: a snake slid out from a crack in a wooden pillar in the palace. Everyone ran from it in a fright; even the king was scared, though in his case it was not fear so much as foreboding. About signs and omens of public import the custom had always been to consult only Etruscan soothsayers; this, however, was a different matter: it was in the king's own house that the portentous sight had been seen; and that, Tarquin felt, justified the unusual step of sending to Delphi, to consult the most famous oracle in the world. Unwilling to entrust the answer of the oracle to anybody else, he sent on the mission two of his sons, Titus and Arruns, who accordingly set out for Greece through country which Roman feet had seldom trod and over seas which Roman ships had never sailed. With them went Lucius Junius Brutus, son of the king's sister Tarquinia.

Now Brutus had deliberately assumed a mask to hide his true character. When he learned of the murder by Tarquin of the Roman aristocrats, one of the victims being his own brother, he had come to the conclusion that the only way of saving himself was to appear in the king's eyes as a person of no account. If there were nothing in his character for Tarquin to fear, and nothing in his fortune to covet, then the sheer contempt in which he was held would be a better protection than his own rights could ever be. Accordingly he pretended to be a half-wit and made no protest at the seizure by Tarquin of everything he possessed. He even submitted to being known publicly as the 'Dullard' (which is what his name signifies), that under cover of that opprobrious title the great spirit which gave Rome her freedom might be able to bide its time. On this occasion he was taken by Arruns and

Titus to Delphi less as a companion than as a butt for their amuse-
ment; and he is said to have carried with him, as his gift to Apollo, a
rod of gold inserted into a hollow stick of cornel-wood – symbolic, it
may be, of his own character.

The three young men reached Delphi, and carried out the king's
instructions. That done, Titus and Arruns found themselves unable
to resist putting a further question to the oracle. Which of them, they
asked, would be the next king of Rome? From the depths of the
cavern came the mysterious answer: 'He who shall be the first to kiss
his mother shall hold in Rome supreme authority.' Titus and Arruns
were determined to keep the prophecy absolutely secret, to prevent
their other brother, Tarquin, who had been left in Rome, from
knowing anything about it. Thus he, at any rate, would be out of the
running. For themselves, they drew lots to determine which of them,
on their return, should kiss his mother first.

Brutus, however, interpreted the words of Apollo's priestess in a
different way. Pretending to trip, he fell flat on his face, and his lips
touched the Earth – the mother of all living things.

Back in Rome, they found vigorous preparations in progress for
war with the Rutuli. The chief town of the Rutuli was Ardea, and they
were a people, for that place and period, of very considerable wealth.
Their wealth was, indeed, the reason for Tarquin's preparations: he
needed money to repair the drain on his resources resulting from his
ambitious schemes of public building and he knew, moreover, that
the commons were growing ever more restive, not only in view of
his tyrannical behaviour generally but also, and especially, because
they had been so long employed in manual labour such as belonged
properly to slaves, and the distribution of plunder from a captured
town would do much to soften their resentment.

The attempt was made to take Ardea by assault. It failed; siege
operations were begun, and the army settled down into permanent
quarters. With little prospect of any decisive action, the war looked
like being a long one, and in these circumstances leave was granted,
quite naturally, with considerable freedom, especially to officers. Indeed, the young princes, at any rate, spent most of their leisure enjoying themselves in entertainments on the most lavish scale. They were
drinking one day in the quarters of Sextus Tarquinius – Collatinus,
son of Egerius, was also present – when someone chanced to mention
the subject of wives. Each of them, of course, extravagantly praised

his own; and the rivalry got hotter and hotter, until Collatinus suddenly cried: 'Stop! What need is there of words, when in a few hours we can prove beyond doubt the incomparable superiority of my Lucretia? We are all young and strong: why shouldn't we ride to Rome and see with our own eyes what kind of women our wives are? There is no better evidence, I assure you, than what a man finds when he enters his wife's room unexpectedly.'

They had all drunk a good deal, and the proposal appealed to them; so they mounted their horses and galloped off to Rome. They reached the city as dusk was falling; and there the wives of the royal princes were found enjoying themselves with a group of young friends at a dinner-party, in the greatest luxury. The riders then went on to Collatia, where they found Lucretia very differently employed: it was already late at night, but there, in the hall of her house, surrounded by her busy maid-servants, she was still hard at work by lamplight upon her spinning. Which wife had won the contest in womanly virtue was no longer in doubt.

With all courtesy Lucretia rose to bid her husband and the princes welcome, and Collatinus, pleased with his success, invited his friends to sup with him. It was at that fatal supper that Lucretia's beauty, and proven chastity, kindled in Sextus Tarquinius the flame of lust, and determined him to debauch her.

Nothing further occurred that night. The little jaunt was over, and the young men rode back to camp.

A few days later Sextus, without Collatinus's knowledge, returned with one companion to Collatia, where he was hospitably welcomed in Lucretia's house, and, after supper, escorted, like the honoured visitor he was thought to be, to the guest-chamber. Here he waited till the house was asleep, and then, when all was quiet, he drew his sword and made his way to Lucretia's room determined to rape her. She was asleep. Laying his left hand on her breast, 'Lucretia,' he whispered, 'not a sound! I am Sextus Tarquinius. I am armed – if you utter a word, I will kill you.' Lucretia opened her eyes in terror; death was imminent, no help at hand. Sextus urged his love, begged her to submit, pleaded, threatened, used every weapon that might conquer a woman's heart. But all in vain; not even the fear of death could bend her will. 'If death will not move you,' Sextus cried, 'dishonour shall. I will kill you first, then cut the throat of a slave and lay his naked body by your side. Will they not believe that you have been caught in adultery with a servant – and paid the price?' Even the most resolute chastity could not have stood against this dreadful threat.

Lucretia yielded. Sextus enjoyed her, and rode away, proud of his success.

The unhappy girl wrote to her father in Rome and to her husband in Ardea, urging them both to come at once with a trusted friend – and quickly, for a frightful thing had happened. Her father came with Valerius, Volesus's son, her husband with Brutus, with whom he was returning to Rome when he was met by the messenger. They found Lucretia sitting in her room, in deep distress. Tears rose to her eyes as they entered, and to her husband's question, 'Is it well with you?' she answered, 'No. What can be well with a woman who has lost her honour? In your bed, Collatinus, is the impress of another man. My body only has been violated. My heart is innocent, and death will be my witness. Give me your solemn promise that the adulterer shall be punished – he is Sextus Tarquinius. He it is who last night came as my enemy disguised as my guest, and took his pleasure of me. That pleasure will be my death – and his, too, if you are men.'

The promise was given. One after another they tried to comfort her. They told her she was helpless, and therefore innocent; that he alone was guilty. It was the mind, they said, that sinned, not the body: without intention there could never be guilt.

'What is due to *him*,' Lucretia said, 'is for you to decide. As for me I am innocent of fault, but I will take my punishment. Never shall Lucretia provide a precedent for unchaste women to escape what they deserve.' With these words she drew a knife from under her robe, drove it into her heart, and fell forward, dead.

Her father and husband were overwhelmed with grief. While they stood weeping helplessly, Brutus drew the bloody knife from Lucretia's body, and holding it before him cried: 'By this girl's blood – none more chaste till a tyrant wronged her – and by the gods, I swear that with sword and fire, and whatever else can lend strength to my arm, I will pursue Lucius Tarquinius the Proud, his wicked wife, and all his children, and never again will I let them or any other man be King in Rome.'

He put the knife into Collatinus's hands, then passed it to Lucretius, then to Valerius. All looked at him in astonishment: a miracle had happened – he was a changed man. Obedient to his command, they swore their oath. Grief was forgotten in the sudden surge of anger, and when Brutus called upon them to make war, from that instant, upon the tyrant's throne, they took him for their leader.

Lucretia's body was carried from the house into the public square. Crowds gathered, as crowds will, to gape and wonder – and the sight was unexpected enough, and horrible enough, to attract them. Anger at the criminal brutality of the king's son and sympathy with the father's grief stirred every heart; and when Brutus cried out that it was time for deeds not tears, and urged them, like true Romans, to take up arms against the tyrants who had dared to treat them as a vanquished enemy, not a man amongst them could resist the call. The boldest spirits offered themselves at once for service; the rest soon followed their lead. Lucretia's father was left to hold Collatia; guards were posted to prevent news of the rising from reaching the palace, and with Brutus in command the armed populace began their march on Rome.

In the city the first effect of their appearance was alarm and confusion, but the sight of Brutus, and others of equal distinction, at the head of the mob, soon convinced people that this was, at least, no mere popular demonstration. Moreover the horrible story of Lucretia had had hardly less effect in Rome than in Collatia. In a moment the Forum was packed, and the crowds, by Brutus's order, were immediately summoned to attend the Tribune of Knights – an office held at the time by Brutus himself. There, publicly throwing off the mask under which he had hitherto concealed his real character and feelings, he made a speech painting in vivid colours the brutal and unbridled lust of Sextus Tarquinius, the hideous rape of the innocent Lucretia and her pitiful death, and the bereavement of her father, for whom the cause of her death was an even bitterer and more dreadful thing than the death itself. He went on to speak of the king's arrogant and tyrannical behaviour; of the sufferings of the commons condemned to labour underground clearing or constructing ditches and sewers; of gallant Romans – soldiers who had beaten in battle all neighbouring peoples – robbed of their swords and turned into stone-cutters and artisans. He reminded them of the foul murder of Servius Tullius, of the daughter who drove her carriage over her father's corpse, in violation of the most sacred of relationships – a crime which God alone could punish. Doubtless he told them of other, and worse, things, brought to his mind in the heat of the moment and by the sense of this latest outrage, which still lived in his eye and pressed upon his heart; but a mere historian can hardly record them.

The effect of his words was immediate: the populace took fire, and were brought to demand the abrogation of the king's authority and the exile of himself and his family.

With an armed body of volunteers Brutus then marched for Ardea to rouse the army to revolt. Lucretius, who some time previously had been appointed by the king Prefect of the City, was left in command in Rome. Tullia fled from the palace during the disturbances; wherever she went she was met with curses; everyone, men and women alike, called down upon her head the vengeance of the furies who punish sinners against the sacred ties of blood.

When news of the rebellion reached Ardea, the king immediately started for Rome, to restore order. Brutus got wind of his approach, and changed his route to avoid meeting him, finally reaching Ardea almost at the same moment as Tarquin arrived at Rome. Tarquin found the city gates shut against him and his exile decreed. Brutus the Liberator was enthusiastically welcomed by the troops, and Tarquin's sons were expelled from the camp. Two of them followed their father into exile at Caere in Etruria. Sextus Tarquinius went to Gabii – his own territory, as he doubtless hoped; but his previous record there of robbery and violence had made him many enemies, who now took their revenge and assassinated him.

Tarquin the Proud reigned for twenty-five years. The whole period of monarchical government, from the founding of Rome to its liberation, was 244 years. After the liberation two consuls were elected by popular vote, under the presidency of the Prefect of the City; the voting was by 'centuries', according to the classification of Servius Tullius. The two consuls were Lucius Junius Brutus and Lucius Tarquinius Collatinus.

BOOK TWO

The Beginnings of the Republic

MY task from now on will be to trace the history in peace and of a free nation, governed by annually elected officers of state and subject not to the caprice of individual men, but to the overriding authority of law.

The hard-won liberty of Rome was rendered the more welcome, and the more fruitful, by the character of the last king, Tarquin the Proud. Earlier kings may all be considered, not unjustly, to have contributed to the city's growth, making room for an expanding population, for the increase of which they, too, were responsible. They were all, in their way, successive 'founders' of Rome. Moreover it cannot be doubted that Brutus, who made for himself so great a name by the expulsion of Tarquin, would have done his country the greatest disservice, had he yielded too soon to his passion for liberty and forced the abdication of any of the previous kings. One has but to think of what the populace was like in those early days – a rabble of vagrants, mostly runaways and refugees – and to ask what would have happened if they had suddenly found themselves protected from all authority by inviolable sanctuary, and enjoying complete freedom of action, if not full political rights. In such circumstances, unrestrained by the power of the throne, they would, no doubt, have set sail on the stormy sea of democratic politics, swayed by the gusts of popular eloquence and quarrelling for power with the governing class of a city which did not even belong to them, before any real sense of community had had time to grow. That sense – the only true patriotism – comes slowly and springs from the heart: it is founded upon respect for the family and love of the soil. Premature 'liberty' of this kind would have been a disaster: we should have been torn to pieces by petty squabbles before we had ever reached political maturity, which, as things were, was made possible by the long quiet years under monarchical government; for it was that government which, as it were, nursed our strength and enabled us ultimately to produce sound fruit from liberty, as only a politically adult nation can.

Moreover the first step towards political liberty in Rome consisted in the fact that the consuls were annually elected magistrates – in the limitation, that is, not of their powers but of their period of office.

The earliest consuls exercised the full powers of the kings, and carried all their insignia, with one exception – the most impressive of all – namely the 'rods'. These were allowed to only one consul of the two, to avoid the duplication of this dreadful symbol of the power of life and death. Brutus by his colleague's consent was the first to have the rods, and he proved as zealous in guarding liberty as he had been in demanding it. His first act was to make the people, while the taste of liberty was still fresh upon their tongues, swear a solemn oath never to allow any man to be king in Rome, hoping by this means to fore-stall future attempts by persuasion or bribery to restore the monarchy. He then turned his attention to strengthening the influence of the Senate, whose numbers had been reduced by the political murders of Tarquin; for this purpose he brought into it leading men of equestrian rank and made up its number to a total of three hundred. This, we are told, was the origin of the distinction between the 'Fathers' and the 'Conscripts': i.e. the original senators and those (the conscripts) who were later enrolled, or conscripted, as members of the senatorial body. The measure was wonderfully effective in promoting national unity and lessening friction between patricians and populace.

Attention was then paid to matters of state worship, and an official appointed with the title *Rex Sacrificolus* – 'King Sacrificer'. Under the monarchy certain public religious ceremonies had been conducted by the kings in person, and the object of this new appointment was to fill the gap now that kings were no more; the office, however, was sub-ordinated to that of the pontifex, to save appearances; for it was felt that, in conjunction with the title of 'King', it might in some way be felt to be anti-republican. I cannot help wondering, myself, whether the precautions taken at this time to safeguard liberty even in the smallest details were not excessive: a notable instance concerned one of the consuls, Tarquinius Collatinus, whose sole offence was the fact that his name – Tarquin – was universally detested. The Tarquins, people felt, were all too much accustomed to absolute power: it had begun with Priscus, and the reign of Tullius had not sufficed to make Tarquin the Proud forget his supposed claim upon the throne, or to regard it as another's property; on the contrary he had resorted to violence to recover what he pretended to consider his rightful inherit-ance. And now, after his deposition, power was in the hands of another Tarquin – Collatinus. To every Tarquin power was the breath of life; it was a name of ill omen, dangerous to liberty. This sort of talk began with a few people anxious to test public opinion; gradually it spread, until, when the whole country was alive with it, Brutus summoned a mass meeting of the commons, whose suspicions were by then thoroughly aroused. He opened his address by repeating the people's oath – that they would allow no man to be king and no man to live in Rome who threatened her liberties. 'The sanctity of this oath,' he continued, 'we must guard with all our might; we must neglect no measure which has any bearing upon it. Personal considerations make it painful to say what I have to say: indeed, only the love I bear my country could have extorted it from me; but the fact is, the people of Rome do not believe in the reality of the freedom they have won. They are convinced that to true liberty an insuperable barrier still remains: the presence, namely, amongst us, and – worse – the promotion to power of a member of the royal family, himself bearing that hated name.'

Then turning to Collatinus, 'Lucius Tarquinius,' he cried, 'Rome is afraid. It is in your hands to allay her fears. Believe us when we say we remember your part in the expulsion of the kings; crown that service now by ridding us of the royal name. I will see to it that you lose nothing; you will keep possession of your property – nay, if it is not enough, we will add to it handsomely. Leave us as a friend; free your country from her fear, however vain it may be. Of this all Rome is convinced – that with the family of Tarquin monarchy will be gone for ever.'

Collatinus was so much astonished by this strange and unexpected request, that for a moment he was speechless. Then, before he could reply, a number of people pressed in on him, begging with the greatest insistence that he would do as Brutus asked. They were all men of distinction, but their entreaties might have had little effect, without the powerful backing of Spurius Lucretius. Lucretius was older than Collatinus and much respected in public life; he was, moreover, the father of Collatinus's wife, so when he began to use all the arts of prayer and persuasion to induce his son-in-law to yield to the unanimous feeling of Rome, he carried his point. Collatinus, fearing that when his year of office was over he would not only still be an object of hostility but might well be publicly disgraced and forced to submit to the confiscation of his property, resigned the consulship and went into voluntary exile at Lavinium, taking with him everything he possessed. Thereupon, in accordance with a decree of the Senate, Brutus brought before the people the proposal that every member of the

Tarquin family should be banished from Rome. Elections were then held, and Publius Valerius, who had assisted Brutus in the expulsion of the kings, was chosen to fill the vacant consulship.

Everybody knew that war with the Tarquins was sure to come; it was, however, unexpectedly delayed, and the first move in the struggle took a form which no one had anticipated. Treason within the city itself nearly cost Rome her liberty. It began with a group of young aristocrats who had found life under the monarchy very agreeable; accustomed to associate with the younger members of the royal family, they had been able to give a freer rein to their appetites and to live the dissolute and irresponsible life of the court. Under the new dispensation they missed the freedom to do as they pleased, and began to complain that what might be liberty for others was more like slavery for themselves. A king, they argued, was, after all, a human being, and there was a chance of getting from him what one wanted, rightly or wrongly; under a monarchy there was room for influence and favour; a king could be angry, and forgive; he knew the difference between an enemy and a friend. Law, on the other hand, was impersonal and inexorable. Law had no ears. An excellent thing, no doubt, for paupers, it was worse than useless for the great, as it admitted no relaxation or indulgence towards a man who ventured beyond the bounds of mediocrity. Human nature not being perfect, to suppose that a man could live in pure innocence under the law was, to put it mildly, risky.

Now it happened about this time, very opportunely for the malcontents, that a mission from the Tarquins arrived in Rome. Its sole ostensible object was to recover the Tarquins' property; no mention was made of their return. The envoys were granted a hearing in the Senate, and for the next few days the matter remained under discussion, the general opinion being that a refusal to restore the property would be taken as a pretext for war, while the result of consent would merely be to add to the resources of the enemy. Tarquin's envoys, meanwhile, did not remain idle, and, still under cover of their original request, began secret negotiations for the recovery of the throne. As if in pursuance of their legitimate mission, they visited a number of the young nobles to find out what their attitude to the situation was likely to be; some showed evident sympathy, and to these the envoys gave letters from the Tarquins and proceeded to discuss arrangements for secretly admitting them into Rome under cover of darkness.

The Vitellii and Aquilii brothers were the first to be entrusted with the project. A sister of the Vitellii had married Brutus, and their two sons, Titus and Tiberius, already on the verge of manhood, were persuaded by their uncles to play a part in the conspiracy. A number of other young men of patrician rank had a share in the secret, but their names are forgotten.

Meanwhile a majority in the Senate had voted for the return of the Tarquins' property. The envoys were allowed by the consuls to prolong their stay in Rome in order to collect transport for the furniture and moveables and they took advantage of this to have frequent consultations with the young conspirators, continually pressing them to give them something in writing which they could show to the Tarquins. For without written evidence, they argued, how in a matter of such importance could the royal family be brought to believe in the truth of their statements? The conspirators allowed themselves to be persuaded. Letters were written and signed – letters which, intended to prove their good faith, proved, in the event, their guilt.

The day before the envoys were due to leave Rome, they and the conspirators met for supper in the house of the Vitellii. During the evening they sent the servants from the room and, supposing that they were alone, began talking over, as men will, the details of their plot, which still had for them all the excitement of novelty. Unluckily, however, a slave overheard what they were saying: he had already guessed what was going on, and was waiting for the delivery to Tarquin's envoys of the letters, the seizure of which would provide him with conclusive evidence. As soon as he was aware that the documents had changed hands, he laid his information before the consuls. The consuls at once left home to arrest the criminals; the plot was nipped in the bud without creating any public disturbance, and particular care was taken to ensure possession of the letters. The traitors were immediately imprisoned; about the treatment of the envoys there was some hesitation: it might well have been argued that their actions put them into the position of an enemy, but they were allowed the customary privilege of representatives of a foreign power.

The question of the Tarquins' property was brought up in the Senate for reconsideration. This time indignation prevailed; the Senate refused to restore it, and refused to confiscate it officially; instead, they let the people loose on it to take what they pleased, hoping that once the lower orders had stained their hands with the gold of kings they would lose for ever all hope of making peace with them again. The tract of land between the city and the Tiber, formerly owned by the Tarquins, was consecrated to Mars, and became known as the Campus Martius. It is said that there was a crop of grain, already ripe, on the land there; and because, for religious reasons, it could not be used for food, it was cut, stalks and all, by hundreds of men all working together, packed into baskets and thrown into the Tiber. The river was low, as it was in the heat of midsummer, and the grain stuck on the bottom in the shallow water and piled up into muddy heaps, so that with the addition of other refuse which floated downstream an island was gradually formed. Later, no doubt, work was done to increase and strengthen it, and to make the whole area high enough and solid enough to carry buildings, even temples and porticoes.

When everything that belonged to the Tarquins had been pillaged and gutted by the populace, the traitors received their sentence, and their punishment. It was a memorable scene: for the consular office imposed upon a father the duty of exacting the supreme penalty from his sons, so that he who, of all men, should have been spared the sight of their suffering, was the one whom fate ordained to enforce it. The condemned criminals were bound to the stake; all were young men of the best blood in Rome, but only the consul's sons drew the eyes of the spectators; the others, for all the interest they aroused, might have come from the gutter. There was pity for their punishment, and greater pity for the crime which had brought it upon them; in every heart was a sort of incredulous sorrow for such treachery at such a time: that these young men, in the very year when Rome was liberated – and by their father's hand – when the newly-created consulship had fallen first to a member of their own family, should have brought themselves to betray the entire population of Rome, high and low alike, and all her gods, to a man who had once been a haughty tyrant and now, from his place of exile, was planning her destruction!

The consuls took their seats on the tribunal; the lictors were ordered to carry out the sentence. The prisoners were stripped, flogged, and beheaded. Throughout the pitiful scene all eyes were on the father's face, where a father's anguish was plain to see.

After the execution, the informer was rewarded; in addition to a gift of money he was granted his liberty with citizen rights. It was hoped that this measure might double the effect of the execution as a deterrent. The informer is said to have been the first slave to be emancipated by touching with the *vindicta* (staff); some think that the word *vindicta* was derived from his name, Vindicius. It was the custom subsequently to regard all slaves who were freed in this way as admitted to the rights of citizenship.

News of these events had a profound effect upon Tarquin; disappointed by the failure of his grand design, he was filled with violent resentment against Rome. One way – the way of treachery – being blocked, he turned to the only alternative, the preparation of open war. For this purpose he visited the various Etruscan towns in order to solicit their support, and his best hopes of success were centred on Veii and Tarquinii. 'I am of the same blood as you,' – so ran his argument – 'yesterday I was a king in no mean kingdom; now I am a penniless exile. Do not let me perish with my young sons before your eyes. Other men have been called from abroad to reign in Rome; I, when the throne was mine, when I was extending Roman dominion by my conquests, was driven from power by a foul conspiracy in which my own kindred took part. My enemies could find no worthy successor, no one man fit to reign; so they snatched at fragments of power – broke it and divided it; they let the rabble, like a gang of thieves, plunder my wealth, that even the lowest might have a share of the guilt. It is my purpose to recover my country and my throne, to punish my ungrateful subjects. I appeal to you for aid. March with me to avenge the injuries you, too, have suffered in the past – your many defeats in battle and the loss of your lands.'

The men of Veii were not deaf to this appeal; it touched them on the quick, and Tarquin's words were met by the sturdy response that every man was ready to wipe out the stain of old defeats and win back what they had lost in war. At Tarquinii the appeal was no less successful but for a different reason: there it was the name that told; all felt it was a fine thing that a man of their blood should reign in Rome. Accordingly two contingents, one from each town, joined Tarquin, bent upon the conquest of Rome and the recovery of the throne for their leader.

As the invading forces crossed the frontier, the consuls marched to meet them, Valerius in command of the infantry in square formation, Brutus feeling ahead with the mounted troops. The dispositions of the enemy were similar, the cavalry under the command of the king's

son Arruns in the van, Tarquin himself following up with the infantry. While the hostile forces were still some distance apart, Arruns
recognized the consul by his lictors, and presently, coming near
enough to distinguish his features, knew without doubt that it was
Brutus. 'There is the man,' he cried in a burst of anger, 'who drove
us from our country! Look how he comes swaggering on, with all
the marks of a power and dignity which by right are ours! Avenge, O
God of battles, this insult to a king!' Setting spurs to his horse, he
made straight for the consul. Brutus was aware of the threat – a
general was expected in those days to play his part in the actual fighting – and eagerly accepted the challenge. The two met with extreme
violence, each without a thought for his own safety, intent only to
strike his enemy down; and such weight was behind their thrust that
the spear of each drove clean through his adversary's shield deep into
his body, and both fell dying to the ground.

By then a general cavalry engagement had begun, and soon afterwards the infantry forces appeared upon the scene. The battle which
followed was indecisive; both armies were successful on the right,
unsuccessful on the left; the contingent from Veii, accustomed to
defeat by Rome, was once more routed, while the men of Tarquinii,
who had no previous experience against Roman troops, not only held
firm but forced the Roman left to withdraw. Oddly enough, however, though the engagement was indecisive, Tarquin and his Etruscans seem to have been suddenly overcome by despair of success, and
the contingents from Veii and Tarquinii both dispersed during the
night and went home, as if all were lost. There is a strange story that
in the silence of the night after the battle a great voice, supposedly the
voice of Silvanus, was heard from the depths of the Arsian wood, saying that the Etruscans had lost one more man in the fight than the
Romans and the Romans were therefore victorious. Legends apart,
there is no doubt that the Romans left the field as conquerors and that
their enemies admitted defeat, for when at dawn next morning not a
man of the Etruscan army remained to be seen, the consul Valerius
marched back to Rome with the spoils of battle, to celebrate his
triumph. Brutus was given as splendid a funeral as those early days
could afford; but an even greater tribute to him was the nation's sorrow, of which the most poignant expression was given by the women
of Rome, who mourned him for a year, as a father. It was their special
tribute to his fierce championship of a woman's honour.

The passions of the mob are notoriously fickle, and Valerius, the surviving consul, soon lost his popularity and came not only to be disliked but suspected on the gravest possible grounds. Rumour had it that he was aiming at the monarchy. The reasons for suspicion were two: first, because he had taken no steps to supply the place of his dead colleague; secondly, because he was building himself a house on the top of the Velia, which might well, in such a position, be turned into an impregnable fortress. Valerius, deeply distressed by the prevalence of these unworthy rumours, called a mass meeting of the people, and, before mounting the platform, ordered his lictors, as a gesture of sympathy with popular feeling, to lower their rods. The gesture was well received; the lowering of the *fasces* – the emblem of authority – in the people's presence was taken as an admission that the majesty of power was vested in themselves rather than in the consul. Valerius then began to speak: he dwelt on the good fortune of his colleague who, having set Rome free, had held the highest office in the state, and had died fighting for his country at the very peak of his fame, before the breath of envy could tarnish its brightness. 'While I,' he went on, 'have outlived my good name; I have survived only to face your accusations and your hate. Once hailed as a liberator of my country, I have sunk in your eyes to the baseness of traitors like the Aquilii and Vitellii. Will you never find in any man merit so tried and tested as to be above suspicion? How could I, the bitterest enemy of monarchy, ever have believed that I should face a charge of coveting a throne? If I lived in the fortress of the Capitol itself, could I ever have thought that my own fellow-citizens would be afraid of me? Can my reputation be blown away by so light a breath? Are the foundations of my honour so insecure that you judge me more by where I live than by what I am? No, my friends: no house of mine shall threaten your liberties. The Velia shall hold no dangers. I'll build my house on the level – more, I'll build it at the very base of the hill, so that you can live above me and keep a wary eye on the fellow-citizen you mistrust. Houses on the Velia must be reserved for men better to be trusted with Rome's liberty than I am.'

The building material was all brought down to the bottom of the hill, and the house erected on the spot where the shrine of Vica Pota now stands.

Valerius then proceeded to propose measures which not only cleared him of the suspicion of monarchical ambitions but actually turned him into a popular democratic figure, and earned him the title of Publicola or the People's Friend. The chief of these measures were the provision of the right of appeal to the people against a decision of the magistrates, and loss of all civil rights for anyone convicted of plotting for the return of the monarchy. As Valerius was anxious to have all the credit for these popular measures, he did not hold elections for the consular office left vacant by Brutus's death until they were carried through. Spurius Lucretius was finally elected, but he was an old man, unfit for the heavy strain the office imposed; he died a few days later and was succeeded by Marcus Horatius Pulvillus. Some old chroniclers make no mention of Lucretius, but state that Brutus was succeeded directly by Horatius. Probably Lucretius's consulship was forgotten as it was not marked by any event of importance.

The temple of Jupiter on the Capitol had not yet been dedicated, and the two consuls now drew lots to determine which of them should perform the ceremony. The lot fell to Horatius, and Publicola proceeded to conduct the operations against Veii. Publicola's relatives were unreasonably hurt that the duty of dedicating so splendid a temple should fall to Horatius, and did everything they could to prevent it. When all else failed, and Horatius, with his hand on the doorpost, was actually in the middle of his prayer, they broke in on the ceremony with the news that his son was dead, implying that while his house was in mourning he was not in a position to dedicate a temple. Horatius either did not believe the message, or showed extraordinary presence of mind – which, we are not told, nor is it easy to guess; but in any case the news had so little effect that he merely gave instructions for his son's funeral and went on to complete the ceremony of dedication.

This completes the tale of Rome's achievements at home and abroad during the first year after the expulsion of the kings. For the year following the consuls were Valerius, for a second term, and Titus Lucretius.

The Tarquins, meanwhile, had taken refuge at the court of Lars Porsena, the king of Clusium. By every means in their power they tried to win his support, now begging him not to allow fellow Etruscans, men of the same blood as himself, to continue living in penniless exile, now warning him of the dangerous consequences of letting republicanism go unavenged. The expulsion of kings, they urged, once it had begun, might well become common practice;

liberty was an attractive idea, and unless reigning monarchs defended their thrones as vigorously as states now seemed to be trying to destroy them, all order and subordination would collapse; nothing would be left in any country but flat equality; greatness and eminence would be gone for ever. Monarchy, the noblest thing in heaven or on earth, was nearing its end. Porsena, who felt that his own security would be increased by restoring the monarchy in Rome, and also that Etruscan prestige would be enhanced if the king were of Etruscan blood, was convinced by these arguments and lost no time in invading Roman territory.

Never before had there been such consternation in the Senate, so powerful was Clusium at that time and so great the fame of Porsena. Nor was the menace of Porsena the only cause for alarm: the Roman populace itself was hardly less to be feared, for they might well be scared into admitting the Tarquins into the city and buying peace even at the price of servitude. To secure their support, therefore, the Senate granted them a number of favours, especially in the matter of food supplies. Missions were sent to Cumae and the Volscians to purchase grain; the monopoly in salt, the price of which was high, was taken from private individuals and transferred wholly to state control; the commons were exempted from tolls and taxes, the loss of revenue being made up by the rich, who could afford it; the poor, it was said, made contribution enough if they reared children. These concessions proved wonderfully effective, for during the misery and privation of the subsequent blockade the city remained united – so closely, indeed, that the poorest in Rome hated the very name of 'king' as bitterly as did the great. Wise government in this crisis gave the Senate greater popularity, in the true sense of the word, than was ever won by a demagogue in after years.

On the approach of the Etruscan army, the Romans abandoned their farmsteads and moved into the city. Garrisons were posted. In some sections the city walls seemed sufficient protection, in others the barrier of the Tiber. The most vulnerable point was the wooden bridge, and the Etruscans would have crossed it and forced an entrance into the city, had it not been for the courage of one man, Horatius Cocles – that great soldier whom the fortune of Rome gave to be her shield on that day of peril. Horatius was on guard at the bridge when the Janiculum was captured by a sudden attack. The enemy forces came pouring down the hill, while the Roman troops, throwing away their weapons, were behaving more like an undisciplined rabble than a fighting force. Horatius acted promptly: as his routed comrades approached the bridge, he stopped as many as he could catch and compelled them to listen to him. 'By God,' he cried, 'can't you see that if you desert your post escape is hopeless? If you leave the bridge open in your rear, there will soon be more of them in the Palatine and the Capitol than on the Janiculum.' Urging them with all the power at his command to destroy the bridge by fire or steel or any means they could muster, he offered to hold up the Etruscan advance, so far as was possible, alone. Proudly he took his stand at the outer end of the bridge; conspicuous amongst the rout of fugitives, sword and shield ready for action, he prepared himself for close combat, one man against an army. The advancing enemy paused in sheer astonishment at such reckless courage. Two other men, Spurius Lartius and Titus Herminius, both aristocrats with a fine military record, were ashamed to leave Horatius alone, and with their support he won through the first few minutes of desperate danger. Soon, however, he forced them to save themselves and leave him; for little was now left of the bridge, and the demolition squads were calling them back before it was too late. Once more Horatius stood alone; with defiance in his eyes he confronted the Etruscan chivalry, challenging one after another to single combat, and mocking them all as tyrants' slaves who, careless of their own liberty, were coming to destroy the liberty of others. For a while they hung back, each waiting for his neighbour to make the first move, until shame at the unequal battle drove them to action, and with a fierce cry they hurled their spears at the solitary figure which barred their way. Horatius caught the missiles on his shield and, resolute as ever, straddled the bridge and held his ground. The Etruscans moved forward, and would have thrust him aside by the sheer weight of numbers, but their advance was suddenly checked by the crash of the falling bridge and the simultaneous shout of triumph from the Roman soldiers who had done their work in time. The Etruscans could only stare in bewilderment as Horatius, with a prayer to Father Tiber to bless him and his sword, plunged fully armed into the water and swam, through the missiles which fell thick about him, safely to the other side where his friends were waiting to receive him. It was a noble piece of work – legendary, maybe, but destined to be celebrated in story through the years to come.

For such courage the country showed its gratitude. A statue of
Horatius was placed in the Comitium, and he was granted as much
land as he could drive a plough round in a day. In addition to public
honours many individuals marked their admiration of his exploit in
the very hard times which were to follow, by going short themselves
in order to contribute something, whatever they could afford, to his
support.

Thwarted in his attempt to take the city by assault, Porsena now
turned to siege operations. He garrisoned the Janiculum, took up a
position on the flat ground near the river, and collected a number of
vessels to prevent supplies from being brought into Rome and also to
ferry troops across whenever, or wherever, an opportunity for a raid
should present itself. His control over the whole outlying territory
was soon so complete that, in addition to other sorts of property, all
cattle had to be brought within the defences of the city, and nobody
dared to drive them out to pasture. In point of fact, however, these
excessive precautions were dictated by policy as much as by fear; for
Valerius was awaiting his chance of really effective counter-measures,
and was prepared to ignore minor raids by the enemy in the hope of
striking a heavier blow, should he succeed in surprising a large body
of them when they were intent only on their depredations and not
expecting an attack. With this in mind, he gave orders that on the
following day cattle should be driven out in large numbers through
the Esquiline gate – the furthest from the enemy lines; the Etruscans,
he was convinced, would soon know what was happening, as slaves
were constantly deserting to escape the shortages of the blockade. Nor
was he mistaken; a deserter took the information to the Etruscan lines,
with the result that they crossed the river in much greater force than
usual, expecting a grand haul. Valerius then issued his orders: Titus
Herminius was to lie concealed with a small body of troops two miles
out on the Gabinian Road, and Spurius Lartius was to take a company
of lightly armed men to the Colline Gate, wait there till the enemy
passed, and then cut off their line of retreat to the river. The consul
Lucretius went out with a few companies by the Naevian Gate, and
Valerius with a picked force, by the Caelian. The consuls and their
parties were the first to be seen by the enemy.

Immediately the engagement began, Herminius fell upon the rear
of the Etruscans, who had turned to meet Lucretius. From the Colline
and Naevian Gates the battle-cry was raised. The raiders were

surrounded; and, being no match for the Roman troops and unable to evade them, were cut to pieces. The Etruscans learned their lesson and attempted no further raids on a similar scale.

The siege none the less continued; food in the city was scarce and dear, and Porsena's hopes rose of being able to starve it into submission without risking an assault. It was in these circumstances that the young aristocrat Gaius Mucius performed his famous act of heroism. In the days of her servitude under the monarchy Rome had never, in any war, suffered the humiliation of a siege, and Mucius was so deeply conscious of the shame of the present situation, when, after winning their liberty, the Romans were blockaded by – of all people – the Etruscans, whom they had so often defeated in the field, that he determined to vindicate the national pride by a bold stroke. His first thought was to make his way, on his own initiative, into the enemy lines; but there was a risk, if he attempted this without anybody's knowledge and without the authorization of the consuls, of being arrested by the guards as a deserter – a charge only too plausible, conditions in Rome being what they were. Accordingly he changed his mind, and presented himself in the Senate. 'I wish,' he said, 'to cross the river and to enter, if I can, the enemy's lines. My object is neither plunder nor reprisals, but, with the help of God, something more important than either.'

The Senate granted him permission to proceed and he started on his way, a dagger concealed in his clothing. Arrived at the Etruscan camp, he took his stand, in the crowd, close to the raised platform where the king was sitting. A great many people were present, as it was pay-day for the army. By the side of the king sat his secretary, very busy; he was dressed much like his master, and, as most of the men addressed themselves to him, Mucius could not be sure which was the secretary and which the king. Fearing to inquire, lest his ignorance should betray him, he took a chance – and stabbed the secretary. There was a cry of alarm; he was seized by the guards as he tried to force his way through the crowd with his blood-stained dagger, and dragged back to where Porsena was sitting. Help there was none, and his situation was desperate indeed: but he never flinched and, when he spoke, his proud words were those of a man who inspires fear, but feels none. 'I am a Roman,' he said to the king; 'my name is Gaius Mucius. I came here to kill you – my enemy. I have as much courage to die as to kill. It is our Roman way to do and to suffer bravely. Nor am I alone in my resolve against your life; behind me is a long line of men eager for the same honour. Gird yourself, if you will, for the struggle – a struggle for your life from hour to hour, with an armed enemy always at your door. That is the war we declare against you: you need fear no action in the field, army against army; it will be fought against you alone, by one of us at a time.'

Porsena in rage and alarm ordered the prisoner to be burnt alive unless he at once divulged the plot thus obscurely hinted at, whereupon Mucius, crying: 'See how cheap men hold their bodies when they care only for honour!' thrust his right hand into the fire which had been kindled for a sacrifice, and let it burn there as if he were unconscious of the pain. Porsena was so astonished by the young man's almost superhuman endurance that he leapt to his feet and ordered his guards to drag him from the altar. 'Go free,' he said; 'you have dared to be a worse enemy to yourself than to me. I should bless your courage, if it lay with my country to dispose of it. But, as that cannot be, I, as an honourable enemy, grant you pardon, life, and liberty.'

'Since you respect courage,' Mucius replied, as if he were thanking him for his generosity, 'I will tell you in gratitude what you could not force from me by threats. There are three hundred of us in Rome, all young like myself, and all of noble blood, who have sworn an attempt upon your life in this fashion. It was I who drew the first lot; the rest will follow, each in his turn and time, until fortune favour us and we have got you.'

The release of Mucius (who was afterwards known as Scaevola, or the Left-Handed Man, from the loss of his right hand) was quickly followed by the arrival in Rome of envoys from Porsena. The first attempt upon his life, foiled only by a lucky mistake, and the prospect of having to face the same thing again from every one of the remaining conspirators, had so shaken the king that he was coming forward with proposals for peace. The proposals contained a demand for the restoration of the Tarquins. Porsena knew well enough that it would be refused – as indeed it was – but out of deference to the Tarquin family he could hardly avoid making it. He was successful, however, in obtaining the return of captured territory to Veii, and in forcing the Romans to give hostages if they wanted the Etruscan garrison withdrawn from the Janiculum. Peace was made on these terms: Porsena withdrew his troops from the Janiculum and evacuated Roman territory. Caius Mucius was rewarded by the Senate with a grant of land west of the river; it was known subsequently as the Mucian Meadows.

The public recognition of Mucius's heroism inspired even the women of Rome to emulate him. A notable instance is the story of Cloelia. Cloelia, an unmarried girl, was one of the hostages, held, as it happened, in the Etruscan lines not far from the Tiber; one day with a number of other girls who had consented to follow her, she eluded the guards, swam across the river under a hail of missiles, and brought her company safe to Rome, where they were all restored to their families. Porsena was furious, and sent to Rome to demand Cloelia's return – adding that the loss of the other girls did not trouble him; soon, however, his anger gave way to admiration of her more than masculine courage: Horatius and Mucius, he declared, were not to be compared with her, and he made it clear that though he would regard the treaty as broken if she were not returned, he would nevertheless, if the Romans surrendered her, himself restore her safe and sound to her family. Both sides acted honourably: the Romans, as the terms of the treaty required, sent the hostage back, and Porsena not only protected the brave girl but praised her publicly, and marked his appreciation of her exploit by handing over to her discretion a certain number of the other hostages, to be chosen by herself. She is said to have chosen the young boys, a choice in accordance with her maiden modesty: the other hostages, moreover, agreed that in liberating them from the enemy those should be first considered who were most subject to injurious treatment. Friendly relations were thus restored, and the Romans paid tribute to Cloelia's courage, unprecedented in a woman, by an equally unprecedented honour: a statue representing her on horseback was set up at the top of the Sacred Way.

The custom which still survives when enemy goods are put up for auction of offering for sale, amongst other formalities, the 'property of King Porsena', is inconsistent with the fact that Porsena withdrew from Roman territory in the peaceful manner above described. The practice may have begun during the war and have been retained afterwards; but it is also possible that it originated in circumstances quite different from what is suggested by a public notice that an enemy's property is up for sale. The most credible explanation is that when Porsena withdrew from the Janiculum he made over to the Romans, who were short of food after the long siege, all the supplies which he had collected at his headquarters from the rich neighbouring lands of

Etruria, and that these supplies were then regularly offered for sale, to prevent them from being pillaged by the populace; they were known as 'Porsena's property', or 'Porsena's stores', from appreciation of the gift rather than because they were Porsena's property up for sale – in any case his property was not in Roman hands.

Having brought his army so far afield, Porsena felt it was a pity to have nothing to show for it, so when he had finally abandoned his attempt upon Rome, he sent a contingent under his son Arruns to attack Aricia. The first effect of this unexpected threat upon the people of the town was consternation; they rallied, however, and the arrival of reinforcements from Cumae and the Latin peoples so raised their hopes of a successful resistance that they ventured to challenge the Etruscans in the field. The engagement began with an Etruscan attack of such weight and fury that the Arician lines were completely dis-organized; but the men of Cumae saved the day. Meeting force by strategy, they moved to the flank to allow the enemy to sweep past them, then turned and attacked them in the rear, with the result that the Etruscans were caught in a trap and cut to pieces almost in the moment of victory. Arruns was killed, and a handful of Etruscan soldiers, having nowhere nearer to go to, found their way to Rome, where they arrived unarmed and helpless and with no resource but to throw themselves on the Romans' mercy. They were kindly received and billeted in various houses. Some, when their wounds were healed, went home to tell their friends of the generous treatment they had received, but the majority of them were induced to stay in Rome by their growing affection both for the city and for their hosts. They were allowed to live in a district which came to be known as the Tuscan Quarter.

The next consuls were Spurius Lartius and Titus Herminius, fol-lowed by Publius Lucretius and Publius Valerius Publicola. In the latter year Porsena made his final effort to procure Tarquin's restora-tion to power. His envoys on their arrival in Rome were told that the Senate would dispatch a mission to the king, and this was immediately done. The members of the mission were all senators of the highest distinction. It would have been easy enough, they declared, to give a curt refusal, on the spot, to Porsena's overtures. That was not the reason why Rome had sent representatives of such distinction rather than answer the Etruscan envoys directly; the reason was that the Romans wished the whole question of the restoration to be closed once and for all. Relations between Rome and Clusium were now excellent; it would be a pity, therefore, to risk the mutual irritation of a repeated request, on the one side, met, on the other, by a repeated refusal; and this would be bound to occur if Porsena continued to ask for what was incompatible with Roman liberty, and the Romans – short of allowing their good nature to prove their ruin – continued to refuse it to a man to whom they would not willingly refuse anything. Rome was no longer a monarchy; she enjoyed free institutions. The people of Rome would sooner open their gates to an enemy than to a king. There was not a man in the city who did not pray that the end of liberty, should it come, might also be the end of Rome. They urged Porsena, therefore, if he had the good of Rome at heart, to accept the fact that she would never surrender her liberties.

Porsena was deeply impressed. 'Since,' he said, 'it is clear that nothing can shake your determination, I will no longer weary you with requests which I now know to be useless; nor shall I deceive the Tarquins with the hope of aid which I have no power to give. They must find – by force of arms or otherwise, as they please – some other place to spend their exile in; for nothing must disturb the friendly relations between myself and Rome.'

His deeds were better than his words: he sent back the remaining hostages, and restored to Rome the Veientine territory which had been ceded to him by the terms of the treaty of the Janiculum. Tarquin, now without any hope of returning to power, joined his son-in-law Mamilius Octavius in Tusculum. Peace between Rome and Porsena remained unbroken.

The consuls for the following year were Marcus Valerius and Publius Postumius. During the year there were successful operations against the Sabines, and the consuls celebrated 'triumphs'. The Sabines then began preparations on a larger scale. At the same time there was danger of a sudden attack from Tusculum, where anti-Roman feeling was suspected though not yet openly declared. To meet this double threat Publius Valerius was elected consul for a fourth term and Titus Lucretius for a second.

At this juncture Sabine unity was split by the rise of a peace party, and this resulted in the transference to Rome of a portion of their strength. Attius Clausus, afterwards known in Rome as Appius Claudius, was a leader of the peace party, and finding himself hard pressed by his turbulent rivals, and no match for them, he left Regillus and fled to Rome, taking with him a large number of his dependants and supporters. They were granted citizen rights and some land on the further side of the river Anio. Later, these people came to be called the Old Claudian Tribe – the original settlers, that is, in the district – after new members had been added to their number. Appius was made a senator, and quickly rose to eminence.

A Roman force under the command of the consuls invaded Sabine territory, which it proceeded to devastate; by that means, and by means of a successful engagement which followed, the Romans broke the Sabines' power of resistance so completely that there was no fear of further hostilities for a long time to come. Returning to Rome, the consuls celebrated their triumph. Next year, in the consulship of Menenius Agrippa and Publius Postumius, occurred the death of Publius Valerius, by universal consent the greatest soldier and states-man of his day; yet in spite of his unprecedented renown he was so poor that his resources were not enough to pay for his funeral. He was buried at the public expense, and the women of Rome went into mourning for him, as they had done for Brutus.

In the same year two Latin colonies, Pometia and Cora, threw off their allegiance and joined the Aurunci. War was declared and Aurun-can territory invaded. A powerful force which gallantly attempted to check the invasion was defeated, and the whole weight of the Roman operations was then concentrated upon Pometia. The battle had been a bloody one; neither during nor after it was quarter given. More were killed than captured, and all prisoners were put to the sword. Not even the hostages, of whom there were three hundred, were spared. This year, too, a triumph was celebrated in Rome.

The consuls of the following year, Opiter Verginius and Spurius Cassius, proceeded at once to attempt the reduction of Pometia, first by assault, then by the use of *vineae*, or mantlets, and other siege en-gines. The Aurunci had little chance or expectation of success; but in sheer blind hatred of the enemy they came pouring out of the town, most of them carrying firebrands instead of swords. Spreading havoc in every direction, they set the mantlets on fire, inflicted heavy casualties in killed and wounded on the Roman troops, and came near to killing one of the two consuls – which, is not recorded. He was flung from his horse and very seriously injured. It was a bad day for Rome, and the army withdrew taking their wounded with them, amongst them the consul hanging between life and death.

Only enough time was allowed to elapse for nursing the wounded back to health and raising new troops, before a second attack was made against Pometia, this time with stronger forces, and greater savagery. The artillery and siege engines had all been reconstructed, and Roman troops were on the point of scaling the walls, when the town surrendered. In spite of its surrender its fate was no less horrible than if it had been taken by storm: the leading men were all executed, the rest sold as slaves; the town was gutted, and its land put up for sale. The war thus concluded had been a minor one; none the less the consuls celebrated a triumph – perhaps to signalize the severity of their revenge.

In the following year Postumus Cominius and Titus Lartius were elected consuls. During the games at Rome a party of young hooligans of Sabine nationality carried off some street-walkers, a piece of foolery which looked like having serious consequences. Crowds gathered; there was a violent quarrel – almost a fight, and it began to seem that there might be a fresh outbreak of war. Moreover, in addition to the chance of war with the Sabines, it was a matter of common knowledge that Octavius Mamilius had been urging the thirty Latin communities to form a league against Rome.

It was in these circumstances of mounting anxiety and tension that the proposal was made, for the first time, of appointing a Dictator. The precise date of this is not known, nor which were the consuls who were suspected of pro-Tarquin sympathies – for that the consuls were indeed so suspected is generally believed. The oldest authorities, I find, state that the first Dictator was Titus Lartius and that Spurius Cassius was his Master of the Horse. Men of consular rank were appointed to these offices, for that was what the law demanded; and for that reason I feel that the ex-consul Lartius is more likely to have been raised to a position which gave him full control over the chief officers of the state than Manlius Valerius son of Marcus and grandson of Volesus, who had never yet been consul at all. Moreover, if people particularly wanted a dictator from that family, they would have been much more likely to choose Marcus Valerius, an ex-consul and a man of proved ability.

The appointment of a dictator for the first time in Rome, and the solemn sight of his progress through the streets preceded by the ceremonial axes, had the effect of scaring the commons into a more docile frame of mind. While there were two consuls sharing power equally, it had been possible to appeal from one to the other; but from a dictator there was no appeal, and no help anywhere but in implicit obedience. The Sabines, too, were alarmed by this new appointment, especially as they were convinced that it was directed against themselves; accordingly they sent envoys to Rome to treat for peace. The envoys urged the Senate not to take too seriously what was only the prank of a few thoughtless young men, and were told in reply that though young men could be pardoned, old men could not, if – as in the present case – they continued to provoke hostilities. Nevertheless negotiations were begun, and the Sabines would have obtained their assurance of peace, if they had been willing to meet the Roman demand that they should guarantee the money which had been spent upon preparations for war. War was formally declared, but for the rest of the year by a sort of tacit agreement no action was taken.

Nothing of importance occurred the following year, when the consuls were Servius Sulpicius and Manlius Tullius; but the year after that, when Titus Aebutius and Gaius Vetusius were in office, saw the siege of Fidenae, the capture of Crustumeria, and the secession of Praeneste from the Latins to Rome. War with the Latins had been smouldering for some time, and it was now no longer possible to postpone it. Aulus Postumius, who had been granted dictatorial power, proceeded with Titus Aebutius his Master of the Horse and a powerful army of combined cavalry and infantry to Lake Regillus near Tusculum, where they encountered the Latin forces already on the march. Report had it that the Tarquins were with them, and their hated presence so inflamed the Roman commanders that nothing would satisfy them but immediate action. The battle which followed was for this reason fought with more determination and greater savagery than usual: officers of high rank, who would normally have confined themselves to directing operations, joined personally in the fighting, and with the exception of the Roman Dictator there was hardly a man amongst the nobility of either side who escaped without a wound. Postumius from his position in the front line was still making his final dispositions and urging his men to do their duty, when Tarquinius Superbus, now an old man with failing strength, came riding straight for him. The attempt failed. Tarquin was struck in the side, but his followers closed in round him and got him back to safety. Similarly on the other wing Aebutius, the Master of the Horse, had charged Octavius Mamilius; the Tusculan commander saw him coming and galloped to meet him; the two met with the utmost fury, Mamilius being wounded in the breast, while his own lance ran clean through his adversary's arm. Mamilius was taken to the rear; Aebutius retired from the fight altogether, as with his wounded arm he could not hold a weapon. The Latin commander continued in spite of his wound to direct operations with full vigour; and seeing his men badly shaken by the Roman onslaught called up a company of Roman exiles under the command of Tarquin's surviving son. Their joining in the action was a steadying influence, at any rate for a time, for they fought with especial fury in that they had especial cause. It was not long before the Romans in that sector began to give way; it was a critical moment, and Marcus Valerius, Publicola's brother, was killed in a gallant attempt to retrieve the situation: the sight of young Tarquin on his horse, in the front rank of the exiles, insolently, as it seemed, inviting attack, set him on fire, and, resolving that the family of the Valerii should have the glory not only of the expulsion of the Tarquins but also of their death, he set spurs to his horse and made for the young prince, to run him through the body. Tarquin moved back as he saw him coming; his troopers rallied closely round him, and one of them, stepping aside as Valerius swept past at a mad gallop, thrust his spear through his body. Valerius fell dying to the ground, his shield and spear on top of him, while the riderless horse galloped on.

The Dictator Postumius now took steps to avert a dangerous situation. The loss of Valerius was in itself a heavy blow; the exiles were moving swiftly and confidently to the attack, and the Romans were giving ground. Accordingly he issued an order to the picked troops who were serving as his personal guard to cut down every Roman soldier whom they saw trying to save his own skin. The measure was successful: threatened simultaneously from front and rear, the Romans turned to face the enemy, and the line was reconstituted. The Dictator's special force then went into action for the first time and with great effect: fresh and vigorous as they were, they attacked the exiles, who were beginning to tire, and cut them to pieces. This led to another notable duel between rival captains: the Latin commander, Mamilius, seeing the exiles almost cut off by Postumius, hurried with a few reserve companies to the front, and as they were marching up Titus Herminius, a Roman general officer, recognized Mamilius, who in his splendid equipment was an unmistakable figure. Instantly Herminius challenged him, riding at him with even greater ferocity than Aebutius had done a little while before. Such was the fury of his assault that he killed him with a single thrust through the body, and a moment later, as he stooped to strip the arms from his fallen enemy, he was himself mortally wounded by a javelin. He was carried to the rear – victorious indeed, but he died as soon as they started to dress his wound.

Postumius now galloped off to make a final appeal to his mounted troops; and urged them to abandon their horses and fight on foot shoulder to shoulder with the exhausted infantry. The appeal was answered; every man leapt from his horse and moved up at the double to the front line, which they covered with their shields. The effect was instantaneous, the infantry fighting with fresh determination, once they saw the young nobles ready to share their dangers on equal terms. From that moment the issue was no longer in doubt; the Latins wavered, and then broke; the Roman cavalry remounted and began the pursuit, followed by the infantry. Even then the dictator Postumius took no chances: to win heaven's help he vowed a temple to Castor, and to get the utmost from his men he offered rewards to the first two soldiers to enter the Latin camp; and such was the ardour of the pursuit that the Roman forces were carried right into the enemy's camp on the same wave that first broke his resistance. So ended the battle of Lake Regillus. The Dictator and the Master of the Horse returned to Rome in triumph.

During the three following years there was neither assured peace nor open war. The consulship was held, first by Quintus Cloelius and Titus Lartius, then by Aulus Sempronius and Marcus Minucius. During the latters' term of office a temple was dedicated to Saturn and the Saturnalia was first instituted as a public holiday. The next consuls were Aulus Postumius and Titus Verginius. Some authorities, I find, assign the battle of Lake Regillus to this year, and state that Postumius was made Dictator after resigning his consulship out of suspicion of his colleague's loyalty. I do not know: the order of magistrates varies so much in different records that there is much confusion about dates during this period, and it is not possible to be certain which consuls followed which or what was done in each particular year. One cannot hope for accuracy when dealing with a past so remote and with authorities so antiquated.

Next to hold the consulship were Appius Claudius and Publius

Servilius. Their year of office was marked by an event of great importance, the death of Tarquin at Cumae. He had gone to the court of Aristodemus in that town after the *débâcle* of the Latins. The news of Tarquin's death came as a profound relief to all classes of society in Rome; it soon proved, however, a mixed blessing, for the patricians welcomed it far too much as an opportunity for self-indulgence at the expense of the masses, who had hitherto, as a matter of policy, been treated with every consideration. Now that the menace of Tarquin was removed, they began to feel the weight of oppression.

This same year the settlement at Signia, originally founded by Tarquin, was freshly established and its population increased. In Rome the number of the tribes was raised to twenty-one. On 15 May a temple was dedicated to Mercury.

During the Latin war relations between Rome and the Volscians had been strained, though actual hostilities had been avoided. The Volscians had raised troops to send to the aid of the Latins in the event of the Roman dictator failing to act promptly; but he did act promptly, to avoid the necessity of having to deal with both peoples at once. By way of reprisal for their hostile intentions, the consuls invaded Volscian territory, and the Volscians, who had not expected to have to pay for a plan which had never materialized, were surprised into submission. They made no resistance, and handed over three hundred hostages, all children of leading families in Cora and Pometia. Roman troops were then withdrawn.

Relieved of immediate anxiety the Volscians soon reverted to their normal practices: once again they began secret preparations for war. They made a military pact with the Hernici, and sent missions to all the Latin communities to stir up rebellion. The Latins, however, were in no mood for war; the recent defeat at Lake Regillus had filled them with such a fury of hatred against anyone who suggested further hostilities, that they actually laid violent hands upon the Volscian envoys and took them forcibly to Rome, where they were delivered to the consuls together with the information that the Volscians and the Hernici were preparing for war. The matter was brought up in the Senate, and so great was the gratitude there for the service done that six thousand Latin prisoners of war were released and the question of a treaty, which had been refused more or less in perpetuity, was referred to the magistrates of the coming year. No one could have been more delighted than the Latins themselves at this result. Praises were showered upon the peacemakers, and to mark their appreciation they sent a golden crown as a gift to Jupiter in the temple on the Capitol. The envoys who brought the gift were accompanied by thousands of the released prisoners of war, who visited the various houses where they had done menial service during their captivity; they thanked their former masters for treating them in their adversity with such liberality and kindness, and promised that for the future the bond between them should be a bond of friendship. Never at any previous time had relations, both public and personal, between Rome and the Latins been closer or more cordial.

Nevertheless a double danger was threatening the City's peace: first, imminent war with the Volscians and, secondly, internal discord of ever-increasing bitterness between the ruling class and the masses. The chief cause of the dispute was the plight of the unfortunates who were 'bound over' to their creditors for debt. These men complained that while they were fighting in the field to preserve their country's liberty and to extend her power, their own fellow-citizens at home had enslaved and oppressed them; the common people, they declared, had a better chance of freedom in war than in peace; fellow Romans threatened them with worse slavery than a foreign foe. Finally, their growing resentment was fanned into flame by a particular instance of the appalling condition into which a debtor might fall. An old man suddenly presented himself in the Forum. With his soiled and threadbare clothes, his dreadful pallor and emaciated body, he was a pitiable sight, and the uncouthness of his appearance was further increased by his unkempt hair and beard. Nevertheless, though cruelly changed from what he had once been, he was recognized, and people began to tell each other, compassionately, that he was an old soldier who had once commanded a company and served with distinction in various ways – an account which he himself supported by showing the scars of honourable wounds which he still bore upon his breast. A crowd quickly gathered, till the Forum was as full as if a public assembly were about to be held; they pressed round the pathetic figure of the old soldier, asking him how it was that he had come to this dreadful pass. 'While I was on service,' he said, 'during the Sabine war, my crops were ruined by enemy raids, and my cottage was burnt. Everything I had was taken, including my cattle. Then, when I was least able to do so, I was expected to pay taxes, and fell, consequently, into debt. Interest on the borrowed money increased my burden; I lost the land which my father and grandfather had owned before me, and then my other possessions; ruin spread like a disease through all I had, and even my body was not exempt from it, for I was finally seized by my creditor and reduced to slavery: nay, worse – I was hauled away to prison and the slaughterhouse.'

The man's story, added to the sight of the weals on his back which still remained from recent beatings, caused a tremendous uproar, which spread swiftly from the Forum through every part of the city. Debtors of all conditions – some actually in chains – forced their way into the streets and begged for popular support; everywhere men flocked to join the rising, until every street was packed with noisy crowds making their way to the Forum. Any senator who happened to be out was in imminent danger, and there is little doubt that the mob would have resorted to violence, had not the consuls, Servilius and Claudius, hastily intervened to attempt to quell the disturbance. But the angry crowd turned on them, forcing them to look at the fetters on their wrists and the other signs of the cruel treatment they had received, and crying out in bitterness of spirit that such was their reward for all the campaigns they had fought in. Every moment their tone grew more menacing. They demanded that the Senate should be convened, and pressed up to the doors of the Senate House that they might themselves witness the proceedings and, if necessary, control them. The handful of senators who chanced to be available were brought by the consuls into the House; the rest were too much alarmed by the way things were going even to venture into the streets, so nothing could be done for lack of a quorum. The mob took this as a mere device to put them off; they refused to believe that fear, or any other such reason, was keeping the absent senators away, and were convinced that it was a deliberate attempt to hold up business. They had no doubt that the consuls' apparent attempt to convene the Senate was a mere empty formality, and that their own grievances were in no way being taken seriously. An explosion was only just avoided by the arrival of the absent senators, who had been unable to decide whether they ran the greater risk by staying away or coming. Had they decided not to come, it might well have been that even the majestic authority of the consuls would have been powerless to control the fury of the mob.

A quorum obtained, the debate began; but no general agreement could be reached, and the consuls were themselves divided: the proud and headstrong Appius was for a settlement by the sheer weight of consular authority – if one or two were arrested, the remainder, he declared, would soon calm down. Servilius, by nature inclined to less high-handed measures, was in favour of trying persuasion, which would, he thought, be both safer and easier than to use force.

On top of this highly critical situation came the alarming news, brought by mounted couriers from Latium, that a Volscian army was marching on Rome. So deeply was the country divided by its political differences, that the people, unlike their oppressors in the governing class, hailed the prospect of invasion with delight. For them, it seemed like an intervention of providence to crush the pride of the Senate; they went about urging their friends to refuse military service – to let the whole community perish rather than one section of it, as was happening in any case. Let the patricians, they argued, do the fighting, if they wished: if there were war, let those face its dangers who alone reaped its profits. The Senate, on the other hand, heard the news with very different feelings: there, in view of the double danger, from within and from without, there was both alarm and depression. Knowing that, of the two consuls, Servilius was more in sympathy with the popular cause, they begged him to do what he could to save the country from the appalling dangers which beset it. Servilius, accordingly, adjourned the meeting and presented himself before the people. He declared that the senators were genuinely anxious to do what they could for the benefit of the commons, who formed the largest part – though still only a part – of the community; but their deliberations upon what measures to adopt had been interrupted by a new fear which concerned the nation as a whole. With the enemy almost at the gates, defence must be the first consideration; even should the danger prove less immediate than it appeared, it was not to the people's credit to refuse to fight for their country except upon terms, any more than it conduced to the honour of the Senate to be forced by circumstances to relieve the sufferings of their fellow-citizens, when they would later have done so voluntarily. Servilius then gave substance to this statement by issuing an edict, to the effect that it should be illegal, first, to fetter or imprison a Roman citizen and so prevent him from enlisting for service, and, secondly, to seize or sell the property of any soldier on active service, or interfere in any way with his children or grandchildren. As a result of the edict all 'bound' debtors who were present gave in their names on the spot, and others from every part of the city hurried from the houses where they could no longer be legally detained, into the Forum where they took the military oath. Their numbers were very considerable, and in the ensuing fight with the Volscians no troops did more distinguished service. The consul then marched, and took up a position not far from that of the enemy.

The Volscians fancied that the political troubles in Rome would facilitate their task, so the next night, under cover of darkness, they made a tentative move in the hope of encouraging deserters from the Roman ranks. Their approach, however, did not escape the Roman sentries, who at once roused the troops. The bugles blew the call to arms; every man took his station, and the Volscians' attempt was frustrated. For the remainder of the night there was no further action. At dawn next morning the Volscians began an assault upon the protective rampart round the Roman position; they filled in the trenches, and before long were at work demolishing the palisades. The consul's men – led by the debtors – urged him in no uncertain terms to give the signal for action; but he held on a few moments longer, to be quite certain of their temper and intentions; then, when there was no longer any doubt that they were spoiling for a fight, he gave the order to advance. They burst out as hungry for blood as the beasts in the circus.

One charge was enough; the enemy fled. The Roman infantry gave chase so far as it could, striking at the fugitives' backs; and the mounted troops pursued them to their camp, which, in its turn, was soon surrounded. Once again there was no resistance, and the camp was taken and stripped of all it contained. The routed Volscians had made for Suessa Pometia, and on the following day the Roman forces marched on the town, which a day or two later was captured. Servilius turned his men loose in it, to take what they pleased, a windfall which by no means came amiss to them.

The victorious consul returned to Rome covered with glory. On his way there he was approached by representatives of the Volscians of Ecetra, whom the capture of Pometia had filled with forebodings. By a decree of the Senate they were granted peace, but their territory was confiscated.

Immediately after this the Sabines caused a certain amount of trouble. It was, however, only a minor incident: news arrived one night that a Sabine raiding party had penetrated as far as the Anio, where it was burning farms and looting over a wide area. Postumius, who had acted as Dictator during the Latin war, was promptly sent out with all the Roman mounted troops, and Servilius followed him with a picked force of infantry. Most of the raiders were rounded up by the cavalry, and the Sabine troops, such as they were, offered no resistance when they saw Servilius's infantry approaching. No doubt they were tired by their long march and their nocturnal activities – most of them, too, were sodden with drink and swollen with food which they had stolen from the farms – and they hardly had strength enough even to run away. Thus the same night which brought the news of the raid saw its end, and there were high hopes of a general peace; but on the following day representatives of the Aurunci informed the Senate that unless Roman troops evacuated Volscian territory they would declare war. The Auruncan forces had left home at the same time as their envoys and a report that they had been seen near Aricia caused a severe shock in Rome. So great was the consequent hurry and confusion that no regular motion could be brought before the Senate and it was impossible to return a pacific answer to the envoys of a people who were already threatening invasion, while Rome herself was hastily preparing her defence. Roman troops at once marched for Aricia. Battle was joined near the town, and in a single engagement the enemy's attempt was foiled once and for all.

Feeling that by this rapid succession of successful actions they had done their duty, the Roman commons now looked to the consul Servilius and the Senate to stand by the promises they had made to them. Appius, however, thought otherwise: in his desire to discredit his colleague, no less than by his own natural arrogance, he began to give the harshest possible judgements in the cases which came before him for the recovery of debts. Men previously bound over were, in consequence of his judgements, abandoned to the mercy of their creditors, and others, previously free, were bound over in their turn. All soldiers thus treated appealed to Servilius; his house was soon crowded with angry men urging him to keep his pledged word, bitterly reminding him of their war service and exhibiting their scars. Either, they declared, he must bring their case formally before the Senate, or help them himself in his double capacity of consul and commanding officer. Servilius was not unaware of the strength of their case, but he was unable wholeheartedly to support them because of the violence of the opposition both of his colleague Appius and of the governing class as a whole. Consequently he temporized, and by trying to make the best of both worlds succeeded in neither: the commons disliked him and thought him dishonest; the nobles distrusted him as a weak consul trying to curry popular favour. Soon it was obvious that he was as much hated as Appius.

About this time the two consuls had begun to quarrel about which of them should perform the dedication ceremony for the temple of Mercury. The Senate referred the decision to the people, and informed them that the man they chose should be instructed to control the distribution of grain, to establish a guild of merchants, and perform the necessary rites on behalf of the pontifex. The people accordingly voted, and gave the dedication to neither of the consuls, but to a senior centurion named Marcus Laetorius – an act obviously intended not to honour Laetorius, whose station in life was quite unsuited to a commission of this kind, but to humiliate the consuls. This time, at any rate, the fury of Appius and the Senate knew no bounds; but popular confidence was growing and the general attitude to the masses was very different from what it had been. They knew now that it was idle to look to the consuls or the Senate for relief: when they saw a debtor carried off to the courts, they took matters into their own hands and rushed to his defence; the noise they made rendered inaudible any order the consul might give; his decrees were ignored, violence reigned, and it was now not the debtors who had to look to their lives but the creditors themselves who were set upon singly by gangs and beaten up in the very presence of the consul.

In this dangerous situation there came the alarming news of a Sabine invasion. The order to raise troops was promptly issued, but there was no response: not a man gave in his name. Appius was beside himself: he accused Servilius of deliberate chicanery and of betraying the country in order to keep the mob quiet; not only, he declared, had Servilius refused to pronounce sentence in cases of debt; he had gone further, and disobeyed the Senate's decree by neglecting to raise troops in the proper manner. 'Nevertheless,' he exclaimed, 'Rome is not utterly deserted; the authority of the consuls is not yet altogether thrown away. I myself will stand up, alone, for the majesty of my office and of the Senate.'

Deeds quickly followed: observing a certain notorious troublemaker in the crowd of men which every day gathered, ripe for mischief, in the Forum, Appius ordered his arrest. The lictors were in the act of dragging him off, when he appealed. Appius knew well enough what the popular decision would be, if the appeal were allowed, and he was at first determined to refuse it; however, in spite of his savage contempt for what people thought of him, he was forced to yield, not so much by popular clamour as by the authoritative advice of the nobles. From then onward the situation grew more and more serious: rioting continued, and – what was much more dangerous – groups of malcontents began to confer in secret. At last the time came for the two consuls to lay down their office. Both had been hated by the popular party – Servilius by the conservative nobility as well, with whom Appius was in high favour.

The consuls for the following year were Aulus Verginius and Titus Vetusius. Not knowing what their attitude to the dispute was likely to be, the people continued to hold meetings to discuss policy; for greater privacy the meetings were held at night on the Esquiline or the Aventine, as it was felt that if they attempted to discuss their affairs in the Forum they might be stampeded into hasty and ill-considered action. The consuls, rightly enough, saw the dangers of this procedure and reported it to the Senate. The report was greeted with uproar and indignation; no orderly discussion of it was possible; the members of the House bitterly resented the attempt to saddle them with a disagreeable task which ought to have been dealt with out of hand by the exercise of consular authority. In their view, if the country had magistrates worthy of the name, there would never have been any question of secret meetings by groups of agitators – the normal Assembly would have sufficed. As things were, the country was split into fragments: instead of the Assembly of the People there were a thousand dissident and petty groups whispering and putting their heads together on the Esquiline or Aventine. What was needed, they declared, was not a mere consul, but a man – a real man, like Appius Claudius: anyone like him would have broken up those treasonous gangs in five minutes.

These were harsh words, and the consuls had to swallow them as best they could: they asked the Senate what steps they wished them to take, adding an assurance that they were prepared to act with all the sternness and vigour which the Senate required. The House replied that the mob having got out of hand through sheer lack of employment, the consuls were to levy troops with the utmost strictness of the law. The Senate then adjourned, and the consuls taking their stand on the tribunal, began proceedings, calling the younger men

individually, by name. No one answered. The crowd swarmed round
the tribunal, and voices were raised saying that the people refused to
be fobbed off any longer: the consuls would never get a single soldier
without a public guarantee of redress for their grievances; every man
must be given liberty again before arms were put into his hands –
for if they were to fight, they were determined to do so not for their
masters, but for their country and their fellow-citizens.

The Senate's instructions to the two consuls had been clear enough;
nevertheless of all the members of the House who had spoken with
such truculence, not one had ventured outside the walls to support
the consuls in the highly invidious task they had asked them to perform. That a violent struggle was imminent was no longer in doubt;
so before proceeding to extremities, the consuls decided once again to
take the opinion of the Senate. The House accordingly met, and immediately the younger members came crowding up to the consuls'
seats with a demand for their resignation of an office which they had
not the courage to implement. The consuls, after weighing carefully
the two courses open to them – namely appeasement or coercion –
said: 'Remember, gentlemen, that you have been warned. We are
threatened with something like civil war. We demand that those of
you who most loudly accuse us of cowardice should stand by us while
we are proceeding with the levy of troops. Then – since that is what
you want – we will carry out our duty as firmly as the most ruthless
amongst you could desire.' They returned to the Forum, mounted the
tribunal, and gave deliberate orders that a particular man, whom they
could see in the crowd, should have his name called. The man did not
answer. A number of others pressed round him, to protect him against
possible violence. Then, by the consuls' order, a lictor was ordered to
arrest him. The lictor was thrust back by the crowd, and the senators
who had left the Curia to support the consuls, enraged at this shame-
less flouting of the consular authority, hurried down from the rostrum
to the lictor's assistance. The lictor, who had merely been prevented
from effecting an arrest, was in no danger, and the crowd at once turned
its attention to the senators. The consuls, however, intervened, and some
sort of order was restored. No stones had been thrown, no weapons
drawn; in fact, there had been more anger and noise than physical
violence.

The position, however, was still critical, and a meeting of the
Senate was called in the utmost haste. Its proceedings, when it met,

were even more disorderly: the members who had been mobbed demanded an inquiry, and the die-hards in the house supported the demand with shouts and general uproar, as they were too angry to make any kind of formal proposal. When at last the atmosphere was calm enough for the consuls to speak, they remarked severely that there was little to choose between the behaviour of members in the House and that of the mob in the streets, after which business was able to proceed normally. Three proposals were put forward: Verginius opposed any measure for general relief, and suggested that only those men should be considered who had fought in the Volscian, Auruncan, and Sabine wars on the strength of the promise made to them by the consul Servilius. Titus Lartius urged that this was no time merely for preferential treatment of the deserving: the commons as a whole were sunk in debt, and the situation could not be remedied without general relief; any sort of preferential treatment, far from allaying, would only aggravate their sense of grievance. Appius Claudius took a different line altogether: naturally harsh as he was, and rendered even more uncompromising by the hatred of the commons and the fervid support of the nobility, he roundly declared that the mob had nothing whatever to complain of: the disturbances were not due to their sufferings but to their disregard for law and order; they were not angry – for they had nothing to be angry about: they were merely out of hand. That, he continued, was the natural consequence of the right of appeal: the appeal had destroyed consular authority; for now that the law allowed an appeal to those who were equally guilty, the consuls could never act – they could only threaten. 'I urge you, therefore,' he said, 'to appoint a Dictator, from whom there is no right of appeal. Do that, and you will quickly enough throw water on the blaze. I should like to see anyone use force against a lictor then, when he knows that the power to scourge or kill him is wholly in the hands of the man whose majesty he has dared to offend!'

The proposal seemed to many, as indeed it was, excessively severe; on the other hand the proposals of Verginius and Lartius were not felt likely to have a salutary effect – certainly not the latter, which would completely undermine credit. The general sense of the House was inclined to the compromise proposed by Verginius; political decisions, however, always have been, and always will be, influenced for ill by party spirit and concern for property. The present case was no exception; Appius carried this point, and came very near to being appointed

Dictator himself. Had this actually occurred, it would have been disastrous: the commons would have been completely alienated at a moment of great national danger when the Volscians, Aequians, and Sabines were simultaneously up in arms. Happily both consuls, supported by the elder members of the Senate, took care that an office, in itself of such formidable power, should be entrusted to a man of moderate temper, and appointed Manlius Valerius, the son of Volesus.

The commons were well aware that the appointment of a dictator was directed against themselves; nevertheless they had little fear of violent or oppressive measures. It was a Valerius, the brother of the Dictator, who had originally given them the right of appeal, and they trusted the family in consequence. Their confidence, moreover, was soon increased when the dictator issued an edict very similar in tenor to that of Servilius, though the effect of it, coming as it did from a man they trusted in an office they were bound to respect, was much greater. They gave up their opposition and enlisted for service. Ten legions were formed, a larger force than ever before; three legions were put under the command of each consul, the remaining four under the command of the Dictator.

By now the Aequians had invaded Latin territory, and action could no longer be deferred. Representatives of the Latins were already in Rome, asking the Senate either for aid or for permission to arm themselves in their own defence. The latter was refused, as Rome was unwilling to allow the Latins to rearm; the safer course appeared to be to send troops. Vetusius was commissioned to lead them, and his arrival marked the end of the raids, as the Aequians withdrew to the hills where they hoped to be safer than in the open country with only their swords to defend them. The other consul proceeded against the Volscians and quickly got down to business, doing his best, chiefly by destroying their crops, to provoke the enemy to battle. In this he was successful; the Volscians advanced to a position close to the Romans, and the two armies, each in front of its own stockade, prepared to engage. Numerical superiority made the Volscians over-confident, so that they advanced to the attack in loose order and a somewhat casual and undisciplined manner. Verginius, the Roman commander, bided his time: he instructed his men to ground their spears and to wait, in silence, until the enemy were upon them. Then they were to be up and at them, using the short sword only, hand to hand. The Volscians had come on at the double, shouting as they came, and persuaded that sheer terror had fixed the Romans to the spot; by the time they were within striking distance they were already tired, and when they found that they were met with vigorous opposition and saw the flash of the Roman swords, the shock was as great as if they had fallen into an ambush. They lost their nerve and withdrew as fast as their blown and breathless condition allowed. It was not fast enough to save them; for the Romans, who had quietly awaited their attack and were in consequence still fresh, easily overtook the panting fugitives, captured their camp by assault and chased them beyond it as far as Velitrae, where both armies, victors and vanquished together, burst simultaneously into the town. The place soon became a scene of indiscriminate slaughter, and more blood was shed than in the actual battle. A handful of men who laid down their arms and gave themselves up, were spared.

Meanwhile the dictator Valerius was no less successful against the Sabines, Rome's most dangerous enemy. The Sabines, by extending their flanks too widely, had weakened their centre, and Valerius, after a devastating cavalry charge, sent in his infantry to finish the work. His forces then swept on to capture the enemy camp, and the operation was over. After the battle of Lake Regillus it was the most distinguished action of that period. Valerius rode into Rome in triumph; in addition to the usual honours a place was reserved for him and his descendants in the Circus, and a chair of state was put there for his use.

As a result of their defeat the Volscians were deprived of the territory belonging to Velitrae, and the town itself was reoccupied by settlers from Rome.

Soon after this there was an engagement with the Aequians. As the ground was unfavourable for a Roman advance, the consul was unwilling to make any move until compelled to do so by his men: they accused him of deliberately prolonging hostilities in order to enable the Dictator to lay down his office before they returned to Rome, in which case the promises he had made them would come to nothing, just as those of the consul Servilius had done. To prevent this, they forced him to undertake a highly risky advance up the slopes of the hills. It was a rash move, but it succeeded through the enemy's cowardice, for they were so badly shaken by what they thought the extreme audacity of the Roman troops, that before they were even within range they abandoned their very strong position and fled for their lives down into the valleys on the further side of the hills. It was a bloodless victory and a good deal of valuable material fell into Roman hands.

In spite of this triple military success both parties in Rome remained as anxious as ever about the issue of the political struggle, for the money-lenders had used all their influence and employed every device to produce a situation which was not only unfavourable to the commons, but tied the hands of the Dictator himself. After the return to Rome of the consul Vetusius, the first business which Valerius brought before the Senate was the case of the commons – who had fought with such distinction in the recent wars. His motion was that the House should declare their policy regarding those who were bound over for debt. The motion was rejected. 'I stand,' Valerius retorted, 'for domestic concord. You will have none of it. But mark my words: the day will soon come when you will wish in vain for men of my way of thinking to plead the cause of the populace. As for myself, I will no longer frustrate the hopes of the citizens of this country; I will resign from my now useless office. Two things made it necessary: war and our own political differences. The wars are won, we have peace abroad; but here at home there are still insuperable obstacles to it. I prefer to meet the real struggle, when it comes, not as Dictator but as a private citizen.' With these words Valerius left the House and resigned his office. It was clear enough to the people that the reason for his resignation was anger at the unfair treatment they had received; he had not actually kept his promise to relieve them, but at least it was through no fault of his that the promise had come to nothing. That was enough to win their gratitude, and they escorted him from the Senate to his house with every sign of appreciation.

The senatorial party now began to fear that if the army were disbanded, representatives of the populace would begin once more to hold their secret and seditious meetings; accordingly, they invented a reason which would justify keeping the men under arms. Actually, the troops had been raised by order of the Dictator, but as they had taken the military oath to obey the consuls as their commanders, it was possible to hold that they were still bound by it; on this assumption, therefore, and on the pretext that the Aequians had recommenced hostilities, the army was ordered to march. The order promptly brought matters to a head: there was talk, we are told, amongst the

soldiers of assassinating the consuls, which would have freed them
from their oath of allegiance; but they abandoned the project when
they were warned that a criminal act could never absolve them from a
sacred obligation. Instead, on the suggestion of a man named Sicinius
and without orders from the consuls, they took themselves off in a
body to the Sacred Mount, three miles from the city across the Anio.
The historian Piso declared that they went to the Aventine, but the
version of the story which I have given is the one which is more
generally accepted. There on the Sacred Mount, without any officer
to direct them, they made themselves a camp, properly fortified in
the usual way, where for a number of days they stayed quietly, taking
only what they needed for subsistence. No hostile move was made
against them.

In Rome there was something like panic; with one party as much
alarmed by the situation as the other, everything came to a standstill.
The commons, abandoned as they were by their friends in the army,
feared violence at the hands of the senatorial party, who, in their turn,
were afraid of the commons still left in the city, and could hardly
make up their minds if they would rather see them stay or go. Moreover, how long would the deserters be content to remain inactive?
What would happen if, in the present situation, there were a threat
of foreign invasion? Clearly the only hope lay in finding a solution
for the conflicting interests of the two classes in the state: by fair means
or foul the country must recover its internal harmony. The senatorial
party accordingly decided to employ Menenius Agrippa as their
spokesman to the commons on the Sacred Mount – he was a good
speaker, and the commons liked him as he was one of themselves.
Admitted to the deserters' camp, he is said to have told them, in the
rugged style of those far-off days, the following story. 'Long ago
when the members of the human body did not, as now they do, agree
together, but had each its own thoughts and the words to express them
in, the other parts resented the fact that they should have the worry
and trouble of providing everything for the belly, which remained
idle, surrounded by its ministers, with nothing to do but enjoy the
pleasant things they gave it. So the discontented members plotted together that the hand should carry no food to the mouth, that the
mouth should take nothing that was offered it, and that the teeth
should accept nothing to chew. But alas! while they sought in their
resentment to subdue the belly by starvation, they themselves and the

whole body wasted away to nothing. By this it was apparent that the belly, too, has no mean service to perform: it receives food, indeed; but it also nourishes in its turn the other members, giving back to all parts of the body, through all its veins, the blood it has made by the process of digestion; and upon this blood our life and our health depend.'

This fable of the revolt of the body's members Menenius applied to the political situation, pointing out its resemblance to the anger of the populace against the governing class; and so successful was his story that their resentment was mollified. Negotiations began and an agreement was reached on the condition that special magistrates should be appointed to represent the commons; these officers – 'tribunes of the people' – should be above the law, and their function should be to protect the commons against the consuls. No man of the senatorial class was to be allowed to hold the office. Two tribunes were accordingly created, Gaius Licinius and Lucius Albinus, who, in their turn, appointed three colleagues, one of whom was the Sicinius who had led the revolt. Who the other two were is uncertain. According to one account, two tribunes only were appointed to office on the Sacred Mount, and it was there that the law was passed which secured their inviolability.

During the 'Secession of the Plebs', as it came to be called, Spurius Cassius and Postumus Cominius began their term as consuls. That year a treaty was made with the communities of Latium, and to preside over the ceremony one of the consuls remained in Rome; the other went on service against the Volscians and heavily defeated them at Antium. They were forced to take refuge at Longula, which shortly afterwards also fell to Rome; the capture of Polusca, another Volscian town, quickly followed, after which a powerful attack was launched against Corioli. Serving in the army at this time was a young aristocrat named Gaius Marcius, an active and intelligent officer, who was presently to earn the courtesy-title of Coriolanus. It so happened that at a critical moment during the operations Marcius was on guard: the last thing the Romans were expecting was any danger from outside the town, upon the siege of which their whole attention was concentrated. Suddenly, however, a Volscian force appeared from the direction of Antium, and to coincide with its attack there was a vigorous sortie from the town. Marcius with a small body of picked men broke up the sortie and then, with great daring, forced his way through the open gate into Corioli itself; there he laid about him to some purpose, and finally seized a blazing firebrand and flung it amongst the houses just within the wall of the town. The cry which arose, and the shrieks of women and children in terror of death were, for the Roman troops, a heartening sound; but for the Volscians it seemed to be the end: the town they had come to relieve was already taken. In this way the men of Antium were defeated, and Corioli fell. Marcius had covered himself with glory, so much so that he completely overshadowed his commander, the consul Cominius; indeed, no one would have remembered that Cominius had fought at all in the action against the Volscians, had it not been for the record, on a brazen column, of the treaty made at that time with the Latins. That record declared that the treaty was signed by one consul only, Spurius Cassius, the other being absent from Rome on service.

During the course of this year Menenius Agrippa died. Throughout his life he had been much loved by both parties in the state, and after the secession he had made himself, to the commons, even dearer than before. His services to his country had been great: sent by the Senate as their ambassador to the people, he had carried through the negotiations which healed the breach between the opposing classes, and had been the means of bringing back to Rome the citizens who had deserted her; yet he died so poor that his estate could not bear the expense of his funeral. He was buried by the commons, who each contributed a few pence for the purpose.

The next consuls to enter upon office were Titus Geganius and Publius Minucius. It was a year of peace, and the political troubles were for the moment over, but Rome, none the less, had to face a situation even more dangerous than war or civil discord. During the secession work on the land had been suspended, and the result was a steep rise in the price of grain; famine followed so severe that Rome might have been a beleaguered city. The slaves and the poorer members of the community would undoubtedly have starved to death, had not the consuls acted promptly and sent agents over a wide area to arrange for the purchase of grain. Bad relations with neighbouring communities had made it necessary to go far afield, and the agents were instructed to travel north-west along the Etrurian coast and south-east along the Volscian coast to Cumae, and even as far as Sicily. Aristodemus, the reigning prince of Cumae, was the heir of the Tarquins, and after supplies had been bought there he retained the

Roman grain-ships in lieu of the property he ought to have inherited. From the Volscians and the people of the Pomptine marshes nothing could be obtained; indeed, the agents were actually in danger of violence. From Etruria supplies reached Rome by way of the Tiber, and this was enough to keep the people alive. Fortunately for Rome the Volscians at this time, just as they were preparing an invasion, were struck down by a serious epidemic; had this not occurred, Rome would have had a disastrous war on her hands, to add to her other difficulties. Volscian morale was so shattered by the effect of the epidemic, that they hardly recovered even after the worst of it was over, and the Romans took advantage of the situation to increase the number of their settlers in Velitrae and to send out fresh settlers to the hill town of Norba, which thus became a fortified point for the defence of the Pomptine region.

In the following year, when Marcus Minucius and Aulus Sempronius had entered on their term of office, large supplies of grain were imported from Sicily, and there was a debate in the Senate on the price which the commons were to be charged for it. Many thought that the time had come for repressive measures and for recovering the privileges which the commons, by their act of secession, had forced the governing class to surrender. Their chief spokesman was Marcius Coriolanus, who was a bitter enemy of the newly instituted power of the tribunes. 'If they want grain at the old price,' he said, 'they must give us back our old privileges. What have I done that I should see upstarts from the mob in office? Am I a slave? Have I been ransomed from brigands? Am I to endure this indignity a moment longer than I need? King Tarquin was not to be borne – are we to bear, then, with King Sicinius? Let him pack up his traps and be gone, and the rabble with him – the road is clear to the Sacred Mount, or any other hills. They can steal grain from our fields as they did two years ago; as for prices, it was their own folly which raised them to their present level, so they must make the best of it. If I am not mistaken, their troubles will soon make them change their tune; they are more likely to get to work on the land again themselves than to go off under arms and prevent others from doing so.'

Whether Coriolanus was actually right is not easy to say; I do, however, think it is possible that the senatorial party might have succeeded in freeing themselves from the various restrictions, including the tribunate, to which they had been forced to agree, if only they had

consented to reduce the price of grain. As it was, the attitude of
Coriolanus seemed to them excessively harsh, while the commons
were so infuriated by it that they almost resorted to violence; to them
it seemed that it was a deliberate threat to starve them by withholding
the bare necessities of life, and that the imported grain, the sole means
of support which an unexpected piece of luck had brought them,
would be snatched from their mouths unless Gaius Marcius were
permitted to work his brutal will upon them, and the tribunes, their
only defence, were sacrificed to satisfy his pride. Marcius, in short,
was little better than their executioner; he offered them the choice
between death and slavery.

As he was leaving the Senate House he would have been assaulted
but for the timely action of the tribunes, who issued a summons
against him. This mollified the fury of the mob, as the position was
now reversed and every man was enabled to see himself as the judge
of his hated enemy, with power over him of life and death. As for
Marcius, his first reaction to the strong measures taken by the tribunes
was one of contempt: their office, he declared, had nothing to do with
the senatorial party; they were not empowered to inflict punishment,
but merely to support the popular cause. Up to a point, however, the
Senate was forced to yield, feeling it wiser to sacrifice one of their
number to appease the popular fury; they did, nevertheless, take steps
to counter their adversaries, employing such resources as they possessed, individual or corporate: for instance, they used their personal
dependants to try to scare people from taking part in popular
meetings in the hope of wrecking their plans; then, when that failed,
they turned to entreaty, hundreds of them going into the streets and
begging the angry populace to give them back their friend – after all,
he was but one, a single member of their order, and, if they could not
acquit him, would they not, as a favour, let him go free? It was a
strange scene, almost as if the whole nobility, as a body, were on their
trial before the people. But it was all to no purpose: Coriolanus failed
to appear in court, and the feeling against him finally hardened. He
was condemned in his absence and went into exile with the Volscians,
bitter as ever and vowing vengeance upon his country. The Volscians,
who gave him a warm welcome, treated him with ever greater consideration as they observed his growing bitterness towards Rome and
listened to the complaints and threats of revenge against her which
were ever more frequently on his lips. He stayed in the house of

Attius Tullius, the most distinguished name amongst the Volscian
peoples and a life-long enemy of Rome. This dangerous pair, the one
moved by inveterate hostility, the other by resentment at his recent
wrongs, began to lay their plans for war. Both knew that the chief
obstacle would be the attitude of the Volscian commons, who after
their many previous defeats would not easily be persuaded, or driven,
to renew hostilities; many men, moreover, of military age had died in
the recent epidemic, and that, added to the war losses of the past few
years, had gone far to break their spirit. Popular hatred of Rome had
cooled with the lapse of time, and it was necessary, in consequence, to
devise something which would once more exacerbate their feelings
against their old enemy.

It so happened that preparations were in progress at Rome for a
repetition of the Great Games. The reason for holding the ceremony
afresh was an incident which, in the first instance, had violated its
sanctity. Early in the morning, before the ceremony opened, someone
had driven one of his slaves, manacled, across the arena, beating him
as he went. The Games then began, as it apparently occurred to nobody that this had been an act of desecration. Soon after, however, a
working man named Titus Latinius dreamed that Jupiter told him
that he was displeased with the 'leading dancer' at the Games, and
then went on to say that unless the festival were started all over again
in the most sumptuous manner, Rome would be in peril. It was his
duty, therefore, the God declared, to go and tell this to the consuls.
Latinius was by no means insensitive to the solemn import of this
dream; but in spite of his alarm he was so much in awe of the consular
office, and so much afraid of being laughed at, that he could not bring
himself to obey the God's command. His hesitation cost him dear, for
a few days later he lost his son; then, as proof, if proof were needed, of
the cause of this sudden calamity, the unfortunate man again dreamed
that he saw the figure of Jupiter, who this time asked him if he
thought he was fairly paid for ignoring the divine command, and
threatened that worse was to come if he did not make haste to tell the
consuls of the warning he had received. The poor fellow now realized
that there was no escape; but, for all that, he continued to hesitate,
until he fell desperately ill and so, at long last, learnt his lesson. Exhausted by sickness and grief, he summoned his kinsmen to his bed-
side and told them how more than once he had seen Jupiter in his
dreams and heard his voice, and how the threats of the angry gods had

been fulfilled in his own misfortunes. All were agreed without any doubt upon what was to be done, and he was forthwith carried in a litter to the consuls in the Forum. The consuls instructed his bearers to take him to the Senate House, and there, to the wonder of all who were present, he repeated his tale. The ending of it was crowned by another miracle; for – if we may believe the traditional account – though he had entered the Senate House a desperately sick man, once his duty was done he walked home unaided.

The Senate issued a decree that the Games should be celebrated anew with all possible splendour, and Attius Tullius arranged for them to be attended by a very large number of his countrymen. Before they began, Tullius, according to a plan which he and Marcius had hatched between them, informed the consuls that he had some business of state which he would like to discuss in private. The consuls agreed and, as soon as they were alone, Tullius began. 'I hesitate,' he said, 'to say anything derogatory about my own countrymen – and indeed I am not here to accuse them, but merely to put you on guard lest they should misbehave themselves. The fact is, there is more instability and caprice in our national character than I like to admit. We have learnt this the hard way, since we owe our preservation less to our own merits than to your forbearance. Now many hundreds of my people are here in Rome; a festival is in progress, and everyone's attention will be occupied in watching it. I have not forgotten what the Sabines did to you on a similar occasion, and I am anxious lest some foolish and re-grettable incident should occur today. I thought it my duty, gentle-men, to mention this to you, for both our sakes. Personally, I propose to go home at once, to avoid being implicated in anything disagree-able that may be done or said.'

The consuls reported this to the Senate as soon as Tullius had gone. The warning was vague, but it came from a reliable source, and for this reason, naturally enough, the Senate, by way of a precaution which might well have proved unnecessary, issued an order to the effect that all Volscians should leave the city at once. Officers were in-structed to order every man to be out before dark. The first effect of this upon the unfortunate Volscians was something like panic, as they scurried to their lodgings to collect their luggage; then, once they were on the road, alarm gave way to indignation at being treated like plague-spotted criminals and driven out at a time of solemn religious festival as if they were unfit to associate with gods or men. Tullius rode on ahead of the long line of angry men and stopped to wait for them at the source of the Ferentina. As the various notables arrived, he accosted them with bitter complaints about what had happened, and they, in their turn, were only too eager to listen to what so well accorded with their own resentment. Meanwhile he led them to a field below the road, whither they had no difficulty in persuading all the others to accompany them. When they were all assembled, Tullius addressed them. 'My friends,' he said, 'you have been insulted. Forget, if you will, the injuries which Rome has inflicted upon us in the past and the many disasters we have suffered. But – I ask you – how do you propose to tolerate what has been done to you today? The opening event in their festival was *our* humiliation! Do you not realize that you have today suffered a most shameful defeat? When they turned you out, did you not feel the curious eyes of every man of them upon you, of Romans and foreigners alike, while your wives and children were laughed to scorn? Is it not obvious that everybody who heard the proclamation, or saw us go, or met this ignominious procession on the road, must believe that there is some dreadful stain upon us, and that we are being expelled from the society of decent men because our presence at the Games would pollute them? Moreover has it not occurred to you that we should probably all be dead if we had not got away – or *run* away, rather – so quickly? Surely you cannot fail to feel that Rome is an enemy city, since another day's delay there would have meant your deaths. Rome has declared war on you; and she will be sorry for it – if you are men.'

Tullius's speech was fuel to the fire of the general indignation. They all dispersed to their various communities, and there, by inflammatory speeches, so effectively roused everybody else that soon the whole Volscian nation was in revolt.

The command in the war which was now imminent was by universal consent entrusted to Attius Tullius and Gaius Marcius, the Roman exile. Of the two, the latter was felt to be the abler man, nor did he in fact disappoint the confidence which was placed in him. Moreover his successes indicated that the strength of Rome lay in her commanders rather than in the armies they commanded. Marcius first marched for Circeii, expelled the Roman settlers, liberated the town, and handed it over to Volscian control; he captured Satricum, Longula, Polusca, and Corioli, all places recently acquired by Rome; then, after taking over Lavinium, he marched across country into the Latin Way and took Corbio, Vitellia, Trebium, Labici, and Pedum. Finally he marched on Rome and took up a position by the Cluilian Trenches five miles outside the walls. From here he sent out raiding parties to do what damage they could to the farms and crops – attaching, however, a special officer to each party with instructions to see that no damage was done to property owned by patricians. Dislike of the populace may have prompted this move; or it may be that he hoped by means of it to sow fresh dissension between them and the Senatorial party. The Roman populace was already out of hand, and the tribunes, by their accusations, were rousing them against their leaders so successfully that a new quarrel would undoubtedly have broken out, had not the common fear of invasion temporarily held things together. Shared danger is the strongest of bonds; it will keep men united in spite of mutual dislike and suspicion.

Upon one point, however, the two parties could not agree: the Senate and the consuls were convinced that the only hope was to meet the threat to the city by force; the commons stood out for any measures rather than a resort to arms, and soon revealed their intention of forcing the senate to their way of thinking. The consuls, Nautius and Furius, were engaged in reviewing troops and posting garrisons and pickets at defensible spots along the walls and elsewhere, when to their consternation they were mobbed by hundreds of men all shouting for peace; not only was the mob in no mood to obey orders, but the angry men who composed it went on to compel the consuls to convene the Senate and formally propose to send envoys to Marcius. The Senate, seeing that the commons were in no mood to fight, accepted the proposal, and the envoys were dispatched to treat for peace. The answer they brought back was an uncompromising one: if, Marcius declared, all their lost territory were restored to the Volscians, then peace terms might be discussed; if, on the contrary, Rome hoped to enjoy her conquests without having to fight to preserve them, she had better realize that he had no forgotten either the insults of his fellow-citizens or the kindness of his present hosts, and would do all in his power to prove that exile, far from crushing his spirit, had strengthened his determination. After their first failure the same envoys were sent to try again. This time they were refused admission to the Volscian lines. Even priests, we are told, wearing the emblems of their office, went to beg for a hearing, but were no more able than the envoys to turn Marcius's inflexible resolve.

In these circumstances the women of Rome flocked to the house of Coriolanus's mother, Veturia, and of his wife Volumnia. Whatever their motive – whether it was fear of impending disaster or a piece of state policy – they succeeded in persuading the aged Veturia and Volumnia, accompanied by Marcius's two little sons, to go into the enemy's lines and make their plea for peace. Men, it seemed, could not defend the city with their swords; women might better succeed with tears and entreaties. The first effect upon Coriolanus when he was told that a number of women had arrived was a hardening of his resolution; and indeed it is not to be expected that women's tears would move a man who had remained inflexible before ambassadors and priests – before the majesty of a national deputation and the awful influence of religion upon eyes and heart. One of his friends, however, recognized Veturia, marked by her look of deep distress, as she stood between Volumnia and the two boys. 'Unless my eyes deceive me,' he said, 'your mother is here, with your wife and children.' Coriolanus was profoundly moved; almost beside himself, he started from his seat and, running to his mother, would have embraced her had he not been checked by her sudden turn to anger. 'I would know,' she said, 'before I accept your kiss, whether I have come to an enemy or to a son, whether I am here as your mother or as a prisoner of war. Have my long life and unhappy old age brought me to this, that I should see you first an exile, then the enemy of your country? Had you the heart to ravage the earth which bore and bred you? When you set foot upon it, did not your anger fall away, however fierce your hatred and lust for revenge? When Rome was before your eyes, did not the thought come to you, "within those walls is my home, with the gods that watch over it – and my mother and my wife and my children"? Ah, had I never borne a child, Rome would not now be menaced; if I had no son, I could have died free in a free country! But now there is nothing left for me to endure, nothing which can bring to me more pain, and to you a deeper dishonour, than this. I am indeed an unhappy woman – but it will not be for long; think of these others who, if you cannot relent, must hope for nothing but an untimely death or life-long slavery.'

His wife and children flung their arms round him; the other women all burst into tears of anguish for themselves and their country, until at last Coriolanus could bear no more. He kissed his wife and the two boys, sent them home, and withdrew his army. There are various accounts of his ultimate fate: he is said by some to have sunk under the burden of resentment which his behaviour brought upon him, though the manner of his death is not known. I have read in Fabius, our oldest authority, that he survived to old age: Fabius states, at least, that he used often to say towards the end of his life that exile was a more bitter thing when one was old.

Rome in those days was free from petty jealousy of others' success, and the men of Rome did not grudge the women their triumph. To preserve the memory of it for ever the temple of Fortuna Muliebris was built and consecrated.

Later the Volscians again invaded Roman territory, this time in alliance with the Aequians. There came a moment, however, when the Aequians were unwilling to continue serving under Attius Tullius, and there was a quarrel about who should command the allied armies. The quarrel led to a bloody battle, in which the good luck of Rome destroyed for her two hostile armies in a bitter and disastrous struggle.

Of the next consuls to enter upon office, Titus Sicinius got the Volscian war for his sphere of action, and Gaius Aquilius the war with the Hernici, who were also up in arms. In the course of the year the Hernici were defeated. The campaign against the Volscians was indecisive.

The following year, in the consulship of Spurius Cassius and Proculus Verginius, peace was made with the Hernici, the surrender of two-thirds of their territory being included in the terms of settlement. Of this land the consul Cassius proposed to make over half to the Latins and half to the Roman commons, and he was anxious, if he could, to increase the gift by the distribution of certain other parcels of state-owned land which he declared were being illegally kept in private hands. The men who held it – a considerable number – were alarmed by this threat to their private interests, while the nobility as a whole were uneasy on political grounds, feeling that Cassius's proposal might lead in the end to a threat to liberty. This was the first occasion on which a proposal for agrarian reform was brought forward in the Senate, and it has never been done since without serious disturbances. The other consul, Verginius, opposed the land-grants, and the Senate supported him; there was some support, too, even from the commons, who resented the fact that the proposed bounty had been extended to include allied communities as well as citizens of Rome; moreover, they had often heard Verginius prophesy in his public utterances that Cassius's bounty would turn out to be a disaster, and that the gifts of land would bring slavery to their recipients. The way, he declared, was being opened to monarchy – for why had the Latins been included, or why was it proposed to restore a third of their territory to the Hernici, who only the other day were the enemies of Rome, if it were not to make Cassius their master in place of Coriolanus? Popular support now began to swing to Verginius, the opponent of Cassius's proposed legislation, with the result that both consuls competed with one another in angling for favour, Verginius declaring that he would allow grants of land to private owners provided that those owners were Roman citizens. Cassius took a different line – and fared worse: by his proposed distribution of land he had hoped to ingratiate himself with Rome's allies, and had thereby destroyed his credit at home; in order, therefore, to recover his lost favour, he put forward another measure which he hoped would prove popular, the repayment, namely, of the money received from the sale of grain imported from Sicily. The commons, however, scornfully rejected this offer, which they looked upon as a direct attempt to purchase power. Fear of the return of the monarchy was deep-seated, and it was this fear which led them to refuse all Cassius's apparently generous offers with as much contempt as if they already had more than they wanted. Immediately Cassius's year of office was over, he was tried, condemned, and executed. According to one story it was his own father who punished him, putting him on trial in his own house, causing him to be first scourged, then put to death, and finally making a gift of his property to the goddess Ceres. A statue was made out of the proceeds of his estate, inscribed with the words: 'the gift of the Cassian family'. Other writers have stated what is probably nearer the truth, namely that he was brought to trial for treason by the quaestors Caeso Fabius and Lucius Valerius; he was found guilty by popular verdict and his house was pulled down by order of the state. The site of the house is the open space in front of the temple of Tellus. But though accounts differ about the circumstances of his trial, there is no doubt of the date: it took place in the consulship of Servius Cornelius and Quintus Fabius.

Popular feeling against Cassius was not of long duration. The idea of agrarian legislation was in itself an attractive one, and once Cassius was out of the way, the commons found it difficult to resist; moreover, their hope of benefiting from it was increased by the action of the Senate, who – meanly, as they thought – had prevented the troops from enriching themselves on the spoils of war taken during the course of the year from the defeated Volscians and Aequians. All the captured material had been sold by the consul Fabius and the proceeds put into the public funds. The family of Fabius was highly unpopular in consequence, nevertheless the senatorial party procured the election in the following year of another member of the family, Caeso Fabius, who assumed office with Lucius Aemilius. This further exacerbated the commons, whose rebellious spirit, with the civil discord it occasioned, encouraged Rome's enemies to take action. Hostilities followed, and for the time being political differences were forgotten; the two parties were united in face of the common danger, and the Roman armies, led by Aemilius, dealt successfully with the Volscians and Aequians who had risen against them. The broken enemy forces were pursued relentlessly, and suffered heavier losses during their retreat than in the actual fighting.

In the same year, on 15 July, the temple of Castor was dedicated. It had been vowed during the Latin war by Postumius, when he held the office of dictator; his son was appointed as one of the two commissioners to perform the ceremony of dedication.

Again during the course of the year the delightful prospect of agrarian legislation brought restlessness and dissatisfaction. The tribunes did what they could to bolster a popular office by urging a popular measure; but the Senate, feeling that quite enough had been ceded already to the mob, shrank from offering further gifts which might well prove a stimulus to still further unreasonable demands. The most vigorous supporters of the senatorial interest were the two consuls, and under their leadership the senatorial party emerged victorious, not only in the immediate dispute but also by their success in procuring the election of the next consulship of Fabius's brother Caeso, and of Lucius Valerius, a man who by his prosecution of Cassius had made himself even more bitterly hated by the commons. The year was a difficult one also for the tribunes: the legislation had fallen through, and their much talk about it combined with little performance brought them into contempt. From this time the reputation of the Fabii was very high; the consulship had been in the family for three years in succession and throughout those years they had been in almost continual conflict with the tribunes. It had been, so to speak, a good investment, and the office was allowed in consequence to remain in the family some time longer.

War with Veii soon broke out, and the Volscians resumed hostilities. Roman resources for waging war were more than sufficient, but they were largely wasted by internal dissensions; the state of things was far from healthy, and to increase the general malaise there was a constant succession in the city and the countryside of odd and inexplicable occurrences which seemed to threaten disaster. The soothsayers made their usual investigations (consulting beasts' entrails and birds' flight), both on their own initiative and by official order, and declared as a result of them that the wrath of heaven was due to the improper observance of religious ceremonies. In consequence of these alarms a Vestal Virgin named Oppia was condemned on a charge of unchastity and put to death.

Next year, the consulship of Quintus Fabius and Gaius Julius, the political troubles were as bad as ever, and the pressure from foreign enemies more severe. The Aequians took up arms; the men of Veii actually ventured a raid into Roman territory. Anxiety increased, and was still increasing when the next consuls, Caeso Fabius and Spurius Furius, entered upon office. The Aequians were attacking the Latin town of Ortona, and the Veientes, who had had enough of casual raiding, were now threatening a move on Rome. Such dangers might have been expected to bring the commons to heel: in fact, they merely made them more intractable. They resorted once more to their old device of refusing military service; on this occasion they were urged to it by the tribune Spurius Licinius, who in the belief that the moment had come for forcing agrarian legislation on the Senate by sheer necessity had been laying his plans to obstruct the preparations for war. The attempt, however, was a failure; for he soon found directed upon himself all the ill-feeling which attached to the tribunate as a whole, and he was attacked hardly more bitterly by the consuls than by the other tribunes, with whose cooperation the consuls were able to proceed with the recruiting.

Troops were enrolled for the two simultaneous campaigns, against the Veientes and the Aequians. In the division of duties, Fabius took charge of the former, Furius of the latter. In the operations against the Aequians there was nothing worth recording. As for Fabius, he had more trouble with his own men than with the enemy; alone, as consul and commander, he upheld the honour of Rome which his disloyal troops were doing their best to betray. He was a skilful commander, and had shown his skill on many occasions both in the preparation and conduct of the campaign; on the occasion of which I am writing he had made his dispositions so effectively that one unsupported cavalry charge broke the enemy's resistance, who retreated in disorder. The infantry refused to press their advantage. Nothing their hated commander could say was able to move them; nor even their own conscience or their country's shame – not even the danger they would be faced with if the enemy found courage for further resistance – could make them bestir themselves, or even, at the worst, to stand their ground. In contempt of orders they withdrew, and marched back to their camp like beaten dogs, muttering abuse of their commander and of the good service done by the mounted troops. Fabius was unable to find any remedy for this disastrous piece of work, which was proof, if proof were needed, that men of outstanding ability are more likely to lack the power of controlling their own people than of defeating an enemy in battle.

The consul returned to Rome. The bitter hostility of his own men outweighed any enhancement of his military reputation; none the less the Senate managed to keep the consulship in the Fabian family: Marcus Fabius was elected, with Gnaeus Manlius as his colleague.

This year another tribune, Tiberius Pontificius, brought forward a measure for the distribution of land. In spite of the failure of his predecessor Licinius, he too attempted to sabotage recruitment. For a while he succeeded, to the acute embarrassment of the Senate. Appius Claudius, however, saved the situation by declaring in the House that the power of the tribunes was, in fact, already done for: the previous year it had been actually overridden, and potentially it was for ever ineffective now that a way had been found to turn it against itself. There would always, he argued, be one tribune who was willing to score a personal victory over a colleague and join the patriots for the good of the country. Several tribunes, should that be necessary, would undoubtedly support the consuls, and even a single one, in opposition to all his colleagues, would suffice. All that the consuls and the leaders of the Senate had to do was to win the support of some of them – if they could not of all. Appius's advice was approved, and the senatorial party began, in consequence, as a general policy to use courteous and friendly language in addressing the tribunes, while those of consular rank who happened to have any personal matter of dispute with one or other of them managed, by a judicious use of private or political influence, to induce them to employ their powers in a wholesome and patriotic manner. In this way, with the support of four tribunes, as against one who was trying to obstruct the necessary measures for public safety, the consuls were enabled to proceed with recruiting.

Roman troops then marched against the Veientes who had been reinforced by contingents from most of the Etrurian towns. These reinforcements had been sent less from any love of Veii than from the hope, which had already begun to crystalize, that Rome might be destroyed by her internal dissensions. In all the councils of Etruria leading men were insisting that Rome was torn apart by political discord, without which her power might well endure for ever; but internal dissension was the poisonous disease of wealthy and powerful communities, the one destructive influence which brought mighty empires low. For a long time, they declared, that evil influence had been kept at bay by wise government action and the willingness of the populace to endure, but now at last it had come to a head: Rome was split in two; each faction had its own representatives, its own laws. Once, though the common people used to obstruct recruiting, they nevertheless obeyed their officers in the field, and, whatever the condition of affairs at home, it was at least possible to have some sort of security, so long as military discipline was maintained; but now the habit of disobeying their superiors had followed the Roman soldiery into the camp as well; during the last war Roman troops, in the middle of a battle, had with one accord handed victory on a plate to their already half-beaten enemy; they had deserted their standards, abandoned their commander in the line, and walked off the field against orders. In short, with a little determination Rome could be defeated by means of her own soldiers; it would be enough merely to declare war, to make them fancy they were about to be attacked, and Fate and the gods would do the rest. Such were the hopes which, after many years of varying fortune in their struggle with Rome, induced the Etruscans to prepare once more for war.

The Roman commanders felt about their men much as the Etruscans did; indeed it was their own troops, and they only, who gave them cause for anxiety. The thought of their shameful conduct in the previous campaign made them shrink from the severe risk of engaging two enemy armies simultaneously; accordingly, to avoid it, they remained within the fortifications of their camp, hoping that time and circumstances would make the men less refractory and bring them to their senses. This made the Veientes and their allies all the more eager to act: their mounted troops rode up to the Roman position, deliberately challenging them to fight; then, when there was no answering movement, they began shouting insults at the soldiers, jeering at the two consuls, and calling out that the Roman army was trying to hide its fear of battle by pretending that it was political difficulties which held it back, and that what the consuls were really afraid of was not that their men were disloyal but that they were cowards. In fact, dead silence and a refusal to budge were, for an army on active service, an odd kind of political demonstration. To all this they added other unpleasant remarks (partly true) to the effect that the Romans were an upstart nation with no roots in the land.

The consuls endured this abuse, shouted at them though it was from right under the wall of the camp, with comparative equanimity; but not so the rank and file: they, more impulsive than their commanders, were overwhelmed with rage and shame, so that they almost forgot their other troubles. Passion was uppermost, and it tore them two ways: they could not bear the thought that the insolent enemy should escape the punishment he deserved, or that the consuls, and the patricians whom they represented, should score a success. At last, however, the mockery and insufferable self-confidence of the enemy proved too much for them: a number of them went to headquarters and demanded instant action.

The consuls thereupon sat for a long time in conference, pretending that it was a matter of strategy which could not be settled off-hand. They wanted to fight, but knew they must check their eagerness to do so, and even conceal it; their men were already roused, but continued opposition to their zeal for action would give it greater punch when the time came. Accordingly the men were told that they must wait; no move would be made yet, as an immediate engagement would be premature. The consuls then issued an order that any man who attempted to fight without orders from an officer would be punished by death. The men were dismissed, their passion for action increased in proportion to the apparent unwillingness of the consuls to let them indulge it. Fuel, moreover, was added to the flames by the behaviour of the enemy, who once it was known that the consuls had decided not to retaliate became even more provocative, certain, as they now were, that they could hurl their insults with impunity; nothing, they supposed, could be clearer than that Roman troops were not to be trusted with arms and that a mutiny was imminent which would mean the end of Roman power. Convinced that this interpretation was correct, they came riding, wave after wave right to the gates of the Roman camp, shouting gibes at the sentries as they came, and barely refraining from a general assault. This proved too much for the Roman rank and file, who could endure such insolence no longer; not a man of them but joined the rush to headquarters. Previously they had put their request cautiously, through the senior centurions; this time it was a very different thing – a noisy and spontaneous demonstration by the whole army. The time to strike had come.

The consuls, nevertheless, continued to temporize, until Fabius realized that his colleague Manlius, afraid that the growing uproar would end in a mutiny, was about to give way. At once, therefore, he ordered his trumpeter to blow a call for silence, and said: 'I know, Manlius, that these men are capable of victory, but I do not know if they are willing to fight. They are themselves to blame for my ignorance. For this reason I am determined not to give the order for action, unless they solemnly swear to return victorious from this battle. On one occasion Roman soldiers betrayed their commander on the field; they will never betray the gods.' A centurion named Flavoleius, who had been as peremptory as any in demanding action, stepped forward. 'Marcus Fabius,' he cried, 'I will return victorious, and if I break my vow, may the anger of Jupiter and Mars and the other gods fall upon my head!' Flavoleius was followed by the entire army in turn, every man swearing the same oath and invoking the same penalty should he break it. The order for action was given; sword in hand, with hot blood and high hopes, they advanced to battle. 'Now gibe and jeer if you dare!' was the thought in every heart; 'here is my sword! Let me find that enemy whose only courage is in his tongue!'

All fought on that day with brilliant courage, whatever their rank, the Fabii with special distinction. The family of Fabius had alienated the commons in the course of many political struggles; in that battle they were resolved to regain their favour and admiration. When the hostile armies faced one another, the enemy showed no sign of weakness or lack of confidence, as they were convinced that the Roman troops meant business no more than on the previous occasion, when they had walked off the field in the campaign against the Aequians; indeed, they felt it was not impossible that the common soldiers might go to even further lengths, the situation being what it was and their attitude being – supposedly – so bitterly hostile to their masters. Events, however, proved otherwise, and every man in the Roman army, roused to fury by the enemy's insults and their own commanders' judicious procrastination, entered the fight with a keener appetite for blood than in any previous campaign.

The Etruscans were given no time even to deploy, before the Romans were upon them. Little use was made of missile weapons; they were got rid of as mere incumbrances in the first swift rush, and in less time than it takes to tell the armies were locked in a struggle of the deadliest kind, sword against sword. The conduct of the Fabii was a thing to envy and admire: one of them, Quintus Fabius, who had been consul three years before, was heading an attack on a massed formation of the enemy, when a big Etruscan, a powerful and practised swordsman, came at him through the press. Fabius was not aware of his danger in time, and the Etruscan stabbed him through the heart. The wound was mortal, and when the blade was withdrawn, he was dead. It was only one man down, but it had its effect upon both armies; the Roman troops would, indeed, have given ground at that point, had not Marcus Fabius leapt astride his brother's body and passionately appealed to them. Covering himself with his shield, 'What of your oath?' he cried. 'Was it as beaten men that you swore to leave the field? Are you more afraid of a cowardly enemy than of Mars and Jupiter by whose names you swore? I swore no oath; but I will either return victorious or die fighting here, Quintus, by your side.' His other brother, Caeso, the consul of the previous year, was near him as he spoke; 'Brother,' he said, 'is it words that will make them fight? No – but the gods by whom they have sworn. Come, let us give them courage for it not by words but by deeds – like leaders, like men who bear the name of Fabius!' No more was said; the gallant pair pressed forward with levelled spears, carried the whole line with them, and, in that quarter of the field, saved the day.

Manlius on the other wing was showing qualities of leadership no less vigorous and effective, when a similar misfortune almost brought disaster. Like Quintus Fabius, he was personally leading the attack; the enemy line was about to break under the powerful pressure of his men, who were supporting him with great gallantry, when he was dangerously wounded and forced to retire from the line. His men thought he had been killed and began to give ground; the moment was critical, and they might have surrendered their advantage

altogether had not Marcus Fabius galloped up with some troops of
cavalry in the nick of time and restored the situation by calling out that
Manlius was still alive and that he himself had come to support them
after a decisive victory in his own sector of the field. Further to
hearten his men, Manlius also managed to show himself, so that the
welcome sight of both their commanders provided just the stimulus
that was required. By this time the enemy line had, moreover, been
somewhat thinned, as their original superiority in numbers had induced them to detach their reserves and send them to attempt the
capture of the Roman camp. They met with little resistance, and
forced an entry; for a while they occupied themselves with taking
what they could find, on the supposition that their battle was over.
But they were mistaken; for the Roman reserves, who had failed to
prevent their entry, got a message through to the consuls, marched
in close order to camp headquarters, and on their own initiative resumed hostilities. Meanwhile Manlius had arrived, and immediately
stationed troops at all the gates to prevent the enemy from getting out.
The effect of this was to fill the Etruscans, penned in as they were,
with the recklessness of despair; they attempted at various points to
burst a way out, but to no purpose, until finally a party of men recognized the Roman commander by his equipment and made a direct
assault upon him. Their first volley of missiles fell amongst the troops
in the consul's immediate vicinity, but it was followed by a determined and overpowering rush. The consul was mortally wounded
and all the men with him took to their heels. This success spurred the
Etruscans to greater recklessness, but for the Romans it was a disaster;
everywhere in the camp discipline broke down and panic reigned,
and things would have been desperate indeed but for the timely action
of the staff officers, who hurriedly removed Manlius's body and
cleared one of the gates to give the enemy a way out. They took the
opportunity promptly, and as they were making their escape in a disorderly rabble were intercepted by the troops of the victorious Fabius.
They were cut to pieces, the survivors making off where and how
they could.

It was a resounding victory for Roman arms, but the death of two
men of such distinction overshadowed the general rejoicing. The
Senate decreed an official Triumph, and Fabius, the surviving consul,
replied to the Senate that if an army could celebrate a triumph without its commanders, then he would have no hesitation in allowing it to

do so in recognition of its magnificent services; but he personally, since his family was in mourning for the death of his brother Quintus, and the country half orphaned by the loss of his colleague Manlius, would be unable to accept a laurel which was blighted both by a national and by a private sorrow. An honour wisely refused may well return with greater lustre to him who refuses it. So it was with Marcus Fabius: no triumph ever celebrated has been more famous in history than this which he rejected.

The funerals of Fabius's brother and colleague followed, and at both Fabius himself spoke the funeral oration. By giving the dead men the chief credit for the victorious campaign he won the admiration of all and the honour he himself richly deserved; nor did he forget his original purpose of attempting to heal the breach between nobility and commons, and with this in view billeted the wounded in various patrician houses to be properly cared for. More were taken by members of the Fabian family than by any other, and nowhere were they better looked after. The name of Fabius began, in consequence, to grow in popular esteem, won – it should be added – by methods wholly consistent with the health and harmony of the country as a whole.

For these reasons the election in the following year of Caeso Fabius to the consulship, with Titus Verginius as his colleague, had as much support from the commons as from the senatorial party. His first concern on taking office was to let slip no opportunity of further cementing that national unity, some hopes of which had already begun to appear. He therefore lost no time in proposing that the Senate should anticipate the tribunes in initiating legislation for the distribution of land. One or other of the tribunes, he suggested, was bound to bring the matter forward, and the Senate would be well advised to get in first and make it their own concern, dividing as fairly as possible amongst the commons all land which had been taken from the enemy in the recent campaigns. It was only right, in his view, that the land should belong to the men who had won it by their own sweat and blood. The proposal was received with anger and contempt; some senators, indeed, remarked that Caeso's wits were going – his mind had been lively enough once, but too much glory had evidently softened it. However, any serious political quarrel was this time avoided. Caeso was commissioned to deal with the situation in Latium, where raids by Aequians were causing trouble. He marched thither with a body of troops, and then crossed into Aequian territory to carry out reprisals. The Aequians withdrew inside the defences of their various towns, and no action of any note was fought.

On another front Rome was less fortunate, for lack of proper caution on the part of Verginius brought about a serious defeat at the hands of the Veientes. His army would have been completely destroyed, had not Caeso come to his assistance in time. Thenceforward Rome's relations with Veii were of a sort of undefined hostility, neither peace nor war. The Veientes continued to carry on a series of plundering raids, retreating within their fortifications at the approach of Roman troops and coming out again upon their withdrawal. One could call the situation neither regular warfare nor settled peace, as their conduct made a mockery of both; it remained, in consequence, necessarily fluid and indecisive.

Trouble was imminent from other quarters as well: the Volscians and Aequians, for instance, were sure to be up in arms as soon as they had recovered from their recent defeat, and it was clear that the Sabines, Rome's inveterate enemies, and all Etruria would before long be on the march. It was Veii, however, which was causing anxiety; Veii's hostility, ever present though not in itself particularly dangerous, and expressed in acts of petty provocation rather than in any serious military threat, could never be ignored, and for that reason prevented Rome from turning her attention elsewhere. It was in view of this situation that the Fabian clan made their proposal to the Senate: 'As you know, gentlemen,' said the consul, who was spokesman for the clan, 'in our dealings with Veii what we need is a regular, permanent force, not necessarily a large one. Our suggestion therefore is that you put the task of controlling Veii into our hands, while you attend to other wars elsewhere. We guarantee that the majesty of the Roman name will be safe in the keeping of our clan, and our purpose is to wage this war at our own expense, as if it concerned our family only. We wish the state to be free of the burden of contributing either money or men.'

The Senate expressed its gratitude for the offer in the warmest terms. The consul then left the House and returned home escorted by a troop of men in marching order, all of them members of the Fabian clan, who had been waiting outside for the Senate's decision. Having received instructions to be present in full military equipment on the following day outside the consul's house, they dispersed to their own homes.

News of what had occurred spread swiftly through the city; the Fabii were lauded to the skies. There was talk everywhere of how a single family had shouldered a burden which by right was the country's as a whole, and how the war with Veii was no longer the responsibility of the state but had passed into private hands. If only, people exclaimed, there were two other families of such gallantry, one might take on the Volscians, the other the Aequians, and the people of Rome enjoy perpetual peace, while all neighbouring nations were being subjected to her rule!

The morrow came, and the Fabii, equipped for service, met at the appointed place. The consul, in the crimson cloak of a commander, stepped from his house; there before his eyes, drawn up in column, stood every male member of the Fabian clan. He took his place amongst them, and gave the word to march. Never before had an army so small and so glorious marched through the streets of Rome: 306 men, all of patrician blood, all kinsmen – men who would have made a fine Senate in any period, and not one of them but was fit for high military command – were on their way to war, resolved to destroy Veii with their own unaided hands. Crowds followed them; many were relatives or friends, their thoughts ranging far beyond the present, with its hopes and fears, to an imagined future big with destiny; the rest exalted by patriotic fervour and almost off their heads with admiration and enthusiasm. 'Brave lads!' they shouted; 'good luck to you all, and success attend your enterprise! Look to us when you are home to reward you well – civic honours, military honours, everything your hearts can desire!' As the column marched past the Capitol and the Citadel and the temples in the streets, the crowd with one accord prayed to all the gods these sacred places brought into their thoughts to bless the heroic band and soon to restore every man of it to his home and country. But alas their prayers were vain.

The little army left the city by the right-hand arch of the Carmental Gate – afterwards named the Unlucky Way – and proceeded to the river Cremera, where they decided to erect a fort. The new consuls, Lucius Aemilius and Gaius Servilius, now entered upon office.

For a while the enemy confined himself to occasional raids, and in these circumstances the Fabii were perfectly competent both to maintain their stronghold and, by patrolling the boundary between Roman and Etruscan territory, to annoy the enemy while giving complete protection to their own people; soon, however, these

incursions were temporarily suspended while the Veientes, with reinforcements from the rest of Etruria, attacked the post of the Cremera
and were engaged in a pitched battle – if that is the word – by a Roman
force under the consul Aemilius. In point of fact, Aemilius hardly gave
them time to deploy; for at the first alarm, while their men were
falling-in behind the standards and their supporters were being posted,
an unexpected charge by a squadron of Roman cavalry on their flank
robbed them of the initiative and threw them into complete confusion.
They fell back as best they could upon the Red Rocks, where their
camp was situated, and sued for peace. Peace was granted. These folk,
however, never knew their own minds for ten minutes together, and,
before the garrison was withdrawn from the Cremera, they were sorry
they had asked for it.

Once again the Fabii found themselves the opponents of the
Veientes. Their little army was neither prepared nor equipped for a
major war; nevertheless, in addition to raids on agricultural land and
swift punitive measures against enemy depredations, they did, on
occasion, try the fortunes of the day in a straight fight, and were more
than once victorious – a remarkable achievement for a single Roman
family against the most powerful community (as power was reckoned
in those days) of Etruria. The Veientes at first bitterly resented their
success as a reflection upon their military prestige, but at last those
very successes suggested a way of catching their audacious enemy in a
trap. Observing, not without satisfaction, that the Fabii were growing
more and more reckless with success, they began, every now and
again, to see to it that cattle should stray, with every appearance of
accident, in the path of the raiding parties; farmers would abandon
their farms, and troops sent out to repel raiders would feign cowardice
and take to their heels. The result of these tactics was that the Fabii felt
such contempt for their enemy that they came to believe themselves
always and everywhere invincible. One day, however, over-confid-
ence brought disaster: a long way from the Cremera, far over the
intervening plain, they saw a herd of cattle. At once they started out
to take them, in spite of the fact that a few parties of enemy troops
were visible here and there in the neighbourhood. The idea of danger
had not occurred to them, and they went hurrying, in no sort of
order, right past an ambush which had been laid for them on both
sides of the track; they were beginning to rope in the scattered and
terrified animals, when, the concealed enemy troops suddenly emerg-

ing, they found themselves surrounded. In consternation they heard
the battle-cry burst from the Etruscans' throats, and the javelins began
to fly. The enemy closed in. All round the little band was an unbroken
wall of armed men, and under its increasing pressure they were
forced inward into an ever-lessening circle, which revealed only too
clearly the smallness of their numbers and the fearful superiority of the
Etruscans, rank behind rank in that narrow space. For a while they
endeavoured to force back at all points the enclosing ring, but to no
purpose; then, concentrating in wedge formation upon a single point
by a tremendous effort they succeeded in breaking through. Making
their way to the top of some rising ground, they turned and stood on
the defensive. It was a good position; it gave them a breathing-space
and a chance to recover from the shattering effect of the peril from
which they had escaped. Confidence returned; they repelled the Etruscan troops who were coming up to dislodge them, and for a time it
looked as if, with the aid of a strong position, that mere handful of
men would be victorious. But it was not to be: an enemy force had
already been dispatched with orders to work round to the further side
of the hill, and now suddenly appeared on the summit in their rear.
The advantage the Fabii had gained was gone; they were all killed,
and their fort taken. Authorities agree that 306 men perished, one only
escaping with his life – he was hardly more than a boy, and survived
to keep alive the Fabian name and to render high service to Rome in
times of need, both in politics and war.

At the time of the defeat of the Fabii Gaius Horatius and Titus
Menenius had already begun their term as consuls. Menenius was
promptly dispatched to deal with the victorious Etruscans. A further
defeat followed. The Etruscans occupied the Janiculum, and Rome,
which in addition to the war was suffering from shortage of supplies, as
the enemy had crossed the Tiber, would have been reduced to a state of
siege, had not the other consul, Horatius, been recalled from operations against the Volscians. None the less, war, on this occasion, came
so close to the actual walls of Rome, that a battle – an indecisive one –
was fought at the temple of Hope, and another at the Colline Gate,
where the advantage, slight though it was, which was won by Roman
troops, was nevertheless enough to restore their confidence for the
future.

The following year saw Verginius and Servilius as consuls. Discour-
aged by their recent defeat, the Veientes turned to minor operations,

raiding Roman territory on a fairly large scale from their fortified base on the Janiculum. For a time neither cattle nor farmers were
safe from them, but they were finally caught in the same trap as that
which they had laid for the Fabii: cattle had been driven out to graze
in various places deliberately to attract them, and, like the Fabii, they
fell into an ambush. As there were more of them, their losses were
proportionately greater. Anger at the humiliation of this reverse led
directly to another, even more serious: having crossed the Tiber under
cover of darkness they attempted an assault upon the camp of the
consul Servilius, but were repelled with heavy losses and struggled
back with difficulty to the Janiculum. Without hesitation Servilius followed them across the river and fortified a position at the base of the
hill. Next day at dawn he was eager for action; the previous day's
success had given him confidence, and, as supplies were short, he was
bent upon moving quickly – even recklessly. For both reasons, therefore – for the latter particularly – he led, without adequate preparation,
an assault upon the entrenched position of the enemy on the top of
the hill. The assault was a more shattering failure than that of the
Etruscans on the previous day, and he and his men were saved only
by the timely arrival of his colleague. The Etruscans thus found themselves caught between two fires; in trying to escape first one contingent and then the other, they were severely mangled. A reckless
move had had a happy ending, and the threat from Veii was over.

With the ending of hostilities the position in Rome with regard to
supplies became easier. Grain was imported from Campania and most
people, now that the threat of famine had passed, brought out what
they had hoarded. Peace and plenty were accompanied, however, by
a return of popular discontent, and troubles abroad having ceased
fresh causes for them were sought at home. Once more the tribunes
injected the familiar poison of agrarian legislation into the body politic;
the Senate resisted and again the tribunes did all they could to rouse
the commons against them. This time, moreover, their attacks were
directed against individuals as well as the senatorial party as a whole.
The two tribunes, Considius and Genusius, who had brought forward the proposal for land reform, issued a summons against Titus
Menenius. What told against him with the commons was the loss of
the position on the Cremera when he had himself been in command
of troops in permanent quarters within easy striking distance; and this,
in fact, was his undoing, though his father Agrippa was still popular

and the Senate exerted itself on his behalf as strenuously as it had done for Coriolanus. In the matter of his punishment, however, the tribunes showed some restraint; for though the charge was a capital one, he got off with a fine of 2000 *asses*. None the less, the affair cost him his life; unable to endure the bitter humiliation, he is said to have fallen into sickness which proved fatal. There was another persecution early next year, when Nautius and Valerius were consuls. This time it was Spurius Servilius, and he was brought to trial by the tribunes Caedicius and Statius immediately he retired from office. His behaviour in court was very different from that of Menenius: instead of defending himself by prayers for mercy – his own or the Senate's – he met the allegations of the tribunes with high confidence in his innocence and popularity. Like Menenius, he too was accused of military incompetence, in his case during the action at the Janiculum. Throughout the trial he showed the same hot courage as he had shown when the country was in danger; in a bold speech he rebutted the charges of the populace and of the tribunes, and poured upon both his anger and contempt for the part they had played in the condemnation and subsequent death of Menenius, reminding them that it was by the good offices of Menenius's father that the commons, not so long ago, had been restored to Rome and now enjoyed the benefit of having their own representative magistrates – a privilege they were using to such savage purpose. His boldness saved him, though he was helped by his colleague Verginius who, when called as a witness, generously gave him a share of his own credit. The trial of Menenius, so strongly had the feelings of the court been swayed, had an even greater influence in his favour.

Political troubles were, for the time being, over; but war broke out again with the Veientes, now in alliance with the Sabines. The consul Valerius was dispatched to Veii with an army reinforced by contingents from the Latins and the Hernici, and with no time wasted led an assault upon the Sabines, who had taken up a position just beyond the walls of the town. The attack was a surprise and completely disorganized the defence; and while small scattered groups were trying ineffectually to deal with it, Valerius got possession of the gate which had been his first objective. Once Roman troops were within the fortifications, what followed can hardly be called a fight; it was a massacre. The noise could be heard as far as Veii, where panic ensued, as if the town were already in enemy hands. There was a rush to arms;

some went to the help of the Sabines, others attacked the Roman troops who, at the moment, had no other thoughts than the work in hand and were temporarily thrown off their balance; but they quickly rallied, and successfully resisted the pressure both on their front and rear, until the cavalry were sent into action and carried all before them. The armies of the two most powerful neighbours of Rome had been simultaneously defeated.

Meanwhile the Volscians and Aequians had invaded Latin territory and caused damage to property there. Acting on their own initiative without waiting for troops or officers from Rome, the Latins, assisted by the Hernici, repelled the invaders and got possession of their camp, thereby not only recovering their stolen property but taking a great mass of valuable material abandoned by the enemy. But in spite of this success the consul Nautius was ordered out against the Volscians: it was, I suppose, a matter of precedent, the Senate being unwilling to allow allied states to wage war independently, unsupported by Roman forces and without a Roman general in command. The Volscians were insulted and provoked in every possible way, but nothing would induce them to risk an action in the field.

The next consuls to take office were Lucius Furius and Gaius Manlius; the latter had Veii as his sphere of action, but there were no hostilities as a forty years' truce was granted at Veii's request, on condition of their paying a cash indemnity and supplying Rome with grain. The peace was promptly followed by renewed political strife, the tribunes applying their old goad of agrarian reform until the commons were, as usual, completely out of hand. The consuls resisted the proposed measures with all the force they could muster, undeterred by the conviction of Menenius or by what might have been the conviction of Servilius. As soon as their term was over, they were arrested by the tribune Gnaeus Genucius. They were succeeded by Lucius Aemilius and Opiter Verginius – or possibly Vopiscus Julius, according to some records, in place of the latter; but that does not affect my story, which concerns, at the moment, the ex-consuls Furius and Manlius. These two men, summoned, as they were, to appear in court, walked the streets of Rome wearing mourning and addressing themselves not only to the commons but to the younger members of the nobility. The latter they urged with the utmost solemnity to have nothing to do with advancement to political office, but to realize the unpleasant truth that the consular rods, the purple-bordered toga, and the chair of state were, in effect, nothing other than the trappings of a funeral: the insignia of power were like the fillets on an animal destined for the sacrifice – they doomed the wearer to death. Anyone who still longed for the sweets of office, had better recognize at once that the consular authority had become enslaved to the power of the tribunes; a consul was no better than the tribunes' flunkey, able to act only at his masters' nod; should he venture an independent move, or dare to consider the class to which he belonged – if he were fool enough to suppose that anyone except the commons existed in the body politic, let him take warning by Coriolanus's exile and Menenius's condemnation and death. Propaganda of this sort was highly successful, and members of the Senate at once began to hold secret meetings to discuss what steps should be taken. In all their discussions one thing was never in doubt, namely that Manlius and Furius must somehow, by fair means or foul, be saved from the necessity of appearing in the courts. The more savage the measures suggested, the more they were applauded, and when, finally, a proposal was put forward to attain their end by criminal violence, an agent was found to do the deed.

On the day of the trial excited crowds gathered in the Forum, awaiting the arrival of the tribune. He did not come. At first people were merely puzzled, but soon, when there was still no sign of him and the delay began to look suspicious, they supposed he had been scared off by the nobles and proceeded to complain of his cowardly desertion of the popular cause. Finally some men who had been to the tribune's house brought the news that he had been found dead in his room. The news was soon all over the Forum, and the crowd melted away like an army on the death of its commander. The other tribunes were more alarmed than anybody else, as the death of their colleague proved only too clearly the inefficacy of the law which was supposed to guarantee the sanctity of their persons. The senatorial party was delighted – more so, perhaps, than was seemly. Not one of them felt any regret for the crime; indeed, even those who had not been implicated wished to assume their share of responsibility, and it was openly said that the power of the tribunes being a bad thing must be put down by bad means.

Under the shadow of this discreditable victory the edict was issued for raising troops; the tribunes were too much alarmed by recent events to venture a veto, and the consuls put the matter through. This time, the fury of the commons was directed less upon the consuls for exercising their power than upon the tribunes for failing to oppose them; they declared that their liberty was gone for ever, that the bad old days were back again and that the authority of the tribunes was dead and buried in Genucius's grave. Other means must be found of resisting the patricians, and their only hope, as they had nobody to help them, was to help themselves. Of what did the consuls' official retinue consist? Of twenty-four lictors, all of plebeian birth! What could be feebler or more contemptible to anyone who had the spirit to see it in its true colours, and not to magnify it in his fancy to something tremendous and awe-inspiring?

As a result of this sort of talk the commons were in a dangerous mood, when, in the course of the recruiting, a man named Publilius Volero refused to be enlisted in the ranks on the ground that he had previously been a centurion. The consuls sent a lictor to arrest him. Volero appealed to the tribunes; none came to his assistance, and the consuls ordered him to be stripped and the rods made ready.

'I appeal to the People,' he shouted, 'since the tribunes would rather see a citizen of Rome flogged than be murdered by you in their beds.' The bolder his defiance, the more roughly the lictor handled him, tearing the clothes from his back. Volero was a powerful fellow, and he had friends to help him; he broke from the lictor's grasp and thrust his way into the thick of the crowd where the uproar was loudest in his support. 'I appeal,' he cried; 'I beg for the protection of the commons. Come friends! Come, fellow-soldiers! Why wait for the tribunes – it is they who need help from you!' There was wild excitement. With the mob apparently preparing to fight, it was clear that a crisis of extreme gravity had come. In another moment all respect for the law of the land or the rights of individuals would be gone.

Faced by this storm the consuls quickly realized the insecurity of high position unsupported by force. The lictors had been manhandled, their rods broken, and they themselves were hustled out of the Forum and compelled to take refuge in the Senate House, still in the dark as to how far Volero would use his victory. At last the uproar in the streets died down, and a meeting of the Senate was called at which many bitter things were said about the insults they had endured from the outrageous conduct of Volero and the violence of the mob. A number of bold and uncompromising proposals were put forward, but the voting went with the older members of the House, who shrank from the idea of a class conflict with nothing but anger on one side and recklessness on the other.

Volero, after this, was in high favour with the commons, and was made tribune at the next election, to serve during the year in which Lucius Pinarius and Publius Furius were consuls. It had been generally supposed that he would use his office to damage in every way he could the out-going consuls, but he did nothing of the kind; putting national welfare before personal grievances and without even a word against the consuls, he brought a bill before the commons to provide that plebeian magistrates should be elected at the Tribal Assembly. At first sight the proposal seemed harmless enough, but in fact it was of great importance, as it would deprive the patricians of the power of using the votes of their personal dependants to secure the election to the tribunate of their own nominees. To the commons, naturally enough, it was entirely welcome, while the Senate put up as vigorous a resistance as it could; it lacked, however, the one means to make the resistance really effective, the veto, namely, of one of the college of tribunes. This neither the consuls nor the nobility had sufficient influence to command. None the less party disputes on the proposal, which was of great intrinsic gravity, continued throughout the year.

Volero was re-elected tribune by the popular vote, and the Senate, convinced that a real trial of strength was about to come, returned Appius Claudius to the consulship. He was the son of the other Appius, and the mutual hatred between him and the commons was the legacy of the struggles of the previous generation. Titus Quinctius was elected as his colleague.

Immediately the new consuls were in office, discussion of Volero's proposal became the first concern of government. The measure found fresh and even more uncompromising support in Volero's colleague Laetorius, another of the tribunes and a man of unparalleled military reputation. No doubt his success as a soldier – there was no finer then living – made him less cautious as a politician; for while Volero confined himself to the merits of the measure as such, and refrained from personal attack upon the consuls, Laetorius launched out into savage abuse of Appius and his family, whom he stigmatized as tyrants and the bitterest persecutors of the people of Rome. He was, however, no orator, and in the middle of a speech in which he was trying to declare that the Senate had elected not a consul but a hangman to bully and murder the working men of Rome, he suddenly broke down. The passion for liberty was in his breast, but his unpractised tongue could not find words to express it. 'Citizens!' he ended, 'I am no speech-maker, but what I have said I can make good. Be here tomorrow; in sight of you all I will get the measure through, or die in the attempt!'

Next day the tribunes were the first to arrive and occupied the speakers' platform. The consuls and the nobility took their places, bent upon stopping the passage of the measure. Laetorius ordered all who were not to vote to be removed. The younger nobles stood their ground and refused to budge. Laetorius ordered some of them to be arrested, and Appius countered by declaring that a tribune had no jurisdiction over anyone who was not a member of the commons, as his office was not a national one but restricted to the affairs of his own class; moreover, even were this not true, ancient precedent would prevent him from forcibly removing anyone at all, the proper formula being, 'Citizens, depart, if such is your pleasure'. Legal arguments of this kind, advanced with the contemptuous ease of a master, infuriated Laetorius, who in a blaze of anger sent his runner to lay hands upon the consul, while Appius in reply ordered a lictor to arrest Laetorius, crying out for all to hear that he was a mere private citizen with no official authority of any kind whatever. The tribune would have been roughly handled but for the universal and determined support of the mob and the rapid filling of the Forum by excited men who ran from every part of the city to swell the crowd. Appius stuck to his guns, ugly though the situation was, and serious bloodshed was avoided only by the action of the other consul Quinctius, who prevailed upon the senators of consular rank to get Appius out of the Forum, if necessary by force. Quinctius himself then addressed the angry mob in words as conciliatory as he could make them, and begged the tribunes to dismiss the meeting. He urged all to give their passions time to cool; a little time for thought would not, he declared, rob them of their power; on the contrary it would give it the backing of wisdom, and they would find that the consul had become the servant of the Senate, just as the Senate was the servant of the people.

Quinctius succeeded in calming the crowd, but it was a hard task; the Senate had even greater trouble with Appius. At last, however, the meeting was broken up, and the Senate was convened. In the House various opinions were expressed, all dictated either by fear or anger; gradually, however, feeling grew calmer, and a revulsion from continuing the struggle became more marked the more coolly members were able to discuss the situation – so much so, in fact, that Quinctius received a vote of thanks for the part he had played in mitigating the violence of the dispute. Appius was asked to consent to the restriction of consular authority within limits compatible with political harmony, on the grounds that in present circumstances the nation as a whole was left helpless between the tribunes on the one hand and the consuls on the other, each of whom were attempting to acquire complete control; the country was being torn two ways, and in the struggle for domination national security was lost sight of. Appius in reply swore by everything he held sacred that, in his view, sheer cowardice was betraying the country and abandoning her to her fate; he as consul was doing his duty and the Senate was failing to support him as it should, while the terms it was prepared to accept were more oppressive and humiliating than those it had assented to on the Sacred Mount. But the Senate was unanimous against him and he was forced to give way. The measure was passed into law without further opposition, and for the first time tribunes were elected in the Tribal Assembly. According to Piso, their number was increased by three, as if there had previously been only two. He also gives their names: Gnaeus Siccius, Lucius Numitorius, Marcus Duellius, Spurius Icilius, and Lucius Maecilius.

While these troubles were still in progress, war broke out with the Volscians and Aequians. They had invaded Roman territory in the hope that the commons might take refuge with them should they decide once again to secede, but they withdrew as soon as they heard that Rome had settled her differences. Of the two consuls, Claudius was given command against the Volscians, Quinctius against the Aequians. In his conduct of the campaign Appius showed the same savage temper as he had shown in political controversy, and it had the freer rein as there were no tribunes to hamper it. His loathing of the commons surpassed even his father's in bitterness; it was intolerable to think that he had been beaten by them, and that when he had been elected to office as the one man capable of standing up to the power of the tribunes, a law had been passed which previous consuls had successfully withstood, with less expenditure of effort and far less hope of success in the senatorial party. He was a proud man at the best of times, and in his rage and indignation at what had occurred he was driven to exercise his authority over his men in the most savage and brutal way.

But they were drunk with insubordination, and nothing he did could bring them to heel. They remained unremittingly idle, negligent, and obstinate; neither shame nor fear could reduce them to obedience. Ordered on the march to quicken their pace, they deliberately dragged their feet; working hard, on their own initiative, at whatever the task might be, they promptly downed tools when their commander appeared on the scene to keep them at it; they refused to look him in the face, they muttered curses as he passed, until even he, who had cared so little for the hatred of the commons, was sometimes shaken. Finally, when all disciplinary measures, however severe, had proved useless, he gave up the men in despair and turned his wrath on the centurions who, he declared, had corrupted them, and whom he contemptuously referred to as his tribunes and Voleros.

All this was well known to the Volscians, who accordingly increased their pressure in the hope that Appius would have to face organized insubordination of the same scale as Fabius had had to face on a previous occasion. In fact it went much further: Fabius's men had refused to conquer; Appius's men actually desired defeat. Ordered into the line, they quite shamelessly turned tail and made for their camp, offering no resistance whatever until the enemy was inflicting severe casualties on the rearguard and obviously preparing to assault the camp's fortifications. The threat of this at last aroused their pugnacity and the Volscians were robbed of their victory and forced to retire; none the less it was all too clear that the loss of the camp was the only thing the Roman soldiers were unwilling to submit to; otherwise they gloated over their ignominious defeat. The conduct of his men in no way diminished Appius's determination to assert his authority; he had every intention of proceeding to the severest measures and was about to order the men to parade, when his officers came to him in a body and warned him on no account to bring his authority to a test, as the whole weight of it necessarily lay in the goodwill of his subordinates. They told him that the men were saying that they would refuse to parade; there were demands throughout the army for a withdrawal from Volscian territory; the victorious enemy had forced his way to the gates of the camp and come within an ace of storming its fortifications, and a disaster of the first magnitude was no longer a mere matter of apprehension but a hideous certainty. Appius allowed himself, for the moment, to be persuaded. After all, the men would gain nothing beyond a postponement of their punishment, so

he gave up the idea of an immediate parade and issued orders for the
army to move on the following day. At dawn the bugles sounded and
the march began. Directly the column was clear of the camp the
Volscians attacked its rear – the signal to march might well have been
their own. The confusion in the Roman rear quickly spread to the
leading columns, till the whole army was in hopeless disorder. Commands were inaudible and there was no chance of forming a line for
effective resistance. In every man's head the one thought was to save
his own skin; all order abandoned, there was a scramble for safety over
piles of dead bodies and discarded weapons, continued even after the
enemy had ceased his pursuit. The consul, who had followed the rout
in a vain attempt to rally his men, did finally succeed in getting what
was left of them together; he then moved to a new position in friendly
territory, ordered a parade, and addressed the troops, calling them,
with full justification, an army who had betrayed military discipline
and deserted its standards. He then asked them individually where
their weapons were, or their standards, as the case might be, and gave
orders that every soldier who had lost his equipment, every standard-
bearer who had lost his standard, every centurion, too, and dis-
tinguished-service man who had abandoned his post, should be first
flogged and then beheaded. The remainder were decimated.

The campaign against the Aequians was conducted in a very different spirit: here the consul and his men vied with one another in goodwill on the one side and generous consideration on the other. Quinctius
was a kindlier man than his colleague, and that he was so was the
greater satisfaction to him when he saw the results of Appius's ill-
starred severity. As a consequence of this close cooperation between
the army and its commander, the Aequians would not risk an action,
but allowed the enemy to raid their territory where and when he
pleased. More valuable material, including cattle, was consequently
taken than in any previous campaign against that people. The whole
of it was distributed amongst the troops. Nor did Quinctius omit to
commend the army's conduct – a thing hardly less gratifying to a
soldier than more tangible rewards. The cordial relationship between
the army and its commander rendered the men, on their return to
Rome, less hostile towards the Senate, which, they declared, had given
to the other army a tyrannical master, but to themselves a father.

What with victory and defeat in war and bitter class conflict both
at home and abroad, the year had been an eventful one; but what made

it most memorable was the new measure about the Tribal Assembly, the importance of which lay less in its practical results than in the victory it represented in the class struggle. In point of fact, the loss of dignity caused by the exclusion of the patricians from the Assembly outweighed any actual shift in the balance of power between the two classes.

A more turbulent year followed, when Lucius Valerius and Titus Aemilius entered upon the consulship. The causes of the trouble were, first, the continuance of the conflict over the distribution of land, and, second, the trial of Appius Claudius. Appius was the most determined opponent of the proposed legislation, and he was engaged in pushing the cause of the present owners of the land under dispute with as much confidence as if he had still been in office when a summons was issued against him by the tribunes Duellius and Siccius. Never had a man more bitterly hated by the commons, both for his own and for his father's offences, faced his trial before the people; nor had the senatorial party ever made such efforts in defence of any other of their order, feeling, as they did, that a champion of the Senate and vindicator of their own dignity, who, albeit with somewhat excessive zeal, had steadfastly opposed every attempt by the tribunes or the people to stir up political trouble, was being offered as a sacrifice to the angry mob. The only senator to remain wholly unperturbed by the whole business was Appius himself: neither the threats of his enemies nor the entreaties of his friends had the smallest effect upon him. Other men in such circumstances might have been induced to wear mourning or to humble themselves by making personal appeals for mercy; but not Appius. Though he had to plead his cause before the people, even so he refused in any way to mitigate or soften his accustomed asperity of speech; his old proud look, his well-known contemptuous glance, the familiar fire and vigour of his words made not a few of the commons as much afraid of him in the dock as they had been when he was consul. He made one speech only in his own defence, and the tone of it was wholly characteristic: one might have thought that he was prosecuting his accusers rather than defending himself against them. Nothing could shake him, and both the tribunes and the commons were so paralysed by his confidence that they voluntarily adjourned the trial without fixing a definite date for its resumption. After a short interval, and before the day finally agreed upon arrived, he fell ill and died. The tribunes tried to stop the eulogy pronounced in his honour, but the people insisted upon giving him his due. He had been a great man, and they refused to rob his dying day of the traditional tribute, listening to the words spoken in his praise now that he was dead with as good a will as they had listened before to his accusers. Thousands of them attended his funeral.

In the course of this year Valerius led an expedition against the Aequians. They refused battle, so he ordered an assault upon their camp, but was prevented from taking it by a sudden and violent storm with hail and thunder. This was quite unexpected, but the men were even more surprised when, the order for withdrawal having been given, the storm was succeeded, no less suddenly, by perfect calm and clear skies, so that it was difficult not to feel that supernatural powers were defending the camp and that it would be impious to attempt a second assault. Operations were therefore diverted to the destruction of crops. The other consul, Aemilius, conducted a campaign against the Sabines, and there, too, operations were confined to the devastation of farmlands, as the enemy refused to leave his defences. Later, thickly populated villages, as well as farms, were burned, and this roused the Sabines to offer some resistance; there was an indecisive engagement, and on the following day they moved back into a safer position. Aemilius felt that this was tantamount to a victory, and left the area though in fact the campaign had hardly begun.

The new consuls, Titus Numicius Priscus and Aulus Verginius, began their term of office while these operations were still in progress. In Rome, political strife continued, and it was beginning to look as if the commons were in no mood to put up any longer with a postponement of agrarian legislation. The storm was on the point of breaking, when the smoke from burning farmsteads and the arrival in the city of farmers and their families fleeing for their lives brought the news that the Volscians were on the march. The threat to national safety checked the outbreak of mob violence just in time. The consuls had prompt instructions from the Senate to take the field with all men of military age, and this had a calming effect on the rest of the commons left in the city. In point of fact the threat proved nothing more than a false alarm; the enemy hastily withdrew, and Numicius proceeded against Antium, while Verginius took control of operations against the Aequians. In the latter campaign the Roman force was ambushed, with results which might well have been calamitous; but it was saved by the valour of the rank and file from a situation of extreme peril into which it had been led by the negligence of its commander. Numicius, at Antium, did better: the enemy was routed in the first engagement and forced to take refuge in the town – a place, for those days, of some wealth and power. Numicius did not risk an assault but contented himself with the capture of the much less important town of Caeno. Meanwhile the Sabines took advantage of the fact that Roman troops were occupied by these two campaigns to send a raiding force right to the gates of Rome. A few days later, however, they had to pay for it; both consuls, by way of reprisal, invaded their territory simultaneously, with the result that the Sabines suffered greater losses than they had inflicted.

The last months of the year brought a period of peace though disturbed, as usual, by the political conflict. The angry commons refused to take part in the consular elections, at which by the votes of the patricians and their dependants Titus Quinctius and Quintus Servilius were returned to office. The new year resembled the old, beginning with internal dissension and ending with foreign war and the patching up of political quarrels. The Sabines swept across the Crustuminan plains bringing fire and sword to the country around the Anio; when almost at the walls of Rome near the Colline Gate they were checked and forced to retreat, taking with them, however, many prisoners and large numbers of cattle. Servilius marched in pursuit; failing to catch the retreating column anywhere where a regular engagement could be fought, he turned his troops over to pillaging; this was carried out over so wide an area and on such a devastating scale that he returned to Rome with a quantity of plunder many times as great as what had previously been lost. Operations against the Volscians, too, were highly successful, through the combined efforts of the troops and their commander: in a hand-to-hand struggle, in which on both sides there were very heavy losses in killed and wounded, the Romans, who were outnumbered and consequently felt their losses more keenly, would have fallen back if the consul had not saved the situation by calling out that on the other wing the enemy were in retreat. This was not true, but the falsehood worked well and put new heart into the men. They resumed the offensive, believing that victory was within their grasp, and the belief was soon a reality. Quinctius, however, was afraid that too vigorous a push might lead to a renewal of fighting all along the line, so he gave the order for withdrawal. For the next day or two all operations were suspended, almost as if by mutual consent, and the enemy employed the interval in very greatly increasing their numbers; large reinforcements drawn from all the Volscian and Aequian communities joined the army in the field, and as all were convinced that the Roman force would, if it knew of their arrival, slip away under cover of darkness they determined to forestall its escape. Accordingly, a few hours before dawn, they moved forward to the attack. There was some confusion in the Roman camp at the unexpected alarm, but Quinctius quickly restored order and then issued instructions for the men to stop in their tents while he took a company of the Hernici to a position outside the defences, and further instructed buglers and trumpeters to get on horseback and by sounding the instruments to keep the enemy on tenterhooks until daybreak. Inside the camp everything remained perfectly quiet for the rest of the night and the men were even able to get some sleep. The Volscians, on the other hand, were kept guessing: the sight of infantry troops equipped for battle, whom they supposed to be Roman and whose numbers they fancied, in the darkness, to be larger than they were, the shrill neighing of horses rendered restless and nervous by riders they were unfamiliar with and by the continuous noise of the bugles, all seemed to point to an imminent attack. Dawn came, and the Roman troops moved out into line of battle; they were fresh and lively after their night's rest, while the Volscians, who had stood to arms throughout the night, were already tired. At the first thrust they were badly shaken; they were not, however, by any means overwhelmed, for there were hills in their rear into which, screened by their front line, the remainder of their men were able to withdraw safely and in good order. Quinctius, following up their retreat, halted his column at the foot of the rising ground, but he had difficulty in restraining his men, who vociferously demanded to be allowed to press their advantage. Most urgent of all were the cavalry: they positively mobbed their commander, shouting their determination to press on in front of the standards. Quinctius was in two minds: on the one hand, his troops could be trusted; on the other, the terrain was against him. While he hesitated, the men with one accord declared their resolution to advance, and promptly did so. Sticking their spears into the ground, to have less to carry up the steep ascent, they moved forward at the double; the Volscians expended their missile weapons in the first few minutes of the fight, but there were rocks and stones lying handy and these they hurled down with great effect upon the Romans as they came on up the slope. The Romans were thrown into disorder and forced back down the hill, and their left wing was nearly overwhelmed; but Quinctius by reproaching his men first for rashness and then for cowardice succeeded in checking their retreat and shaming them into facing their dangerous situation with confidence. They stood their ground firmly, then, resuming the offensive, and raising once more the battle-cry, pressed forward to the attack. One more rush and they were over the worst, with the steep and broken ground behind them, and they were about to gain the summit of the hill when the enemy fled. Pursuers and pursued were hardly separated as, moving with all the speed they could muster, they reached the Volscian camp which, in the resulting panic and confusion, was captured. The Volscian survivors made for Antium, and the Roman army followed. After a few days' siege the town surrendered without any further operations having been undertaken against it. From the moment of their recent defeat and the loss of their camp the enemy had no heart for continuing their resistance.

BOOK THREE

The Patricians at Bay

THE next consuls to enter upon office after the capture of Antium were Titus Aemilius and Quintus Fabius – the latter being the one survivor of the disaster suffered by his clan at the river Cremera. Aemilius during his previous term of office had brought forward a measure for making grants of land to plebeian families, and for that reason, on his being re-elected, hopes were high that a law would at last be put through, and the tribunes took the matter up with renewed confidence, in the belief that a measure which had so often been opposed by the consuls might now, with a consul's support, be actually carried into effect. Aemilius himself had not, moreover, changed his mind on the subject. The owners – or, rather, occupiers – of the land in question comprised most of the patrician families of Rome; they, by indignantly asserting that a leading officer of state, allying himself with the party policies of the tribunes, was trying to be generous with other people's property in order to curry popular favour, succeeded in diverting to the consul the whole onus of ill-feeling which would otherwise have fallen upon the tribunes. A bitter struggle was imminent, but Fabius saved the situation by a proposal which neither party found unacceptable: a certain amount of land, he reminded them, had been taken from the Volscians in the preceding year by Roman armies under the command of Titus Quinctius; Antium was a town with an excellent position on the coast; settlers might well be sent there, and in that way plebeian families might obtain farms without giving cause for complaint to the patrician landlords in Rome, and political harmony would not be disturbed. The suggestion was adopted. Three commissioners, Titus Quinctius, Aulus Verginius, and Publius Furius, were appointed, and all who wished to receive grants were instructed to give in their names. Human nature, however, does not change: the mere fact that there was plenty for everyone blunted the edge of appetite and so few applied for a grant that Volscian families had to be included in order to bring the number of settlers to a satisfactory figure. The bulk of the plebeian families preferred to demand land in the neighbourhood of Rome rather than to accept the offer of it elsewhere.

The Aequians, meanwhile, were causing trouble. Quintus Fabius had invaded their territory. They admitted defeat and asked for a truce. The truce was granted, but they promptly broke it by a sudden raid into Latium. In the following year Quintus Servilius who, with Spurius Postumius, had been elected to the consulship, was ordered against them. He constructed a permanent fortified post on Latin territory, where enforced inactivity caused serious sickness amongst the troops. The campaign dragged on into its third year, into the consulship of Quintus Fabius and Titus Quinctius, to the former of whom, on the strength of his previous success, was given the command against the Aequians: the usual drawing of lots was, in this case, waived. Fabius marched from Rome fully confident that his name alone would be enough to bring the Aequians to terms; he sent envoys to their national council with instructions to announce that he, Quintus Fabius the consul, the man who had brought peace to Rome after his victory, was now returning thence with a sword in that same right hand which had previously been offered them in friendship. Whose was the treachery, whose the perjury answerable for the change, was already clear in the sight of heaven, who would soon wreck venegeance on the offenders. Nevertheless he had hopes that the Aequians would, even now, avoid the distresses of war by freely admitting the error of their ways; if they did so, they would find safe refuge in the clemency they had experienced once already; if they clung to their perjury, they would find themselves at war not with a human enemy only but with the angry gods.

Fabius's stern message had no effect whatever. The envoys who carried it were more or less roughly handled, and a force was dispatched against the Romans at Algidus. When the news reached Rome the insult was deeply resented, and, though the military situation did not really demand it, the other consul marched to join his colleague, so that two consular armies were approaching the enemy together, both bent upon immediate action. It so happened, however, that before anything could be done there was very little daylight left and a sentry on watch in one of the enemy outposts called out, 'What's this, my fine fellows? Action stations at nightfall? All for show, no doubt – for it does not look like business to me! As for ourselves, we shall need rather more daylight for the coming battle: form your line again at dawn tomorrow, and you will have plenty of chance for fighting, never fear!' The taunt went home; the Roman troops were marched back to their quarters in no very amiable frame of mind to await the morrow, and not a man but felt that the coming night would be all too long. They ate and slept, and at daybreak were first in the field; later the Aequian force made its appearance and a hard-fought action ensued. No quarter was given by either side, as the Romans were exasperated by the insult they had received, while the Aequians were driven to utter recklessness both by the knowledge that they had brought their peril on themselves and by despair of ever being trusted again. Nevertheless recklessness and despair did not enable them to withstand the pressure of the Roman armies, and they were forced to retreat to their own territory. But they were a tough crowd, and even then were no more inclined to admit defeat; on the contrary the rank and file abused their commanders for their folly in risking an action in the field: that – they urged – was the form of fighting in which Rome admittedly excelled; their own advantage lay, on the other hand, in raiding operations: for them, successful warfare involved small units operating over a wide area rather than massed attack by an organized army. Accordingly they garrisoned their camp and crossed the Roman border; the incursion was so rapid and so violent that alarm was felt even in Rome: everyone in the city was on edge, and the more so from the unexpectedness of the move, as of all things the least to be feared was a sudden raid by a more or less beleaguered and defeated enemy. Families from outlying farms, who came scrambling into the city for protection, brought stories wildly exaggerated by their terror, magnifying small units and raiding-parties into legions and armies marching on Rome with terrible swiftness in a full-scale invasion. The rumours grew wilder and more absurd as they passed from mouth to mouth; men ran through the streets calling for a last stand; panic spread as if the enemy were already within the gates.

Fortunately Quinctius had returned to Rome from Algidus and was able to remedy the situation. Having restored some semblance of order, he pointed out, not without indignation, that the enemy everyone was so much afraid of had already been defeated. He then took the precaution of posting pickets at the city gates, convened a meeting of the Senate, and, with the Senate's backing proclaimed a *justitium*, or general suspension of public business. That done, he marched to the defence of the frontier, leaving Quintus Servilius as City Prefect, but found no enemy on Roman soil.

The other consul was highly successful: knowing the route which the enemy was bound to take, he fell upon them in circumstances very advantageous to himself, as their movement was impeded by the plunder they had collected during their raid. That plunder was their undoing; it was all recovered, and few of them escaped alive from the trap which had been set for them. The *justitium*, which had lasted four days, consequently came to an end upon Quinctius's return to Rome.

The census was then taken, and Quinctius conducted the ceremonial purification which marked its conclusion. The number of citizens registered, apart from widows and orphans, is said to have been 104,714. In the campaign against the Aequians nothing further happened worth mentioning: they withdrew into their towns and offered no resistance to the burning and plundering of their farms. On several occasions the consul marched his men through the length and breadth of their territory taking everything he could pick up, and finally returned to Rome laden with plunder and with his reputation greatly enhanced.

The consuls for the next year were Aulus Postumius Albus and Spurius Furius Fuscus – some writers spell the name Fusius instead of Furius, a point I mention to preclude the mistake of supposing that it was a different person. There was no doubt that one of the consuls would lead a campaign against the Aequians, who accordingly appealed for help to the Volscians of Ecetra. The help was eagerly granted, these two peoples having always vied with one another in their hatred of Rome, and vigorous preparations for war were set going. The Hernici were aware of what was happening and warned Rome of the defection of Ecetra; the settlement at Antium was also under suspicion, as it was supposed that a large number of men had escaped from the town at the time of its capture and sought refuge with the Aequians, and they had, in fact, done very good service all through the Aequian campaign. Later, when the Aequians had been forced to take shelter inside their towns, these men dispersed and returned to Antium, where they won over the Roman settlers who were already at heart disloyal to their compatriots. Things had not yet come to a head when the proposed defection was reported to the Senate, and the consuls were instructed to summon the leading men amongst the settlers to Rome for questioning. They came readily enough, but their answers to the questions they were asked in the Senate left them, by the time they were dismissed, under graver suspicion than before. From that moment war was regarded as inevitable. The command against the Aequians was entrusted to the consul Furius, who marched from Rome and encountered marauding enemy forces in the territory of the Hernici; having seen only scattered bands, he was ignorant of their total strength and rashly offered battle against what proved to be superior numbers. At the very beginning of the engagement he was forced to retire within the fortifications of his camp. Even then the danger was by no means over, for throughout the night and the following day his position was subjected to such pressure from enemy attacks and so closely blockaded that it was not possible to get a message through to Rome. The defeat and subsequent blockade of Furius and his men were reported to the Hernici, and the impact of the news upon the Senate was so shattering that a state of emergency was formally declared: the form of the decree *that the consul shall see to it that the state takes no harm* – has always been held to signify a real threat to the nation's life. In this case the consul was Postumius, Furius's colleague, and to him was entrusted the task of dealing with the emergency.

It was decided that Postumius himself should remain in Rome to enroll every man capable of bearing arms, while Titus Quinctius, acting on his behalf, was dispatched to the relief of the beleaguered camp with a contingent of allied troops drawn from the Latins, the Hernici, and the settlement at Antium, all of whom received orders to supply drafts of 'crisis men', as hurriedly raised reinforcements were called in those times. Crowded days followed; there was marching and countermarching, and no one knew where the next blow would fall; the enemy's numerical superiority led them to harass and divide the Roman forces – inadequate, as they knew, to deal successfully with every threat – by simultaneous operations on different fronts, sending one contingent to assault the camp, another to devastate farmland in Roman territory, another to attack Rome itself if it got the chance.

Valerius was left in charge of the city, Postumius sent out to protect the frontier. Every possible precaution was taken: watches were set in the city, pickets posted outside the gates, the walls manned, and – a necessary measure in so critical a time – all public business was suspended for several days. Furius meanwhile had been taking no action against the enemy forces which surrounded his camp, until he found a chance to catch them off their guard and made an unexpected sortie by way of the gate in the rear of his position. He might have followed up his advantage, but failed to do so for fear of an assault upon the camp from the other direction. His brother, serving under him as an officer pressed his advance to a considerable distance and in the heat of action failed to observe either that his comrades were falling back or that the enemy were moving to the attack in his rear. Thus he found himself cut off, and after many fruitless but gallant attempts to fight his way back to the camp, he was killed. The consul had no sooner learned that his brother was surrounded than he, too, resumed the offensive and plunged into the thick of things with less caution than the circumstances demanded; he was wounded, and dragged to safety – but only just in time. This was a shock to his men and a great encouragement to the enemy: to have wounded the consul and killed his brother acted as fuel to the flame of their courage, and from that moment nothing could stop them; the Romans, dispirited and outnumbered, were forced back within the fortifications of their camp, where they were once again blockaded. Only the arrival of Quinctius with the allied contingents of the Latins and Hernici saved the army from total destruction.

The Aequians, when Quinctius appeared on the scene, were wholly intent upon the beleaguered troops in the camp, to whom with triumphant savagery they were displaying the severed head of the consul's brother. Quinctius attacked them in the rear; upon a signal from himself there was a simultaneous sortie from the camp and a large part of the enemy force was surrounded. On Roman territory there was a further success, where the invading Aequians were even more soundly defeated, though their losses in killed were not so great; scattered groups of them were engaged in stripping the farms of whatever of value they could find, when they were attacked by Postumius simultaneously at various points where he had stationed troops to await their chance; trying to make their escape without any order or cohesion, they fell in with Quinctius as he was returning with the wounded consul from his successful action. That wound and the deaths of the lieutenant and his men were nobly avenged in the battle which ensued.

Throughout these operations heavy losses were inflicted and received by both sides. In describing events so distant in time, it is difficult to make a precise or trustworthy estimate of the size of the forces engaged or the number of casualties; none the less Valerius of Antium does venture to do so: according to his account Roman losses in the territory of the Hernici amounted to 5,200 killed, and those of the Aequian raiders in their engagement with Postumius to 2,400 killed; the rest of them, who fell into Quinctius's trap as they were on the way home with their plunder, suffered far worse, losing no fewer (as Valerius says with punctilious exactitude) than 4,230 men.

When the campaign was over and normal business in Rome had been resumed, strange things began to happen: lights blazed in the sky, and other inexplicable phenomena were either seen or, perhaps, imagined by frightened people. So seriously was this taken that a three days' *feriae* was proclaimed – shops were shut, the courts closed, and all work forbidden, while every shrine and temple was, throughout the period, packed with men and women praying for the pardon of heaven. The troops from Latium and the Hernici were thanked by the Senate for the services they had rendered and sent home, and the thousand men from Antium who had arrived late, after the battle was over, were dismissed more or less in disgrace. Elections were then held, and Lucius Aebutius and Publius Servilius began their term of office on 1 August – at that epoch the beginning of the year. It was an unhealthy season and in both town and country there was a great deal of sickness. Cattle suffered as much as men, and the incidence of disease was increased by overcrowding, as farmers together with their livestock had been taken into the city for fear of raids. The smell of this motley collection of animals and men was distressing to the city folk, who were not accustomed to it; the farmers and yokels, packed as they were into inadequate quarters, suffered no less from the heat and lack of sleep, while attendance upon the sick, or mere contact of any kind, continually spread the infection. The unhappy people were already almost at the end of their tether, when a report suddenly arrived from the Hernici that a combined army of Aequians and Volscians had crossed their border and established a base from which very powerful forces were overrunning the countryside. The Hernican envoys who brought the news together with their request for assistance received a melancholy answer – though it was already only too clear, by the diminished numbers in the Senate, that the plague had reduced Rome to desperate straits: they were told, in short, that with what aid the Latins could give they must fend for themselves. The gods had visited Rome with sudden wrath and were destroying her; but should any relief be granted, then she would help her friends as she had always done in the past. Thus the envoys had even worse news to take home than what they had brought with them, for it meant that they would have to bear alone the whole weight of a war, which even with Roman assistance would have been almost beyond their strength.

The invaders did not stop at the territory of the Hernici but swept on into that of Rome, where the farmlands needed no enemy to render them desolate. In all the countryside they found not a single man, armed or unarmed; there was no sign of defenders, not a trace of cultivation. Passing through what might have been a desert, they advanced to the third milestone on the Gabinian Way.

In the city, the consul Aebutius had died; his colleague Servilius was in a lingering state, almost despaired of. Most of the leading men, the majority of the Senate, almost everyone of military age were down with the disease. The situation called for military counter-measures, but such, in the circumstances, were utterly impossible; there were hardly enough fit men left to mount guard at the gates. Watches were kept by those of senatorial rank who were young enough, and fit enough, to do so, while the duty of doing the rounds of inspection fell upon the plebeian aediles, into whose hands had passed the lofty responsibility normally wielded by the consuls.

Her strength gone and with no one to lead her, Rome lay helpless. Only her tutelary gods could save her – and her own abiding Fortune. And so it was: the enemy proved to be no soldiers after all, but merely thieves. They were very far, as it turned out, from hoping to capture, or even to get within striking distance of, the city; the mere sight from far away of its hills and houses so effectively extinguished their martial ardour, that with one accord they began to grumble about wasting their time amongst the rotting carcases of men and cattle in a stricken desert where nothing was to be found worth taking, while they might just as well be turning their attention to the rich and wholesome lands of Tusculum. So, on the spur of the moment, they got moving again, and passed by cross-country tracks through the territory of Labici to the hills near Tusculum, which from then on became the focal point of their operations.

The Latins and Hernici, meanwhile, showed their sympathy in a practical manner. Ashamed to allow a common enemy to march on Rome without making any effort to stop him, or bringing any aid to their beleaguered friends, they joined forces and proceeded to the scene of action. Finding the enemy gone, they gathered what information they could and followed his tracks until they finally came upon him approaching the valley of Alba from the direction of the hills near Tusculum. A battle ensued in circumstances greatly to their disadvantage, so that, for the present at least, their loyalty to their friends cost them dear. Their losses were heavy, but not greater in number than the victims of the plague in Rome, which included the surviving consul, and other distinguished men such as the augurs Marcus Valerius and Titus Verginius Rutilus, and the president of the Ward-Priests Servius Sulpicius, while amongst the nameless and humble its ravages were indeed terrible. The Senate, despairing of human aid, turned the people to their prayers, bidding them go with their wives and children and supplicate heaven for a remission of their sorrows. It was an official command, but no more than what each was impelled to do by his own distress: every shrine was packed; in every temple women lay prostrate, their hair sweeping the floor, praying the angry gods to grant them pardon and to put an end to the plague.

It may be that the prayers were granted; in any case, the sickly season was now over, and from this time, little by little, those in whom the disease had run its course began to recover, and it was once more possible for people to turn their thoughts to public affairs. Several *interregna* had expired, when Publius Valerius Publicola, three days after assuming office as *interrex*, declared the election to the consulship of Lucius Lucretius Tricipitinus and Titus Veturius (or Vetusius) Geminius. They entered office on 11 August, by which time the general health of the population was so far re-established that, in addition to the defence of the city, it was possible to undertake offensive operations. Accordingly upon receipt of a report from the Hernici that their territory had been invaded, assistance was promptly offered: two consular armies were enrolled, Veturius being commissioned to proceed against the Volscians, while Tricipitinus, ordered to protect allied territory from invasion, marched eastward to the Hernici. Veturius was completely successful in his first engagement; Tricipitinus failed to intercept an enemy raiding party which had crossed the mountains of Praeneste and, after doing much damage to the countryside about Praeneste and Gabii, had then turned left for the Tusculan hills. Rome herself had a moment of acute anxiety: not that she was incapable of defending herself, but because the threat was totally unexpected. Quintus Fabius was in command in the city; all men of military age were, by his instructions, armed; all strong points were manned, and everything made safe and kept under orderly control. In consequence of these precautions the enemy after taking whatever of value they could find in the immediate neighbourhood did not venture to approach the city, but by a circuitous route made for home. The further away they got, the more careless they became, until they unexpectedly fell in with the consul Lucretius, whose scouts had already ascertained the route they were likely to take. Lucretius's men were deployed for battle and ready to engage. To them, the sudden action came as no surprise; the enemy, on the contrary, were taken completely off their guard; they panicked at the first attack, albeit by somewhat inferior numbers, and their whole force – a very large one – was flung into disorder. The victorious Romans drove them down into the deep gullies from which escape was difficult, and surrounded them. In what followed the Volscian name almost ceased to exist: in some records I find that 13,470 were killed during the battle and the subsequent rout, 1,150 prisoners were taken, and 27 regimental standards captured. These numbers are perhaps exaggerated; none the less, they did, without doubt, suffer terribly. The victorious consul, laden with the spoils of war, returned to the permanent camp he had previously occupied. The two consuls then joined forces, and the Volscians and Aequians did the same with what was left of their own. There was another battle – the third that year. The result was as before: Rome's enemies were defeated in the field, and their camp fell into Roman hands.

In the course of these events history was repeated and the successful conclusion of a war was once again immediately followed by political disturbances. Amongst the tribunes for the year was a certain Gaius Terentillus Arsa, and he it was who began to stir up trouble, taking advantage of the consuls' absence from the city. On several successive days he made inflammatory speeches to the mob, inveighing bitterly against the arrogance of the patricians as a whole and more particularly against the excessive powers of the consuls, which he denounced as intolerable in a free community. Consul, he declared, might be a less hateful word than King, but in actual fact consular government was even more oppressive than monarchy, in that the country had taken two masters in place of one, both of them men with irresponsible and unlimited powers who without any sort of check upon themselves used the whole terror of the law with all the penalties it sanctioned for the crushing of the common people. 'Therefore,' he said, 'it is my intention to propose a measure which will put a stop to this tyranny. Five commissioners must be appointed to codify the laws which limit and define the power of the consuls; that done, the consuls will be bound to use against the people only the authority granted to them by popular assent, instead of giving the force of law, as they do at present, to their own arbitrary passions.'

The effect of the tribune's proposal was highly disturbing to the patricians, who were afraid that, as neither consul was at the moment in Rome, they might be compelled to submit; but the situation was saved by the City Prefect, Quintus Fabius, who convened the Senate and delivered a violent attack both upon the measure itself and on the character of the man who proposed it: indeed if both consuls had been present in person to face the tribune, they could have added nothing to the strength of his denunciation. 'Traitor that you are,' he cried, 'you have timed your attack upon the government with the utmost cunning. If last year, when we had war and pestilence to contend with, the angry gods had cursed us with a tribune like you, nothing could have saved us: with the consuls dead, the country prostrate with disease, and everything in hopeless confusion, he would have brought in a measure for abolishing the consular authority, and would thereby have shown our enemies the road to their assault on Rome. Think again, my friend: if a consul is guilty of a tyrannical or oppressive act against any individual, does not the law allow you to call him to account, to accuse him in court where he will be tried by men of the same class as his victim? It is not the consular authority which you are making hateful and intolerable; it is the power of the tribunes, a power once brought into harmony with the Senate so that it no longer conflicted with the Senate's proper functions, but now degraded again to its former state. I will not ask you to abandon the course you have begun. No; it is you other tribunes whom I would implore never to forget that the power you wield was given you to help individuals where help was needed, not to destroy the commonwealth as a whole. You were appointed not as enemies of the Senate, but as tribunes of the people. That the government should be attacked now, when the consuls' absence renders it helpless, is for us a bitter thing; but on your heads it will bring hatred. Diminish that hatred, I beg you – for it will in no way diminish your rights – by urging your colleague to postpone discussion of this matter until the consuls are back in Rome. Even the Aequians and Volscians, when the consuls last year had died of the plague, spared us the full horrors of war.'

The other tribunes used their influence with Terentillus to secure a postponement of his proposed measure – though in point of fact it was temporarily dropped.

The consuls were immediately recalled to Rome. Lucretius entered the city covered with glory and laden with the spoils of war. The enthusiasm which greeted his arrival was further increased by his generous

behaviour in having all the captured material laid out in the Campus
Martius for a period of three days, for public inspection: anyone who
recognized property of his own, could take it away; whatever was not
claimed was sold. Lucretius had, by general consent, earned the distinction of a Triumph, but since in his own view discussion of Terentillus's
proposal for political reforms was of more immediate importance, the
celebration was postponed. For a number of days the political issue was
debated both in the Senate and before the people, until Terentillus
finally yielded to the authority of the consul and ceased to urge his case.
The commander and his army were then able to receive the official recognition they had so truly earned, and Lucretius celebrated his
Triumph over the Volscians and Aequians, his chariot followed through
the streets of Rome by the legions who had fought at his side. Veturius,
the other consul, was granted the lesser distinction of an Ovation,
entering the city unaccompanied by his troops.

The consuls of the following year, Volumnius and Sulpicius, had no
sooner entered upon office than they were faced with the necessity of
dealing all over again with Terentillus's proposed measure, which this
time was brought forward with the backing of the whole college of
tribunes. The year was marked by ominous signs: fires blazed in the
sky, there was a violent earthquake, and a cow talked – there was a
rumour that a cow had talked the previous year, but nobody believed it:
this year they did. Nor was this all: it rained lumps of meat. Thousands
of birds (we are told) seized and devoured the pieces in mid-air, while
what fell to the ground lay scattered about for several days without going putrid. The Sybilline Books were consulted by two officials, who
found in them the prediction that danger threatened from a 'concourse
of alien men', who might attack 'the high places of the City, with the
shedding of blood'. There was also found, amongst other things, a
warning to avoid factious politics. This annoyed the tribunes, who
swore the prophecies were a fake, deliberately invented to stop the passage of the proposed law. A dangerous clash was imminent, and only
avoided by – would you believe it? – a report from the Hernici that the
Volscians and Aequians, in spite of their recent losses, were on the war-
path again. The old cycle was being repeated.

This time, the nerve-centre of the threatened attack was, according
to the report, Antium, and at Ecetra settlers from Antium were openly
meeting to discuss plans. In the Senate a decree was promptly issued for
the raising of troops, and the consuls received instruments to assume

direction each of his own sphere of the coming operations. The tribunes loudly asserted in public that the war-scare was a blind: it was a piece of play-acting staged by the Senate, who had hired the Hernici to play a part in it. The liberty of the Roman people, they declared, had once been suppressed by strong measures, the open hostility of men against men: now worse means were being employed – bare-faced trickery. As no one could possibly believe that the Aequians and Volscians after their crushing defeat would be already capable of aggression, a new enemy had to be invented; so a neighbouring colony of known loyalty to Rome was accused of treachery. War had been declared, indeed, against the innocent Antiates; but the real enemy which the Senate meant to fight was the common people of Rome; they proposed to drive them, loaded with military equipment, helter-skelter out of the city, and by getting rid of as many of them as possible to revenge themselves upon their representatives, the tribunes. The people, they asserted, had better realize that the Senate's one object was to quash the proposed legislation, and that the object was already achieved – unless they themselves acted promptly. The matter was still open; they had not yet changed civilian dress for the soldier's: let them, therefore, take immediate steps to avoid expulsion from the city which belonged to them, and the slavery which would follow. Let them show courage, and help would not be wanting: the tribunes were unanimous; there was no danger to be feared from foreign enemies, and their liberties could be safely defended – under the eye of heaven, as the gods had shown the previous year.

The consuls in reply to the tribunes' outburst ordered their chairs of state to be placed full in their view and proceeded with the levy. The tribunes pressed towards them with a mob at their heels. A few names were tentatively called, and a riot began. If the consul ordered an arrest, a tribune countered by ordering the prisoner's release. Rights and duties were forgotten; force, and what it might achieve, was the only arbiter of conduct.

The question of the proposed legislation was brought up on each successive day that the Assembly could be legally held, and the Senate employed similar tactics in blocking it to those the tribunes had employed in blocking recruitment. Senators and aristocrats refused to budge when the tribunes issued their order to divide into *centuries* for voting, and this started the brawling. The older men, indeed, in the senatorial party took little part in an affair with which statesmanship obviously had nothing to do, but which had become the mere battleground of conflicting passions, and the consuls, too, dissociated themselves from it as far as they reasonably could, to avoid any affront to their exalted office such as might well occur in the general confusion.

There was a young nobleman named Caeso Quinctius, a man of action, tall and strongly built, whose physical endowments were enhanced by a distinguished record both as a soldier and a forensic orator. In short, it was generally felt that if either words or deeds were called for, there was no better man in Rome than he. To the Senatorial party he was a tower of strength: standing amongst his friends, head and shoulders above them all, strong as an ox and with a commanding voice which seemed to suggest all the powers of state rolled into one, he was indeed a champion of the patrician cause, ready single-handed to meet the attacks of the tribunes and to weather the storms of popular fury unaided and alone. Many a time under his vigorous leadership the tribunes had been hounded out of the Forum and the mob scattered like a beaten enemy, while anyone who dared to cross him soon found himself creeping away the worse for wear, or with his clothes stripped from his back, so that it was sufficiently obvious that, if this sort of thing was allowed to go on, there was little chance of Terentillus's proposal ever being passed into law.

The only one of the tribunes who was not cowed into submission was Aulus Verginius, who, accordingly, summoned Caeso to stand his trial on a capital charge. Caeso was not a whit disturbed; on the contrary, the summons was fuel to the flame of his haughty and uncompromising nature, so that with increased virulence he continued to oppose the passage of the law, harrying the mob and doing battle with the tribunes more vigorously than ever. Verginius made no attempt to check the headlong career of his intended victim; he allowed him to fan the flames of popular fury and to supply further matter for the charges he meant to bring against him in court, and continued meanwhile to urge the measure less in the hope of getting it through than with the deliberate intention of goading Caeso to lose control of himself. Caeso was by now a notorious character, and was often, in these circumstances, held personally responsible for things done or said – regrettably, in the heat of the moment – by the younger nobles.

Resistance to the proposed law was none the less not allowed to drop, and Verginius took every opportunity to continue his provocative speeches to the people. 'I presume, my good friends,' he would say, 'that you are now aware that the law you wish to see passed is incompatible with the presence of Caeso in your midst. Caeso – or the law: you cannot have both. But why say 'law'? It is your liberty that this man is trying to destroy – this tiger compared with whom the Tarquins were but lambs. Nobody though he is, you can see him playing the tyrant over you – but wait till he becomes consul or dictator!' Such words found ready listeners amongst the numerous people who complained of rough treatment at Caeso's hands, and now urged Verginius to proceed to business.

The day fixed for the trial drew near. Amongst the masses the belief was clear enough that liberty depended upon Caeso's being found guilty. In consequence he was at last forced to the disagreeable necessity of canvassing for the support of individual citizens, and went about amongst them accompanied by his distinguished friends. Titus Quinctius Capitolinus, who had been three times consul, reminded people of the fine record of Caeso and his family, declaring that never before in the Quinctian clan – or, indeed, in any other throughout Rome's history – had there been a nobler example of native genius which had ripened so soon into the best qualities of manhood. Caeso, he said, had been his finest soldier, and many was the fight he had fought under his eye. Spurius Furius testified that Caeso, sent by Capitolinus to help extricate him from a dangerous situation, had succeeded magnificently and that the subsequent victory was due to no one man more than to him. Lucretius, the consul of the previous year, still in the full glory of his recent victories, attributed to Caeso a share in his success and told over again the story of the campaigns and of Caeso's splendid service on raids or in the field, urging his hearers with all the eloquence at his command to remember that Caeso was a man of true quality, blessed with every gift of nature and fortune, who would inevitably exert the greatest influence on the affairs of any country where he happened to be, and begging them, in consequence, not to let him become an alien in exile, but to keep him as their own, in Rome. After all – he added – that fervid impetuosity to which they objected was diminishing daily as he grew older, while the wisdom and stability of judgement, which he at present wanted, proportionately increased. Steadily the bad in him was withering away, and the good growing to maturity: surely, therefore, they should allow a man of such sterling worth to grow old amongst them? Another man to put in his plea was Caeso's father, Lucius Quinctius, surnamed Cincinnatus. Afraid of adding to his son's unpopularity if he, too, did nothing but sing his praises, Lucius took another line and asked indulgence for his son's youthful extravagances, begging the people to pardon him as a favour to himself, who had never done or said anything to hurt anyone. He met, however, with no success; so strong was the feeling against Caeso that some were afraid of listening to Lucius's pleading; others were embarrassed, while others, again, countered with complaints of the rough usage they had received, and that so bitterly as to make very clear what their verdict would be.

Apart from the general dislike in which Caeso was held, there was one particular charge which told heavily against him. It was brought up by a certain Marcus Volscius Fictor, who had been tribune a few years previously, and the story was that this Fictor shortly after the epidemic, had encountered a riotous party of young aristocrats in the Subura; a quarrel broke out during which his elder brother, who had not yet fully recovered his health, was knocked down by a blow from Caeso's fist; he was carried home in a fainting condition, and subsequently died as a direct result of his injury. Under the consuls of the last few years he – Fictor – had not been able to obtain satisfaction for this atrocious crime. This story, told by Fictor at the top of his voice in the crowded street, caused such excitement that Caeso was nearly torn to pieces on the spot. Verginius ordered his arrest and imprisonment. The patricians resisted the order no less vigorously. Titus Quinctius loudly asserted that it was illegal to lay hands on a man who was shortly due for trial on a capital charge, before the case had been heard or sentence passed. Verginius replied that he had no intention of punishing the prisoner before he was condemned: he was determined, however, to keep him in custody till the case came on, to make sure that the people of Rome were not deprived of their chance to punish a homicide. The other tribunes were then appealed to, and decided on a compromise: exercising their right to protect the person of the accused, they refused to allow him to be gaoled and ordered that he should appear before the court; in the event of his failing to appear a sum of money should be pledged to the people. The question of the amount, being in doubt, was referred to the Senate, and the accused was detained in custody until it could be consulted. The Senate declared their intention of providing sureties, each for a sum of 3,000 *asses*. The number of sureties was to depend upon the decision of the tribunes, who fixed it at ten. Verginius then admitted the accused to bail. It was the first case on record of a defendant giving sureties to the people.

Caeso, having liberty of movement after these arrangements were made, left Rome for Etruria on the following night, and on the day of the trial his supporters pleaded that he had gone into voluntary exile. Verginius was none the less determined to try him in his absence, but failed to do so when the other tribunes, on being appealed to, dismissed the Assembly. Caeso's father was ruthlessly compelled to pay up; in order to do so, he had to sell everything he possessed and leave the city. He found a deserted hovel across the river, and lived there like a banished man.

In spite of peace abroad, the trial of Caeso and the dispute about Terentillus's proposed reform had, throughout this period, kept the whole country in a ferment. The tribunes were exultant; the patrician cause having received a severe setback from Caeso's exile, they felt that the law was as good as passed already; and it was undoubtedly true that the older patricians, at any rate, had loosened their hold upon the conduct of affairs. The younger nobles, however, especially those amongst them who had been hand in glove with Caeso, showed no signs of softening; but though their animosity against the commons was more bitter than ever, the methods they adopted to achieve their ends showed a certain moderation, which largely contributed to their success. As soon as the attempt was made, after Caeso's exile, to reintroduce the question of Terentillus's law, they took the field, as it were, with a great army of their personal dependants, bent upon the destruction of the tribunes. Immediately the tribunes tried to clear them off the streets, they went for them tooth and nail; which of their number was the doughtiest champion in the brawl – which of them went home with the largest share of glory or blame – it is impossible to say. The action was admirably concerted, and drew from the populace the angry comment that whereas they had had only one Caeso before, they now had a thousand. On the days when there was no business regarding the proposed legislation, these same young gentlemen behaved very differently: then, they were models of decorum; they would bid their friends of the working class good morning, talk to them kindly, and invited them to their homes; they strolled about the Forum with an air of good-fellowship and made no attempt to obstruct any meeting on different matters which the tribunes might wish to hold. In short, they showed no hostility whatever, either as individuals or as a class, except when the question of the reform came up for discussion; on all other occasions the young noblemen acted like convinced democrats. The tribunes, moreover, were not only able to put through their other business without opposition, but were re-elected to office for the following year; the people, for their part, were brought to heel without even a harsh word; of violence there was no question; it was, in fact, all done by kindness. Such was the successful policy by which the objectionable legislation was put off to the end of the year.

When Appius's son Claudius and Publius Valerius Publicola entered upon the consulship, they found public affairs in a more settled state. The new year had brought no fresh problems, Terentillus's proposed measure, and the possible passing of it into law, being still the centre of the conflicting interests of the two parties. The more the young patricians ingratiated themselves with the commons, the fiercer became the opposition of the tribunes, who did their utmost to discredit them by all sorts of slanders – that a plot was brewing, that Caeso was back in Rome, that plans were prepared for the murder of the tribunes and a general massacre, that the elder patricians had commissioned their young friends to get the tribunate abolished and restore the government to what it had been in the bad old days before the occupation of the Sacred Mount. There were two further causes of trouble: first, the fear of attack by the Volscians and Aequians, which by now had almost become an annual event, and, secondly, a new danger which unexpectedly raised its head much nearer home. Under the leadership of a Sabine named Appius Herdonius an army of slaves and exiles, 2,500 strong, seized under cover of darkness the Fortress on the Capitol, and butchered every man they found there who refused to join them. Some escaped in the confusion and ran down pell-mell into the Forum. Panic spread; cries of 'To arms!', 'the enemy is upon us!' rang through the streets. The consuls were in a dilemma: to arm the people, and not to arm them, seemed equally dangerous, as the cause and origin of the sudden attack were still obscure; it might, for all they yet knew, be a foreign enemy – or an attempt on the city by the angry mob – or a treacherous uprising of the slaves. They did their utmost to restore calm but without much success, for the panic-stricken mob was out of control and in no state to listen to orders. However, they did finally distribute arms, though on a limited scale – sufficient, so far as they could guess with their present inadequate knowledge, to deal with whatever might occur with reasonable confidence. What remained of the night proved, in the general uncertainty about the nature and numbers of the enemy, a time of acute anxiety, and the hours till dawn were spent in picketing strategic points in all parts of the city.

Daylight made the situation clear: Herdonius, in possession of the Capitol, was calling upon the slaves to assert their freedom, and proclaiming himself the champion of the oppressed with the object of restoring to their country all who had been unjustly sentenced to exile, and of freeing the slaves from their cruel yoke. He would prefer, he declared, to achieve his purpose with the approval of the Roman people; but, should that approval be withheld, he would stop at nothing and, if necessary, call in the Volscians and Aequians.

To the Senate and the consuls no doubt now remained about the magnitude of the crisis, though its implications were not yet fully resolved: they were afraid, in spite of the threats of Herdonius, that the whole thing might be a plot of the Veientes or the Sabines, and that at any moment, with so large a hostile force already in the city, there might be an attack by a combined Sabine and Etruscan army – or, again, that their traditional enemies the Volscians and Aequians might go one better than their usual frontier raid and, encouraged by the presence of enemy forces within the walls, venture an assault upon the city itself. But of all causes of alarm the worst was the slaves – the universal dread of having an enemy in one's own house; no slave could be safely trusted, and to show open suspicion was equally dangerous, as it might only exacerbate his hostility. So serious was the situation that it seemed beyond the power even of a united people to face it with confidence; it was as if a flood were sweeping over Rome, and drowning men had no thoughts to spare for politics; fear of the tribunes, fear of the populace was forgotten – it was a tame thing by comparison, a recurrent inconvenience which cropped up when times were otherwise quiet and now seemed lulled to sleep by the terror which threatened from a foreign enemy.

In point of fact, however, it was precisely the political division of the country which, in the present crisis, was most fraught with danger; for the tribunes were so blinded with passion that they insisted that the seizure of the Capitol was a mere piece of play-acting got up to divert the attention of the commons from the question of political reform; the friends and retainers of the nobility would, they declared, melt away even more silently than they had come, once the passing of the reform had proved the futility of their attempt. They then called the people from their military duties and convened an assembly with the object of getting the law passed.

Meanwhile the Senate was sitting, and the members were showing even more alarm at the behaviour of the tribunes than they had shown at the seizure of the Capitol during the night. Presently the news came that the men were laying down their arms and leaving their posts; instantly Valerius, leaving his colleague to keep the Senate together, hurried from the building to where the tribunes were holding their meeting. 'Come, gentlemen,' he cried; 'what is the meaning of this? Is it your intention to follow Herdonius and wreck the country? Has this blackguard who failed to raise the slaves against us been so successful in bribing you to support him? The enemy are on top of us – yet you want, it seems, to down swords and discuss politics!' Then turning to address the crowd, 'Friends and citizens,' he went on, 'though you feel no concern for your city or yourselves, fear at least your gods whom the enemy hold captive! Jupiter, Lord of all, Juno the Queen, Minerva, and all the company of heaven are beleaguered; an army of slaves hold in their hands the divinities who guard your country. A hostile force, many hundreds strong, is within the walls – nay, more: it is in the Citadel – up there, above the Forum and the Senate House: and what do we do? A public meeting in the Forum – a session of the Senate – senators propose motions – the commons vote – all as if peace and security reigned supreme! Does this look like a country in its senses – or is it lunacy? No, no, my friends: at a moment like this every man in Rome, regardless of rank, patrician and plebeian alike – consuls, tribunes, the gods themselves – should have marched sword in hand to the Capitol, to restore liberty and peace to the awful House where Jupiter dwells. Father Romulus, hear my prayer, and give your children the courage which burned in your breast when you wrested from these same Sabines the Citadel they had captured with their gold! Bid them go forward where once you led, on the road which once your soldiers trod. I will be the first to follow your divine footsteps, so far as a man may. Citizens of Rome, I take up my sword, and call upon every man of you to do the same!'

To this stirring appeal Valerius added that if anyone stood in his way, rank and dignity should count for nothing; regardless of consular authority, tribunician power, the sanctity of person as established by law, he would regard any man, anywhere, on the Capitol or in the Forum, who tried to stop him as a public enemy. 'If the tribunes,' he cried, 'forbid you to march against the traitor Herdonius, let them order you to march against me, your consul. I shall not hesitate to deal with them as the founder of my family once dealt with kings.'

It was clear that an appeal to force was imminent, and that the enemy would soon be enjoying the spectacle of civil war in Rome. Things had reached an *impasse*: it was as hopeless for the tribunes to continue their attempt to get the law passed as for the consul to proceed to the Capitol. Darkness, however, averted the immediate danger, and the tribunes, fearing the armed strength of the consuls, retired as night closed in.

As it was the tribunes who had incited the people to insurrection, the patricians, once they were out of the way, took their opportunity: moving about the city still crowded with people they joined groups of men excitedly talking, and put in a wise word or two, urging their listeners to realize the terrible danger into which they were bringing the country, and insisting that it was no longer merely a question of class conflict but that the whole nation, nobles and commons alike, together with the Citadel and its temples, the tutelary gods of every household in the city and of the City itself, was being surrendered to the enemy. The consuls, while these efforts were being made in the streets to bring the people to their senses, had gone off to inspect the defences of the gates and walls, in case of some hostile movement from Veii or the Sabines.

In the course of that night news reached Tusculum of the various troubles in Rome, including the occupation of the Capitol and the seizure of the citadel. Lucius Mamilius, who at that time enjoyed supreme power in the town, promptly called a meeting of his Council; the messengers from Rome were brought in, and Mamilius urged with all the force at his command that it would be wrong to withhold action till Rome sent a formal request for aid; the situation spoke for itself – her desperate danger, the oaths of alliance they had sworn in the sight of God, demanded that they should act promptly. They would never be given a better chance of earning the gratitude of their powerful neighbour. The Council voted in favour; troops were enrolled and arms issued.

By dawn the Tusculan contingent was in sight of Rome; they were taken at first for a hostile force of Aequians or Volscians, but when on their near approach it proved a false alarm, they were admitted into the city and proceeded in column to the Forum, where Valerius, having left his colleague to guard the gates, was already engaged in preparing his men for action. The fact that he was able to do so was something of a personal triumph; for he had declared that if they would allow him, once the Capitol was recovered and peace restored, to explain to them the real dangers which underlay the proposal which the tribunes were trying to pass into law, he would be their friend for ever: remembering the services his family had rendered to the people long ago and the name of Publicola, or People's Friend, which he still bore and by which he had, as it were, inherited the duty of protecting their lawful interests, he would never seek to rob them of their right to assemble for political purposes. The promise had its effect; the men followed him in spite of the efforts of the tribunes to stop them, and with the support of the troops from Tusculum the march up the slope of the Capitoline hill began. The Tusculans were as determined as the citizen soldiers of Rome; each contingent was the rival of the other for the honour of recovering the Citadel.

With attack imminent the enemy were ill at ease. Only the strength of their position gave them any confidence. Then, before they could pull themselves together, the assault was delivered. The Temple court was forced, but a moment later Valerius, fighting at the head of his men, was killed. Volumnius saw him fall and, ordering a party to cover his body, dashed forward to take his commander's place. In the heat of the assault the rank and file were unaware of their loss, grievous though it was, and the battle was won before the men knew that they were fighting without their captain. Many of the exiles stained the temple with their blood; many were taken prisoner. Herdonius was killed. The prisoners, both freemen and slaves, received the punishment appropriate to their rank and station. Tusculum received formal thanks for her aid, and an act of purification was performed on the Capitol. It is said that the common people flocked to the house of the dead consul and that each man tossed in a copper to enable his funeral to be solemnized on a more sumptuous scale.

With the restoration of peace the tribunes pressed the Senate to honour Valerius's promise, and the consul Claudius to justify the departed spirit of his colleague by allowing discussion of the law to be resumed. Claudius in reply refused to do so until the vacancy in the consulship had been filled, and the dispute continued until the day of the election, in December, when with the enthusiastic support of the senatorial party Caeso's father, Lucius Quinctius Cincinnatus, was returned as consul, to enter upon his duties forthwith. To the commons the election came as a shock; for they were aware that they would have in Cincinnatus a consul of great ability who was powerfully backed by the Senate and far from friendly to themselves – a man, moreover, who was the father of three sons, all of whom yielded nothing to Caeso in haughtiness and surpassed him in the ability to show restraint when reasons of state might make it advisable to do so. Cincinnatus began his period of office with a series of speeches in which his castigation of the Senate was even more vehement than his attempts to repress the commons. According to him, it was the feebleness of the senatorial party which had allowed the tribunes to hold office for an indefinite period and by their scurrilous talk and reiterated charges to exercise a tyranny fitter for a disorderly household than for the political life of a city like Rome. Courage, constancy, all the virtues which, in civil or military life, were the true glory of manhood, had followed his son Caeso into banishment. 'And what,' he cried, 'have we in their stead? The tribunes! Those men of many words, those trouble-mongers and fomenters of political strife, who by underhand methods get themselves elected for a second, or even a third, term of office and lord it amongst us as irresponsibly as kings! Did Aulus Verginius deserve less punishment than Herdonius, simply because he was not in the Capitol? By any just account he deserved more. Herdonius at least proclaimed himself an enemy – and that was as good as a call to arms; but this fellow told you there was nothing to fight about, and thereby robbed you of your swords and exposed you unarmed and helpless to a rabble of exiles and the fury of your own slaves. And you – with due respect to Claudius and his dead colleague let me say it – you marched up the Capitoline hill before turning *these* enemies of your country out of the Forum. Shame on you all! With the Fortress on the Capitol in enemy hands, with a leader of slaves and exiles desecrating by his hateful presence the holy shrine of Jupiter Greatest and Best, it was in Tusculum, not in Rome, that swords were first drawn, and nobody knew whether Mamilius of Tusculum or our own consuls, Valerius and Claudius, would strike the blow which would liberate our Citadel! He who once refused to let the Latins arm even in their own defence against an invader, would, on this fateful day, have been utterly destroyed had they not on their own initiative taken up arms to save us. I ask the tribunes – is *that* what you call "helping the people" – to deliver them, helpless and unarmed, into the enemy's hands to have their throats cut? Why, if the humblest of your people – *your* people, whom you have cut away from the rest of us to make a sort of state within the state, all of your own – if, I say, the obscurest of them all sent you word that his servants had possessed themselves of arms and were besieging his house, you would think it your duty to rescue him; and is Jupiter himself unworthy of any human aid, when ringed round by the swords of exiles and slaves? Yet these precious tribunes expect their persons to be sacred and inviolable, though God himself, in their view, is neither! Sunk as you are in a morass of impiety and crime, you yet continue to assert that you will get the law through before the year is out; if you do, then, by Heaven, it was a bad day for Rome when I was made consul – worse, by far, than when Valerius was killed.

'And now,' he ended, 'the first resolve of myself and my colleague is to take the field against the Volscians and Aequians – for God seems to smile more kindly upon this country of ours when we are at war. How dangerous those peoples would have been, had they known that a band of exiles had succeeded in occupying the Capitol, is pleasanter to guess from what has already happened than to wait for bitter experience to prove.'

The effect of this harangue upon the populace was very great, and to the senatorial party it brought renewed confidence that public affairs were at last moving in the right direction. The other consul, ready enough to support Quinctius though unwilling himself to take the lead, offered no objection to his colleague's initiative; though in carrying out the important measures he had proposed, he claimed his share of the duties of his office. The tribunes, for their part, were contemptuous: Quinctius's speech was, they said, all sound and no sense – for how could the consuls lead an army into the field, when no one would permit them to raise troops? Quinctius, however, had his answer ready. 'We have no need,' he said, 'to do so. We have the men already; for when Valerius armed the people for the recovery of the Capitol, every man took the oath to parade upon orders from the consul and to remain on service till orders came for his dismissal. Our instructions therefore are that all of you who took the military oath of obedience present yourselves, armed, at Lake Regillus tomorrow.' The tribunes, in the hope of releasing the men from their obligation, resorted to the quibble that Quinctius was not actually in office when the oath was administered. Fortunately, however, in those days authority, both religious and secular, was still a guide to conduct, and there was as yet no sign of our modern scepticism which interprets solemn compacts, such as are embodied in an oath or a law, to suit its own convenience. The tribunes, accordingly, were forced to give up hope of directly thwarting the consul's design; instead, they did what they could to postpone the departure of the troops – and all the more eagerly in that a rumour was abroad that the augurs had received instructions to go to Lake Regillus; this meant that, after all due and proper formalities, political questions would be able to be brought up there for public discussion, with the object of repeating by popular vote any measures which had been forced through by the tribunes in Rome. Everyone, they were convinced, would vote as the consuls wished, for there was no right of appeal outside a radius of one mile from the City, and the tribunes themselves, if they were present, would be subject like everybody else to the consular authority. All this was alarming enough; but worst of all was the fact that Quinctius was continually saying that he did not intend to hold the consular election, because, in his view, the country was much too sick to be cured by ordinary remedies: what was needed was a dictator. Political troublemakers would soon realize the fact that from the word of a dictator there was no appeal.

A meeting of the Senate was held on the Capitol; thither went the tribunes followed by an excited crowd, who with a deal of noise and shouting called upon the consuls and the members of the Senate to stand by them, but were unable for all their importunity to turn Quinctius from his purpose, until the tribunes had guaranteed to submit to the Senate's authority. Thereupon Quinctius brought up the demands of the tribunes and of the people, and a resolution was passed forbidding the tribunes, on the one hand, to proceed with the law that year, and the consuls, on the other, to take troops out of the city. As for the future, it was, in the Senate's opinion, contrary to the national interest that the same person, whether a tribune or anyone else, should hold office for successive terms.

In spite of the protests of the consuls, who were forced to acquiesce in the Senate's authority, the tribunes were re-elected, and the Senate, to allow no advantage in the game to their opponents, were anxious to secure the return of Quinctius to the consulship the following year. Quinctius, however, resisted this measure in the most uncompromising speech he had made since his election. 'Can I be surprised, gentlemen,' he said, 'that you have little authority over the commons? Your own actions nullify it: because the commons ignore a decree of the Senate against the re-election of magistrates, is that a reason for your wishing to do the same? Do you wish to compete with the commons in disregard of principle? Or imagine that political power is commensurate with irresponsibility? It was your decree, not theirs; and to ignore one's own declared policy is, for sheer levity, worse than to fly in the face of a measure passed by somebody else. You are merely copying the mob – whom no one expects to be politically adult; you are taking your cue in folly from the very people to whom you should be an example of political rectitude. Well, do as you will: I at least refuse to follow the tribunes' lead or to allow myself to be re-elected in contravention of the Senate's decree. As for you, Gaius Claudius, I beg you to put every restraint upon this irresponsible behaviour; and you may rest assured that I shall not resent your standing in the way of my election: on the contrary, I shall feel my reputation enhanced by my refusal of office, when standing for a second term would only have brought odium upon me.'

The two consuls then issued a joint edict that no one should vote for Quinctius in the consular election, and that if anyone did so his vote should be discounted. The consuls actually elected were Quintus Fabius Vibulanus and Lucius Cornelius Maluginensis. The former had held the office on two previous occasions. This year a census was held, but it was felt more proper to omit the usual ceremony of purification, because of the capture of the Capitol and the death in battle of the consul Valerius.

The new year was from its inception a stormy one. Apart from continued efforts by the tribunes to rouse the commons to revolt, there were reports from the Latins and Hernici of hostile preparations on a large scale by the Volscians and Aequians. Volscian troops, it was said, were already at Antium, and there was acute anxiety lest the Antiates themselves should break their allegiance to Rome. In these dangerous circumstances it was only with difficulty that the tribunes were persuaded to allow national defence to take precedence over party politics.

In the operations which followed it fell to Fabius to command the army in the field, while Cornelius remained in Rome in case the Aequians should repeat their usual tactic of sending raiding-parties into the immediate vicinity. The Latins and Hernici were called upon to furnish men according to the terms of their treaty, and the resulting force consisted of two-thirds allied troops and one-third Roman. Once the allied contingents had joined, Fabius moved from Rome and encamped outside the Capena Gate, where the ceremony of purification was performed; he then marched for Antium and took up a position near the town and the permanent camp of the enemy. The Volscians, who had not yet been joined by their Aequian allies, did not venture to offer battle but remained on the defensive within their fortifications. The initiative was taken by Fabius, who on the following day divided his force into its national units – Latin, Hernican, and Roman – each under its own officer, and ordered it into position close to the enemy's outer line of defence. He himself took the centre, in command of the contingent from Rome. His orders then were for all three divisions to watch for the signal, to ensure that the assault should be simultaneous – and also the withdrawal, if the order to withdraw should be given. Each division was supported by its cavalry, stationed in its rear. The attack, when it came, was thus simultaneous on three sides, and it was delivered with such vigour that the Volscian defenders were flung back from their position on the outer rampart, and Fabius's troops, forcing their way over all the defences, drove the remainder in a disorderly rout before them until the whole camp was cleared. The cavalry, unable to get over the rampart, had, up to this point, played little more than a spectator's part in the action. Now it came into its own: in the open ground it rode down the more or less helpless fugitives, and thus enjoyed its share of the victory. Both inside the camp and during the subsequent pursuit the enemy losses were heavy; but the quantity of plunder which fell into Fabius's hands was even more remarkable, as the enemy had been able to take nothing with them, scarcely even their arms. Had they not found shelter in the woods, they would have perished to a man.

The Aequians, meanwhile, had proceeded against Tusculum; picked troops by an unexpected attack under cover of darkness had captured the inner fortress of the town, and the rest of the force, to distract and disperse the defence, had taken up a position not far from the walls. News of the operation quickly reached Rome, and was passed on to the army at Antium. The effect of it was hardly less than if the Capitol itself had been taken; every man had fresh in memory the service Tusculum had rendered, and now she was herself in similar peril. The debt of honour must assuredly be repaid. In Fabius's mind there was but one thought: hurriedly conveying the material captured in the Volscian camp to Antium, he detailed a party to guard it and set off with all possible speed for Tusculum. The men were forbidden to take anything with them beyond their weapons and such bread as happened to be on hand: further supplies were to be sent from Rome by the other consul Cornelius.

The campaign continued for some months; part of his forces Fabius employed in operations against the entrenched position of the enemy outside the town, the remainder were turned over to the Tusculans to attempt the recovery of the inner fortress, which nevertheless proved too strong to be carried by assault. Eventually, however, the invaders were starved out, and, unable to hold out longer for lack of supplies, were stripped of their arms and equipment and sent 'under the yoke'. They then set out for home, a shamed and beaten army, but were caught by the Roman consul on the slopes of Algidus and all killed. The victorious Fabius withdrew to a place called Columen and there encamped, while his colleague Cornelius, now that the threat to Rome was removed, also took the field. Enemy territory was thus invaded simultaneously at two points, and the Volscians and Aequians became the unhappy victims of the two consuls' rivalry in destruction.

I find in most records that in the course of this year Antium revolted and that the situation was dealt with by Cornelius, who captured the town. However I should not venture to state this as a fact, as there is no mention of it in the older chroniclers.

The campaign was no sooner over than the senatorial party had to face another – this time against the tribunes, who accused them of sharp practice in keeping the army in the field with the deliberate intention of stopping the passage of the law, and reaffirmed, at the same time, their determination to see the matter through. Lucius Lucretius, however, the City Prefect, held out for the postponement of any measures the tribunes might take until the return of the consuls to Rome. A fresh cause of disquiet was the prosecution of Marcus Volscius by the quaestors Cornelius and Servilius on a charge of giving patently false evidence at the trial of Caeso. It was becoming known from many sources that Volscius's brother had never appeared in public from the moment he fell ill; indeed, he had never even left his bed, but after lingering many months had died of a consumption; moreover, throughout the period to which the witness had referred the crime, Caeso had not once been seen in Rome; many who had served with him stated that he had been constantly with them in the lines, and had never been home on leave. To prove this, many offered Volscius to refer the decision to a private arbitrator, and his refusal to accept the offer told heavily against him: in fact his refusal, added to the other confirmatory evidence, made his condemnation as certain as his own evidence had made Caeso's. Once again, however, the tribunes employed their delaying tactics and declared that they would permit the quaestors to hold an assembly for the trial only on condition that they first held one to discuss the passage of the law. Both matters, accordingly, were kept in abeyance till the consuls' return.

The two consuls with their victorious army entered the city in triumph, and, as nothing for the moment was said about the law, most people supposed that the tribunes had received a set-back. However, they had other plans; the official year was nearly over, and they were anxious to secure a fourth successive term, and with this object in mind they shifted their ground from the dispute over the law to a dispute over the coming elections. The consuls were as violently opposed to the principle of successive tenures of the tribunate as they would have been if a measure had been proposed with the express purpose of curtailing their own authority; but their opposition was unavailing and the tribunes carried the day.

During this year the Aequians asked for, and obtained, a treaty of peace. The previous year's census was completed – it was the tenth lustral sacrifice to be celebrated since the city was founded. The number of people registered was 117,319. It was a year in which the consuls won high distinction at home and abroad; their military campaigns they brought to a successful conclusion, and the political atmosphere at home they at any rate improved. The troubles were not over, but they were less acute than at other times.

The consuls for the following year, Lucius Minutius and Gaius Nautius, inherited the two main problems of their predecessors. They continued, as before, to obstruct the passage of the law, while the tribunes continued to obstruct Volscius's trial. Now, however, there were new quaestors – Marcus Valerius, son of Manlius and grandson of Volesus, and Titus Quinctius Capitolinus, who had thrice been consul – and both were men of outstanding personality and influence. Capitolinus, unable any longer to restore Caeso to his family or the greatest of her young men to his bereaved country, yet honoured the ties of kinship by unremitting warfare against the perjuror who had robbed an innocent man of the power of defending himself against a false charge. Of the tribunes, Verginius was the most active in working for the passage of the law; nevertheless the consuls managed to obtain two months' respite to examine its implications, after which they were to explain their views to the people on the sinister consequences it might involve, and then – and only then – allow them to vote. This was, at least, a breathing-space, and tranquillity was for the time being restored; but it was not to last long, for the Aequians broke the treaty of peace which had been made the previous year, entrusting the command of their renewed offensive to their most distinguished soldier Cloelius Gracchus. Under Gracchus they invaded the territory of Labici, whence they proceeded to Tusculum, doing heavy damage in both places and carrying off much valuable property; they then fortified a position on Algidus, where they were visited by Fabius, Volumnius, and Postumius who came as envoys from Rome to lodge a complaint and demand restitution, according to the terms of the treaty.

Close by Gracchus's headquarters was an enormous oak, whose branches gave a cool and pleasant shade. When the Roman envoys arrived, Gracchus said to them: 'Give the Senate's message to that tree there – I happen to be otherwise engaged.' The envoys turned to go, and one of them before he left exclaimed: 'May this holy tree and whatever gods there are hear me when I declare that it is you who have broken the treaty between us; may they listen now to our words, and give strength to our hands when, as soon we shall, we avenge the violation of all that should be sacred to God and man.'

The Senate, on the envoys' return, instructed one consul to proceed against Gracchus and the other to direct an invasion of Aequian territory. The tribunes proved true to form by trying to obstruct the raising of troops – and might, indeed, have succeeded, had not a fresh cause for alarm presented itself in an unexpected move by the Sabines. A large force of these people penetrated nearly to the walls of Rome; crops in the countryside were ruined and everyone in the City felt his safety seriously threatened. In these circumstances the commons were willing enough to enlist and despite the tribunes' protests two large armies were enrolled, one of which, under Nautius's command, took the field against the Sabines. Nautius fortified a position at Eretum and proceeded to send out a series of raiding-parties, usually under cover of darkness, into enemy territory; these parties, none of which was numerically strong, did so much damage that the Sabine raids on Roman territory seemed to have been comparatively harmless. Minucius, on the other hand, whether by ill luck or lack of enterprise, was less successful than his colleague; for after an unsuccessful, but quite minor, engagement he refused to take any further risks and stayed within the fortifications of his camp, not far from the enemy lines. Such timidity, naturally enough, was a fillip to the enemy's confidence, and they boldly attacked Minucius's camp during the night. The attack failed, but next day they set to work to wall him in with earthworks; before these were completed and every exit barred, five men were ordered out to ride through the enemy posts and carry to Rome the news that the consul and his army were under siege. Nothing could have been more unexpected. The city was thrown into a state of turmoil, and the general alarm was as great as if Rome herself were surrounded. Nautius was sent for, but it was quickly decided that he was not the man to inspire full confidence; the situation evidently called for a dictator, and, with no dissentient voice, Lucius Quinctius Cincinnatus was named for the post.

Now I would solicit the particular attention of those numerous people who imagine that money is everything in this world, and that rank and ability are inseparable from wealth: let them observe that Cincinnatus, the one man in whom Rome reposed all her hope of survival, was at that moment working a little three-acre farm (now known as the Quinctian meadows) west of the Tiber, just opposite the spot where the shipyards are today. A mission from the city found him at work on his land – digging a ditch, maybe, or ploughing. Greetings were exchanged, and he was asked – with a prayer for God's blessing on himself and his country – to put on his toga and hear the Senate's instructions. This naturally surprised him, and, asking if all were well, he told his wife Racilia to run to their cottage and fetch his toga. The toga was brought, and wiping the grimy sweat from his hands and face he put it on; at once the envoys from the city saluted him, with congratulations, as Dictator, invited him to enter Rome, and informed him of the terrible danger of Minucius's army. A state vessel was waiting for him on the river, and on the city bank he was welcomed by his three sons who had come to meet him, then by other kinsmen and friends, and finally by nearly the whole body of senators. Closely attended by all these people and preceded by his lictors he was then escorted to his residence through streets lined with great crowds of common folk who, be it said, were by no means so pleased to see the new Dictator, as they thought his power excessive and dreaded the way in which he was likely to use it.

Next day, after a quiet night in which nothing was done beyond keeping careful watch, the Dictator was in the Forum before dawn. He appointed as his Master of Horse a patrician named Lucius Tarquitius – a man who had the reputation of being the best soldier in Rome, in spite of the fact that he was too poor to keep a horse and had served, in consequence, as an infantryman. Accompanied by Tarquitius, the Dictator then appeared before the assembled people, to issue his instructions: legal business was to be suspended, all shops closed and no private business of any kind transacted; all men of military age were to parade before sunset in the Campus Martius with their equipment, each man bringing with him a five days' bread ration and twelve stakes. All men over military age were to prepare the food for their younger neighbours, who would employ themselves meanwhile in looking over their equipment and collecting their stakes.

The Dictator's orders were promptly executed: stakes were hunted out by the soldiers and taken from wherever they were found, nobody objecting to their removal; every man presented himself punctually. Then column of march was formed, all prepared, should need arise, for instant action, and moved off with Cincinnatus at the head of the infantry and Tarquitius in command of the mounted troops.

In each division, infantry and cavalry, could be heard such words of command or encouragement as the occasion demanded: the men were urged to step out, reminded of the need for haste, in order to reach the scene of action that night, pressed to remember that a Roman army with its commander had already been three days under siege; no one could tell what the next day or the next night might bring, and events of tremendous import often hung upon a single moment of time. The men themselves, too, to show their spirit and gratify their officers, exhorted each other to every effort, shouting to the standard-bearer to move faster and to their companions to follow him.

At midnight the army reached Algidus and halted not far from the enemy's position. The Dictator rode round it on his horse, to inform himself, so far as he could in the darkness, of the extent and lay-out of their camp, and then ordered his officers to instruct their men to pile their baggage in a selected spot and return to their ranks with only their weapons and the stakes which each was carrying. Then, in the same formation as on the march from Rome – a long column, that is – he so manoeuvred them as to form a complete ring round the enemy's position. Their orders then were to raise the war-cry on a given signal, and then to begin digging, each man at the spot where he stood, and to fix his stakes, so as to form a continuous trench and palisade. The signal soon came and the work began. The shout which rose from the Romans' throats told the enemy that they were surrounded, and carried beyond their lines into the beleaguered camp of Minucius, bringing alarm to the one and joy to the other. Minucius's men knew it was the voice of friends; with satisfaction and relief they told each other that help had come, and their sentries and outposts began to assume the offensive. Minucius himself, aware that instant action was vital, urged that the welcome cry meant not only that their friends had come but that they were already engaged, and had almost certainly started an assault on the outer ring of the enemy's position. So he ordered his men to draw their swords and follow him.

It was still dark when the fight began, and the relieving troops of Cincinnatus knew by the war-cry of their beleaguered friends that they, too, were in action at last.

The Aequians were preparing to resist the work of circumvallation, when Minucius started his offensive. To prevent his troops from forcing a way right through their lines, they were compelled to turn inward to face them, thus withdrawing their attention from the troops of the Dictator, who were, in consequence, left free to continue all night the construction of their trench and palisade. The battle with Minucius lasted till dawn; by that time the circumvallation was completed, and Minucius's men were beginning to get the upper hand. For the Aequians the moment was critical: the Dictator's troops, their work finished, promptly began an assault on the outer defences, thus forcing the Aequians to fight on a second front while still heavily engaged on the first. Caught as it were between the two fires, they soon gave up the struggle and begged both Cincinnatus and Minucius not to proceed to a general massacre but to disarm them and let them go with their lives. Minucius referred them to the Dictator, who accepted their surrender, but on humiliating terms: their commander Gracchus, with other leading men, was to be brought before him in chains; the town of Corbio was to be evacuated; the Aequian soldiers were to be allowed to go with their lives, but, to force a final confession of absolute defeat, they were to pass 'under the yoke'. A 'yoke' was made from three spears, two fixed upright in the ground and the third tied across them, and the Aequian soldiers were made to pass under it.

As the Aequians had been stripped before their dismissal, their camp, when it fell into the Dictator's hands, was found to contain much valuable property. All this Cincinnatus turned over to his own men exclusively; Minucius's men, and Minucius himself, got nothing. 'You,' the Dictator remarked severely, 'shall have no share of the plunder taken from an enemy who nearly took *you*.' Then, turning to Minucius, he added: 'Until, Lucius Minucius, you learn to behave like a consul and commander, you will act as my lieutenant and take your instructions from me.'

Minucius resigned the consulship and remained with his troops as second in command; his men were quick to appreciate the military qualities of the Dictator, and gave him implicit obedience; they forgot their disgrace in the memory of the service he had done them, and voted him a gold circlet of a pound in weight, and when he left them saluted him as their protector.

In Rome the Senate was convened by Quintus Fabius the City Prefect, and a decree was passed inviting Cincinnatus to enter in triumph with his troops. The chariot he rode in was preceded by the enemy commanders and the military standards, and followed by his army loaded with its spoils. We read in accounts of this great day that there was not a house in Rome but had a table spread with food before its door, for the entertainment of the soldiers who regaled themselves as they followed the triumphal chariot, singing and joking as befitted the occasion, like men out to enjoy themselves. The same day Mamilius of Tusculum by universal consent was granted Roman citizenship.

Only the impending trial of Volscius for perjury prevented Cincinnatus from resigning immediately. The tribunes who were thoroughly in awe of him made no attempt to interfere with the proceedings, and Volscius was found guilty and went into exile at Lanuvium. Cincinnatus finally resigned after holding office for fifteen days, having originally accepted it for a period of six months. Nautius, meanwhile, fought a successful action against the Sabines, adding defeat in the field to what they had already suffered from the previous raids. Quintus Fabius was sent to relieve Minucius on Algidus. At the close of the year the question of the law was again brought forward by the tribunes, but the Senate succeeded in preventing the submission of any measure to the popular vote on the ground that two armies were absent from Rome. The commons scored a point in obtaining the election of the same tribunes for a fifth term. Wolves are said to have been seen this year on the Capitol: they were being chased by dogs. It was taken as an ominous sign and the Capitol was officially 'purified'.

The next year, with Quintus Minucius and Gaius Horatius Pulvillus as consuls, began without trouble from foreign enemies, though political warfare continued as before. There was the old cause of dispute and the same tribunes to keep it alive. Passions were so inflamed that this time things might have gone to greater lengths but for what was, in the circumstances, the providential news of a night attack by the Aequians on Corbio, and the loss of the garrison. The Senate was convened, and the consuls received instructions to raise an emergency force and proceed at once to Algidus. The business of the law was for the moment shelved, but a fresh dispute arose, as always, about the raising of troops, and the efforts of the tribunes to obstruct it, in opposition to the consular authority, were on the point of succeeding when a further alarming report arrived that a Sabine force had descended upon Roman territory and was approaching the city. The tribunes had then no option but to let the recruiting go through, though only on condition that their number should thenceforward be increased to ten – a demand which they justified on the ground that, as they had been baffled for the past five years in their attempts to get Terentillus's proposal passed into law, the support they were able with their present numbers to give the popular cause was not adequate. The Senate agreed under pressure of circumstances, but stipulated that re-election of the same tribunes should not continue. To prevent this concession from being revoked, as others had been, when the campaign was over, elections were held immediately, and ten tribunes, two from each class – an arrangement which it was decided should become permanent – were appointed. Since the election of the first tribunes thirty-five years had passed.

Troops were then enrolled; Minucius proceeded against the Sabines but made no contact with them; the Aequians who, after butchering the garrison at Corbio, had taken the town of Ortona, were successfully engaged by Horatius on Algidus. Their losses were heavy and they were forced to withdraw not only from Algidus but from Corbio and Ortona as well. Horatius razed Corbio to the ground in revenge for its betrayal of the garrison.

The following year, when Marcus Valerius and Spurius Verginius succeeded to the consulship, was uneventful both at home and abroad. A wet season made grain very scarce, and a measure was passed opening the Aventine to settlement; the same tribunes were re-elected to

office, and in the year which followed, in the consulship of Titus
Romilius and Gaius Veturius, they lost no opportunity of urging the
passage of the law, repeating, in all their public speeches, that they
would be ashamed of the pointless increase of their number if during
the two years of their office this vital measure received no further
advancement than in the preceding five.

The agitation was at its height, when the alarming news arrived that
the Aequians were on Tusculan soil. In view of Tusculum's recent
services to Rome honour demanded that aid should be sent immediately, so both consuls were ordered out. They made contact with
the enemy on Algidus, their usual base; in the engagement which
followed the Aequians were heavily defeated, losing more than 7,000
men and a great deal of material and equipment, all of which the
consuls sold, to replenish the depleted treasury. The sale, however, was
not approved by the troops, and the tribunes jumped on it as an excuse
for prosecuting the consuls, both of whom, accordingly, as soon as
their year of office was over, were called to appear in court. The tribune Claudius Cicero acted as plaintiff against Romilius, and Alienus,
the aedile, against Veturius. In both cases, to the great indignation of
the senatorial party, the verdict was guilty, Romilius being fined
10,000 *asses*, Veturius 15,000.

The new consuls, Spurius Tarpeius and Aulus Aternius, continued
their opposition undismayed by their predecessors' misfortune, declaring that they were quite prepared to be found guilty by the courts, but
that the one thing which could never happen was the passage of the
law by the people and tribunes. Finally, out of sheer disgust and weariness, the whole question was allowed to drop, and the tribunes began
to adopt a less provocative attitude. They called, at long last, for a
truce in the struggle, and suggested that, if the Senate disliked popular
legislation, both parties might unite in allowing the appointment of a
board of legislators, consisting of plebeians and patricians, serving
jointly, and qualified to propose measures which should benefit both
parties and secure the liberties of each.

The Senate was prepared to accept this suggestion in principle,
though it insisted that the right to propose a law should rest solely with
the patricians. This being the only point in dispute, and the principle
being accepted by both sides, three representatives, Spurius Postumius
Albus, Aulus Manlius, and Publius Sulpicius Camerinus, were sent to
Athens with instructions to take down in writing the laws of Solon

and acquaint themselves with the way of life and the political institutions of other Greek communities.

The year, with no threats from abroad, had been a quiet one, and the next, when Publius Curiatius and Sextus Quinctilius succeeded to the consulship, was quieter still. From the tribunes there was not a word – a silence due, first, to the fact that they were waiting for the commissioners to bring back their report from Athens, and, secondly, to two terrible disasters – famine and plague – which had simultaneously struck the country down. Men and cattle suffered equally; farms were devastated; death after death drained the city's strength. Many distinguished families were in mourning: Servius Cornelius, Priest of Quirinus, and the augur, Gaius Horatius Pulvillus, died. To succeed the latter the augurs appointed Gaius Veturius – and were the more glad to do so because of this recent condemnation by the people. The consul Quinctilius died too, and four of the tribunes. It was a gloomy year, but free, at least, from the distress of foreign wars.

The new consuls were Gaius Menenius and Publius Sestius Capitolinus; this year, like the last, was undisturbed by foreign wars, though there was a recurrence of political strife. The return of the commission from Athens with a copy of Solon's laws led the tribunes to redouble their insistence that a beginning should at last be made upon the task of reducing Roman law to a written code, and to this end it was decided to abolish, for the one year, all the normal offices of government and to appoint instead *decemvirs* – a Board of Ten – who should not be subject to appeal. There was a certain amount of argument about whether men not of patrician birth should be allowed to serve, but the senatorial party finally carried their point, on the understanding that the Icilian law about the Aventine and all 'sacred' laws – those, namely, the breach of which carried the penalty of outlawry – should not be abrogated.

Thus it happened that 302 years after the foundation of Rome the form of government was for the second time changed; once power had passed from kings to consuls, now it passed from consuls to *decemvirs*. This second change, however, was less important than the first, as it proved of short duration; for the Board of Ten, after a flourishing start, soon proved itself a barren tree – all wood and no fruit – so that it did not last, and the custom was resumed of entrusting two men with the name and authority of consuls.

The *decemvirs* were the following: Appius Claudius, Titus Genucius,

Publius Sestius, Lucius Veturius, Gaius Julius, Aulus Manlius, Publius Sulpicius, Publius Curiatius, Titus Romilius, and Spurius Postumius. Claudius and Genucius were elected by way of recognition of the fact that they were consuls designate for the year, and Sestius, who had been consul the year before, because he had brought the measure before the Senate in spite of the opposition of his colleague. Next were the three commissioners who had gone to Athens: these were chosen partly as a reward for having taken so long a journey in the public service, and partly because it was felt that their knowledge of foreign institutions would be of value in helping them to frame a new code. The other four had no special qualifications – it is said that old men were chosen, as being likely to offer vigorous opposition to the proposals of their colleagues. The leading spirit of the whole Board was Appius, and it was to his popularity with the commons that he owed his influence – a remarkable change, indeed, in a man who had once been their most violent persecutor and opponent; but he had assumed, for the moment, a new character, stepping, all of a sudden, on to the stage as the People's Friend, and catching at every breath of popular applause.

The *decemvirs* sat in the courts in rotation, one each day, and the one on duty was attended by twelve lictors, his nine colleagues by a single orderly only. Amongst themselves they maintained an absolute harmony – such as has proved, on occasion, by no means to the advantage of the mass of a population which has no share in government; but at the same time their decisions were always perfectly fair and unprejudiced. A single example will serve: a corpse was found buried in the house of a patrician named Publius Sestius and produced before the assembly. Sestius's guilt was as obvious as the crime was atrocious, yet the *decemvir* Julius, who had the legal right to pronounce summary judgement, summoned him to trial and himself appeared before the people as his prosecutor. By this act Julius surrendered his own prerogative, increasing the liberty of the subject by deliberately curtailing the power vested in himself by virtue of his office. And all this, be it remembered, in spite of the fact that by law there was no right of appeal from the Board of Ten.

This prompt justice, of an almost superhuman purity and enjoyed alike by the highest and lowest in the country, was one aspect of the *decemvirs'* work; at the same time they were busy with framing a code, until a day came when, in the midst of tremendous public excitement, they published ten Tables of Law and, with a solemn prayer for heaven's blessing on themselves, their country, and their children invited the whole population of Rome to come and read the statutes which were there offered for approval. They were anxious to impress everyone with their conviction that, though they had been completely impartial so far as the wits of ten men could foresee how their provisions would work out, many minds engaged upon the problem might well have important contributions to make; it was their wish, therefore, that every citizen should first quietly consider each point, then talk it over with his friends, and, finally, bring forward for public discussion any additions or subtractions which seemed desirable. The object was for Rome to have laws which every individual citizen could feel he had not only consented to accept, but had actually himself proposed. Certain amendments were made, and when, to judge by what people were saying about the various sections of the new code, it had been reduced to as great a perfection as was possible, a meeting of the *comitia centuriata* – or Assembly by Centuries – was held and the Laws of the Ten Tables were adopted, which still today remain the fountain-head of public and private law, running clear under the immense and complicated superstructure of modern legislation. It was soon generally believed that, to complete the whole corpus of Roman Law, two Tables were lacking, and the hope of remedying this deficiency underlay the desire, as election day approached, of appointing *decemvirs* again, for the following year. The commons, moreover, who hated the word 'consul' as bitterly as the word 'king', had already ceased to look for support from the tribunes, because the *decemvirs* themselves were seldom rigid in their judgements, but, when an application was made to one of their number against the decision of another, the latter would usually give way.

The election was announced to take place in twenty-four days' time. Canvassing began, and was conducted with passionate urgency: even the leading men in Rome – from fear, no doubt, that, if they stood aside, a position which involved such tremendous power might pass into unworthy hands – could be seen in the streets buttonholing passers-by and humbly soliciting the votes of their old enemy the mob for an office which they themselves had exerted all their influence in opposing. As for Appius, the risk, at his time of life and after such a distinguished career, of losing his position goaded him to feverish activity, hardly compatible with the dignity of a *decemvir*. Indeed his behaviour was more like that of a candidate seeking election than of a magistrate in office: he blackened the character of the nobility, sang the praises of all the most socially disreputable and insignificant candidates, hung about the Forum in the company of ex-tribunes like Duellius and Icilius, by way of advertisement to sell himself to the mob, until even his colleagues, who till then had been his most devoted adherents, could not but raise an eyebrow and wonder what it all could mean. That there was a crack somewhere was all too clear: Appius was a proud man, and such excessive affability to inferiors could hardly be without some ulterior motive; such deliberate and self-conscious humility, such determination to reduce himself to the level of the populace hardly suggested a man in a hurry to retire from office – it was suspiciously characteristic of someone anxious to serve another term. The other *decemvirs*, not venturing openly to oppose his desire for re-election, tried to blunt the edge of it by a show of complaisance, and unanimously offered him, as their youngest colleague, the honour of presiding at the election – a piece of policy intended to prevent him from declaring himself elected, a thing which nobody except tribunes had ever done, and which, even in their case, was the worst possible precedent. Appius, however, was equal to the occasion: with the customary prayer for heaven's blessing, he accepted the presidency and then proceeded to turn his disability to his own advantage; by a collusive redistribution of votes he succeeded in keeping out the two Quinctii, Capitolinus and Cincinnatus, his uncle Gaius Claudius, a firm supporter of the aristocratic cause, and certain other equally outstanding men, and procured the election of infinitely less distinguished candidates, with himself at the head of the list. Nobody had believed he would dare to do it; however, it was done – and the impropriety of such conduct was clear to all who had any sense of political decency. Appius's colleagues were the following: Marcus Cornelius Maluginensis, Marcus Sergius, Lucius Minucius, Quintus Fabius Vibulanus, Quintus Poetilius, Titus Antonius Merenda, Caeso Duellius, Spurius Oppius Cornicen, Manlius Rabuleius.

From that moment Appius threw off the mask and showed his true character. At once, even before their term of office began, he set about the task of moulding his colleagues to his own pattern. Every day there were private meetings; plans for getting into their hands absolute and irresponsible power were secretly matured; they began openly to display arrogance, to refuse interviews without strict formalities, to be cold and repellent in conversation. And so it went on until 15 May, the date (in that period) upon which new magistrates entered upon office.

The day, the very first of their office, was made memorable by a terrifying revelation. Their predecessors had limited the 'rods' – the emblem of royal power – to one of their members at a time, each enjoying in rotation this signal mark of the dignity of his office; now, without any preparations, all ten of them appeared in public, attended each by his own twelve lictors. The Forum was crowded with lictors – a hundred and twenty of them; and, what was more, they carried axes bound up with their rods, an ominous sign which was taken as emphasizing the fact that there was no right of appeal. Had they been ten kings, the menace would have been no more terrible; and the fear they inspired in high and low alike was intensified by the belief that what they most desired was a pretext for beginning their bloody reign – that if anyone in the Senate or the streets spoke a word for liberty, the rods and axes would promptly be made ready, if only to teach the rest a bitter lesson. The right of appeal was gone; the people could no longer help a fellow-citizen wrongfully accused; moreover the new tyrants had agreed never to upset each others' decisions – unlike the first *decemvirs*, who had allowed their judgements to be modified on appeal to a colleague, and had even, on occasion, referred matters which might well have been thought to be within their own competence to a popular vote.

For a time one class seemed to have as much to fear as another; but little by little the whole weight of the terror began to turn against the commons. The nobility was spared, while the humbler folk were subjected to treatment at once arbitrary and brutal. For the *decemvirs*, personal favour was equated with justice; the man was everything, the cause nothing. They cooked up their decisions in the privacy of their homes, and pronounced them in the Forum; if a man ventured to appeal from one to another, he went away sorry that he had not accepted the judgement of the first. Worse still, there was a rumour abroad that this evil conspiracy was no temporary affair, but that the *decemvirs* had bound each other by a secret oath not to hold elections but by making the decemvirate permanent to keep for ever the power they had acquired. This was the fear which made common men in the streets look with anxious inquiry into the faces of the patricians, hoping to catch some breath of liberty even from their one-time enemies and dreaded masters, by terror of whose tyranny they had brought the country to its present pass. As for the senatorial party, its leaders hated the *decemvirs* as much as they hated the populace; they could not like the way things were going, though they felt at the same time that the commons were getting what they deserved, and were in consequence unwilling to help them. Their blind and greedy stampede for liberty had ended in servitude – very well: might it not be best to allow their sufferings to accumulate, till in utter desperation they came to wish the old days back again, with two consuls and everything as it used to be?

In the latter part of the year the two supplementary tables of laws were added to the existing ten, so that once they were passed, as the previous ones had been, by the Centuriate Assembly, there would be no further legal justification for continuing the decemvirate, and everyone was waiting to see how soon a date would be announced for the consular elections. The one thing which worried the popular party was how they were to recover the bulwark of their liberties, the tribunate, which had been suspended. Meanwhile, however, there was no mention of an election; the *decemvirs*, who had begun, as a popular gesture, by ostentatiously showing themselves in the company of ex-tribunes, had now taken to going about with an escort of young nobles. Groups of them blocked the tribunals; they bullied and robbed the commons; luck went to the strong – and if they wanted anything, they took it. Soon the rods began to be used: men were beaten, others executed. Cruelty had its reward, and, often enough, a victim's property was turned over to his murderer. The *decemvirs'* young toadies were easily corrupted by such pay, and, far from making any attempt to check their masters' brutal conduct, openly rejoiced in it; for them, personal immunity in crime was a more agreeable thing than national liberty.

15 May – election day – came. Technically, the *decemvirs'* term of office was over; but no new magistrates were nominated, and the Ten appeared in public with the same ruthless determination to dominate, and still with the insignia which symbolized their power. This was tyranny confessed, and nothing could any longer disguise it. Men mourned for liberty now gone for ever; no champion, it seemed, now or hereafter, would step forward in her defence.

Rome's spirit was crushed; but that was not all, for the nations beyond her borders were now beginning to despise her and to resent the fact that a slave state – as they thought her – should exercise imperial power. The Sabines invaded Roman territory with a considerable force, doing much damage, driving off cattle, and taking prisoners without encountering resistance; they then withdrew to Eretum, where they fortified a position, confidently expecting that political discord in Rome would prove their best ally, and prevent troops being raised. The messengers who brought the news were quickly followed by refugees from burnt-out farms, crowding the City and spreading dismay. The *decemvirs* met to deliberate, alone – the solitary Ten, hated by all alike. Then came a second alarm: the Aequians, from the eastward, occupied Algidus and began to use it as a base for raids on Tusculum, whence messengers hurried to Rome with a request for assistance.

With the City threatened on two sides, the *decemvirs* were badly shaken; driven to face the necessity of consulting the Senate, they issued orders for the members to be called, well aware of the storm clouds of hatred which were gathering over their heads. Nothing could be clearer than that the whole responsibility for the devastation of Roman territory and for the other dangers which now threatened would be laid to their charge, and that this would lead to an attempt to get rid of the decemvirate, unless they offered a united resistance and forestalled any concerted move against them by savage repression of the few bold spirits who seemed likely to take the initiative.

It was so long since the Senate had been convened for consultation that the voice of the crier in the streets calling the members to attend came to people almost like a memory from the distant past; they wondered what could have happened that their new rulers should suddenly revive a custom long fallen into abeyance, and were inclined to be grateful to the action of an enemy, which apparently allowed something, at any rate, to be done in accordance with free institutions. They looked in every corner of the Forum to see if they could recognize a senator, but hardly one was to be found; then they turned their eyes upon the Senate House and its empty benches, the *decemvirs* sitting there alone – a state of things which they put down to the fact that the *decemvirs*, not legally holding office, had not the right of convening a meeting, while the *decemvirs* themselves took it as a sign of the hatred in which their tyrannical domination was held. The moment was propitious, and the first step in the struggle to regain liberty might have been taken, if only the commons and the Senate had been willing to work together, the commons refusing to enlist just as the Senate had ignored the order to meet. This was what the popular party wanted, though they did not openly express their desire; but the patricians had nearly all left Rome; in public not one was to be seen, for finding the political situation unendurable the great majority of them had gone to their country estates, where they were occupying themselves with their private affairs, in the belief that the greater the distance between themselves and their tyrannical masters, the better was their chance of escaping injury and insult.

Finding their summons ignored, the *decemvirs* sent their officers to the senators' houses with the double purpose of collecting fines and of ascertaining if the refusal to attend had been deliberate. The officers reported that the senators were in the country, which the *decemvirs* were better pleased to hear than they would have been, had the members been in Rome and deliberately disobeyed the order. They then issued a second order, and announced a meeting for the following day. It was somewhat better attended than they expected, which the commons felt as a betrayal of liberty, as the senators had obeyed the summons of men who, apart from force, no longer held any official position just as if it had legal sanction behind it. We are told, however, that the views expressed during the session by no means matched the submissiveness shown by members in consenting to atttend; it is on record, for instance, that Lucius Valerius Potitus, after Appius Claudius had proposed his motion and before comments were asked for from the House, demanded leave to debate the political situation, and, when the *decemvirs*, with threats, refused, raised an uproar by declaring that he would go before the people. Marcus Horatius Barbatus crossed swords no less courageously, calling the *decemvirs* ten Tarquins and reminding them that it was under the leadership of the Valerii and Horatii that the kings had been expelled: it was not, he declared, the name of king that men resented in those days – how could it be, when religious orthodoxy applied it to Jupiter, when Romulus, their Founder, and his successors bore the name, which was still, moreover, used as the title of a religious functionary? No; what men hated was not the name of king but his pride and his violence. If these evil things were felt to be intolerable in a king or the son of a king, who was likely to endure them in men who held no legal office at all? They had better beware, he continued, lest by forbidding free speech in the Senate they set tongues wagging in the streets. Since neither he nor they held any official position, was it less legal for him to call a mass meeting of the people than for them to convene the Senate? 'Put it to the test,' he cried, 'any time you please, and you will soon see that the self-seeking and cupidity of tyrants is no match for honest indignation fighting to throw off its chains. You talk of the Sabine invasion – that paltry affair.

The real war which the people of Rome must fight is of a very different kind, if only you knew it: it is a war against those who, appointed to office in order to give us laws, have left our country at the mercy of their own caprice; it is against those who have abolished free elections, annual magistracies, which, by ensuring the regular transference of power, are the sole guarantee of liberty for all, and, without any mandate from the people, flaunt the insignia, and exercise the power, of kings. When Tarquin was expelled, patrician magistrates were appointed; later, after the secession of the commons, plebeian magistrates were added: on which side are you? Which party do you support – the popular? Not one thing have you done through the agency of the people! The aristocratic? For nearly a year you never once convened the Senate, and today, when we are met, we are forbidden to debate the political situation! Do not, I warn you, trust too much to men's fear of consequences if they rebel: what we are suffering now is worse than anything we fear may come.'

During this impassioned harangue the *decemvirs* were far from comfortable. Ignorant of what it might lead to, they could not be sure how far they could afford to express resentment or how far it would be safe to let it pass. But when Horatius had stopped speaking, Gaius Claudius, the uncle of Appius the *decemvir*, rose to his feet and made a speech in a very different tone, pleading rather than abusive. As his father's brother, he begged Appius, in the name of that father's departed spirit, to think of the civil society in which he had been born and forget the abominable compact he had made with his colleagues. 'I make this appeal,' he went on, 'more for your own sake than the country's; for Rome will seek her rights whether you and your colleagues are willing to grant them or not. Be warned: the struggle will be bitter, and bitter the passions it will arouse. I shudder to think what the outcome may be.'

Though the *decemvirs* had forbidden discussion of anything but the proposal they had themselves brought forward, they were nevertheless unwilling to interrupt Claudius, who ended his speech by moving that no action should be taken. All members took this to imply that, in Claudius's view, the *decemvirs* held no official position, and many of consular rank signified their assent. Another motion, apparently harsher, directed the patricians to proclaim an *interrex*; actually, however, this second motion was less uncompromising than the first, as the mere fact of taking a decision was equivalent to admitting that the men who

presided at the session held official rank, whereas Claudius, by proposing that no action should be taken, had thereby assumed the opposite.

The *decemvirs'* position had already been considerably shaken by
these moves, when Lucius Cornelius Maluginensis, the brother of the
decemvir Cornelius, rose to speak. He had been purposely kept as the
last speaker amongst the ex-consuls, and he now proceeded to feign
anxiety about the military situation in order to protect his brother and
the other *decemvirs*. 'I cannot but wonder,' he said, 'what strange conjunction of circumstances has brought it about that the *decemvirs* are
being attacked solely – or almost solely – by the men who themselves
hoped to be appointed to that office. Why, when during months of
continuous peace nobody ever bothered to question the legality of
their power, do they stir up trouble now – when the enemy is almost
at our gates? I can but suppose they are trusting to the fact that what
goes on in a muddy stream is less easily detected. Be that as it may; at
the moment we can hardly prejudge the matter, important though it
is, as we are occupied with something more important still, so I propose that we postpone discussion of the charge, brought by Horatius
and Valerius, that the *decemvirs* concluded their official term of office
on 14 May to a more suitable occasion: let us wait till the coming campaign is over and peace is restored, and then refer it to the Senate for
settlement. Meanwhile Appius Claudius must prepare himself to clear
up all doubts about the decemviral elections – which he presided over
despite the fact that he was himself one of the Board: he must tell us
whether, in fact, the *decemvirs* were appointed for one year, or were
intended to remain in office until the two supplementary tables of law
had been adopted. For the moment all our attention should be directed
to the defence of our country; if you think that the reports of enemy
activity are mere rumour or that the men who brought them – not to
mention the envoys from Tusculum – are liars, I suggest that you send
a reconnoitring party to investigate: they, at least, will return with the
facts. If, on the contrary, you believe the reports to be true, let us raise
troops at the first possible moment, so that the *decemvirs* may proceed
at once to such strategic points as they think fit. Nothing else should
take precedence of this.'

The younger members of the Senate were trying to force a division
upon this motion, when Valerius and Horatius sprang to their feet
again and addressed the house in an even more combative tone than
before, demanding a debate on the state of the nation, and declaring

their intention of addressing the people if illegal repression prevented them from speaking their minds in the Senate. Never, they asserted, would a handful of private persons, with no legal authority to back them, stop them from saying what they pleased either at a mass meeting of the people or in the House, nor would they ever yield to rods and axes which were a mere mockery of power. Appius saw that he must act quickly, for it was evident that the decemvirate was done for unless he met the attack with equal boldness. 'It will be wiser,' he said, 'to restrict your remarks to the subject of our motion.' Undismayed, Valerius refused to be silenced by a person without authority, whereupon Appius ordered a lictor to arrest him. Valerius moved to the steps of the House and was already appealing to the men in the street for protection, when Lucius Cornelius flung his arms round Appius, in pretended concern for Valerius and stopped what looked like becoming an ugly scene. By his intervention Valerius was then permitted to say what he wished to say, but as words were not followed by deeds, the *decemvirs'* position remained unshaken. Moreover, there was a further reason why no immediate action was taken: the ex-consuls and older members of the Senate still thought with abhorrence of the tribunate; they were convinced that the commons desired its restoration much more than that of the Consulate, and were therefore more willing to see the *decemvirs* retire voluntarily from office at a later date than to face another popular rising such as the hatred of their tyrannical conduct might cause. If, they thought, a moderate and cautious policy brought the consuls back into power without a popular upheaval, then, perhaps after a period of war, perhaps by means of a milder and more beneficent exercise of consular authority, the commons might be brought to forget the tribunes altogether.

The order for raising troops was then given. No objection was raised. The younger men answered to their names, as the *decemvirs'* authority was not subject to appeal. In consultation with each other the *decemvirs* arranged their duties and divided the army commands, assigning the most important tasks to their two most influential members, Appius Claudius and Quintus Fabius. On the assumption that the real struggle was at home rather than in the battlefield, they decided that Appius with his ruthless and uncompromising methods, was the better man of the two for crushing civil disturbances. Fabius was given command of the operations against the Sabines, with Manlius Rabuleius and Quintus Poetilius to assist him. Fabius was a lesser character than

Appius – not actively vicious, but unreliable; in former days he had distinguished himself both as statesman and soldier, but the influence of his colleagues in the decemvirate had so changed him that he forgot his honourable record and took the violent Appius as his model. Marcus Cornelius was sent to Algidus with Lucius Minucius, Titus Antonius, Caeso Duellius, and Marcus Sergius; Spurius Oppidus was appointed as adjutant to Appius in Rome, each to have full decemviral powers.

Military operations under the *decemvirs* were no less disastrous than their peace-time record had been. The commanders in the field were not incompetent, but they had made themselves universally hated: that was their only fault; for the rest, the whole responsibility for failure rested upon the men, who, rather than succeed under the command of officers they so detested, preferred to disgrace them – and themselves – by deliberately courting defeat. They were beaten by the Sabines at Eretum and by the Aequians on Algidus. In the silent hours of darkness they fled from Eretum and entrenched themselves on high ground not far from Rome between Fidenae and Crustumeria; the enemy followed up their retreat, but they refused to engage; trusting for their lives not to their soldierly virtues but to the ditch and rampart which protected them. On Algidus the conduct of the troops was more disgraceful still: the camp was lost, and the whole force, stripped of all its gear, fled to Tusculum in the hope that the compassionate loyalty of that friendly town would feed and support it – as indeed it did. So alarming were the reports which reached Rome, that the Senate forgot their hatred of the *decemvirs* and set about taking active measures for defence. Watch posts were established; all men of military age were ordered to guard the walls and man pickets outside the gates; arms and reinforcements were sent to Tusculum; the *decemvirs* were advised to move their men from Tusculum and hold them ready in camp outside the town; instructions were issued for the other force to leave Fidenae and proceed to Sabine territory, so that by assuming the offensive it might be possible to check the enemy's plans to attack Rome.

Military defeat was not the only thing the *decemvirs* had to answer for: there were also two revolting crimes, one committed on the battlefield, the other in Rome. During the operations in Sabine territory a certain Lucius Siccius took advantage of the feeling against the *decemvirs* to spread talk amongst the soldiers about the possibility of electing tribunes and refusing service. Getting wind of this, the commanders of the army sent him out to reconnoitre a site for a camp, with a party of men whom they instructed to take the first opportunity of killing him. The instructions were obeyed, but he did not die unavenged; for he was a powerful man, as brave as he was strong, and when his assailants closed in on him in a ring, he fought back with great vigour and some of them fell. The rest returned to camp with the story that they had fallen into a trap set by the enemy and that Siccius, fighting bravely, had been killed together with some of his men. At first the story was believed; but later a party went out, with the commanders' permission, to bury the bodies, and finding none of them stripped and Siccius, with his equipment intact, lying surrounded by the other bodies, all of which were turned towards him – and not a single enemy corpse or any trace of their withdrawal – they returned with Siccius's body to camp and unequivocally asserted that he had been murdered by his own men. Amongst the troops there was fierce indignation and it was determined that Siccius should at once be taken to Rome; this, however, was forestalled by the *decemvirs*, who hastened to give him a military funeral at the public cost. The troops grieved profoundly for the loss of their comrade, and current talk about the *decemvirs* was about as bad as could be.

Hard upon this followed the second crime, in Rome. Its origin was lust, and in its consequences it was no less dreadful than the rape and suicide of Lucretia which led to the expulsion of the Tarquins. The *decemvirs*, in fact, met the same end as the kings and lost their power for the same reason. What happened was as follows: there was a girl of humble birth whom Appius wished to debauch; her father Lucius Verginius, who was serving with distinction on Algidus as a centurion, was a man with an excellent record in both military and civilian life, and his wife and children had been trained in the same high principles as himself. He had betrothed his daughter to an ex-tribune named Lucius Icilius, a keen and proven champion of the popular cause. This, then, was the girl – at that time a beautiful young woman – who was the object of Appius's passion. His attempts to seduce her with money and promises failed, so when he found her modesty proof against every kind of assault, he had recourse to a method of compulsion such as only a heartless tyrant could devise. Taking advantage of her father's absence on service, he instructed a dependant of his own, named Marcus Claudius, to claim the girl as his slave and to maintain the claim against any demands which might be made for her liberty. One morning, therefore, when she was entering the Forum to attend the school, Claudius – the *decemvir*'s pimp – laid hands on her, and, asserting that she, like her mother before her, was his slave, told her to follow him, and threatened to take her by force if she refused. The poor girl was dumb with fright, but her nurse shouted for help and a crowd quickly gathered; for as both Verginius and Icilius were well known and well liked, there were plenty of people to support her, either out of personal regard or simply because the whole proceeding was so disgraceful. There was now no likelihood of her being carried off by force, as there were plenty of people to protect her; Claudius, however, called out that there was no need for the crowd to get excited, as what he was doing was perfectly legal. He then asked Verginia to come before the court. The bystanders advised her to comply with the request, and the two of them presented themselves at Appius's tribunal. The farce which Claudius then acted was of course familiar to the judge, who was, indeed, the author of it – the girl, he said, had been stolen from his house, where she was born, and palmed off on Verginius as his daughter. He had this on excellent evidence, and was prepared to prove it before any judge in the land – even before Verginius, who had been worse used in the matter than himself. Meanwhile Verginia – the slave-girl – was surely bound to go with her master. Verginia's advocates urged that her father was absent on national service; he could be home in two days if he were sent for, and it was unfair to involve a father in a law-suit about his children when he was not present to conduct his case; accordingly they asked that the hearing should be postponed till Verginius could return to Rome, and that meanwhile Appius, in accordance with the law he had himself sponsored, should grant the defendants custody and not permit a young woman to risk her reputation before her status in society was legally decided. Appius prefaced his judgement by remarking that his championship of liberty was made plain enough by that very law which Verginius's friends cited in support of their demand and added that it would prove a sure defence of liberty only if its application were fixed and invariable. Anyone was entitled to bring an action, and in other cases in which people were claimed as free, the demand was legal; but in the present case, where the girl was subject to her father, there was nobody else to whom the master could surrender custody, and for that reason he gave judgement that the father should be sent for and that meanwhile the claimant – Claudius – should not relinquish his right but should take charge of the girl and promise to produce her in court when the person said to be her father arrived in Rome. The judgement was patently unjust, but though there was plenty of muttering and indignation nobody ventured to speak openly against it.

At this juncture Verginia's uncle, Numitorius, and her betrothed lover, Icilius, arrived on the scene. The crowd made way for them, and most people were beginning to hope that Icilius's intervention might be more effective than anything else in thwarting Appius's design, when a lictor called out that, judgement having been given, the case was over, and tried to shove Icilius, despite his loud protests, out of the way. Even the mildest of men would have been enraged at such an insult. Icilius turned on Appius. 'Get rid of me?' he cried; 'only naked steel will do it – if you are to get away with your loathsome secret, and no one be the wiser. I am to marry this girl, and I mean to have a virgin for my bride. Call every lictor in the city – let them get out their rods and axes – I refuse to let my promised wife pass the night away from her father's house. You have made slaves of us all – you have robbed the people of their right to appeal and of the protection of their tribunes; but that does not mean you have the lordship of your lusts over our wives and children. Fulfil your savage pleasure on our backs and necks; at least our chastity shall be safe from you: assault that, and I will call upon every man in Rome to defend my bride – Verginius will raise the army on behalf of his only daughter – all of us will move heaven and earth to help us, and never shall you get away with the infamous judgement you have given unless you kill us. I conjure you, Appius, to think seriously where you are going. Verginius can decide what to do about his daughter when he comes; but I wish him to know that, if he yields to this fellow's claim, he will have to look for another son-in-law. For my part, in defence of my bride's freedom, I will die sooner than betray her.'

There was intense excitement, not without a threat of violence. The lictors had surrounded Icilius, but they took, as yet, no definite action. It was not, Appius declared, a question of Icilius's defence of Verginia; it was a question of a disorderly demagogue, looking in the true spirit of the tribunate for a chance to stir up trouble – which chance he would certainly not get that day. He had better realize, however, that his reckless behaviour was by no means being overlooked – on the contrary, his freedom from immediate arrest was a concession to a

father's rights – Verginius being absent– and to the liberty of the subject; and, to prove it, judgement in the case would be postponed.
Appius went on to say that he would ask Claudius to waive his rights
and allow Verginia to go free till the following day, adding at the same
time a warning, for the benefit of Icilius and his like, that, if the girl's
father failed to appear, the *decemvir* would certainly not lack firmness
in administering the law which he had himself proposed. He concluded by remarking that his own lictors were quite adequate to the
task of dealing with disturbances of the peace – so there was no need to
send for those of his colleagues.

A little time had now been gained, and Verginia's friends decided
that the first thing to be done was to get a message through to her
father. Icilius's brother and a son of Numitorius were accordingly
commissioned to go straight to the city gate and ride with all possible
speed to the camp where Verginius was serving, as the girl's safety
depended upon her father's punctual arrival in Rome. They were both
active young men, and having covered the distance at a gallop, they
delivered their message.

Claudius, meanwhile, was pressing Icilius to provide sureties for the
surrender of Verginia, and Icilius was doing his utmost to delay matters
in order to allow the messengers to get well on their way to the camp;
nevertheless, he replied to Claudius that it was precisely the question of
sureties that he was considering, whereupon people on every side
began to raise their hands to signify their readiness to go bail for him.
Icilius was touched. 'I thank you,' he said with tears in his eyes. 'I will
need your services tomorrow. I have sureties now in plenty.' This
being settled Verginia was surrendered on the security of her kinsmen.

Appius did not wish to give the impression that he had sat for the
sole purpose of this case, so he waited a little while to see if there were
any other business. There was none, everybody's attention and interest
having been totally absorbed in Verginia. Accordingly Appius went
home and wrote to his colleagues in command of the army telling
them to refuse Verginius leave, or – better – to put him under arrest.
Happily, the letter containing these vile instructions arrived too late:
Verginius had already got his leave and had started for Rome soon
after dark. The letter with its now useless orders to stop him was
delivered early on the following morning.

At dawn next day the excitement in the city reached a new height.
Verginius entered the Forum leading his daughter by the hand – he in

mourning, she in rags. With them were a number of women, and well-wishers in plenty. Moving about amongst the crowd, Verginius accosted one man after another and begged for their support – or, rather, demanded it as his due; for, as he did not fail to tell them, it was for their wives and children that he stood every day in the battle-line, and no soldier had to his credit a better war record than he. But what price patriotism, if his children were doomed to suffer within the safe walls of Rome the worst horrors of a captured town? Icilius made similar appeals for public sympathy; but the women's silent weeping was more moving than any words. On Appius alone – who was, indeed, more like a man demented than a lover – this touching scene had no effect whatever. He mounted the tribunal. Claudius, the plaintiff, started to complain of unfair treatment at the previous day's session, but before he could finish what he had to say or Verginius be given a chance to reply, Appius interrupted him. What he said by way of justification of his decision our ancient writers have recorded, some of them – maybe – truly; personally, in view of the enormity of the decision itself, I find all the accounts implausible. I can but state, therefore, the bare and indisputable fact, that Appius gave judgement for the plaintiff and declared Verginia to be his slave.

This monstrous decision was received with stupefaction, and for several minutes nobody uttered a word. Presently Claudius began to push his way through the group of women to where Verginia was standing – to claim his property. The women burst into tears, and suddenly Verginius shook his fist at Appius and called out: 'I betrothed my daughter to Icilius, not to you – I meant her for a marriage-bed, not for a brothel. Are men and women to copulate like goats and rabbits? Whether these people will endure it, I do not know; but I know very well that no man will who has a sword!' Claudius was being jostled away by the women and Verginia's other friends who were crowding round her, when an officer of the *decemvirs* blew his trumpet for silence. Appius then spoke, and his words were those of a man whose passions had turned his wits. 'I have incontrovertible evidence,' he said, 'quite apart from Verginius's violent behaviour yesterday and the abusive words uttered by Icilius – to which everyone here could bear witness – that throughout last night meetings were being held in the City for seditious purposes. Forewarned of the coming struggle I have therefore brought an armed escort with me – not that I would interfere with any law-abiding citizen, but simply to check disturbers of the peace, as the majesty of my office demands. It will be wiser to keep quiet. Lictor, clear the crowd. Let the master through, to take possession of his slave.' The loud and angry tones in which these words were uttered had their effect: the crowd instinctively shrank back, and the poor girl was left standing alone, a helpless victim. Verginius looked round for help, but there was none. In a moment his mind was made up: 'Appius,' he cried, 'if I spoke too harshly, a father's heart was to blame, and I ask your pardon. This whole business bewilders me – let me question the nurse here, in my child's presence; then, if I find I am not her father, I shall understand and be able to go more calmly.' Permission was granted, and he took Verginia and her nurse over to the shops by the shrine of Cloacina – the New Shops, as they are called today. Then he snatched a knife from a butcher, and crying: 'There is only one way, my child, to make you free,' he stabbed her to the heart. Then, looking behind him at the tribunal, 'Appius,' he said, 'may the curse of this blood rest upon your head forever!'

The uproar which followed the dreadful deed shook Appius profoundly. Instantly he ordered Verginius's arrest, but the knife was still in his hand and cutting his way through the crowd he succeeded, with the help of friends, in reaching the city gate. Icilius and Numitorius lifted the lifeless body for the crowd to see, with imprecations upon Appius's guilt and tears for the girl's ill-starred beauty and the awful necessity which drove her father to his crime. Women pressed round – were children, they cried, begotten and born only for this? Was this the reward of chastity? – and much more that grief, at such a time, will wring from women's hearts, the more pitiful to hear from their very weakness. As for the men – Icilius especially – one thought was uppermost in their minds, one theme, above all, on their lips: the loss of the tribunate and the right of appeal, and the tyrannous oppression of the people.

The atrocious conduct of Appius, combined with the hope that some chance was offered of regaining their liberty, kept the mob at fever pitch. Appius ordered that Icilius should be called to the court, then, when he resisted the summons, ordered his arrest; the attendants, however, could not get anywhere near him, whereupon Appius himself with a number of young patricians thrust his way through the crowd and told them to drag him off to prison. But Appius was too late; for already the press around Icilius had been joined by the popular leaders Valerius and Horatius; they stopped the lictor and said they would not allow the arrest of Icilius on the order of a man without any official standing, even if the form of the arrest were in accordance with law; if, on the other hand, force were attempted, they would be quite equal to the occasion. A riot at once broke out. The lictor made a dash at Valerius and Horatius, but the mob seized his rods and smashed them. Appius mounted the platform to speak, but was shouted down; Horatius and Valerius followed, and got a hearing. Valerius took advantage of the momentary authority he had gained to order the lictors to refuse service to Appius who had no official rank – and at that moment Appius's resistance collapsed and, in fear for his life, he gave his enemies the slip by wrapping his head in his cloak and disappearing into a nearby house.

Spurius Oppius hurried into the Forum by a street on the opposite side to help his colleague, and saw that vigorous action had won the day. The next step, however, was far from clear: everyone suggested something different; undecided and on edge, he agreed to each proposal as it came, but finally made up his mind to call a meeting of the Senate. This was oil on the troubled waters, for as nearly all the nobility were believed to be hostile to the *decemvirs*, the populace hoped that the Senate would bring their power to an end.

The Senate passed a resolution that the people must be carefully handled, adding that it was even more vital to prevent Verginius's return to the army from causing disaffection amongst the troops. For this purpose some of the younger senators were sent to the camp on Mount Vecilius to urge the *decemvirs* to do all they could to keep their men under control. As it was, however, Verginius caused a greater upheaval in the army even than he had done in Rome. His arrival was immensely impressive: long before he reached the camp he could be seen because of the crowd of some four hundred citizens who accompanied him out of sympathy for his lacerated feelings; his naked weapon was still in his hand, and his clothes were covered with blood. There was not a man but had his eyes riveted upon him. Moreover the presence in camp of so many men not in uniform made the number of civilians seem greater than it actually was. When the soldiers asked him to explain his strange appearance, for a while he was unable to answer, and stood weeping silently, while more and more men came hurrying and jostling to the scene. At last the excitement calmed down, and as soon as there was silence he told his whole story. Then, the story ended, he raised his hands as if in prayer, and made a moving appeal to his comrades. 'Fellow-soldiers,' he said, 'I beg you not to hold me guilty of a crime for which Appius is to blame. Do not turn from me as if I were the murderer of my child. Had my daughter been allowed to live in freedom, and like an honest woman, her life would have been dearer to me than my own; but when I saw her being dragged like a slave-girl to a brothel, she was already lost to me – and better, I thought, by death than by dishonour. It was pity that drove me to what looked like cruelty, nor should I ever have survived her death, but for the hope of avenging it by your help. You too, my friends, have daughters, sisters, wives; though my Verginia is dead, the lust of Appius still lives, and will grow the hungrier if it goes unpunished. Learn by another's sorrow to avoid it for yourselves. As for me, I have no wife – she died a natural death; I have no daughter – for, unable to live chaste, she met a piteous yet honourable end. In my house, therefore, there is nothing now for Appius's lust, and should he threaten me in any other way, I will defend myself as unshrinkingly as I defended my daughter's chastity. Do the same, fellow-soldiers, for your own selves and for your children.'

Verginius spoke with passion and he was answered by cries of sympathy from his hearers, and assurances that they would fail neither to support him in his distress nor to vindicate their own liberty. The civilians who were present echoed his complaints; they told the soldiers that merely to hear of these dreadful events was bad enough, but had they actually seen them, they would have felt them more deeply still; finally by reporting that in Rome the *decemvirs* had been overthrown – together with news which came soon afterwards that Appius had narrowly escaped with his life and had gone into exile – they prevailed on the troops to muster on parade and to march forthwith for Rome. The *decemvirs* in command, greatly alarmed by this turn of events and by the reports from the city, made hurried and anxious efforts to restore discipline. Mild methods proved useless, and were met with stubborn silence; attempts to exercise authority were greeted with the reply that they were dealing with men – and armed men at that. The whole force then marched in column to Rome and occupied the Aventine, where they urged every man of the common people they met to recover their liberties and restore the tribunate. Beyond this, no proposals were made for violent measures.

Oppius convened the Senate. A resolution was passed in favour of conciliatory action, as the occasion of the mutiny came from their own –

the aristocratic – party. Three representatives of consular rank, Spurius Tarpeius, Gaius Julius, and Publius Sulpicius, were commissioned to inquire, in the name of the Senate, by whose orders the troops had deserted and what they intended by their armed occupation of the Aventine, the abandonment of their military duties, and the capture, so to speak, of their own country. The troops, though they had their answer ready, had nobody who was qualified to give it, for as yet they had no recognized leader and each man individually shrank from taking on what would certainly prove a dangerous and invidious task; with one voice, therefore, they demanded Valerius and Horatius – let them be sent, and to them they would give their answer. Verginius, when the Senate's representatives had gone, pointed out to the troops that lack of recognized leadership had, only a moment ago, involved them in confusion over a comparatively trivial matter; an answer had been given, nor was it a bad one, but it was the result, none the less, not of concerted policy but merely of a lucky consensus of opinion. He proposed, therefore, that ten men should be invested with supreme authority, with the title of Military Tribunes. The proposal was accepted, and Verginius himself was the first man to whom the new office was offered. In the present circumstances, however, he was unwilling to accept it: 'Reserve your good opinion of me,' he said, 'until matters improve, both for me and yourselves. While my daughter's death is still unavenged, no position of responsibility can give me pleasure, and it would not be wise during the present political crisis to have the men most likely to get into trouble as your leaders. If I can be of service to you at all, the fact of my not holding official rank will make no difference.' Ten military tribunes were then appointed.

Meanwhile things had been moving in the other army, in Sabine territory. Icilius and Numitorius had not been idle; by reminding the men of the murder of Siccius, which roused them to hardly less fury than the subsequent story of the brutal attempt to rape Verginia, they got them to mutiny. Icilius, who had a good working knowledge of mob psychology, hearing that the army on the Aventine had created military tribunes, was afraid that their lead would be followed in the city elections and the same men be elected tribunes of the people. Now he had designs on the tribunate himself, so to prevent his fears being realized he had another ten military tribunes, with similar powers, appointed by his own troops as well, before they started for Rome.

They entered the city in marching order by the Colline Gate and proceeded straight through to the Aventine, where they joined the other army and directed the twenty military tribunes to elect two of their number for the supreme command. The two elected were Manlius Oppius and Sextus Manilius.

For the Senate the situation was an anxious one: they were in session daily, but spent more time in quarrelling than in fruitful deliberation. They bitterly blamed the *decemvirs* for the murder of Siccius, the monstrous conduct of Appius, and the disgrace of the armies in the field; finally they decided to send Valerius and Horatius to the Aventine, but both men refused to go unless the *decemvirs* abandoned the insignia of an office which had in fact terminated the previous year. The *decemvirs* objected to what they called a summary dismissal and refused to resign until the laws, the codifying of which had been the purpose of their appointment, had been formally enacted.

When the common soldiers were told by an ex-tribune named Marcus Duellius that the endless quarrels in the Senate were leading nowhere, they left the Aventine and moved to the Sacred Mount, as Duellius assured them that the senatorial party would never take the situation seriously until they saw the City empty; moreover the associations of the Sacred Mount would remind the patricians that the people were capable of firmness, and they would be made to realize that without the restoration of the tribunate national unity was impossible. The men left by the Via Nomentana – then known as the street of Fig Trees – and on the way to the Sacred Mount observed the same decency and restraint as their fathers had done some fifty years before. The army was followed by the whole civilian population – all but the too young or too old – and they were seen on their way by their women and children asking in piteous tones who they supposed would protect them now, in a city where there was no respect for chastity or freedom.

Rome was empty. The city, a moment before so full of life, had suddenly become a desert. In the Forum no one was to be seen but a few old men – when the Senate was sitting it was indeed a solitude. It was no longer only Horatius and Valerius who protested, or gloomily asked the senators what they imagined was to happen next. 'If,' was the cry, 'the *decemvirs* still refuse to yield an inch, will you let everything fall to ruin or go up in smoke? We would ask the *decemvirs* themselves what they suppose *is* the office to which they cling so desperately. Come now, gentlemen – do you fancy laying down the law to a blank wall in an empty house? Are you not ashamed to see your lictors outnumber the rest of us in the Forum? What do you mean to do if the City is attacked? Or if the populace, finding, as soon they may, that secession is inadequate to move us, rises in armed rebellion? Do you want your power to end with the collapse of Rome? The plain truth is that either we must have the tribunate, or do without the commons – for we ourselves are more likely to dispense with our patrician magistrates than ever they are with theirs. When they forced us originally to grant them the tribunate, it was an untried experiment; but now that they have tasted the sweetness of the power it confers, they will never willingly give it up, especially when we make no attempt whatever in the exercise of our own powers to lessen their need of protection.' Bitter attacks of this sort were so general that the *decemvirs* could not but bow to a weight of hostile opinion now almost universal; accordingly, they gave assurances that they would accept the ruling of the House and submit themselves to the Senate's authority. One request – or one warning – they added: namely, that their persons should be protected from the popular fury, lest their blood should set an evil precedent for the murder, on future occasions, of Senators by the people.

Valerius and Horatius were entrusted by the Senate with the task of settling with the commons upon what terms they would consent to return to Rome, and they were urged at the same time to see that the *decemvirs* were protected from the violence of the mob. They left the city forthwith and on reaching the Sacred Mount received a tremendous welcome as the champions of popular liberty, both at the outset of the recent troubles and in the sequel. They were formally thanked in a speech which was delivered by Icilius on behalf of the commons as a whole. They then proceeded to the discussion of terms, and asked what demands the commons proposed to make. Again it was Icilius who spoke, and his answer, in accordance with an understanding reached before Valerius and Horatius arrived, made it clear that the people based their hopes for the future upon equity rather than force. What they required was, first, the restoration of the tribunate and the right of appeal, to which they had trusted for protection before the *decemvirs* came to power, and, secondly, that no one should be liable to prosecution for having incited the army or the populace to recover their liberties by secession. Their only harsh demand concerned the punishment of the *decemvirs*; justice, they declared, required their surrender, and they threatened to burn them alive.

The commissioners from Rome replied to the following effect: 'Your demands have been dictated partly by judgement, partly by passion; as to the former, they are so equitable that they deserve to have been granted on our own initiative, for by them you seek only to safeguard your liberty, and not at all to put yourselves into a position to make irresponsible attacks upon other people. As to the latter, we can, indeed, understand your anger, but we must not therefore indulge it. Because of it you are tumbling headlong into that very vice you profess so bitterly to hate, and almost before you yourselves are free you are showing your desire to play the tyrant against your enemies. Will our country never have done with these everlasting bloody reprisals? A shield is what you need, not a sword. Surely it is enough for any ordinary man to enjoy his rights in a free country, hurt by none and hurting no one. Moreover, if the time should come when you can make yourselves feared – when by the recovery of your own magistrates and the laws they may pass you have power in your hands to fine us or exile us – then you will be in a position to judge every case on its merits. For the time being it is enough to seek the recovery of your liberty.'

The people were willing that the Senate's representatives should do as they wished, so they gave the assurance that they would settle matters in Rome and return without delay. All the *decemvirs* except Appius, when the demands of the commons were presented to them, were so much relieved to find no mention made of their own punishment that they agreed unconditionally. Appius, on the contrary, the most savage and the worst hated of them all, measured the revengefulness and brutality of others by what he found in his own breast. 'I know well enough,' he said, 'what is coming to us. It is obvious that the fight against us is postponed only till our enemies have arms. Hatred must have its offering of blood. Not even I hesitate any longer to resign my powers.' Decrees were then passed by the Senate ordering, first, the resignation of all the *decemvirs* at the earliest possible moment; secondly that tribunes should be elected under the presidency of the Pontifex Maximus, Quintus Fabius; thirdly, that no one should be liable to prosecution either for the mutiny in the army or for the departure of the commons to the Sacred Mount. The Senate then adjourned and the *decemvirs* publicly handed in their resignations amidst general rejoicing. A report of all these proceedings was sent to the Sacred Mount, and the men who carried it were escorted on their way by every man left in Rome; they were met by a similar happy crowd from the camp and mutual congratulations ensued upon the restoration of liberty and domestic peace. The official representatives who had brought the news addressed the people: 'In the name of our country – and may she, and you, for ever prosper,' they said, 'we invite you to return to your homes, your wives, and your children. One thing we beg: here, though much has been needed to support so many of you, you have exercised exemplary self-control and nobody's land is any the worse for your presence; observe, then, the same discipline when you enter the city. Go back now to the Aventine. It has happy associations for you, as it was the place where you took the first step on your road to political liberty. There, once more, you will elect your tribunes, and the Pontifex Maximus will be present to preside at the election.' All this was joyfully and unanimously approved. Without delay the march to Rome began, soldiers and civilians alike exchanging with all whom they met expressions of triumph and delight. Once in the city, the troops proceeded to the Aventine in silence, and there, under the presidency of Quintus Fabius, the election was held.

First on the list of new tribunes was Lucius Verginius; then came Icilius and Publius Numitorius, the great-uncle of Verginia, the two men responsible for the secession; then Gaius Sicinius, son of the Sicinius who is said to have been the first tribune elected on the Sacred Mount; then Marcus Duellius, who had served with distinction in the same capacity before the period of the *decemvirs* and in the subsequent conflict with them had remained a staunch friend of the people. The other five – Marcus Titinius, Marcus Pomponius, Gaius Apronius, Publius Villius, and Gaius Oppius – were elected on promise rather than on past performance.

As soon as he entered upon office Icilius laid a motion before the commons that no man should be held guilty at law for defying the authority of the *decemvirs*. The motion was carried, and immediately afterwards Duellius got another motion through for the election of consuls, with the right of appeal. All these transactions took place in the Circus Flaminius – then known as the Flaminian Meadows.

Valerius and Horatius were elected to the consulship through an *interrex*, and began their official duties forthwith. Their policy had a popular bias without being anti-aristocratic; it did not, however, avoid giving offence to the aristocratic party, who felt every measure intended to safeguard popular liberty to be a diminution of their own power. Their first measure concerned the disputed legal question as to whether or not the Senate was bound by resolutions passed by the commons: with a view to this, they put through a bill, at the Centuriate Assembly, to the effect that any resolution passed by the commons at their Tribal Assembly should be binding upon the whole people, thereby giving a cutting edge to all measures brought forward by the tribunes. As to the right of appeal – the one real safeguard of liberty – they went further than the mere restoration of what it had been before its abolition by the *decemvirs*, and strengthened the whole basis on which it stood by the solemn enactment of a new measure, which provided that no one should declare the election of any magistrate without the right of appeal, and that anyone who did so could be killed without offence to law or religion. Then, having adequately strengthened the position of the commons by the two safeguards of the tribunate and the appeal, they revived, in the interest of the tribunes themselves the almost forgotten principle of their 'sacrosanctity'; this they did by reintroducing certain religious sanctions long fallen into disuse, and then proceeded to make the principle of inviolability legal as well as religious by a further enactment that an assault upon a tribune, an aedile, or a member of the board of Ten Judges should carry a penalty of death or exile, the property of the offender to be sold by public auction. Jurists deny that by this law anyone is sacrosanct; it means, they maintain, that an assault upon any of these officials carries a penalty of outlawry – the guilty person being, in the legal phrase 'forfeit to Jupiter'. Thus an aedile may be arrested and imprisoned by a superior magistrate, an act which, though illegal according to the law in question, is none the less a proof that aediles are not considered as sacrosanct. The tribunes, on the other hand, are – according to this school of thought – sacrosanct by virtue of an ancient oath sworn by the people at the time of the original creation of this magistracy. There were other jurists who offered a different interpretation: according to these, the consuls and praetors (as being created under the same auspices as the consuls) were also protected by this law, the consuls being known as 'judges'. But the fallacy here lies in the fact that a consul was not called a 'judge' at that period, but a 'praetor'. It was Horatius and Valerius, too, who started the practice of having the decrees of the Senate delivered to the plebeian aediles in the temple of Ceres, whereas previously they had been suppressed or falsified by the consuls to suit their own convenience.

The tribune Duellius then brought forward a motion that anyone who left the people without tribunes or declared the election of magistrates without the right of appeal should be first scourged and then beheaded. The motion was passed. All these measures were disliked by the aristocratic party, but they offered no definite opposition as, up to the present, no attacks had yet been made against individuals.

Political liberty was now firmly established on the basis of the restored tribunate, and the tribunes felt themselves strong enough to proceed against individuals. Their first victim was, of course, Appius, and Verginius was put up to conduct the case against him. The summons was issued. Appius entered the Forum with a strong escort of young patricians, and the sight of him there with his satellites was a bitter reminder of the frightful tyranny which had so recently been suppressed. Verginius spoke. 'Oratory', he said, 'is all very well when there are no facts to go on: it was invented to conceal our doubts. I will not waste your time in presenting a case against a man from whose bestial conduct you found freedom by force of arms, nor will I let him at this juncture add to his other crimes the impudent hypocrisy of defending himself. Very well then: I have nothing to say at the moment, Appius, of all the countless vile offences which during the past two years you have committed against the dictates of decency and law; one charge only I bring against you: unless you can produce a referee to establish your innocence of having illegally given custody of a free person to one who claimed her as his slave, I shall order you to prison.' What the people's verdict would be was all too obvious, and in the protection of the tribunes Appius could have no hope whatever; nevertheless he called on the tribunes and, when none of them offered to stay the proceedings and he was arrested by an officer of the law, he cried out: 'I appeal'. The sound of the word, so intimately associated with popular liberty, on the lips of the man who so short a time before had pronounced that monstrous judgement which no one could forget, struck everybody dumb. Soon every man present was muttering to himself indignant comments – there were gods in heaven, who did not neglect the doings of this world – punishment, though late not light, found out at last the proud and remorseless amongst men. Here, they murmured, was the very man appealing who had robbed the nation of the right to do so – begging for the people's aid, when he himself had trampled under foot every privilege they possessed – being hauled to prison without the protection which every

man in a free society should enjoy, in just retribution for his own foul
deed.

Suddenly above the murmurings of the crowd Appius's own voice
was heard, raised in supplication to the people he had once enslaved.
'Will you not remember,' he said, 'the services my family has rendered our country in politics and war, or my own unhappy involve-
ment in the popular cause? It was for that that I braved the Senate's
displeasure and resigned the consulship, simply to codify the laws in a
form that would be just to all. And what of those laws themselves –
the Twelve Tables – which will be there for ever to protect your interests, while I, who am responsible for them, am taken to prison? As
for my own personal acts – good or bad – I mean to put them to the
proof when I am given the chance formally to plead my cause; for the
moment I confine myself to demanding the common privilege of a
Roman citizen accused of an offence to speak, and to await the judgement of the people. You hate me, but I am not so afraid of your hatred
as to have no confidence in the mercy and the sense of justice of my
fellow-citizens. I will call a second time upon the tribunes if I am taken
to prison unheard, and I warn you not to imitate those whom you
hate. Moreover, if the tribunes declare that they are bound not to
listen to an appeal – the very crime with which they charge the *decemvirs* – then I appeal to the people, and invoke the protection of the
laws passed this year for the safeguarding of this privilege, on the
motion both of consuls and of tribunes. Who – I ask you – do you
expect to appeal, if not a man who has been refused the right of pleading his cause and has never been legally found guilty? What humble
working man do you suppose will find protection in the laws of our
country, if I cannot? Your treatment of me will show clearly enough
whether it is liberty or tyranny which has been strengthened by the
new legislation, and whether the right of appeal either to the tribunes
or to the people against injustice in high places is a reality or a mere
parade of empty words.'

Verginius replied: 'This man – Appius Claudius – is not as other
men: he alone can claim no share in the beneficence of law; he alone
has no part in the mutual compact of civilized men. Turn your eyes
to the tribunal where he sat, like a murderous brigand in his stronghold – remember him there, a self-appointed tyrant in perpetuity,
robbing, beating, killing, threatening us all with his bloody rods and
axes, attended, in his contempt for God and man, by the twelve exe-

cutioners he called his lictors, and turning, at last, from rapine and murder to the lust which drove him, before the eyes of the Roman people, to tear a freeborn girl from her father's arms and give her to his pimp, like a helpless prisoner of war. From that tribunal he pronounced the savage decree – the judgement of unspeakable baseness – which armed a father's hand against his daughter, and ordered to gaol her lover and her uncle even as they were lifting her body from which life had scarcely flown – and why? in anger for her death? No indeed; but in rage for the loss of his own pleasure. Appius, the prison which you called in savage jest the working man's home, was built for you as well as for him; appeal as often as you will, and I, as often, challenge you to prove before a referee that you did not give custody of a free citizen to a person who claimed her as his slave. If you refuse to do this, I shall take it as a verdict against you and order you to prison.'

Appius was flung into gaol. No one, indeed, raised a protest, but there was, nevertheless, considerable uneasiness in most people's minds. Appius was a very distinguished man – and might not this summary treatment of him be a sign that the newly won freedom of the common people had already gone too far? The tribune fixed a date for the formal legal proceedings.

Meanwhile representatives from the Latins and the Hernici arrived in Rome to express the good wishes of their governments on the restoration of political harmony. To mark the occasion they brought with them a gold crown, to be presented to Jupiter, Lord of Heaven and Earth, in his temple on the Capitol. The crown was a small thing in itself, as neither state was wealthy, the offices of religion being observed in each with piety rather than splendour.

The same envoys also brought the news that the Aequians and Volscians were again mobilizing on a large scale, and steps were at once taken to meet the threat: the consuls, on the Senate's instructions, settled their respective commands, Horatius obtaining control of operations against the Sabines, Valerius against the Aequians and Volscians. Troops had then to be raised, and as soon as the order for enlistment went out, so great was the popular enthusiasm that in addition to the younger men a large number of volunteers who had already served their time presented themselves for further service, so that the resulting force was, by the admixture of veteran troops, not only stronger in numbers than usual but also better in quality. Before it left the city, the consuls had the decemviral laws – the 'Twelve Tables' – engraved on bronze and permanently exhibited in a place where all could read them. Some historians declare that this service was performed by the aediles, acting on orders from the tribunes.

Appius's uncle, Gaius Claudius, had always strongly disapproved of the *decemvirs'* crimes, especially of the tyrannical behaviour of his nephew, and to mark his disapproval had retired to his old home at Regillus; but now, in spite of his advanced age, he returned to Rome to plead for the man whose vicious conduct had been the cause of his exile. Dressed as a mourner, he appeared in the Forum with his dependants and various other members of his clan and solicited the support of everyone he chanced to fall in with, begging them not to brand the Claudian family with the ignominy of imprisonment and chains. Appius, he urged, was a man whose bust would be honoured by future generations as that of the great founder of Roman law, and it was intolerable to think that such a man should be languishing in gaol amongst sneak-thieves and cut-throats. 'Forget your anger,' he said, 'for a little while, and try to see things as they really are; it would surely be better to forgive one man at the entreaty of so many members of the Claudian family than to let hatred of one stop your ears to the prayers of all. I am doing this for the sake of my family and my name; Appius was no friend of mine, and I never made up my quarrel with him – but he is in trouble, and I wish to help him. By your own determination you recovered your liberties; aristocracy and people have composed their differences, and harmony between them can be maintained on firm foundations only if you show clemency.'

Some were more affected by the old man's loyalty to his family than by the actual object of his appeal; Verginius, however, was adamant: he insisted that he and his daughter were the only worthy objects of pity; other men should listen not to the entreaties of those born tyrants the Claudii, but of Verginia's kinsmen, the three tribunes, who held their position solely in the interest of the common people whose loyal support they now implored. Of the two appeals for pity, that of Verginius was felt to be more just. It was the end of all hope for Appius: he refused to face his trial, and killed himself.

Immediately afterwards a warrant was issued by Numitorius for the arrest of Spurius Oppius, who, after Appius, was the chief object of popular detestation, as he had been in Rome when his colleague gave the infamous judgement in the case of Verginia. Actually, however, the feeling against Oppius was due less to his failure to prevent the miscarriage of justice than to a piece of brutality for which he was himself responsible. A witness was produced to prove the fact: he was an old soldier who had served in twenty-seven campaigns and had been eight times decorated. Wearing his decorations so that everyone present could see them, he tore his tunic open and revealed his back frightfully disfigured by a beating, and declared that if Oppius, the defendant, could mention any misdemeanour of which he had been guilty to deserve such punishment, he would let him repeat the beating, even though he no longer had any official authority to do so. Like his colleague, Oppius was flung into gaol, and put an end to his life before formal judicial proceedings could begin. His property, together with that of Appius, was confiscated by the tribunes. The remaining *decemvirs* went into exile, with fortfeiture of all they possessed. Marcus Claudius, the man who had claimed Verginia, was prosecuted and condemned, but was spared the extreme penalty at the request of Verginius himself and went into exile at Tibur. Thus not a single man who had any share in the guilt of Verginia's death remained, and her ghost, which so long had wandered from house to house in search of satisfaction, found rest at last.

To the aristocratic party the preceding events had caused something like terror, for the tribunes, like the *decemvirs* before them, had already a murderous gleam in their eyes. It was a relief, therefore, when the tribune Duellius took steps to place a salutary check upon the excessive powers they had acquired. 'Our battle for freedom,' he said, 'is already won, and we have punished our enemies enough. For the rest of the year I do not propose to allow any man to be prosecuted or imprisoned. Now that the recent offences of our political enemies have been sufficiently atoned for by the punishment of the *decemvirs*, there is no point in raking up old and forgotten troubles; and, so far as the future is concerned, the unceasing care of both consuls in the safeguarding of your liberties will ensure that no lawless act calling for the intervention of the tribunes will be attempted.' This move towards a more moderate policy relieved the natural apprehensions of the nobility; at the same time, however, it increased their dislike of the consuls who, in their view, had shown a disproportionate interest in the popular cause: so much so, in fact, that the safety and dignity of the patrician order had been the concern of the tribunes rather than of their own representative magistrates, and their opponents had wearied of revenge before the consuls had shown spirit enough to attempt any

check upon the arbitrary use of their powers. It was commonly said
that the Senate had shown weakness in supporting the consuls' policy
– and perhaps truly; for there was no doubt that the political situation,
difficult as it was, had compelled them to temporize.

The position of the commons was now defined, and the settlement
of domestic affairs enabled the consuls to take up their respective
military commands. The Volscians and Aequians had already joined
forces on Algidus, and Valerius, with proper caution, did not immediately engage them; had he done so, one can well believe that, in
view of the effect of the *decemvirs'* disastrous command in the previous
campaign upon the morale of the Romans and their enemies, his rashness would have cost him dear. Taking up a position a mile from the
enemy, he waited within his defences, and though enemy troops on
several occasions advanced into the open ground between their respective positions, the challenge was not accepted. Waiting around for
a fight which never came off proving tedious to the Volscian and
Aequian forces, they took the Roman reluctance to engage as a confession of defeat and dispersed on plundering raids against the Latins
and Hernici, leaving to protect their original position a small garrison
quite inadequate for a general engagement. This was Valerius's opportunity: reversing the previous position of affairs, he marched out from
his entrenchments and assumed the offensive, the enemy, for their part,
refusing to engage from an uncomfortable sense of their numerical
inferiority. This was a great fillip to the morale of the Romans, to
whom an enemy too scared to leave the cover of his entrenchments
seemed already as good as beaten. They did not withdraw until nightfall, having stood to arms throughout the day. Eating their rations that
evening they were full of confidence, in marked contrast to the enemy
troops, who in great alarm sent riders all over the countryside to recall
their comrades who had gone off on the raids. Some were successful,
and the raiders who had not gone far afield returned; no contact was
made with the rest.

At dawn next morning the Romans again took the field with the
intention of assaulting the enemy's defences if he still refused to engage
in the open, and when the greater part of the day had passed without
any move being made, Valerius ordered his men to the attack, and the
advance began. Nothing was better calculated to arouse the indignation of the Volscians and Aequians than to find their victorious armies
forced to cower behind an earthen rampart in order to save their lives.

They too, therefore, confident that their safety lay in their own courage and their own swords, demanded from their officers the order to advance. The order was given, and acted upon, but with unexpected results; for the Roman commander attacked before they were properly organized to receive him, only the leading files having got clear of the camp while the remainder, in good order, were still coming down the slope to their assigned positions on the open ground below. Even the sections which were clear of the entrenchments in time were not yet adequately deployed, so what the Romans encountered was, to all intents and purposes, little better than a mob of men in appalling confusion, trying desperately to form some sort of defensive line and looking to every side for support which was not there. Valerius struck hard, and the weight of his attack, and the war-cry of his men, added to their difficulties, so that they were compelled to give ground; soon, however, they rallied, partly by their own efforts, partly in response to their officers who roundly abused them for running from an enemy they had so recently defeated. A stern struggle ensued; Valerius called upon his troops to remember that they were free men, fighting their first battle for a free Rome: 'For none but yourself,' he cried addressing the infantry, 'the victory will be – not this time will it fill the pockets or swell the pride of the *decemvirs*! Not Appius commands you now, but I, your consul – I, Valerius, who brought you freedom like my ancestors before me. Show by your deeds that in former fights it was the commanders who failed, not the men. What? Will you stoop to have shown more courage against Romans than against a foreign foe? To have feared political domination more than defeat? Before this war began, Verginia might have been raped – the lust of Appius was a menace to all. Yes, Appius and Verginia – *one* man, *one* girl! But now, should things go ill, the children of every one of us will have to fear the worst from thousands. God avert the omen! Such things, indeed, Jupiter and Mars will never let happen to a city founded as ours was founded. Remember the Aventine and the Sacred Mount! bring back to the place where a few months ago you won your freedom a power and empire not a jot diminished, and prove today that the heart of a Roman soldier is what it always was before the *decemvirs* came to their accursed power, and that a Roman's courage is none the less for his equality before the law!'

Valerius then galloped off to the cavalry lines for a final word, urging them to match their superiority of rank and honour by the quality of their performance. 'Come, my lads,' he said, 'the infantry have shifted them already – now it is your turn: charge, and drive them from the field. They will not stand against you – even now their apparent resistance is no more than hesitation.'

Off went the squadrons at full gallop; some of the work having already been done by the infantry, they burst clean through the enemy's lines, while other units riding round beyond their flanks, and finding the entire force bent upon nothing but saving their skins, cut across their line of retreat and prevented all but a few from reaching their entrenchments. Valerius and the infantry then concentrated their whole strength upon the camp itself, which was captured with heavy losses in men and immense losses in material.

News of the action quickly reached Rome and the other army which was engaged against the Sabines. In Rome there was rejoicing, but the effect of the news was even more notable on the troops under Horatius's command, as it fired them to emulation. Horatius had already put his men through a period of training, sending out raiding-parties and seeking occasions for minor engagements, and by these means had given them confidence and helped them to forget their disgraceful defeat under the *decemvirs'* command, until successes on a small scale had encouraged their hopes of victory in the campaign as a whole. The Sabines, for their part, were hardly less active: the previous year's success had heightened their morale and they were now constantly trying to provoke a battle; they found it irritating in the extreme that their opponents should content themselves with what was, in effect, mere banditry, sending out and as rapidly recalling small groups of raiders, and dissipating what should have been an all-out struggle in a succession of trivial skirmishes. They would have greatly preferred a major action – a bold throw of the dice for victory or defeat. The Romans, for their part, had a double reason for impatience: first, the confidence they had by now acquired, and, secondly, the feeling that they were hardly being treated fairly. They knew that Valerius's army would be returning to Rome with the laurels of victory, while their own opponents were still being permitted to treat them with mockery and contempt. But when would they be equal to them, if not now? Horatius, aware of his men's restlessness, took the opportunity to address them. 'I suppose,' he said, 'that you know the result of the action on Algidus. It was everything that a battle fought by the soldiers of a free people should be: by the skill of my colleague

and the valour of his men victory was won. As for myself, the nature
of my strategy and the quality of my determination will depend upon
you: it is in our hands either to prolong this campaign or to bring it
to a quick conclusion. Either course could lead to success; if we adopt
the former, I shall continue to raise your confidence and heighten your
morale by the same sort of discipline and training as heretofore; if,
on the other hand, you are truly ready and ripe for a final trial of
strength, then show it now in soldierly fashion – give a cheer, my men,
as rousing as your battle-cry will be, to show that you have indeed the
will and the stomach for a fight.'

Instantly the cheer was raised, and Horatius, with a prayer for luck,
told his men that he would accept their decision and lead them into
action on the following day. The rest of that day was spent in preparation and in final attentions to the men's equipment.

At dawn the Sabines saw the Roman troops moving into battle
positions. What they had long wanted had come at last, and they lost
no time in following suit. The fight that followed was fiercely con-
tested; the confidence of each army in its own superiority was based
on sufficient reason: on the one side, a long past of unbroken military
glory, on the other a recent and hardly expected victory. The Sabines
showed tactical skill as well as fighting power, keeping in reserve a
detached force, 2,000 strong, to attack the Roman left wing after the
main bodies of the two armies had become engaged. This force duly
executed the movement assigned to it, with the result that the Roman
left was under serious pressure and almost surrounded, when the
cavalry of two Roman legions, some 600 in number, dismounted and
pressed forward on foot to the support of their badly shaken comrades.
In any action it is the infantry who face the greatest danger, so this
move on the part of the cavalry was doubly effective; for in addition
to increasing the weight of resistance the mere fact that they were now
engaged on equal terms shamed the infantry to further effort. Indeed,
their pride could not endure to see their mounted comrades doing
double service, or to feel that an honest footslogger was not a match
for a dismounted cavalryman. As a result they resumed the offensive
and recovered their lost ground, and in less than no time the immediate danger was not only averted, but the enemy's wing was
actually being forced back. The cavalry, covered by the infantry, took
their chance to withdraw and remount, and then galloped across to
the Roman right with news of the success, executing, immediately

afterwards, a charge with devastating effect upon an enemy whose spirit was already partly broken by the defeat of his best troops. No other troops in the whole course of the engagement did finer service.

Horatius, in command, had his eyes everywhere; he was as quick to praise valour as to castigate the shirkers. A word of rebuke from him was enough to make a man of anyone – shame was as strong an incentive to the laggard as praise was to the valiant. Once again the battle-cry rang out, and a concerted thrust by every unit in the army had its reward; the enemy wavered, and from that moment the weight of the Roman attack was irresistible. The Sabines broke and fled for their lives, leaving their camp to be plundered at will. This time the Romans recovered property of their own, lost in previous raids – not, as was the case on Algidus, the property of their allies.

The behaviour of the Senate at this double success, in two separate battles, was ungenerous in the extreme: it decreed, in the name of the consuls, a period of national thanksgiving for one day only. The people, however, on their own initiative, took a second, and flocked to the temples to offer up their prayers – and indeed this second day of thanksgiving, though unofficial and purely the issue of popular sentiment, showed the greater earnestness and enthusiasm. The two consuls had agreed to return to the city within a day of each other, and on their arrival they called a meeting of the Senate in the Campus Martius to render an account of their exploits. During the session certain leading senators objected to its being held in the presence of troops, declaring that it was a deliberate attempt to terrorize the government; the protest was successful, and the consuls, to clear themselves, adjourned the session and called another in the Flaminian Meadows, where the temple of Apollo now stands (even in those days the place was known as Apollo's Precinct). At this second meeting the Senate unanimously refused to grant the victorious consuls the public honour of a Triumph, whereupon the tribune Lucius Icilius submitted the question to a popular vote. Many came forward to dissuade the people from reversing the Senate's decision, the most vehement of all being Gaius Claudius, who maintained that what the consuls really wanted was a 'triumph' not over the enemy but over the aristocratic party, their object being favour in return for personal services to a tribune rather than a public honour for military services to the state. He stressed the fact that the decision as to whether a Triumph had been earned by a successful commander had always, in the past, rested with the Senate, never with the people, and that not even the kings had impaired the dignity of the highest order in the state. It would be intolerable, he urged, if the power of the tribunes swelled to such proportions that there was no room left for any national deliberative body, as the very existence of fair laws and a free society demanded that every class within it should have, and keep, its own appropriate dignity and rights. Similar views were expressed by many others of the older Senators, but to no purpose. All the tribes voted in favour of Icilius's motion. It was the first time in history that a Triumph was celebrated at the bidding of the people, without the Senate's authorization.

The tribunes had won another victory for the popular cause, and this time it nearly resulted in a serious abuse, as it was followed by a secret agreement to procure the election of the same tribunes for the following year. To deflect attention from their own ambitions, the consuls, too, were to be elected for another term. The justification for this move was the united determination of the aristocratic party to discredit Valerius and Horatius and thus, by implication, to impair the influence of the tribunes. What – their argument ran – would happen if, before the laws were firmly established, the new tribunes were attacked through the agency of consuls belonging to the patricians' own party? There would not always be consuls like Valerius and Horatius, to set popular liberty before their own interests. The immediate danger was, however, averted by the happy result of the drawing of lots for the presidency of the elections. The lot fell to Duellius, the very man for the purpose in view of the political good sense which enabled him to foresee the passions which would inevitably be aroused if magistrates were re-elected for a further term. Duellius declared that he would not consider the candidacy of any of the former tribunes, and his colleagues replied by insisting that he must either take a free vote from the tribes, with no conditions imposed, or resign the presidency to his colleagues, who would conduct the election according to law and not according to the wishes of the patricians. This conflict was precisely what Duellius wanted, and his next move was to ask the consuls, in due form, what their intentions were with respect to the consular elections. They replied that they would not seek re-election, whereupon Duellius, having gained popular supporters for his unpopular policy, went with them before the assembly. There the consuls were publicly asked what they would do if the Roman people, in regard for their military successes and for their help

in the recovery of political freedom, re-elected them to office. Both
men stuck to their decision, and said they would refuse the honour.
Duellius expressed his warm approval of their determination not to
imitate the conduct of the *decemvirs*, and proceeded to hold the election.
Five tribunes were elected, and when, because of the ill-concealed
efforts of the existing tribunes to obtain re-election, no other candidates succeeded in polling enough votes, he dismissed the assembly
and held no further ones for election purposes. He maintained that his
procedure was perfectly legal, as the law had never prescribed a definite
number of tribunes but only the necessity for not leaving the office
vacant, together with the duty of the successful candidates to co-opt
colleagues. He then read aloud the legal formula, part of which ran:
'If I shall call for your votes for ten tribunes, and you today shall elect
less than ten, then those whom the elected tribunes co-opt as their colleagues shall be tribunes no less legally than those whom today you
shall have elected.' Duellius had stuck to his point; by refusing to admit
the legality of having fourteen tribunes he succeeded in defeating the
selfish ambition of his colleagues. He then resigned, having won the
warm approval of both parties in the state.

In co-opting their colleagues the new tribunes allowed themselves
to be guided by the wishes of the patricians, and even went so far as
to select two, Spurius Tarpeius and Aulus Aternius, who were themselves of noble birth and ex-consuls. The consuls for the year were
Spurius Herminius and Titus Verginius Caelimontanus; neither man
had very pronounced leanings either to the aristocratic or to the
plebeian interest, so their period of office was a tranquil one.

The fact that two patricians had been co-opted was resented by one
of the tribunes named Trebonius, who felt he had been cheated in the
matter by the aristocratic party and betrayed by his colleagues; he
accordingly brought forward a proposal that whoever called upon the
commons to elect tribunes should continue to do so until ten had been
elected. Indeed, the grudge he bore against the patricians made him
throughout his year of office such a thorn in their flesh that he was
nicknamed Asper – 'the Prickly'.

The next consuls, Marcus Geganius Macerinus and Gaius Julius,
managed to pour oil on the troubled waters of strife between the tribunes and the young nobles without any hostile action against the
tribunate or any sacrifice of their own party's dignity. They kept the
restlessness of the commons within bounds by suspending a recruiting

order which had been issued for a campaign against the Volscians and Aequians, maintaining that political tranquillity at home went hand in hand with good relations abroad, just as domestic discord was always the cue for potential enemies to start fire-eating. Their peace policy also led to a diminution of tension within the state. Nevertheless the fundamental hostility between the two orders remained; either was always quick to take advantage when the other showed moderation, and if the commons were apparently content, it was only a signal for the young nobles to start fresh persecutions. The tribunes attempted to protect the humble and obscure, but their intervention was hardly successful, and as time went on they were not even safe from attack themselves, especially in the latter months of the year when powerful cabals began to be formed against them, and their own influence, like that of all magistrates, was tending to diminish as the end of their term approached. Tribunes like Icilius would indeed have been something for the commons to put their trust in: but what were the tribunes now? For two years they had been no more than names. As for the older members of the nobility, the position was somewhat equivocal: they knew that the young men in their party were going too far, but could not help feeling, at the same time, that if there must be excesses, it was better to have them practised by their own party than by their opponents. True moderation in the defence of political liberties is indeed a difficult thing: pretending to want fair shares for all, every man raises himself by depressing his neighbour; our anxiety to avoid oppression leads us to practise it ourselves; the injustice we repel, we visit in turn upon others, as if there were no choice except either to do it or to suffer it.

The next consuls to take office were Titus Quinctius Capitolinus (for the fourth time) and Furius Agrippa. They were fortunate in not having to deal either with a popular revolt or a foreign war, though both came all too near for comfort. The hostility of the tribunes and the commons against the nobility was again on the increase; prosecutions of one or another member of the aristocratic party were continually reducing the public assemblies to uproar, and party strife of the most embittered kind seemed inevitable. These disturbances were the signal for the Volscians and Aequians to prepare for war; their leading men, eager to enrich themselves at Rome's expense, had persuaded their peoples that Rome had failed to raise troops the previous year because the commons had deliberately refused service, and for that reason no expedition had been sent out against them. Roman discipline was a thing of the past; her people had lost the habit of war, and she was no longer a united nation. All the pugnacity which once found satisfaction in foreign wars was now turned inward; the Roman wolves, as they put it, were blinded by a rabid hatred of each other, and this was the chance to crush them.

Their combined forces first invaded Latium with devastating effect. Finding no serious opposition they then, to the infinite satisfaction of the men responsible for their aggressive policy, advanced, spreading desolation in their path, to the very walls of Rome near the Esquiline Gate, where with triumphant insolence they called upon the inhabitants of the City to cast their eyes over their ruined farms and abandoned fields. Nothing was done to avenge the insult, and they marched back to Corbio with their plunder.

This was the moment for the consul Quinctius to intervene: he called a mass meeting and addressed it (I am informed) to the following effect. 'Fellow Romans, though my conscience is clear, I meet you in this place with bitter shame. To think that you know – and that history will record – that in the fourth consulship of Titus Quinctius an armed force of Volscians and Aequians, who were recently hardly a match for the Hernici, advanced with impunity to the walls of Rome! For years now the sort of life we Romans have lived and the sorry state of our affairs have given me little cause to foresee a happy outcome; nevertheless had I known that such a disgrace was in store for us this year of all years, I should have shunned it by any means in my power – by exile or death, if there was no other way of avoiding office. If those who stood armed at our gates had been worthy of the name of men, Rome might have been captured in my consulship! I had had honours enough already, and enough – more than enough – of life; it would have been better to have died in my third consulship.

'Our dastardly enemy has held us in contempt; but – I ask you – who was it he despised? Was it we, your consuls, or yourselves? If we are in fault, strip us of the command we do not deserve: nay, if that is not enough, bring us to justice to cut off our heads; if it is you who are guilty, then, my friends, it is my prayer that neither God nor man may punish you, but only that you may repent. Is the enemy confident of his valour and contemptuous of your cowardice? No indeed: he has too often been beaten, too often driven from his camp, stripped of his lands, sent under the yoke, not to know himself and you. The truth is that our communal life is poisoned by political discord and party strife, and it was that which raised his hopes of destroying us, seeing, as he did, your lust for liberty in perpetual conflict with our lust for power, and each party's loathing of the representative magistracies of the other. What, in God's name, do you want now? Once it was tribunes, and to preserve the peace we let you have them; then it was *decemvirs*, and we permitted their appointment. Soon you were sick of them; we forced them to resign, and then, when you continued to pursue them into their private lives with your rage and resentment, we permitted men of the noblest birth and highest political distinction to suffer exile or death. Again you wanted tribunes – and got them; you wanted consuls who would support the popular cause, and, though we knew how hard it would hit us, the great patrician magistracy was offered on a plate to our opponents. You have your tribunes to protect you, your right of appeal to the people, your popular decrees made binding on the Senate, while in the empty name of justice all our privileges are trampled under foot: all this we have borne, and are still bearing. How is it to end? Will the time ever come when we can have a united city, a united country? You have beaten us, and we accept our defeat with more equanimity than you your victory. Is it not enough that we must fear you? *We* were the enemy when you took the Aventine and occupied the Sacred Mount; now we have seen the Esquiline within an ace of capture, and Volscian troops swarming up the ramparts of Rome – and not a man stepped forward to repel them. Only against us do you play a soldier's part; only against us have you drawn the sword.

'Let me give you a piece of advice: when you have besieged the Senate House, made the Forum unsafe for honest men, filled the gaol with your hated aristocrats, just take a trip, swashbucklers as you are, outside the Esquiline Gate – or, if that is too much for your courage, climb on the walls and look at your farms destroyed with fire and sword, watch the smoke rising, far as your eyes can reach, from burning buildings, and your cattle being driven off. Maybe you will say that it is only the state which is the sufferer – crops are being burned, the City besieged by a victorious enemy. God help you! Aren't your own pockets affected too? Soon enough the reports will come in and every man of you will know his losses. What resources have you got to make them up with? Will your precious tribunes give you back your wrecked or stolen property? They'll give you words, sure enough

– as many as you like – and other fine things – writs against leading
statesmen, public meetings, and half a hundred new laws. But not your
property. Public meetings, indeed! Who ever left them better off in any
real or practical way, or took anything home from them for his wife and
children except hatred and bitterness and food for fresh quarrels either
with the government or his neighbour – troubles too great, apparently,
for yourselves as brave and honest men to cope with, as you always
expect somebody else to get you out of them. But – God in Heaven!
– in the days when you were soldiers under our command, not political agitators whom your tribunes lead by the nose – when you used
your throats not for political slogans to scare the Roman senators, but
for the battle-cry to strike terror into the hearts of the enemy in the
field – then indeed you would return in triumph to your hearths and
homes loaded with spoils from captured lands and full of success and
glory, each for himself and each for all, while now the foreigner is
carrying away all your treasure, all you possess – and you let him go!
Stick as you will to your assemblies and your petty politics, the necessity of military service, which you try to avoid, will pursue you.
Action against the Volscians was not to your taste – so what? The
enemy are at the gates. If he is not forced back, we shall soon be fighting in the streets; Volscian troops will be climbing the Capitol and
chasing you into your very homes. Last year the Senate ordered the
raising of troops and an expedition to Algidus – but here we still are,
doing nothing, screaming at each other like fishwives, thankful to be
at peace and blind to the bitter truth that we shall pay for the few short
months of it by a many times more desperate war. What I am saying
is not, I know, of the pleasantest sort; but I cannot help it. Harsh necessity, as well as my own character, compels me to tell the truth, not
to flatter you with agreeable lies. I should like to please you, my friends,
but I should much prefer to save you, whatever your feelings to me,
personally, may be. It seems to be a law of nature that a speaker who
speaks only for himself is more popular with a crowd than one who
has nothing in his mind but the public welfare – unless perhaps you
believe in the disinterestedness of those flattering demagogues, those
yes-men and self-styled friends of the people, and suppose that it is for
your sakes that they rouse your wrath and urge you to action. Your
passions are their profit – to fill their pockets or get them promotion.
In an ordered and harmonious society they know they are nothing,
and they would rather lead a bad cause than none at all. Only tell me

that now, at long last, you are sick and weary of this state of affairs –
that you are willing to go back to your old ways, like your fathers before you – and I give you leave to gaol or behead me as you please if
I fail within a week to beat these marauders, capture their camp, remove the threat to the gates and walls of Rome and carry to their cities
the whole terror of war which now makes you tremble.'

They were the words of the sternest of consuls, yet seldom had the
mob greeted the speech even of a popular tribune with greater enthusiasm. Even the young men who were accustomed in such moments of
crisis to consider the refusal to enlist as their best weapon against the
nobility, now began to turn a favourable eye upon the prospect of war.
Resentment rose as refugees began to come in from the countryside,
some badly wounded, others who had lost all they possessed, and all
with stories of atrocities worse than anything that people in the city
could be directly aware of. In the Senate everyone looked to Quinctius
as the sole champion of the majesty of Rome, and the leading senators
declared that his speech had been in the true tradition of consular authority and worthy of a man who had so many times held that eminent
position and lived a life crowded with honours often enjoyed and
oftener deserved. It was the unanimous opinion of the House that while
other consuls had either betrayed the dignity of the Senate to curry
favour with the populace, or, on the other hand, had exacerbated its
opposition by their bullying and high-handed determination to safeguard the privileges of their own order, Titus Quinctius had delivered
a speech which was consistent no less with the friendly cooperation
between parties than with the majesty of the Senate, and which – more
important still – was aptly timed to meet the circumstances. He and his
colleague Agrippa were requested to assume control; the tribunes were
urged to cooperate loyally with the consuls in removing the immediate
threat to Rome, and to see to it that the commons throughout the crisis
obeyed the orders of their superiors. It was emphasized that the appeal
to the tribunes came from the country as a whole: both parties equally
implored their assistance in a situation of exceptional danger.

By general consent a decree was issued, and acted upon, for the raising of troops. The consuls, addressing the assembled people, said that
it was no time to consider appeals for exemption; all men of military
age were to present themselves at dawn the following day in the
Campus Martius; only when the war was over would they fix a date
for hearing the appeals of men who failed to register, and anyone

whose appeal was not satisfactory would be treated as a deserter. At the appointed time every man without exception presented himself.

The cohorts selected their own centurions, and two senators were put in command of every cohort. The whole process of mobilization was, we are told, so rapid that though the quaestors had brought the standards from the treasury only that morning the troops were on the move by ten o'clock; a few veteran cohorts accompanied the army of fresh recruits, and the whole force encamped for the night ten miles out of the City on the Latin Way. The next day brought them in sight of the enemy and they took up a position within easy striking distance of them, near Corbio; on the third day the engagement took place – neither side wishing to postpone matters, as the Romans' blood was up and the enemy, having broken the peace on so many previous occasions, was rendered reckless by the knowledge of the injustice of his cause.

The tradition in the Roman army was that the two consuls shared the command equally; on this occasion, however, Agrippa by mutual agreement conceded the supreme command to his colleague Quinctius – a concession likely to prove most salutary when important decisions have to be made. Agrippa stood down without any feelings of resentment, and Quinctius in reply showed no less courtesy in discussing with him all his plans and admitting him, as if he were his equal, to a share in all his achievements.

When the armies engaged, Quinctius commanded the Roman right, Agrippa the left; Spurius Postumius Albus, a senior officer, had charge of the centre, and another, Publius Sulpicius, of the cavalry. On the right the infantry fought a distinguished action against fierce resistance; Sulpicius with his mounted troops broke through the enemy's centre and then made a quick decision, though the way was open for withdrawal, to attack them in the rear before they could re-form. By this movement, which would have subjected them to simultaneous pressure on both front and rear, he might in less than no time have completely broken their resistance, had not the Volscian and Aequian cavalry, taking a leaf from his own book, swiftly intervened. For some time they managed to check him; but he was a determined fighter and called for instant and vigorous action. They were cut off and surrounded, he cried, and would remain so unless an immediate and desperate effort were made. To rout the enemy cavalry was not enough: they must not escape alive – men and horses must be killed – not one must be allowed to get away or to fight again. 'At them, men!' he ended; 'how can they stand against us, when their massed infantry broke before our charge?'

Sulpicius's appeal did not fall on deaf ears. A single charge was enough; the whole enemy brigade was cut to pieces – men in hundreds flung from their mounts to perish, man and beast, at the point of the Roman lances. The cavalry engagement was over. Sulpicius then turned his attention to the infantry, at the same time sending the consuls a report of his success. The enemy line opposed to Quinctius was already beginning to crack, and the good news put fresh heart into the Roman battalions and brought dismay to the hard-pressed Aequians; it was their centre which had first begun to go, where Sulpicius's victorious charge had thrown their ranks into confusion; then their left, too, had been forced to withdraw before the weight of Quinctius's attack. On the enemy right was the hottest work: Agrippa, a magnificent fighter and still in the prime of life, aware that things were going worse in his own sector than anywhere else, snatched the standards from their bearers and pressed forward with them in his own hands – and even, to shame his men to greater efforts, flung some of them into the thick of the enemy ranks. The ruse succeeded; a furious onslaught followed, and victory along the whole front was won.

At that instant there arrived a message from Quinctius saying that he, too, had been successful and was within striking distance of the enemy's camp, which he was nevertheless unwilling to enter until he knew that on the left wing too all had gone well. If, the message added, Agrippa had already proved victorious, he was to join him immediately so that all divisions of the army might take possession of what the camp contained. Close to the camp the two victorious commanders met, with mutual congratulations. There was no further fighting; the small remaining garrison was quickly overwhelmed and the Roman armies burst in; an immense mass of material was captured, including what had been lost in the recent raids, and the two armies started back on their march to Rome.

I find in the accounts of this campaign that the consuls did not ask for an official Triumph – nor was it offered them by the Senate. No reason is given for their refusing, or not expecting, this honour; my own guess – tentative, indeed, as all this happened so long ago – is that the attitude of Quinctius and Agrippa was not uninfluenced by the case of Valerius and Horatius in the preceding campaign: Valerius and

Horatius had achieved the distinction of a victory not only over the
Volscians and Aequians but over the Sabines as well, but were none
the less refused a triumph by the Senate; and in view of this Quinctius
and Agrippa hesitated to demand a triumph for a victory only half as
great, lest, if they were granted it, it should have the appearance more
of a personal favour than of a reward for services rendered to the state.

The lustre of the victorious campaign was somewhat dimmed by a
disgraceful incident which followed. It arose out of a request from the
communities of Aricia and Ardea, both allies of Rome, that the Roman
people should act as arbitrators in a dispute about the ownership of a
piece of territory, for which the two towns had fought so often that
they were both exhausted. Representatives duly arrived in Rome; the
Roman magistrates granted an Assembly to hear them put their case,
and each side advanced its claims with the utmost vehemence. When,
after the evidence had been heard, the moment came for the tribes to
be called upon and the people to give their decision, a certain aged
Roman of humble birth, named Publius Scaptius, suddenly intervened.
'If,' he said, addressing the consuls, 'I may be permitted to speak on
the national interest, I shall not allow the Roman people to make a
mistake in this matter.' The consuls, who thought he was an old dot-
ard with no right whatever to express an opinion, ordered his removal;
but he continued to shout at the top of his voice that the country was
being betrayed, and finally appealed to the tribunes for a hearing. The
tribunes – as always, the servants rather than the masters of the mob –
aware that everybody was bursting with curiosity, gave the old man
leave to say what he pleased. At once he began to speak: 'I am eighty-
two years old,' he said, 'and once long ago I fought in that bit of land
you are talking about. I wasn't young even then, for it was my twen-
tieth year of campaigning – at Corioli it was. So what I'm telling you
is something rubbed out of your memories by lapse of years, though
in my own it is fixed clear enough. Now this land they are arguing
about belonged to Corioli, and when Corioli was taken it became the
property, by right of conquest, of the Roman people. The men of
Ardea and Aricia had no control whatever over this land while Corioli
remained independent; yet now they hope to rob us of it – us, the
rightful owners, whom they have asked to arbitrate! Can you beat that
for impertinence? I have not much longer to live; but I helped years
ago, like a good soldier, to take that land with the strength of my arm,
and I cannot believe that now I am old I should not defend it with my

tongue – the only weapon I have left. I beg you therefore not to spoil your chances by a squeamishness which will do you no good.'

Scaptius's advice was listened to not only with close attention but with a high measure of approval, and the consuls, to whom this was all too clear, swore by everything they held sacred that the thing was an outrage, and hurriedly sending for the leaders of the Senate went round the assembly with them beseeching everybody they spoke to not to be guilty of this infamy: for an arbitrator to convert disputed property to his own use was a crime revolting in itself, and would set a precedent even worse. 'Moreover,' they added, 'even if there were nothing to prevent a judge from attending to his own interest, by no means as much would be gained by the seizure of this territory as would be lost by the consequent, and deserved, alienation of our friends. Who can reckon the cost of the loss of honour, of the loss of our good name? What a story for these men to take home to Aricia and Ardea! Everyone will hear of it – our friends and enemies alike – our friends with what grief, our enemies with what delight! Do you think for a moment that any foreigner will put this down to Scaptius – an old fool who likes the sound of his own voice? No indeed: it would make a fine epitaph for Scaptius, no doubt – but as for the Roman people, they would be playing the unwonted role of petty swindlers in the fraudulent conversion of other men's property. What judge in a private case would ever have awarded the disputed property to himself? Not even Scaptius would do such a thing, however dead to shame he may be.'

Unhappily such arguments, though passionately urged both by the consuls and the senators, were of no avail. Cupidity prevailed – and the man who had recommended it. The tribes were called upon and pronounced their decision that the land was the public property of the Roman people. It is not denied that the verdict would have been the same, had the case gone to another court; as it was, it was wholly shameful, with no extenuating circumstances whatever, and the Roman senators felt it to be no less cynical and base than did the men of Ardea and Aricia.

The remainder of the year was undisturbed by civil dissension or foreign war.

BOOK FOUR

War and Politics

THE next consuls were Marcus Genucius and Gaius Curtius. War and political dissension made the year a difficult one. Hardly had it begun, when the tribune Canuleius introduced a bill for legalizing intermarriage between the nobility and the commons. The senatorial party objected strongly on the grounds not only that the patrician blood would thereby be contaminated but also that the hereditary rights and privileges of the *gentes*, or families, would be lost. Further, a suggestion, at first cautiously advanced by the tribunes, that a law should be passed enabling one of the two consuls to be a plebeian, subsequently hardened into the promulgation, by nine tribunes, of a bill by which the people should be empowered to elect to the consulship such men as they thought fit, from either of the two parties. The senatorial party felt that if such a bill were to become law, it would mean not only that the highest office of state would have to be shared with the dregs of society but that it would, in effect, be lost to the nobility and transferred to the commons. It was with great satisfaction, therefore, that the Senate received a report, first that Ardea had thrown off her allegiance to Rome in resentment at the crooked practice which had deprived her of her territory; secondly, that troops from Veii had raided the Roman frontier, and, thirdly, that the Volscians and Aequians were showing uneasiness at the fortification of Verrugo. In the circumstances it was good news, for the nobility could look forward even to an unsuccessful war with greater complacency than to an ignominious peace. Accordingly they made the most of the situation; the Senate ordered an immediate raising of troops and a general mobilization on the largest possible scale and with even greater urgency than in the previous year, in the hope that the revolutionary proposals which the tribunes were bringing forward might be forgotten in the bustle and excitement of three imminent campaigns. Canuleius replied with a brief but forceful statement in the Senate to the effect that it was useless for the consuls to try to scare the commons from taking an interest in the new proposals, and, declaring that they should never, while he lived, hold a levy until the commons had voted on the reforms which he and his colleagues had introduced, immediately convened an assembly. The battle was on: the consuls and the Senate on the one side, Canuleius and the populace on the other, were in the full flood of mutual recriminations. The consuls swore that the lunatic excesses of the tribunes were past endurance, that it was the end of all things, that war was being deliberately provoked far more deadly than any with a foreign enemy. 'The present situation', they said, 'is not, we admit, the fault of one party only: the Senate is not less guilty than the people, or the consuls than the tribunes. In all communities the qualities or tendencies which carry the highest reward are bound to be most in evidence and to be most industriously cultivated – indeed it is precisely that which produces good statesmen and good soldiers; unhappily here in Rome the greatest rewards come from political up-heavals and revolt against the government, which have always, in con-sequence, won applause from all and sundry. Only recall the aura of majesty which surrounded the Senate in our father's day, and then think what it will be like when we bequeath it to our children! Think how the labouring class will be able to brag of the increase in its power and influence! There can never be an end to this unhappy process so long as the promoters of sedition against the government are honoured in proportion to their success. Do you realize, gentlemen, the appalling consequences of what Canuleius is trying to do? If he succeeds, bent, as he is, upon leaving nothing in its original soundness and purity, he will contaminate the blood of our ancient and noble families and make chaos of the hereditary patrician privilege of 'taking the auspices' to determine, in the public or private interest, what Heaven may will – and with what result? that, when all distinctions are obliterated, no one will know who he is or where he came from! Mixed marriages forsooth! What do they mean but that men and women from all ranks of society will be permitted to start copulating like animals? A child of such intercourse will never know what blood runs in his veins or what form of worship he is entitled to practise; he will be nothing – or six of one and half a dozen of the other, a very monster!

'But even this is not enough: having made hay of the dictates of religion and the traditions of our country, these revolutionary fire-eaters are now out for the consulship. They began merely by suggest-ing that one of the two consuls might be a plebeian, but now they have brought in a bill which would enable the people to elect consuls as it pleased, from either party – plebeian or patrician. And whom are they likely to elect? Obviously, men of their own class, and the most tur-bulent demagogues at that. We shall have men like Canuleius and

Icilius in the highest office of state. God forbid that an office invested with an almost kingly majesty should fall so low! We should rather die a thousand times than allow such a shameful thing to happen. We are very sure that our forefathers too, had they guessed that by wholesale concessions they would exacerbate, rather than appease, the hostility of the commons and lead them to make further demands each more exaggerated than the last, would have faced at the outset any struggle, however fierce and embittered, rather than permit such laws to be imposed upon them. The concession in the matter of tribunes only led to another, and so it goes on. It is impossible to have tribunes side by side with a governing class in the same community; either the nobility or the tribunate must go. Now – better late than never – we must make a firm stand against their reckless and unprincipled conduct. Are we to take no action when they first deliberately embroil us, thus inviting a foreign invasion, and then prevent us from arming for defence against the danger for which they were themselves responsible? Or when, having more or less invited an enemy to attack us, they refuse to allow us to raise troops – nay, worse, when Canuleius has the audacity to declare in the Senate that unless the members of the House permit his proposals to be accepted as law, as if he were a conquering hero, he will rescind the order for mobilization? What is such a statement but a threat to betray his country, to submit passively to the storming and capture of Rome? It is indeed a timely word of encouragement to the Volscians, to the Aequians, to the men of Veii – but hardly to the common people of Rome. The enemy may well be confident in their ability to climb, with Canuleius in command, to the Citadel on the heights of the Capitol! Gentlemen, unless the tribunes, when they robbed you of your dignity and privilege, robbed you of your courage too, we are ready to put first things first: we will lead you against criminal citizens of Rome before we lead you against an enemy in arms.'

While opinions of this sort were being vented in the Senate, Canuleius was defending his proposed reforms and attacking the consuls elsewhere. 'Men of Rome,' he said, 'the violence with which the Senate has been opposing our programme of reform has made me realize more vividly than ever before the depth of the contempt in which you are held by the aristocracy. I have often suspected it, but now I know: they think you are unworthy of living with them within the walls of the same town. Yet what is the object of our proposals? It is merely to point out that we are their fellow-citizens – that we have the same country as they, even though we have less money. We seek the right of intermarriage, a right commonly granted to other nations on our borders – indeed, before now Rome has granted citizenship, which is more than intermarriage, even to a defeated enemy. By our other proposal we intend no innovation, but merely seek the recovery and enjoyment of the popular right to elect whom we will to positions of authority. What is there in this to make them think that chaos is come again? Is this enough to justify what came near to being a personal assault upon me in the Senate, or their threat to use violence against the sacrosanct office of the tribunes? If the people of Rome are allowed to vote freely for the election to the consulship of whom they please – if even a man of their own class, provided that he is worthy of it, may hope to rise to this high honour – does that mean that our country's stability and power are necessarily done for? We propose that a man of the people may have the right to be elected to the consulship: is that the same as saying some rogue who was, or is, a slave? Such is their contempt for you that they would rob you, if they could, of the very light you see by; they grudge you the air you breathe, the words you speak, the very fact that you have the shape of men. They declare – if I may say so without irreverence – that a plebeian consul would be a sin in the sight of heaven.

'We common folk may not be allowed, as our betters are, to consult the Calendar of work days and holidays or the Pontiff's records, but – I ask you – don't we know what is familiar to everyone, even to foreigners, namely that here in Rome consuls succeeded kings and possess no dignity or privilege which did not belong to the kings before them? Come, come! One might fancy that nobody knew the story of how Numa Pompilius, who was not only not of noble birth but not even a Roman citizen, was invited, on the authority of the people and with the Senate's consent, to leave the country of the Sabines and assume the crown in Rome. And what of Lucius Tarquinius? He was no Roman – he was not even an Italian, but the son of Demaratus of Corinth; yet coming here as an immigrant from Tarquinii he was made king. Then Servius Tullius, son of a prisoner of war from Corniculum – a man with nobody for his father and a slave for his mother– reigned over us simply by his native ability and manly virtues. Need I go on? What of Titus Tatius the Sabine, whom our founder Romulus himself took to share his throne? History speaks, my friends: so long as nobody who had conspicuous ability was despised, whatever his origin might be, Rome's power grew. Would you hesitate today to have a consul of humble birth, when in the past no one raised an objection to having foreigners on the throne, and when even after the expulsion of the kings we never closed our doors against any foreigner with ability? Take the Claudian family: after the abolition of the monarchy we not only gave its members citizen rights, strangers though they were from the Sabine country; we even admitted them to the patriciate. If a foreign immigrant can become first a patrician, then consul, what sort of justice is it to preclude a native-born Roman from all hope of the consulship simply because he is of humble birth? Perhaps we find it hard to believe that people like Numa, or Tarquin, or Servius Tullius, men of vigour and determination, good statesmen and soldiers, could ever spring from an obscure family – or perhaps, even if the miracle happened, we should refuse to let such a person lay his hand upon the helm of the ship of state, and look forward instead to having consuls like the *decemvirs* – who were all blue-blooded, let me remind you, and all monsters – in preference to such as resemble the best of our kings, self-made men though they were. A likely supposition indeed! However, you may take a different line, and point out that there has never, in fact, been a plebeian consul since the abolition of the monarchy. But haven't you heard of progress? Are we never to make changes? Because a thing has not been done before – and in a young country there are lots of things which have not been done before – is that a reason for never doing it, however great the benefits it may bring? In Romulus's reign there were no priests and no augurs: Numa Pompilius created both. Before Servius Tullius introduced it, the census had never been heard of, nor the registration of centuries and classes. There were no consuls till the kings were expelled and the consulate created; it was only recently that the office of dictator came into being – previously the very word was unknown; tribunes, aediles, quaestors were all new once; barely ten years ago we appointed *decemvirs* to codify the laws – and then gave them the sack. In a city built to last for ever, a city whose future expansion is beyond all reckoning, changes must inevitably come: new powers, new priesthoods, new privileges for families or individuals must at some time or other be introduced. This very measure we are discussing – the ban on intermarriage between the nobility and commons – was brought in only a few years ago by the *decemvirs*, with the worst effect upon the community and the gravest injustice to the commons. One could hardly offer a more signal insult to one section of the community than to consider it unfit to marry with, as if it were too dirty to touch: it is like condemning it to exile and banishment within the city walls. They take every precaution against the dreadful risk of becoming related by blood to us poor scum. Come, come, my noble lords – if such a connection is a blot on your fine escutcheon – though I would mention that many of you were originally Albans or Sabines, not of noble birth at all, and got your present rank as a reward for services either at the hands of the kings or, later, of the people – could you not keep your precious blood pure simply by determining on your own initiative, not to marry plebeian wives and not to let your sisters and daughters marry out of the patriciate? No patrician girl need, I assure you, fear for her virtue so far as any of us are concerned: rape is a patrician habit. No one would have forced a marriage contract upon an unwilling party – but to set up a legal ban upon the right of intermarriage, *that*, I repeat, is the final insult to the commons. Why not go further and propose a ban on marriages between rich and poor? Marriages have always been a matter of private arrangements between families, and now you propose to subject them to the restraint of a law which is the very reflection of your own arrogant conceit, for the purpose, I presume, of splitting society in two and of turning united Rome into two separate communities. I wonder you do not pass a law to stop a plebeian living next door to a nobleman, or walking in the same street, or going to the same party, or standing by his side in the Forum. What difference does it make if a patrician marries a plebeian wife, or a plebeian a patrician one? There is no loss of privilege whatever, as children admittedly take the rank of the father; we expect to gain nothing from marrying into your class except to be considered as human beings and citizens of Rome; and your opposition is wholly unreasonable – unless you take pleasure merely in humiliating and insulting us.

'Finally tell me this: does the ultimate power in the state belong to you or to the Roman people? When we finished with the monarchy, was it to put supreme authority into your hands or to bring political liberty to all alike? Have the people, or have they not, the right to enact a law, if such is their will? Or are you to quash every proposal of ours by proclaiming a levy of troops immediately it is brought up, and as soon as I, in my capacity as tribune, begin to call upon the tribes to vote, is the consul to reply by administering the military oath and ordering mobilization, with threats against me and my office and the commons in general? Do not forget that twice already you have learned by experience the value of your threats in face of our united resolution – do you wish to pretend that on those occasions you abstained from actual physical conflict purely out of tender feelings towards us? or was the reason, perhaps, that the stronger party happened to be the one to exercise restraint?

'My friends and citizens, there will be no swords drawn this time either; your opponents will continue to try your resolution but they will never put the strength of your right arms to the proof. Here, then, is my last word – and I speak it for the consuls to hear: The commons are ready for the campaigns which – truly or falsely – you talk so much about, if by restoring their right of intermarriage you unify the country at last; if you enable them by entering into private and domestic alliances to become one people with yourselves; if the hope of political advancement is held out impartially to vigorous and courageous men; if, finally, we are granted a share in the government with the opportunity, inherent in free institutions which are founded upon the principle of annual magistracies, to govern and to be governed in turn. But should anyone deny these conditions and prevent these reforms, you may tell us of a hundred imminent wars and not a man of us will register for service or take up arms: not one of us will fight for the benefit of arrogant masters with whom we have nothing in common either in domestic relationships or in the rewards of public life.'

The consuls finally left the Senate House and went before the assembled populace. Further speeches were, in the circumstances, out of the question, and violent altercation began; and when a tribune demanded a reason for keeping plebeians out of the consulship, Curtius, on the spur of the moment, said it was because only the nobility enjoyed the privilege of 'taking the auspices' – or ascertaining, by certain ceremonies, the will of heaven; the children of mixed marriages would be of somewhat equivocal status, and this might adversely affect this important aspect of religious observance. To prevent this was what the *decemvirs* intended when they forbade intermarriage. Now this was probably true enough, but as things were it was both irrelevant and unfortunate: the commons were furious at what they took to be the worst possible insult – the suggestion, namely, that they were so hateful to the gods that they were unfit to take the auspices.

And so the controversy continued to rage – the populace rivalling with their own determination the passionate advocacy of Canuleius – until at last the patricians were forced to yield, and permitted the removal of the ban on intermarriage to pass into law. By this concession they hoped to bring the tribunes either to abandon altogether their other contention – for plebeian consuls – or at least to shelve it until after the war, while the people, satisfied for the time being with what they had actually achieved would, they thought, be prepared to register for service.

By this triumph over the patricians and his consequent popularity Canuleius now found himself a great man. This fired the other tribunes to continue their struggle, and they fought tooth and nail for their proposed reform, preventing mobilization in spite of the fact that the rumours of war grew every day more insistent. The consuls, rendered powerless by the tribunes' veto to get anything done through the normal procedure in the Senate, held private meetings for discussion at the houses of leading senators. It was clear that they must admit defeat either by the enemy or by the popular party. The only ex-consuls not present at these discussions were Valerius and Horatius; Claudius expressed the opinion that the consuls should prepare to use force, but the Quinctii – Cincinnatus and Capitolinus – opposed this policy, maintaining that blood must not be shed or any violence employed against the tribunes, whose sacrosanctity had been accepted after a solemn covenant had been made to that effect with the people. The discussions ended in a resolution to permit the appointment of 'military tribunes' – senior military officers – with consular authority, to be chosen from either party indifferently. The matter of the consuls they left as it was. This satisfied both people and tribunes.

The day was announced for the election of the new officers – three in number – and at once all the ex-tribunes and anybody else who had spoken or acted against the government set about canvassing for votes; in the white togas of candidates they were here, there, and everywhere in the Forum, to the acute annoyance of the patricians who at first despaired of obtaining office in the present exacerbated state of popular feeling and then, in sheer disgust at the thought of working in harness with such intolerable colleagues, threw in their hands altogether. However, their leaders finally compelled them to stand, in order to avoid the appearance of having surrendered control of the government to their opponents. Men fighting for their own liberty and prestige are very different creatures from men who are called upon to use their judgement, unclouded by passion, when the fight is over. The result of the election was a signal proof of this, for the three candidates returned by the people's votes were all patricians: the fact that plebeians had been allowed to stand was enough to satisfy them. Such decency of feeling, such fairness and magnanimity characterized, on that occasion, the whole body of the Roman commons – where would you find it today in one single man?

Thus 310 years after the foundation of Rome military tribunes with consular power first entered upon office. The three men were Aulus Sempronius Atratinus, Lucius Atilius, and Titus Cloelius. During their term there was no political dissension and – consequently – no threat of foreign invasion.

According to some writers the creation of military tribunes was not connected with the proposal to throw open the consulship to plebeians. These writers say that the appointment of the three new officers of state with the insignia and authority of consuls was due to the inability of the two consuls to cope with three simultaneous campaigns, a quarrel with Veii having arisen in addition to the war with the Volscians and Aequians and the revolt of Ardea. In any case the new magistracy was still only a tentative arrangement, as after three months it was temporarily suspended in consequence of a decree of the augurs that there had been a technical flaw in the election: the magistrate who presided at the election, Gaius Curtius, had, it was said, incorrectly sited the tent from which the sky had to be watched for the traditional signs from heaven.

Meanwhile a deputation arrived in Rome from Ardea to complain about the recent judgement in the matter of the disputed territory; at the same time they made it clear that if the land were restored to them – its rightful owners – they were prepared to abide by their treaty and remain on friendly terms. The Senate replied that they were unable to rescind a judgement given by the people as a whole: there was neither authority nor precedent for such a thing, and were they to do it now it would imperil the relations between the two parties in the state; none the less, if the Ardeates were willing to wait a little and allow the Senate to decide upon a way of compensating them for what they had suffered, the time would come when they would be glad of their self-control and would know that the Senate had been as much concerned to prevent the original injury as they now were to limit the duration of its effects. The deputation promised to refer the whole question to the government at home, and was then courteously dismissed.

As the country had now no senior magistrate – none, that is, entitled to sit in the Chair of State – the patricians met to appoint an *interrex*, and his appointment continued for a number of days in consequence of a dispute as to whether the new government should be entrusted to military tribunes or consuls. The *interrex* himself with the support of the Senate was in favour of consuls, while the tribunes and commons as a whole held out for military tribunes – the recently created office. The dispute ended in a victory for the Senate, because the commons, feeling that there was little to choose between one office and the other as it would in either case be held by a patrician, gave up their opposition; moreover, their leaders preferred an election in which they were not qualified to stand as candidates to one in which they might fail to secure a majority. The tribunes too saw that further opposition was useless, and gave way in favour of the patrician leaders. Under the presidency, therefore, of the *interrex*, Titus Quinctius Barbatus, Lucius Papirius Mugilanus, and Lucius Sempronius Atratinus were elected to the consulship. During their term the treaty with Ardea was renewed, which proves that these man did hold the consulship that year, though their names do not appear in the ancient annals or in the official lists. Presumably the omission was due to the fact that the military tribunes were treated as if they had been in office throughout the year, though actually their tenure lasted for only three months. Licinius Macer is our authority for the statement that the names of these consuls appeared both in the treaty with Ardea and in the Linen Rolls in the temple of Moneta. The year was a quiet one both at home and abroad, in spite of the numerous threats from neighbouring states.

There are no such doubts about the nature of the chief officers of state for the following year: it is on record without question that the consuls were Marcus Geganius Macerinus (for the second time) and Titus Quinctius Capitolinus (for the fifth). This year also saw the beginning of the censorship, that important magistracy which from a trivial origin subsequently grew to exercise jurisdiction over the whole range of our social proprieties, to determine membership of the classes of Senators or Knights according to property and desert and to have complete control over the regular state revenue and the location of public and private buildings. The office originated in the fact that a census of the population had not been taken for many years and could no longer be postponed, while the consuls were too busy with threats of war from a number of directions to be able to undertake to organize it. The subject was brought up in the Senate, where the opinion was expressed that the service, which was a laborious one and beneath the dignity of a consul, required a special magistrate of its own with a staff of secretaries, who should take custody of the records and determine the form of the census. It was a small matter, but the Senate welcomed the suggestion as it would mean an increase in the number of patrician magistrates – and also, I fancy, because they already foresaw that the distinction of the men who held the office would soon add lustre and significance to the office itself. Even from the tribunes there was no opposition, for they looked upon the new magistracy – rightly enough, as it then was – as merely fulfilling a need rather than as conferring any particular lustre on the holder of it, and they had no wish to be tiresomely provocative in matters of minor importance. The leading men in the country, though invited to stand, considered the post beneath them, and the task of administering the census was given by popular vote to Papirius and Sempronius (the men whose consulship is questioned) to enable them to make up by this appointment for their uncompleted year as consuls. The object of the appointment being what it was, they were given the title of censors.

Meanwhile a deputation arrived from Ardea. The town was threatened with irretrievable disaster, and its people in the name of their ancient alliance with Rome, cemented afresh by the recent renewal of the treaty, were sending an urgent appeal for help. They could no longer enjoy the peaceful relations they had maintained with Rome owing to civil war, which arose, we read, out of political rivalry – the perennial curse of nations and destroyer of more peoples than foreign wars, famine, pestilence, or any other scourge men fancy that the angry gods have sent to ruin them. A young girl of humble birth and well known for her beauty had two rivals for her affections: one belonged to her own class and counted on the approval of her guardians, who were of the same social standing; the other was a young nobleman, attracted solely by her physical charms. The latter had the support in his suit of the aristocratic interest, and the result was that the clash of political faction penetrated into the girl's own household. Her mother, who would have liked as splendid a match as possible for her daughter, preferred the nobleman; her guardians, who could not keep politics even out of match-making, held out, so to speak, for their own candidate. The dispute continued and when it could not be settled within doors it was taken into court, where, the disputants having put forward their respective pleas, the magistrates gave judgement for the girl's mother, permitting her to arrange her daughter's marriage as she pleased. Might, however, was stronger than right, and the angry guardians, after holding forth in the streets to their political sympathizers on the injustice of the verdict, collected a party and carried the girl off from her mother's house. The noble lover was outraged; under his leadership an army of young aristocrats, out for blood, marched to confront the robbers. There was a savage battle, in which the popular party had the worst of it, and then – unlike the Roman commons on a famous occasion – having withdrawn from the town, sword in hand, and entrenched themselves on a hill outside the walls, proceeded to make destructive raids on the outlying farms of their aristocratic opponents; nor was this all, for having induced by the hope of plunder the whole body of artisans, who had previously been unconcerned in the quarrel, to come to their aid, they actually threatened to lay siege to the town. It was war indeed, with all its horrors, and the whole community seemed to have caught the plague and to be as rabid for blood as the two young men, each of whom was determined to get his girl though it meant the ruin of his country.

Before long neither side found its own resources adequate, and each applied for external aid, the aristocrats appealing to Rome for help in raising the siege, the popular party to the Volscians for reinforcements for the assault. The Volscians were the first to answer the call, and a detachment of them under the command of the Aequian Cluilius ringed the town with a trench and wall to prevent sorties. The consul Geganius, immediately the report of this reached Rome, marched with his troops to a position three miles from the Volscian force, where, as dusk was already swiftly falling, he ordered the men to rest; then at the beginning of the fourth watch he moved forward again and began the construction of a ring of earthworks around the enemy's position. So rapidly was the work done that by dawn the Volscians found themselves more securely pinned in by the Romans than was the town by themselves – for in point of fact the circumvallation of the town was incomplete, and Geganius was able to construct a fortified 'arm' or passage-way, leading from the town-wall, to enable his friends inside to pass in or out.

Cluilius, who had arranged no regular supplies for his men but had fed them hitherto on what he could get from the countryside, now suddenly found himself destitute of any sort of provision, and in this desperate situation invited Geganius to a parley, at which he said that, if the Romans had come with the object of raising the siege, he was willing to withdraw. Geganius replied that it was not the part of a defeated army to propose terms but to accept them: the Volscian force had come of its own free will to attack an ally of Rome – but its departure would be a very different matter. He then gave orders that the beaten men should surrender their commander, lay down their arms, and obey his instructions with a full admission of defeat; if they refused, he would, he said, continue hostilities whether they went or stayed, as he preferred to return to Rome with a victory to his credit, instead of a truce in which nobody would have any confidence. The Volscians, cut off from all outside aid, had no hope but in their swords – and that was not much; to add to their difficulties, the ground where they had to fight was all against them, while retreat was impossible. Surrounded as they were, they were cut to pieces and soon gave up the struggle and begged for quarter. Cluilius was handed over as a prisoner, their weapons were surrendered, and every man, stripped to his tunic, was sent 'under the yoke'. The remnants of the force, crushed and humiliated, were then allowed to go, but when they had got as far as the neighbourhood of Tusculum they were set upon in their defenceless condition by their old enemies of that town and so terribly punished that hardly a man was left to tell the tale.

Geganius restored peace to the distracted town of Ardea by executing the ringleaders of the recent troubles and turning over their property to the public funds. Though the inhabitants of the place felt that the generous help they had received amply compensated for the territory they had been so unjustly deprived of, the Senate was still convinced that not enough had been done to efface the memory of that notorious act of national avarice.

The consul returned to Rome in triumph, Cluilius the Volscian captain walking before his chariot, while in the procession were displayed the spoils of war, taken from the enemy after his surrender. Quinctius achieved the rare and difficult distinction of performing at home service as notable as his colleague had performed in the field; acting with perfect equity and discretion towards all classes of society, he was so successful in preserving good relations between the political parties that the Senate found in him a strict disciplinarian and the commons a kindly friend. Even in his dealings with the tribunes he avoided contention and got his way by the force of his personality. Quinctius was indeed a remarkable character: five consulships, all inspired by the same high principles, and a life lived throughout with the dignity of a high officer of state won him the awed respect of all not merely as a consul, but still more as a man. That year, with two such consuls, there was no mention of military tribunes.

The consuls for the following year were Marcus Fabius Vibulanus and Postumus Aebutius Cornicen. The year just closed had been remarkable for its fine achievements both in war and in the political arena, and had been rendered memorable abroad, to both friends and enemies by nothing so much as by the whole-hearted assistance given to Ardea in the crisis of her fortunes; the realization of this was an additional spur to the new consuls to blot out, once for all, from men's minds the memory of the infamous decision of the Roman populace in the matter of the disputed territory. For this purpose they issued a decree authorizing the enrolment of settlers who, as Ardea had been sadly depopulated by the civil war, would help to defend the town against the Volscians. This was the form in which the decree was published, as a blind to the tribunes and the populace who would otherwise have known that a plan was afoot to upset the judgement about the disputed territory; privately, however, the consuls had agreed, first, that the great majority of the settlers should be Rutulians (Ardea was a Rutulian town), secondly, that there should be no grants of land except from the sequestrated territory, and, thirdly, that no Roman should be given a single clod until all the Rutulians had been provided for. In this way the sequestrated territory reverted to Ardea. The commissioners for organizing the new settlement were Menenius Agrippa, Titus Cloelius Siculus, and Marcus Aebutius Helva; they had a most unpopular duty to perform, and not only angered the commons by distributing to an allied state grants of land which the Roman people had by a considered judgement declared to be their own, but also by a strict avoidance of any sort of favouritism failed to satisfy the great nobles; they were summoned by the tribunes to stand their trial before the people, but managed to avoid trouble by remaining in the settlement and thereby giving sufficient evidence of the justice and integrity of their administration.

Both in this year and the following – when the consuls were Gaius Furius Pacilus and Marcus Papirius Crassus – there was peace at home and abroad. The Games which the *decemvirs* had promised in accordance with a decree of the Senate during the secession of the commons were celebrated. One Poetilius tried to stir up trouble, but without success: he had got himself elected tribune for the second time by promising to force the consuls to bring before the Senate a proposal for the distribution of land to the commons; but he failed to do so, and when, after a great struggle, he managed to get the Senate to vote on whether consuls or military tribunes should be appointed for the succeeding year, the vote was in favour of consuls. He then threatened to obstruct recruiting, which amused people considerably as there was no prospect of war and no call for mobilization.

The next year, when Proculus Geganius Macerinus and Lucius Menenius Lanatus were consuls, was far from continuing the tranquillity of the last. On the contrary, it was a black one in almost every respect – a year of death and danger, of famine and sedition, while starving men were so grateful for gifts of food – given with an ulterior motive – that they almost fell to the lure and bowed their necks to the yoke of sovereignty. Had war been added to the list of miseries, scarcely by the help of all the gods in heaven could the country have survived. It began with famine caused, it may be, by a bad season or – as some say – by the pleasures of city life and the excitement of politics which had kept people from attending to their farms. The nobles accused the working population of idleness, the tribunes blamed the consuls for dishonesty and negligence. Finally, with no opposition from the Senate they induced the commons to procure the appointment of Lucius Minucius as Controller of Supplies, a man who was to prove during his tenure of office less successful in actual administration than as a guardian of public liberties, in spite of the fact that he did finally succeed in relieving the situation and was deservedly popular and respected in consequence. He began by sending missions all round the neighbouring states in the hope of purchasing grain, but except for a little he was able to obtain from Etruria his hopes were disappointed and he found the position as bad as ever; he accordingly fell back upon an attempt to distribute more evenly the burden of the shortage by various devices, such as forcing people to declare their stocks and, if they possessed more than a month's supply, to sell the surplus, cutting the slaves' daily ration and, finally, accusing the dealers of sharp practice and rousing popular fury against them. In effect however these inquisitorial methods did less to relieve the scarcity than to reveal its extent, and many of the poorer people, their last hope gone, covered their heads and drowned themselves in the Tiber to escape the anguish of prolonging their miserable lives.

Things had reached this pass, when a man named Spurius Maelius, who was rated as a cavalryman and was, for those days, exceedingly rich, undertook what should have been a useful service had it not set a very bad precedent and originated in motives which were even worse. At his own expense he bought grain in Etruria through the agency of friends and dependants in that country – a proceeding which in itself, I believe, had adversely affected government efforts to bring prices down – and then started to distribute it free amongst the poor. Such generosity won their hearts, and crowds of them followed him wherever he went, giving him an air of dignity and importance far beyond what was due to a man who held no official position. Their devoted support seemed to promise him the consulship at least, but – so rarely are the fair promises of fortune enough to satisfy the human heart – he was soon nursing a loftier – and a criminal – ambition. Even the consulship he would have had to fight for against the united opposition of the nobility; but it was no longer the consulship he wanted: it was the throne. Nothing less, he felt, would pay him adequately for all his elaborate plans and for the dust and heat of the great struggle which lay before him.

The consular elections took Maelius by surprise, as his plans were not yet fully matured; he was unfortunate, moreover, in the fact that Titus Quinctius Capitolinus, a difficult man for a revolutionary to deal with, was returned for the sixth time, with Menenius Agrippa, surnamed Lanatus, as his colleague. Lucius Minucius was reappointed Controller of Supplies – or perhaps given that position for an indefinite period, as circumstances should demand; for apart from the appearance of his name in the Linen Rolls amongst the magistrates for both years there is no definite agreement on that point. But however that may be, he was, in fact, officially concerned with the same task as Maelius had undertaken in a private capacity, with the natural result that the same type of men – corn-merchants and so on – were constantly in and out of both their houses. This led to the discovery of what was afoot, and Minucius reported to the Senate that Maelius was building up a store of arms in his house and secretly talking to certain groups of people. There was no doubt in Minucius's mind that plans were going on to set up a monarchy, and that though the time to strike had not yet been fixed everything else had been arranged – the tribunes bribed to betray the country's liberty and the mob leaders all assigned their tasks. He had, he said, put off giving this information rather longer than public safety required; but he had been anxious to wait until rumours became certainties.

The Senate was both angry and alarmed by this revelation. The leaders of the House blamed the consuls of the previous year for allowing the free distribution of grain and for not stopping suspicious assemblies of the commons in a private house, while at the same time they were no less critical of the new consuls for having waited for a revelation of such importance, which required a consul at least not only to report it but also to take action upon it, to be made to the Senate by a mere Controller of Supplies. Quinctius, on the other hand, maintained that the consuls were not to blame, for, fettered as they were by the Appeal laws, deliberately designed to break their authority, they had less power than will to punish an offence of that sort in the summary fashion it deserved. What was needed, was not merely a resolute man, but a man who was also free from the net of legal controls. Such being the circumstances, Quinctius declared that he would nominate Lucius Quinctius Cincinnatus as Dictator, convinced that in him were courage and resolution equal to the majestic authority of that office. The proposal was unanimously approved, but Cincinnatus, hesitating to accept the burden of responsibility, asked what the Senate was thinking of to wish to expose an old man like him to what must prove the sternest of struggles; but hesitation was vain, for when from every corner of the House came the cry that in that aged heart there was more wisdom – yes, and courage too – than in all the rest put together, and when praises, well deserved, were heaped upon him and the consul refused to budge an inch from his purpose, Cincinnatus gave way and, with a prayer to God to save his old age from bringing loss or dishonour upon his country in her trouble, was named Dictator by the consul. Having appointed Gaius Servilius Ahala as his Master of Horse, on the following day he picketed the city and made his appearance in the Forum, where the unusual and surprising sight turned all eyes upon him. Maelius and his fellow conspirators knew well enough that it was against themselves that the powers of that exalted office were directed, but all who were not in the plot asked in bewilderment what sudden rising or unexpected threat of attack could have rendered necessary so drastic a step – a Dictator in all his majesty, the aged Cincinnatus (he was over eighty) in supreme control of the country's fortunes. On Cincinnatus's orders Servilius then addressed to Maelius the ominous words: 'The Dictator requires your presence'. Maelius, turning pale, asked what he wanted, and was told in reply that he would have to answer in a court of law to a certain charge which Minucius had brought against him in the Senate. The wretched man shrank back amongst his friends, looking desperately around for some way of escape, and when Servilius's sergeant attempted to arrest him he was dragged away by some of the bystanders and fled, calling for help from the common people he had befriended. 'Save me!' he cried. 'The nobles have united to put me down because I was your friend. Help me now in my deadly peril – do not let me be butchered before your eyes!' His cries availed nothing. Servilius caught him and cut him down, then, spattered with his blood and guarded by a group of young patricians, went back to report to the dictator: Maelius, he said, on a summons to attend him had forcibly eluded the sergeant and was trying to raise a popular revolt. He had been punished as he deserved. 'Sir,' the dictator replied, 'I congratulate you. You have saved the country from tyranny.'

Uncertain of the significance of what had happened, the crowd was in a state of great excitement, when Cincinnatus called for silence and addressed them. 'Maelius,' he declared 'has been justly killed, even if he was not guilty of aiming at the throne; he was summoned by the Master of the Horse to present himself before the Dictator, and refused: that in itself was a capital offence. I had taken my seat to hear his cause, and he would have been treated in accordance with the verdict, had the trial proceeded; but having used force in an attempt to avoid trial, by force he has been dealt with. How could we treat such a man as one of ourselves? He was born here amongst a free people protected by just laws; he knew, as we do, that the kings were expelled; he knew that in the same year Tarquin's nephews, sons of the consul who set our country free, were executed for a plot to restore the monarchy; he knew that the consul Tarquinius Collatinus was forced to resign office and leave Rome simply because he bore the hated name of a king, and that a few years later Spurius Cassius suffered the supreme penalty for conspiring to seize the throne; he knew that only the other day the *decemvirs* were punished with confiscation, exile, and death for arrogating to themselves the air and authority of kings; all this Maelius knew, yet in this same city of ours he himself dared hoped to reign. And what was he? To be sure, noble blood, high office, distinguished services are not, in Rome, the means of smoothing the path to tyranny; yet we must admit that men like Appius Claudius or Cassius had some reason, at least, to aspire to forbidden heights – they had splendid estates, and family traditions of public service; they had been consuls or *decemvirs*. But Spurius Maelius! a fellow who might have hoped – and hoped in vain – to be made a tribune – a rich corn-dealer of humble birth – *this* was the man who thought he could buy our liberty with a bag of flour, and that Rome, the mistress of Italy, could be lured into servitude by tossing her a biscuit! He fondly imagined that we, who could hardly think of him as a senator without a pain in the belly, would endure him as a king with the power and insignia of our founder Romulus – of Romulus, descended from the gods and now returned to their blessed company! Why, the thing is not a crime merely, it is a monstrosity – nor is his blood enough to pay for it: the house where he lived, where he first conceived this piece of criminal lunacy, must be utterly demolished and the fortune he tainted in the attempt to buy a throne must be confiscated. It is my order, therefore, that the quaestors sell everything he possessed and turn over the proceeds to the public funds.'

Cincinnatus then issued instructions for the immediate demolition of the house, the site, which came to be called Aequimaelium, to be left empty as a permanent reminder of the plot that failed.

Minucius was presented with an ox with gilded horns; the presentation took place outside the Porta Trigemina, and the common people made no objection as he let them have for a penny a bushel all the grain which had been bought up by Maelius. I find in some records that Minucius changed his standing to that of a plebeian, was co-opted as tribune in addition to the statutory number of ten, and stopped an incipient riot arising out of Maelius's death. But it is hardly credible that the senatorial party would have permitted an increase in the number of tribunes, and still less that such a precedent should have been set by a man of patrician birth; and the commons, once they had got the concession, would surely have held on to it, or at least tried to do so. But the strongest argument for the inaccuracy of the inscription on his portrait-bust is the fact that a few years previously a law had been passed forbidding the tribunes to co-opt a colleague.

Quintus Caecilius, Quintus Junius, and Sextus Titinius were the only tribunes who had not supported the proposal to honour Minucius, and ever since they had been constantly bringing charges against both him and Servilius on the grounds that Maelius had been illegally executed, and by this means they succeeded in forcing through a measure providing for the election the following year of military tribunes instead of consuls, convinced as they were that some at any rate of the six elected (six now being the statutory number) would be plebeians, provided that they declared their purpose of avenging Maelius's death. The commons, however, in spite of all their troubles during the past year, elected only three military tribunes, one of whom was Lucius Quinctius, son of the very man whose dictatorship people were trying to use as a cause of resentment, to stir up further trouble. Aemilius Mamercus, a man of high distinction, headed the poll, with Quinctius second and Lucius Julius third.

During their year of office the Roman colony of Fidenae threw off its allegiance and went over to Lars Tolumnius, king of Veii. Worse than the defection was the crime which followed – the murder of four envoys from Rome. These men – Gaius Fulcinius, Cloelius Tullus, Spurius Antius, and Lucius Roscius – had visited the town with instructions from the Roman government to demand a reason for the change of policy, and were all murdered by Tolumnius's orders. An attempt has been made to whitewash the crime: Tolumnius (it is maintained) was playing at dice and, upon a lucky throw, made some remark or other which was taken by the Fidenates as an order to kill the envoys, and that this mistake was the cause of their death. But it is incredible that Tolumnius should not have had his attention distracted from a game of dice by the arrival of a mission from Fidenae – new allies come to consult him about a murder which would violate the law of nations. The idea of attributing the crime to a mere mistake must surely have come later. It is far more likely that Tolumnius wanted to involve the people of Fidenae in the guilt of the murder, and and so to render their break with Rome final and absolute. Statues of the murdered envoys were set up on the Rostra in the Forum.

The struggle, now about to begin, with Fidenae and Veii was bound to be a desperate one, not only because they were close neighbours of Rome but also, and especially, because of the unspeakable brutality of the occasion for it which they had themselves provided; in view of this neither commons nor tribunes attempted to raise any dispute about the supreme command, and the two consuls elected were Marcus Geganius Macerinus (for the third time) and Lucius Sergius, later sur-

named Fidenas – presumably for his services in the campaign, for he
was the first commander to fight a successful battle with the king of
Veii south of the Anio. The victory was a costly one and caused more
grief for Roman lives lost than joy for the enemy's defeat, and the
Senate, following the usual practice in times of crisis, decreed the appointment of Mamercus Aemilius as Dictator, who, in his turn, named
as Master of the Horse a man who had been military tribune with him
the previous year – Lucius Quinctius Cincinnatus, a fine young soldier
worthy of his eminent father. The troops raised by the consuls were
stiffened by the addition of centurions with long experience of active
service, and the casualties of the last battle were made good. As his
senior officers, or seconds in command, the Dictator appointed
Quinctius Capitolinus and Marcus Fabius Vibulanus.

The majestic authority of the dictatorship in the hands of a man fully
capable of exercising it was enough to make the enemy withdraw
from Roman territory and re-cross the Anio, after which they took up
a position on the hills between the river and Fidenae, not venturing
down until they were reinforced by troops from Falerii, when they
moved to a fresh position before the walls of Fidenae. The Roman
Dictator fortified a position a few miles south at the confluence of the
Anio and the Tiber, throwing up an earthwork from bank to bank,
at a point where the distance was not too great, between himself and
the enemy; then, on the following day, he marched out into battle
position. The enemy were not agreed upon the best tactics to adopt:
the contingent from Falerii was for immediate action, as the men were
confident and inclined to grumble at the prospect of a long campaign
so far from home, while their allies from Veii and Fidenae both
thought success more likely if they felt their way cautiously and waited
on events. Tolumnius himself shared this latter view, but preferred,
nevertheless, to humour the men of Falerii lest they should find the
conditions of a campaign so far away intolerable; he accordingly said
that he would fight next day. Mamercus and his troops were encouraged by the fact that the enemy had not at once accepted their
challenge, and on the following day the rank and file swore to assault
the enemy's camp and the town of Fidenae if he still refused to fight it
out in the open. However, he left his defences, and both armies
marched in battle order to their stations between the two camps. The
Veientes, who were numerically strong, sent a detachment round
the back of the hills to attack the Roman camp during the coming

engagement, the main body of their force holding the right of the allied armies, with the contingent from Falerii on the left and that from Fidenae in the centre; on the Roman side, the Dictator commanded the right, and Capitolinus the left, while the Master of the Horse led out his squadrons in front of the centre.

For some minutes there was neither sound nor movement. The Etruscans had no intention of attacking unless they were forced to it, and the Dictator kept glancing behind him at the citadel in Rome, waiting for the agreed signal from the augurs which they were to send him as soon as the omens were favourable. The instant he saw it he ordered his cavalry to charge; off they went, shouting their battle-cry, and the infantry followed. The weight of both attacks was tremendous and in no part of their line could the Etruscans stand against them; the Etruscan horse offered the stiffest resistance, and of all their mounted troops none fought with such courage as Tolumnius the king, who kept the fight going by repeated individual attacks upon Roman cavalrymen as they galloped in loose order in pursuit of the fugitives.

The conduct of Aulus Cornelius Cossus must here have special mention. Cossus was a cavalry officer of high rank, a magnificent figure of a man, strong as an ox and as brave as he was strong; proud of his distinguished name, he left it to his descendants with an added lustre. This officer had observed the effect of Tolumnius's attacks upon the Roman squadrons, which everywhere reeled and hesitated under them, and his regal dress and equipment as he rode, wheeling and swooping swift as a bird, now here, now there, soon revealed his identity. At once Cossus made up his mind. 'So this is he,' he cried, 'who broke the compact of man with man and violated the law of nations! If it is God's will that there should be anything sacred in this world, I will appease with his blood the ghosts of the men he murdered!' Putting spurs to his horse he rode at his enemy with levelled spear. The blow struck home and Tolumnius fell; instantly, Cossus dismounted and as Tolumnius struggled to rise struck him down again with the boss of his shield and with repeated thrusts of his spear finally pinned him to the ground. Then he stripped the lifeless body of its armour, cut off its head and, sticking it on the point of a lance, returned to the fight with his spoils. At the sight of their dead king the enemy broke and fled. That ended the resistance of the Etruscan cavalry, which had been the only arm to keep the issue in doubt. The Dictator pressed on in pursuit of the routed legionaries, drove them to the walls of their camp, and cut them to pieces; though a large part of the contingent from Fidenae, fighting as it was on familiar ground, managed to escape into the hills. Cossus crossed the Tiber with his cavalry and brought back to Rome immense quantities of valuable material from the territory of Veii. Tolumnius, it will be remembered, had sent a brigade round the back of the hills to the Roman camp, so here, too, there was fighting while the main action was in progress. Fabius Vibulanus manned the rampart with a thin line – 'crowned' it, as the phrase is – and then, when the enemy were fully engaged in their efforts to storm it, marched his veteran reserves out of the main gate on the right and delivered a surprise attack. The effect was devastating: fewer were killed than in the main action as fewer were engaged, but the rout was no less complete.

In recognition of all these victories the Senate with the support of the whole population granted the Dictator a Triumph. On his return to Rome the finest sight in all the procession was Cossus carrying the 'spoils of honour' – the arms and equipment of King Tolumnius, slain by his hand – while the troops roared out impromptu songs comparing him to Romulus. He afterwards solemnly dedicated the spoils in the temple of Jupiter Feretrius, hanging them on the temple wall near those which Romulus had taken – the first, and, up to that time, the only ones to be known as 'spoils of honour'. During the procession the Dictator's chariot had been almost ignored – it was Cossus who was the cynosure of every eye, and the honours of the festival and the plaudits of the crowds were, to all intents and purposes, his alone. The Dictator at the people's request offered to Jupiter on the Capitol a golden crown, a pound in weight, paid for out of public funds.

I have followed all previous chroniclers in saying that Aulus Cornelius Cossus was a senior officer – 'army tribune' – when he deposited the 'spoils of honour' in the temple of Jupiter Feretrius; but there is a difficulty here, for in addition to the fact that the expression 'spoils of honour' is properly applicable only when they are taken by the supreme commander from the supreme commander of the enemy, and that we recognize no supreme commander apart from the man under whose auspices the campaign is fought, the actual inscription on the spoils proves that Cossus was consul when he took them. I have heard that Augustus Caesar, founder and restorer of all our

temples, entered the shrine of Jupiter Feretrius, which he had caused
to be rebuilt after many years of neglect and dilapidation, and himself
read the inscription on the linen corslet, and I have felt, in consequence, that it would be almost sacrilege to deprive Cossus of so
great a witness to his spoils as Caesar, the restorer of that very shrine.
By what error the ancient annals and the Linen Rolls of magistrates in
the temple of Moneta, cited again and again as his authority by
Licinius Macer, only record Cossus as having shared the consulship
seven years later with Titus Quinctius Pennus, is anybody's guess.
Again, it is impossible to shift the date of such a famous battle to this
subsequent year, because Cossus's consulship (to assume the later date)
fell within a three-year period during which, owing to famine and
epidemics, there were no wars at all – indeed certain annals of the time,
as dismal as death-registers, give us nothing beyond the names of the
consuls. In the third year after his consulship Cossus is mentioned as
Military Tribune with consular powers, and in the same year as Master
of the Horse, in which capacity he fought another distinguished
cavalry action. In all this there is room for conjecture, though in my
own view it is unnecessary; for one need hardly attend to other
people's guesses when the man himself who fought the battle, having
laid his newly won spoils in their sacred resting-place, in the visible
presence, if one may say so, of Romulus and of Jupiter to whom he
dedicated them – awful witnesses whom no forger would take lightly
– inscribed his name and title as *Aulus Cornelius Cossus, consul.*[1]

Next year – in the consulship of Marcus Cornelius Maluginensis and
Lucius Papirius Crassus – there were expeditions against the territory
of Veii and Falerii, resulting in a number of prisoners and some captured cattle. There was no fighting, as enemy troops were nowhere
encountered, and no attempt was made upon the towns as an epidemic
had started in Rome. The tribune Spurius Maelius tried, but without
success, to stir up political trouble; he knew his name was popular with
his own class, and hoping it might be enough to start something he
issued a summons against Minucius and at the same time put forward
a proposal to confiscate the property of Servilius Ahala, on the grounds
that his namesake Maelius, the corn-merchant, had been falsely accused by Minucius, while Servilius was guilty of the crime of killing a
citizen who had not been condemned in the courts. However, nobody

1. This paragraph appears to have been added after the book was completed.
In ch. 32 Cossus is again referred to as an ' army tribune'.

paid any attention to him – and even less to his charges; there were other and more important causes of concern. The virulence of the epidemic was on the increase; odd and frightening things were happening – most notably frequent earth-tremors which, the reports said, had been causing the collapse of buildings in the countryside – and a day of public prayer was held under the direction of the *duumvirs*, the two officials in charge of the Sibylline books.

The following year, when Gaius Julius (for the second time) and Lucius Verginius were consuls, the epidemic was worse still. Fears of its ultimate effects in both town and country destroyed all enterprise: no raids were undertaken, no thought of aggressive operations entered anyone's mind in any class of society; and – even more sinister – the men of Fidenae, who had previously kept to their mountains or within their walls, now ventured down into Roman territory, eager to take what they could find. Presently they got reinforcements from Veii (as for Falerii, neither the distresses of Rome nor the entreaties of her friends could induce her to resume hostilities) and the combined armies crossed the Anio and advanced almost as far as the Colline Gate. The alarm in the outlying districts was now felt no less acutely in the City itself; the consul Julius manned the walls and the outer defences; his colleague Verginius convened the Senate in the temple of Quirinus, and a resolution was passed to appoint Aulus Servilius Dictator (authorities differ about Servilius's surname; it was either Priscus or Structus). Verginius waited to consult his colleague and then, with his permission, that night named the Dictator, who thereupon took Postumus Aebutius Helva as his Master of the Horse. Servilius's first order was that all available men should report at dawn outside the Colline Gate, and it was promptly obeyed by everyone in a fit state to bear arms. The standards were then fetched from the treasury and brought to him.

Such evidence of activity induced the enemy to withdraw to higher ground, and without delay Servilius was on their tracks. Near Nomentum he caught them, beat them soundly and forced them to take refuge in Fidenae, which he then proceeded to ring with an earthwork. Fidenae was a fortified hill-town and could not be taken by means of scaling-ladders, nor, as it happened, could anything have been done by blockading it, as it was full of supplies which had been collected some time before – far more than enough for its immediate needs. Servilius, however, knew the locality well, as Fidenae was quite near Rome, and on this knowledge he based his plan of campaign. Realizing the impossibility either of taking the place by storm or of starving it into surrender, he had a sap constructed on the far side, where the conformation of the ground made a natural defence, so that few, if any, in that quarter would be on the look-out for danger. To distract attention from the work he split his remaining force into four divisions which he sent successively to threaten the walls of the town at widely separated points, keeping the enemy continuously engaged night and day, until the sap was completed and a passage-way opened right up into the citadel. The Etruscans meanwhile, intent upon dealing with what were merely feints, were quite unaware of the real danger, until the triumphant cheer of the Romans, far above them in the citadel, told them that the town was captured.

During that year the censors Gaius Furius Pacilus and Marcus Geganius Macerinus approved the erection of a building at the public expense in the Campus Martius, and the census was held there for the first time.

According to the historian Licinius Macer the same consuls were elected for the year which followed: Julius for the third time and Verginius for the second. Valerius Antias and Quintus Tubero, on the contrary, state that the consuls for that year were Marcus Manlius and Quintus Sulpicius. In spite of the discrepancy both Tubero and Macer quote the authority of the Linen Rolls, and neither of them conceals the fact that previous chroniclers had recorded that there were military tribunes that year, not consuls at all; Licinius chooses unhesitatingly to follow the Linen Rolls, Tubero admits to uncertainty. So we must leave it in doubt – the mists of antiquity cannot always be pierced.

The capture of Fidenae caused great alarm in Etruria, especially in the towns of Veii and Falerii – the former from dread of a similar fate, and the latter from the uneasy consciousness of having supported Fidenae when the war started, even though in the second outbreak she had stood aside. Accordingly when these two communities obtained the consent of the Twelve Towns for a general council of all Etruria to meet at the temple of Voltumna, the Senate in Rome expected a serious rising and, to meet it, decreed that Mamercus Aemilius should again be appointed Dictator. Mamercus named Aulus Postumius Tubertus Master of the Horse, and the danger from a united Etruria being so much greater than last time, when only Veii and Fidenae were involved, mobilization began on a proportionately greater scale. However the whole affair ended more peacefully than anyone expected; traders came back with news that Veii had failed to secure support: having started the war on her own initiative she must carry it on with her own resources, and not expect friends to share her troubles when they had not been offered a share in the prospect of success. Mamercus, in this changed situation, was nevertheless unwilling to allow his dictatorship to lapse with nothing accomplished, even though the opportunity of military fame was gone; hoping, therefore, to render his office memorable by some service in the political field, he planned to curtail the power of the censorship, either because he thought it excessive or, perhaps, merely because he felt it to be a mistake that the censors' term of office should be such a long one. With this in view he declared before an assembly that, the gods having evidently undertaken to protect the interests of the country in foreign affairs, he himself proposed to turn his attention to domestic matters and to do what he could to ensure the liberties of the People. The greatest safeguard, he said, of those liberties was to see that great powers should never remain long in the same hands: positions of political eminence could not be limited in the scope of their jurisdiction, but they could be limited in duration. The censorship was tenable for five years, other magistracies only for one, and it was not an acceptable thing to have the same people in control for so long over so many aspects of one's life. He intended, therefore, to introduce a bill limiting the censorship to a period of a year and a half. The bill was carried through next day with enthusiastic popular support, whereupon Mamercus instantly resigned the dictatorship – 'to give', as he put it in a speech to the people, 'concrete evidence of my disapproval of the extended tenure of power'. The commons were delighted; the new law and Mamercus's resignation had alike won their warm approval, and crowds escorted him like a public hero to his residence.

The censors, on the other hand, were furious at what Mamercus had done; they struck his name from the register of his tribe, octupled his assessment for tax and reduced him to the lowest class of citizens, thus disfranchising him and making him ineligible for any public office. This vindictive punishment he is said to have borne with remarkable fortitude, which allowed the degradation he had suffered to sink into insignificance beside the memory of the act which led to it; the leaders of the patrician party, though they had not approved the weakening of the censorship, nevertheless greatly disliked this example of its ruthlessness in action – aware, no doubt, of the obvious fact that individually they would all have to suffer the jurisdiction of the censors much more often and for much longer periods than they would have a chance of exercising it. As for the populace, they were so fiercely indignant that nothing could have saved the censors from their fury except the restraining influence of Mamercus himself.

The tribunes steadily opposed the holding of consular elections for the succeeding year; a little longer and it would have been necessary to appoint an *interrex*, but, just in time, they carried their point and procured the election of military tribunes with consular power; they did not, however, get what they hoped for from their victory, namely the election of a plebeian: the successful candidates – Marcus Fabius Vibulanus, Marcus Foslius, and Lucius Sergius Fidenas – were all patricians.

During the year more sickness distracted men's minds from political agitations. On behalf of the public health a temple was vowed to Apollo; by direction of the Sibylline Books, the officials in charge of those documents did much to attempt to placate the wrath of the gods and avert the curse of the epidemic, but in spite of all both men and cattle died and there were terrible losses in town and country. The farmers, too, were falling sick, and in fear of famine delegations were sent to buy grain in Etruria and the Pomptine, and finally as far as Sicily. No mention was made of consular elections; again military tribunes with consular power were appointed, and again they were all patricians – Lucius Pinarius Mamercus, Lucius Furius Medullinus, and Spurius Postumius Albus. Then at last the virulence of the epidemic began to abate, and that year there was no fear of famine, steps having been taken to lay in supplies. War plans were discussed in the councils of the Volscians and Aequians, and also in Etruria at the shrine of Voltumna, where a decision was postponed for a year and a decree issued forbidding any further meeting until the year was over, in spite of the urgent and bitter representations of Veii that she was threatened with the same disaster as that which had brought destruction to Fidenae.

In Rome meanwhile the leaders of the popular movement, continually disappointed of their hopes of further political advancement so long as the country was not at war, began to arrange secret meetings in the tribunes' houses to discuss their plans. The attitude they took was one of indignation against their own party for the apparent contempt in which they, the leaders, were held: year after year military tribunes had been appointed, yet never once had a plebeian candidate been returned. The original precaution that patricians should not be eligible for plebeian magistracies was indeed a wise one, for had it not been taken they would, no doubt, have had to put up with patricians in the tribunate – such, at least, was the natural inference from the attitude towards them of their own class, which despised them as heartily as the patricians did. Another line of argument tried to fix the blame on their patrician opponents: according to this, plebeian candidates found their road to office blocked by the skilful canvassing of their noble rivals, and if only the common people could get a respite from those veiled menaces masquerading as a humble request for votes, they might remember their own friends when they went to the polls and so have representatives with real power as well as the right, which they already possessed, of helping them in trouble. They therefore proposed to abolish canvassing, and for this purpose urged that the tribunes should bring forward a bill prohibiting candidates for office from whitening their togas.[2] This may hardly seem a serious matter nowadays, but it was a burning question at the time and caused the fiercest of struggles between the opposing parties. In the end the tribunes got their proposal passed into law, and it was soon evident that the commons in their present exacerbated mood would rally to the support of their own candidates. To prevent them from doing so, the Senate, on the strength of a report from the Latins and the Hernici of an Aequian and Volscian rising, issued a decree for the election of consuls. The men elected were Titus Quinctius Cincinnatus, son of Lucius and also surnamed Poenus, and Cnaeus Julius Mento.

War was obviously imminent. Both the Volscians and Aequians had been raising troops by their surest method – under the sanction, that is, of a law which carried the penalty of outlawry; the forces of each were in consequence numerically strong, and, having proceeded to Algidus, they took up separate positions, constructed elaborate defences, and began a more intensive period of training than ever before. Reports of these activities increased the alarm in Rome, and the Senate resolved on the appointment of a Dictator; there were three reasons for this step, first that the enemy, though often previously defeated, was this time planning aggression on a greater scale than ever before; secondly, the drain on Roman military strength owing to the epidemic; thirdly, and most particularly, the general anxiety caused by

2. A candidate wore a white (*candidus*) toga.

the incompetence of the consuls who were perpetually at loggerheads
and could never agree in any of their plans. Some historians have put
forward the view that they lost a battle on Algidus, and that that was
the reason why a Dictator was appointed; but however that may be, it
is certain that in one point at least the two men were in agreement,
namely in their opposition to the Senate over the appointment of a
Dictator. Finally when the news became more and more alarming and
the consuls refused altogether to submit to the Senate's direction, a
distinguished public servant named Quintus Servilius Priscus turned to
the tribunes for a way out of the impasse. 'We are at the end of our
tether;' he declared, 'so the Senate calls upon you to use your powers
in this crisis to compel the consuls to name a Dictator.' The tribunes
saw in this appeal an opportunity of increasing their power, and after
a private conference announced their unanimous resolution that the
consuls should obey the Senate, adding that if they continued to flout
the united will of that honourable body they would order them to
prison. The consuls found it less unpleasant to have to yield to the
tribunes than to the Senate; so they gave way, not without the angry
comment that the supreme office of the state had been betrayed and
that through the weakness of the Senate the consulship had been forced
to capitulate to the power of the tribunes; for what other meaning
could be attached to the fact that consuls could be subjected to the
compulsion of a tribune and even suffer the intolerable indignity of
being sent to gaol?

The duty of naming a Dictator fell by lot to Titus Quinctius – for
the two 'colleagues' (if one may so call them without irony) could not
agree even on this small matter. Quinctius named his father-in-law,
Aulus Postumius Tubertus, a well-known disciplinarian and martinet.
Lucius Julius was made his Master of the Horse. Immediately the order
went out for the raising of troops, and at the same time all legal business was suspended and all activities forbidden which might in any
way hamper mobilization; the hearing of claims for exemption was
postponed till the war was over, which had the effect of inducing possible malingerers, or those whose claims were doubtful, to register.
The Latins and Hernici were also instructed to raise troops, and the
Dictator's orders were in both cases eagerly obeyed. All this was done
with the utmost dispatch; the consul Cnaeus Julius was left to guard
the City, with Lucius Julius, Master of the Horse, in charge of emergency supplies so that the troops on service might not be held up by

shortages. The Dictator then vowed – repeating the formula after the Pontifex Maximus – to celebrate votive games by way of thanks to heaven in the event of victory, and, putting the consul Quinctius in command of one-half of the army, marched from Rome.

Seeing on their approach that the enemy had fortified two positions a little way apart, the Roman commanders followed suit and encamped separately, about a mile away, the consul in a position south of the Dictator's; there was thus space between the four armies and their re-spective entrenchments for irregular skirmishing – and indeed for full deployment in a pitched battle. As for skirmishing, it went on con-tinuously from the moment the Roman positions were established over against their adversaries, for the Dictator was more than willing to let his men try out what they could do and by success in minor engage-ments come gradually to have confidence in a major victory. The enemy, for their part, soon lost hope of succeeding in a straight fight, and had recourse to the very risky procedure of a night attack on the consul's camp. The sudden noise put the sentries on the alert, and a moment later the whole army was awake. The Dictator, too, had heard it. Instant action was necessary, and the consul was equal to it both in judgement and resolution, losing no time in strengthening the guards at the gates and 'crowning' his defences with armed men. In the Dic-tator's camp, where things were naturally quieter, it was easier to de-termine precisely what steps were necessary to meet the emergency, and reinforcements were promptly sent under the command of Pos-tumius Albus, while the Dictator himself took a party of men round to a spot well away from the main action, from which he would be able to deliver a surprise attack in the enemy's rear. Sulpicius was put in command of the camp, and the other lieutenant Marcus Fabius was given charge of the cavalry with strict orders not to move before day-light, to avoid the confusion in which mounted troops are so easily involved during night fighting. The Dictator, in fact, took all the neces-sary steps and precautions which any forceful and prudent commander would take in similar circumstances; but he went further than mere normal efficiency, and proved his really original tactical enterprise by sending Geganius with picked troops to storm the enemy camp from which, as his scouts had ascertained, most of the men had already gone. Geganius and his party found the remainder intent upon the issue of the enterprise in which their friends were engaged and with no thought for any peril which might threaten themselves; they had consequently neglected all ordinary precautions against surprise, and their camp was in Roman hands almost before they knew that the assault had begun. The instant the Dictator saw the prearranged smoke-signal he had the news of the success announced to every man under his command.

The coming of daylight soon revealed how things were going: Fabius had delivered a cavalry charge; the consul had made a sortie from the camp against the enemy who were already showing signs of distress, and the Dictator had come in on their rear with an attack on their supporting troops in the second line. The din of battle was everywhere in their ears, and desperately they tried to meet the sudden simultaneous threats from so many points at once, but all to no purpose; they were surrounded, and every man of them would have paid the penalty of rebellion had it not been for the courageous act of the Volscian soldier, Vettius Messius, a man of obscure birth but a great fighter. Seeing his comrades forming a circle for their final hopeless stand, he raised his voice above the din and roared out his challenge. 'Do you mean', he cried, 'to offer your throats to the Romans' steel without a blow struck in your own defence? What are your swords for? Why did you start this war, if you can do no better than this? Shame on you for peace-time soldiers, who shrink from action when it comes! What hope while you stand cowering here? Do you think some god will help you and let you out of this trap? Come, hack your way out – follow my lead, if you ever hope to see your homes and wives and parents and children again. There is no wall of earth or stone to stop you – but armed men like yourselves; in courage you are as good as they – in the ultimate and most powerful weapon of all – desperation – you have the advantage!'

Messius was as good as his word: his comrades raised the battle-cry once more and followed his lead, flinging themselves against the Roman cohorts under Postumius Albus with such effect that they forced them to give ground until the Dictator arrived upon the scene. All the fighting was now concentrated upon this one sector, and the fate of the enemy hung upon one man – Messius. Many fell on both sides, wounded or dead; even the Roman commanders bled as they fought. The Dictator was wounded in the shoulder, Fabius's thigh was pinned to his horse by a lance, the consul had an arm shorn off, but the fight was critical and all three fought on. Only Postumius left the field, his skull fractured by a stone. Messius with a gallant company thrust his way over the bodies of the dead and dying to the Volscian camp which was not yet in Roman hands, and upon that point all the fighting converged: the consul began his assault upon the outer defences, quickly followed in another section by the Dictator. The assault was no less vigorous than the preceding struggle; the consul is said to have spurred his men to fiercer efforts by throwing his standard inside the rampart and that it was in their determination to recover it that the first onslaught was made, almost at the moment when the Dictator breached the defences and carried his troops through into the camp itself. That was the end: resistance was over and the enemy began on all hands to lay down their arms and give themselves up. With the capture of the camp every man in the enemy army, with the exception of senators, was sold into slavery. Of the material taken, that portion which the Latins and Hernici identified as their own was restored to them, and the rest was sold by auction on the instructions of the Dictator, who then, having left the consul in charge, drove back in triumph to Rome and resigned his dictatorship.

The memory of these splendid achievements is darkened by a story that the dictator's son, who, seeing a chance of distinguishing himself, had left his post without orders, was executed for insubordination in the very moment of success. One hesitates to believe this tale, and as opinions differ about it one may, I suppose, take it or leave it as one pleases; an argument against it is the existence of the phrase 'Manlian discipline': we do not speak of 'Postumian discipline', and it is surely most probable that a phrase expressive of extreme severity would be derived from the person who, of the two, was the first to give a notable example of it. Again, it was Manlius who was given the sobriquet of 'the Martinet', while Postumius was never distinguished by any mark or title of disagreeable significance.

The consul Julius dedicated the temple of Apollo in the absence of his colleague. The formality of drawing lots was omitted, to the annoyance of Quinctius who after disbanding his forces returned to Rome and laid a complaint before the Senate, but to no purpose. One other thing happened in the course of this eventful year: the Carthaginians – destined one day to be our bitterest enemies – crossed for the first time into Sicily to take sides in a local dispute. This seemed at the time to have no significance for Rome!

Next year Lucius Papirius Crassus and Lucius Julius were elected to the consulship in spite of attempts by the tribunes to procure the appointment of military tribunes with consular powers. The Aequians

sent a delegation to the Senate to ask for a treaty between the two
states; the Senate began by suggesting unconditional surrender but
finally granted them an armistice for eight years; the Volscians fared
worse, for in addition to their defeat on Algidus they found themselves involved in violent internal quarrels between the peace-party
and the war-party. In Rome all was tranquil. The consuls got information, which one of the college of tribunes allowed to slip out, that the
tribunes were contemplating a very popular bill to regulate the assessment of fines, and took the opportunity thus offered to anticipate their
opponents by introducing the measure themselves.

The next year, the consulship of Lucius Sergius Fidenas and Hostius
Lucretius Tricipitinus, saw no events of importance and was followed
by the election to office of Aulus Cornelius Cossus and Titus Quinctius
Pennus (for the second time). Raiding parties from Veii entered Roman
territory and it was said that a number of people from Fidenae parti-
cipated in the raids; three men, Sergius, Servilius, and Aemilius, were
commissioned to look into the truth of this rumour and as a result
certain people were banished to Ostia, as no satisfactory reason could
be found for their absence from Fidenae at the time in question. Fresh
settlers were sent to the settlement and were given land which had
belonged to men killed in the war. The year was marked by a serious
drought; not only was the rainfall inadequate, but there was barely
sufficient moisture in the earth to supply the perennial streams; in some
places it was so bad that cattle lay dying of thirst near the dried-up
springs and along the banks of the parched brooks; others died of scab
and the infection was passed on by contact to human beings, the
country-folk and slaves being the first to go down, after which the
City was infected. Men's minds fell sick as well as their bodies; they
became possessed by all sorts of superstitions, mostly of foreign origin,
and the sort of people who can turn other men's superstitious terrors to
their own advantage set up as seers and introduced strange rites and
ceremonies into private houses, until the debased state of the national
conscience came to the notice of the leaders of society, who could not
but be aware in every street and chapel of the weird and outlandish
forms of prayer by which their hagridden compatriots sought to appease the wrath of heaven. Then the government stepped in, and the
aediles were instructed to see that only Roman gods were worshipped
and only in the traditional way.

The punishment of Veii was postponed to the following year, when the consulship was held by Gaius Servilius Ahala and Lucius Papirius Mugilanus. Even then, however, a certain difficulty connected with religious observance prevented the prompt declaration of war and the dispatch of troops, and the decision was taken to precede hostilities by sending the fetials to demand compensation for all property taken in the recent raids. Not long before there had been a clash with Veii at Nomentum, and also at Fidenae, after which only an armistice, not a peace, had been signed; the period of the armistice had already expired and, moreover, the Veientes had renewed hostilities before the date when it was due to end; none the less the fetials were sent on their mission, but without effect, for their demand for compensation, duly made after the traditional oath, was ignored. In Rome the question then arose whether war could be properly declared by a decree of the Senate or whether it would be necessary to obtain the consent of the people as a whole; there was some controversy on this point, ending in a victory for the tribunes who, by declaring their intention to stop recruiting, succeeded in forcing the consul to bring the question before the people. All the centuries voted for war. In addition to this the commons scored a second success in preventing the election of consuls for the ensuing year, and military tribunes were appointed, four in number: Titus Quinctius Pennus, Gaius Furius, Marcus Postumius, and Aulus Cornelius Cossus. The last named was made City Prefect, while the other three marched with their forces to Veii, where they gave signal proof of the inefficacy of a divided command. Unable ever to agree with his colleagues, each man persisted in following his own judgement, to the obvious advantage of the enemy who chose his time well: when he attacked, the Roman force was all at sixes and sevens, and hopelessly confused by conflicting orders, with the result that it turned tail and retreated in disorder to its camp which, luckily, was not far distant. The losses were not, indeed, heavy – but it was a shameful performance. The distress throughout the country, unaccustomed as it was to defeat, was great. Feeling against the military tribunes rose high and there was a general demand for a Dictator, who seemed in the circumstances to offer the only hope of national recovery. But the augurs had first to be consulted, for there was a solemn tradition, backed by religious sanctions, that a Dictator could be named only by a consul – and there was no consul in office. The augurs, however, put the matter upon a proper footing, and Aulus Cornelius named Mamercus Aemilius for the dictatorship, being himself appointed Master of the Horse.

This goes to show that the moment the country had need of a truly great man, other considerations were forgotten: the fact that the censors had humiliated – and undeservedly humiliated – Mamercus in the past was now no obstacle to his appointment as supreme head of the state.

The Veientes were proud of their success and sent representatives to the various Etruscan communities with the boast that three Roman commanders had been beaten in a single battle; nevertheless they failed to win any general support from the league and had to content themselves with such volunteers as were attracted to their cause by hopes of loot. The only town to decide upon a renewal of hostilities was Fidenae; the people of the place butchered the new settlers before joining Veii, just as on a previous occasion they had murdered the envoys from Rome – almost as if they felt in duty bound to take the field only when their hands were already stained with blood.

The leaders of the two states, discussing which town to make their base, decided upon Fidenae as the more convenient, and that involved the crossing of the Tiber by the Veientine army. In Rome there was something like panic; troops were hurriedly recalled from Veii – troops already badly shaken from their recent defeat – and went into camp outside the Colline Gate; guards were stationed on the city walls, legal business was suspended, and all shops closed, and the city itself rapidly assumed the appearance of an armed camp. The Dictator, aware of the bad state of public morale, sent criers along every street to call a mass meeting of the population, which he proceeded to address in no very complimentary terms: 'It seems to take very little,' he said, 'to make you lose your presence of mind. What! After one minor reverse, which was in no way due either to the enemy's courage or to the cowardice of our own troops, but solely to the fact that our commanders could not agree upon tactics, are you scared of the Veientines whom we have already thrashed half a dozen times, or of Fidenae which we have captured – if I may so put it – twice for every once we have tried to do so? We and our enemies are the same as we have always been, for years and years – the same hearts, the same hands, the same swords. Nor have I changed either: I am still Mamercus Aemilius, the Dictator who crushed the combined armies of Veii, Fidenae, and Falerii at Nomentum, and Aulus Cornelius, our Master of Horse, will fight again as he fought before, when as a senior officer in our armies he killed Lars Tolumnius, the king of Veii, in sight of all and brought the spoils of honour to the temple of Jupiter Feretrius. Remember, when you draw your swords, that yours have been the triumphs, yours the spoils, and yours the victory, while the men you fight are burdened with the misery of guilt – our envoys murdered in violation of the law of nations, our settlers at Fidenae in peace-time savagely butchered, a treaty broken and a solemn compact foolishly flouted for the seventh time. Remember this, and take courage. Only let us get within striking distance, and I am very sure that our guilty foe will not long enjoy the pleasure of having humiliated a Roman army, while you, on the other hand, will soon see that the men who made me Dictator for the third time were better patriots than those who allowed my second dictatorship to end in dishonour, because I had stripped the censors of the excessive power they then enjoyed.'

Then, having prayed to heaven for success, Mamercus marched and took up a position a mile and a half south of Fidenae, protected on the right by the hills and on the left by the Tiber. Titus Quinctius Pennus, a brigade officer, was ordered to secure the hills and to occupy a ridge to the enemy's rear, behind which his men would be effectually screened. Next morning the Etruscans took the field in all the confidence of their previous exploit – which had been, in truth, more a matter of luck than of military prowess; Mamercus waited till the report came in from his scouts that Quinctius was firmly established on the ridge near Fidenae, and then gave the order for his infantry to advance in battle formation at the double, at the same time forbidding his Master of Horse to engage until he received instructions to do so, which instructions would be given as soon as cavalry support was needed; then – the Dictator added – when the moment came, let him fight as he fought with king Tolumnius, inspired by the memory of his glorious gift of the spoils of honour to Romulus and Jupiter Feretrius.

The legionaries of the opposing armies met, and the shock was terrific. The rage in the Romans' hearts found its satisfaction in their swords, and in the taunts they hurled at the godless brutes of Fidenae, and the brigands of Veii – treaty-breakers with the stain of murder still on their hands, dripping with the blood of slaughtered settlers – treacherous friends, cowardly foes.

The Etruscans were already reeling under the weight of the Roman attack, when suddenly through the open gates of Fidenae came pouring a stream of men armed with fire. It was like an army from another world – something never seen or imagined before that moment. There were thousands of them, all lit by the glare of their blazing torches, and like madmen, or devils, they came rushing into the fray. For a brief moment the sheer unfamiliarity of this mode of attack made the Romans waver, but the Dictator's prompt action saved the situation: sending orders to the Master of Horse to join him with the cavalry and to Quinctius to bring his men from the hills, he galloped across to the left wing, where the scene was like a city on fire and his troops were already giving ground before the terrifying onset of the flames. Raising his voice above the din, 'What', he shouted, 'will you let yourselves be smoked out like a swarm of bees? The enemy is un-armed, and you have swords – use them, and put out their fire! Or if we must fight with fire instead of steel, can you not wrest their torches from them and attack them with their own weapon? Remember the name of Rome – remember your fathers' valour and your own – turn this conflagration to its proper use and destroy Fidenae with her own flames, since generous kindness could not make her your friend! It is not I who urge you to this revenge: it is your devastated fields – it is the blood of your envoys and of your comrades who sought there a new home.'

Throughout the army there was immediate response; men sprang forward to tear the burning brands from their adversaries, or to snatch them up from where they smouldered on the ground. Soon both armies were armed with fire. The Master of Horse, not to be outdone, and employing a new tactic of his own, took off his horse's bridle and ordered his troopers to do the same; then he put himself at their head and with a touch of the spur and nothing to check the headlong speed of his mount galloped into the thick of the flames, followed by his men. Clouds of smoke and dust almost blinded both men and beasts, but the sight which had shaken the soldiers had little effect upon the horses, and the charging squadrons everywhere left ruin and destruc-tion in their path.

Suddenly, from another quarter, the battle-cry rang out – what could it mean? For a moment both armies paused to wonder; then the Dictator called out that it was Quinctius and his men, who were at-tacking the enemy in their rear; from his own troops a cheer went up and with greater vigour than ever he pressed his advantage. The Etruscans were now surrounded – caught in the pincers and hard pressed both front and rear; no way of escape remained open, either back to their camp, or into the hills where Quinctius was blocking their path, and their mounted troops had scattered, out of control; in this desperate situation most of the Veientes made for the Tiber as best they could, while such of their allies as survived tried to reach Fidenae. The Veientes, far from saving their skins, ran into the very jaws of death; some were cut down on the river bank, some driven into the water and swept away, even the swimmers, wounded as most of them were and exhausted and terrified, being dragged under and drowned. Few got across in safety. The Fidenates reached the town by way of their camp, whither the Romans swept on in pursuit of them, Quinctius in the van doing the hottest work, as the contingent he had brought down from the hills was still fresh, having been engaged only towards the end of the battle; they forced their way through the town gate side by side with the fugitives, mounted the wall, and signalled to their comrades that the town was taken. The Dictator had already entered their abandoned camp, but at the sight of Quinctius's signal he checked his men's natural desire to loot it and marched them out again to the town gate, consoling them with the assurance that they would find more and better loot in the town itself; then, once within the walls, he made for the central fortress, where he could see that the mob of fugitives were hoping to find refuge. Heavy as the enemy's losses had been in the battle, hardly fewer were killed inside the town, until at last the end came: they threw down their arms and surrendered, asking for nothing but their lives. The town and the camp were both sacked; next day every cavalry trooper and every centurion drew lots for a prisoner apiece – two prisoners being granted as a reward for specially distinguished service – and the remainder were sold by auction. The Dictator marched his victorious army, enriched with its plunder, back to Rome, where he celebrated his triumph, formally dismissed his Master of Horse as the need for his services was over, and himself resigned from office. He had served for sixteen days, and was able to surrender in peace the supreme power which, amidst the alarms and anxieties of war, he had undertaken to wield.

Some historians have stated that ships were also engaged near Fidenae in the fight with the Veientes. This, however, would have been difficult – and surely no one could believe it really happened, for even today the river there is not wide enough and at that time, according to our older authorities, it was narrower still. Possibly a few boats were assembled to help stop the Veientes from getting across the water, and this circumstance was exaggerated (as often happens) into the claim for a naval victory when the inscription under the portrait-bust of Mamercus was composed.

For the following year four military tribunes with consular powers were appointed, Aulus Sempronius Atratinus, Lucius Quinctius Cincinnatus, Lucius Furius Medullinus, and Lucius Horatius Barbatus. Veii was granted a truce for twenty years and the Aequians for three years, though they tried to obtain an extension. In Rome there were no political disturbances. The year after that was also an uneventful one so far as war and politics were concerned, but is nevertheless to be remembered for the celebration of the Games which had been vowed at the outset of the previous war; the Games were magnificently staged by the army generals and attended by large crowds from neighbouring communities. The military tribunes for the year were Claudius Crassus, Spurius Nautius Rutilus, Lucius Sergius Fidenas, and Sextus Julius Julus. The Games were much appreciated by the foreign visitors, not least because of the courtesy which their hosts had agreed to extend to them. On their conclusion the tribunes started their usual sort of trouble-making, addressing meetings at which they abused the mob for allowing their absurd admiration of their political enemies to keep them in perpetual servitude, too craven-spirited either to aspire to a share in the consulship or even to spare a thought for themselves or their friends at the election of military tribunes, in spite of the fact that candidates from either party were eligible. 'Do not be surprised,' they went on to say, 'if nobody bothers to consult your interests; a man will work hard and face risks when he can hope for profit and place as a result, and he will shrink from nothing if only he knows that the reward is likely to be worthy of the attempt; but you can neither ask nor expect a tribune to shut his eyes and go charging, with great peril and no profit, into a struggle which will inevitably subject him to the remorseless persecution of the senatorial party, while you yourselves, for whom he risks all, do not lift a finger to add to his honours. No, no: ambition cannot live upon air – aspiration must have something to aspire to. No plebeian will despise himself, once you, as a class, get proper recognition. It is high time we proved in a practical way whether some plebeian is fit for high office – or whether we are to assume that vigour or ability in men of our class is a sort of monstrosity only fit to make people gasp with astonishment.

'We did storm the fortress of privilege in procuring the legalization of our candidature for the office of military tribune with consular powers, and we did put forward candidates with fine military and political records; but with what result? They were kicked around, rejected and jeered at by the patricians, so that as time went on they stopped exposing themselves to such insulting treatment. It seems to us that one might as well abrogate a law, if its sole purpose is to legalize something which can never happen; surely there would be less shame in submitting to injustice and in accepting inequality than in being passed over because nobody thinks we are worth their notice.'

Speeches of this sort, and the approval with which they were received, inspired a few plebeian candidates to offer themselves for the military tribuneship, and various promises were made of what they would do for the popular cause if they were elected: hopes, for instance, were held out of distributions of public land, of planting new settlements and of taxing the nobles who at present occupied the public land, in order to raise money for the payment of men on military service. The military tribunes, however, had their answer ready: waiting until people were out of town, they secretly recalled the senators and got a decree passed in the absence of the People's tribunes authorizing an investigation of a report that the Volscians had invaded the territory of the Hernici, and the holding of consular elections. The military tribunes accordingly started on their mission, leaving as City Prefect Appius Claudius, the *decemvir*'s son, a young man of great natural force and imbued from the cradle with passionate hatred of the mob and its representatives, who, now that the matter was a *fait accompli*, found that they had no grounds of dispute either with the absent commissioners who had got the decree passed, or with Appius. Gaius Sempronius Atratinus and Quintus Fabius Vibulanus were accordingly elected consuls.

During this year an incident is said to have taken place, which, though not connected with Roman history, is nevertheless of interest. The Etruscan town of Volturnum was seized by the Samnites, who gave it its modern name of Capua. The name is supposed to have been derived from their leader, Capys; but it is more likely to have been descriptive of the region in which it lies – *campus*, or 'plain' country. The seizure of the town took place in peculiarly horrible circumstances: the Samnites had been allowed by the Etruscans, whose strength had been drained by war, to share in the amenities of the town and in the working of the land belonging to it, and one night, after a public holiday, when the native Etruscans were sleeping off the effects, they set upon them and butchered them.

But to return to my story: the consuls I mentioned took up their duties on 13 December, to be faced not only with the report from the commissioners that war with the Volscians was imminent, but also with the arrival of envoys from the Latins and Hernici, who brought the alarming information that never before had the Volscians been making their preparations with such single-minded intensity. They were all saying, apparently, that the crisis of their destiny had come: either they must submit to the permanent domination of Rome and give up for ever all thought of military enterprise, or make themselves a match – now – for their great rivals in the soldierly qualities of courage, discipline, and endurance.

All this was perfectly true: it was a dangerous situation, but the Senate took it in a strangely casual way. Sempronius, who was appointed by lot to the command, was inclined simply to trust to luck; having led Roman troops to victory against the Volscians on a previous occasion, and supposing, it seems, that his luck would hold, he made his preparations with such absurd negligence that the traditional Roman discipline was more in evidence in the Volscian army than in his own. The natural result followed, and success went to the men who deserved it. The very first battle was typical of Sempronius's carelessness and neglect of all reasonable precautions: no reserves had been posted to support the front line, no trouble taken to place the cavalry where it would be most effective. The first indication of how things were likely to go was in the quality of the respective battle-cries: loud and confident rose the cheer, again and again, from the Volscian throats, but the Romans' wavering morale was all too obvious in their reply – in that ragged shout, ill-sustained, and with each repetition feebler. The inevitable result was to increase the enemies' confidence; on they came, shields thrusting and swords flashing, in terrible contrast to their undisciplined adversaries whose helmets could be seen feebly bobbing as heads turned this way and that in bewilderment and alarm, and isolated groups, seeking safety in numbers, made for wherever they saw any sign of cohesion amongst their comrades; sometimes the standards were advanced with a show of fight, only to be abandoned by the shock-troops falling back; often they were hurriedly withdrawn. So it went on, a half-hearted business, not yet either a Roman defeat or a Volscian victory; on the Roman side the offensive spirit was wholly

absent: it was the Volscian troops who attacked – and attacked with
vigour – but, though they inflicted heavy casualties, they failed, for a
time, to break completely such resistance as the Romans offered. But
only for a time: for soon a general withdrawal began, and Sempronius
could do nothing to check it either by exhortation or abuse; not even
the inherent and majestic authority of the supreme commander availed
to stop the rot, and in another moment the Romans would have been
on the run but for the prompt and courageous intervention of a cavalry
decurion named Sextus Tempanius. Seeing that things were pretty
well desperate, Tempanius on his own initiative roared out an order
to every cavalryman who had the safety of his country at heart to dismount immediately. The troopers of every squadron jumped to the
order as if it had come from the consul himself, whereupon Tempanius
called upon the men to follow him. 'Unless you,' he cried, 'with those
little round shields of yours, hold up the attack, Rome's dominion is
done for. Look, here is my lance: take it for your standard and follow
where it goes. Show the enemy – and our comrades too – that mounted
you are a match for any cavalry in the world, and that dismounted no
mere footsloggers can touch you!' His words were greeted with a
cheer and he plunged forward, holding his lance high above his head;
his men followed; nothing could stop them, and wherever the Roman
battalions were hardest pressed, there those little round cavalry shields
could be seen thrusting forward. At every point where they struck,
Rome's tottering cause was on its feet again, and if only that small
band had been endowed with the gift of ubiquity, the Volscians would
certainly have turned tail and fled.

The Volscian commander, seeing that the round shields (Rome's
new weapon, as it were) were invincible, changed his tactics and
ordered his men to cease resistance and let them through, in order to
cut them off from their friends. This was done, and the gallant little
company found themselves isolated and unable to force their way back
through the massed Volscian infantry which had closed in behind them.
A moment before the whole Roman army had owed them their lives
– now they had vanished. Desperately the consul and his legionaries
pressed forward in the attempt to save, at any cost, their heroic comrades from annihilation, and the Volscians, endeavouring to check this
fresh attack, found themselves fighting on two fronts, as they were
forced at the same time to exert what pressure they could on Tempanius and his troopers in their rear. Tempanius had repeatedly tried to

break through and rejoin Sempronius, and when all his attempts failed he had withdrawn to a low hill, where his men, in circular formation, now stood on the defensive – though their aggressive spirit was by no means broken.

The battle did not end before dark, Sempronius relaxing no effort to hold the enemy as long as any daylight remained. When night fell, there was still no decision, and both armies found their nerves so frayed by the general uncertainty of the position, that first one and then the other assumed defeat and, abandoning its wounded and most of its gear, sought safety in the nearest hills. The elevation, however, on which Tempanius and his troopers were holding out, remained surrounded by enemy forces till after midnight, when a message came through to them that their camp had been abandoned; they supposed, by this, that the main body of their army had been defeated, and accordingly made their own escape, each man slipping away through the darkness in whatever direction his fears suggested. Tempanius, suspecting a trap, stayed where he was till dawn, and then, with one or two others, went cautiously off to investigate; he soon discovered by questioning enemy wounded that the Volscian camp was abandoned, whereupon he returned with the good news to his comrades on the rise and marched them off to the camp of the Romans. He found it in precisely the same state as the other – empty and abandoned, and everything in a mess. In which direction the consul had gone he had no idea, so before the Volscians could learn of their mistake and return he set off with as many of the wounded prisoners of war as he could manage, by the shortest route for Rome.

Bad news had preceded him and there were already rumours in the city that the army had been beaten and the camp abandoned, but nothing caused more general distress, apart from any personal bereavement which was involved, than the supposed loss of Tempanius and his gallant troopers. The city itself was in a state of acute alarm and the consul Fabius was on guard at the gates, when suddenly in the distance a troop of cavalry was seen; at first, as nobody knew who they were, fears were intensified, but as the strange horsemen drew nearer and were recognized, the relief was so great that a shout of joy echoed through the city as people everywhere thanked their lucky stars for the safe return of their victorious troopers. From houses which but a moment before had been mourning their menfolk for dead, women came pouring into the streets, and wives and mothers, almost afraid to believe their eyes and in utter forgetfulness of self, ran to meet the advancing column and flung themselves, in complete abandonment and almost mad for joy, into the arms of their husbands and their sons.

The tribunes had already issued a summons against Marcus Postumius and Titus Quinctius for their failure at Veii three years previously, and they saw a good chance of reviving public feeling against them in the bad name which the consul Sempronius had brought upon himself by his conduct in the recent campaign. At a mass meeting they declared, with all the eloquence at their command, that at Veii the country had been betrayed by its generals and, as a direct consequence of the fact that the guilty generals had not been brought to justice, the army had been betrayed by the consul in the Volscian campaign, the heroic cavalry abandoned to their fate, and the camp basely deserted. One of the tribunes, Gaius Julius, had Tempanius called as a witness and proceeded to interrogate him. 'Is it your opinion,' he asked, 'that the consul Gaius Sempronius timed his attack skilfully, or posted his reserves in a proper manner, or carried out any of the duties to be expected of a competent commander? Did you on your own initiative, when our legionaries were hard pressed, order the cavalry to dismount, thus preventing the total disintegration of our forces? When you and your party were cut off, did the consul come to your aid, or send troops to attempt your rescue? Had you any assistance whatever on the following day, or did you and your men get through to the camp solely by your own efforts, and, when you got there, did you find either the consul or his army, or was the camp deserted except for the wounded, who had been left to their fate? I appeal to your honour as a soldier – which alone in this unhappy affair prevented a national disaster – to answer these questions here and now. Where are Sempronius and our legions? Has it been a case of your deserting them, or of their deserting you? In short, have we been defeated, or have we not?'

Tempanius was no orator, but he is said to have replied in a soldierly and impressive manner, making no attempt to blame other people and scrupulously avoiding self-praise. 'As for Sempronius's military qualifications,' he declared, 'it is not for a private soldier to sit in judgement on his commander's abilities – that is the responsibility of the nation, when it elects him to his post. You must not look to me for the wisdom of a commander-in-chief or for the knowledge and skill

313

proper to a consul, all of which call for mental and moral capacities of a high order merely to assess; what I actually witnessed I can, however, tell you: before we were cut off, I saw the consul fighting in the front line; he was inspiring his men to do their best, and I saw him with the standards and under fire. Then when I could no longer see what the position was, I could tell by the noise and shouting that the fight was continued till dark, and I am convinced that the enemy's superior numbers precluded the possibility of a break-through to the hill I was holding. Where the army now is, I do not know: I should imagine, however, that for his men's sake the consul has found some safer spot to camp in, just as I myself, when things began to get awkward, looked for a place where I could better defend both myself and my comrades.

'Nor, in my belief, have the Volscians come out of it any better than we have; what with the darkness, and the luck of the game, there was pretty general error and confusion on both sides.'

Tempanius asked not to be any longer detained, as he was tired, and his wounds were troublesome, whereupon he was allowed to go, not without expressions from everyone present of the highest admiration for his soldierly conduct, and especially for his generous refusal to involve his commanding officer in trouble.

Meanwhile the consul Sempronius had reached the temple of Peace on the Labici road. As soon as his whereabouts was known, wagons and pack-animals were sent from the city to aid in the transport of the men, exhausted as they were by fighting and by marching all night, and after a short interval Sempronius himself entered Rome, where he gave Tempanius his full due of praise and made comparatively little effort to exculpate himself.

While the country was still mourning over the recent defeat and popular resentment against the generals still ran high, Marcus Postumius, who had been one of the military tribunes concerned with the affair at Veii, was brought to trial and fined 10,000 *asses* – in the old 'heavy' currency. His colleague Titus Quinctius, in view of the fact that he had fought successfully first against the Volscians under the dictator Tubertus and then again at Fidenae as lieutenant of the other dictator Mamercus, managed to shift the blame for the campaign in question on to Postumius, who had already been condemned, and was acquitted by the votes of all the tribes. It is said that a powerful factor in his acquittal was the honoured memory of his father Cincinnatus, and also the earnest entreaties of Quinctius Capitolinus, then a very old man, to be spared in the few hours he had left to live, the duty of carrying to Cincinnatus such cruel news.

The commons chose for their tribunes Sextus Tempanius, Aulus Sellius, Sextus Antistius, and Spurius Icilius; they were not in Rome when they were appointed, and they were the same men whom the cavalry, at Tempanius's suggestion, had asked to act as their centurions in the recent battle, after they had dismounted and were serving as infantrymen. The Senate, feeling that the odium against Sempronius had brought the consulship into disrepute, decreed the election for the coming year of military tribunes with consular powers, and those elected were Lucius Manlius Capitolinus, Quintus Antonius Merenda, and Lucius Papirius Mugilanus.

The new year had hardly begun when the tribune Hortensius brought an action against Sempronius for his misconduct of the previous year's campaign. At a full assembly of the people Hortensius's four colleagues begged him to drop his prosecution of their commanding officer – a man, they declared, who could be blamed for nothing but ill luck. Hortensius, however, refused to listen, and took their plea as a test of his own determination; moreover he was convinced that the defendant was really relying upon the other tribunes' veto, not upon their entreaties which they made only to cover their purpose of using it. So turning to Sempronius, 'What,' he said, 'has become of the famous patrician pride? Where is that noble spirit which trusts to its own innocence? Can it be that a former consul is hiding under the protecting shadow of the tribunate?' Then to his colleagues, 'And as for you,' he went on, 'what do you mean to do if I persist? Will you rob the people of their rights and undermine the authority of our office?' The tribunes replied that supreme authority over every member of the community, Sempronius included, was indeed in the people's hands, and that they themselves had neither the wish nor the power to override any decision the people might make; nevertheless, should the prayers they offered on behalf of their commander, whom they regarded as a father, prove unavailing, then, like him – and like all men standing their trial – they would go into mourning. Such evidence of feeling touched Hortensius; 'The people of Rome', he said, 'shall never see their tribunes in mourning. I will not detain Sempronius, since in the course of his command he won from his soldiers such affection.' People of all classes were as much pleased with

Hortensius's generosity in submitting where submission was due as with the loyalty of the four tribunes to their commanding officer.

The Aequians, who had taken the Volscians' dubious success as a victory for their own cause, had had a run of luck; but it was not to last, as the following year – which was by no means a notable one – saw their ignominious defeat. The consuls for the year were Cnaeus Fabius Vibulanus and Titus Quinctius Capitolinus, the former of whom was in command of the operations, which fizzled out in the complete collapse of the Aequian force almost before it had begun to fight. Fabius got little credit and was refused a triumph, though he was granted an 'ovation' as he had at least done something to mitigate the disgrace of Sempronius's defeat.

In contrast to this campaign which was so much more easily settled than people feared it might be, a short period of political tranquillity at home was unexpectedly broken by a number of serious disputes originating in a proposal to double the number of quaestors. The proposal – to add to the two City quaestors two more who should be responsible to the consuls for supplies in time of war – was introduced by the consuls and strongly supported by the Senate, but the people's tribunes fought hard for an amendment to provide that two of the quaestors should be plebeians, instead of all patricians, as the law then stood. The Senate, headed by the consuls, began by offering the strongest possible opposition to the amendment, but moved later towards a compromise and were willing to concede that the voting should be free, and without regard to which class the candidate belonged to, as in the case of the military tribunes. However, the offer did not prove acceptable, and they dropped the whole question, whereupon the tribunes promptly took it up again and followed it by various other anti-government proposals, including one for the distribution of publicly owned land. In view of these disturbances the Senate would have preferred to appoint consuls for the ensuing year rather than military tribunes, but successive vetoes by the people's tribunes made it impossible to get a resolution passed, so there was nothing for it but to allow the government to pass into the hands of an *interrex* – though even that solution was reached only after a violent struggle, as the tribunes tried to prevent the patricians from meeting.

There were new tribunes for the next year, and most of it was marked by incessant bickerings; the tribunes were continually preventing the patricians from meeting to appoint an *interrex* – there were several of them during the course of the year – or else pronouncing their veto on the one who happened to be in office, in order to stop the Senate passing a resolution to hold consular elections. Finally an *interrex* was appointed who had the courage to face the situation squarely – Lucius Papirius Mugilanus; he showed no tenderness to either party, and boldly declared that patriotism was dead, and that without God's providence and the lucky accident of the truce with Veii and the unadventurous policy of the Aequians the country would long ago have been done for. 'But suppose', he said, 'a threat should come from that quarter – would you want us to be caught without any patrician in a position of authority? Or without an army – or a general to raise one? Civil war is hardly a good weapon for repelling an invader; and were we to be faced with both at once, God himself would hardly be able to avert our total destruction. Why cannot each party yield a point and agree upon a compromise – the Senate allowing the appointment of military tribunes instead of consuls, and the people's tribunes refraining from putting their veto on the proposal for free elections of four quaestors without regard to which class they belong to?'

The appeal had its effect: the elections for the military tribuneship were held first, and the successful candidates were all patricians – Lucius Quinctius Cincinnatus (for the third time), Lucius Furius Medullinus (for the second time), Marcus Manlius, and Aulus Sempronius Atratinus. The last-named presided over the election of quaestors, at which there were several plebeian candidates, amongst them a son of the tribune Antistius and a brother of another tribune, Sextus Pompilius; but the support of these men was not of sufficient influence to procure their protégés' election, and only aristocratic candidates, men whose fathers and grandfathers had been consuls, secured a majority of votes. All the tribunes were furious, but especially Pompilius and Antistius whose relatives had been defeated at the polls. That their own services they declared, to the popular cause, and the equally great disservices of the nobility, not to mention the natural desire of exercising a right to which a change in the law had recently entitled them, should have failed to procure the election of a single plebeian quaestor – far less a military tribune – simply did not make sense. What could it mean? Here were two men – two tribunes, holders of a sacrosanct office created for the protection of liberty – of whom one begged votes for a brother and the other for his son. And what was the result? Both were ignored! No, no: it could only mean that there was dirty work somewhere and that Sempronius had rigged the election; it was his dishonesty which was responsible for their relatives' defeat. Sempronius was, of course, innocent, and the office he held protected him from direct attack, so the two irate tribunes diverted their attentions to his uncle, Gaius Sempronius, whom with the support of their colleague Canuleius they summoned to appear in court to answer for the disgraceful campaign against the Volscians. The same two men brought up in the Senate the question of distributing the publicly-owned land, a measure which Gaius Sempronius had always vigorously opposed, as they thought – rightly – that he would either withdraw his opposition and thus weaken his case in the eyes of the senatorial party, or by continuing to maintain it up to the time of his trial give offence to the popular party. The latter, however, was of little account to him and he preferred to injure his own chances of acquittal rather than prove false to his political principles, refusing to abandon the position that there should be no gifts of public land – which would merely, in his view, be a feather in the cap of three tribunes, as what they wanted was not really land for the people at all, but simply a chance to arouse resentment against himself. Personally, he declared, he was quite ready to face that storm without shrinking, and no individual citizen, either himself or anybody else, ought to be so highly valued by the Senate that its efforts to protect him involved damage to the interests of the country as a whole. When the day of his trial came, he faced it with the same confidence and the same pride; he pleaded his own cause, and the Senate did everything in its power to mollify the feelings of the commons against him, but to no effect. The verdict went against him and he was fined 15,000 *asses*.

It was during this year that a Vestal Virgin named Postumia was put on trial for a sexual offence. Actually she was innocent, but the fact that she dressed well and talked rather more freely and wittily than a young girl should, up to a point justified the suspicion against her. She was remanded, and afterwards acquitted, with a warning from the Pontifex Maximus, in the name of the college of priests, to stop making jokes and to dress in future with more regard to sanctity and less to elegance.

This year also saw the capture by the Campanians of the Greek settlement of Cumae.

Next year military tribunes were appointed: they were Agrippa Menenius Lanatus, Publius Lucretius Tricipitinus, and Spurius Nautius

Rutulus. It was a year made memorable by an appalling danger which threatened the country, but was – by the good fortune of Rome – averted. A plot was hatched by the slaves to start fires at widely separated points in the City and to seize the Citadel and Capitol while people were everywhere occupied in saving the burning buildings. Jupiter himself intervened to prevent the abominable crime; two slaves turned informer, and the guilty ones were arrested and executed. The informers were rewarded with their liberty and a gift from public funds of 10,000 *asses* (old currency) each, in those days a very considerable sum.

The Aequians began once more to prepare for war, and a report reached Rome on reliable authority that a new enemy, the town of Labici, had joined up with the old ones. The Aequians had by now grown to expect a war every year; they sent representatives to Labici, but got little satisfaction as the answer they brought back seemed to indicate that, though there were at present no actual preparations for war, peace was none the less unlikely to continue long; accordingly they asked the people of Tusculum to watch on their behalf to see that no unusual disturbances arose in Labici. Early the following year a delegation from Tusculum visited the military tribunes in Rome and reported that Labici was in arms and in conjunction with an Aequian force had raided Tusculan territory and was now encamped on Algidus. The military tribunes for the year were Lucius Sergius Fidenas, Marcus Papirius Mugilanus, and Gaius Servilius – son of the Priscus who had been Dictator when Fidenae was captured – and as soon as the report from Tusculum was received war was declared on Labici and a decree issued by the Senate to the effect that two of the military tribunes should proceed to the scene of operations while the third should remain behind in charge of affairs in Rome. The decree at once started a quarrel, each of the tribunes being convinced that he was the right man to command the army in the field, while the charge of home affairs was an ungrateful and ignoble task and far beneath his dignity. The quarrel, to say the least, was an unseemly one, and in the Senate eyebrows were raised. Quintus Servilius, however, quickly settled it: 'Since,' he remarked, 'there seems to be no respect either for the dignity of this institution or for the welfare of the country, a father's authority will have to put an end to this dispute: my son shall remain in control here – that is my will, and the customary drawing of lots shall not take place. I can only hope that the other two who are so eager for active service will conduct themselves in the field with more consideration and mutual deference than they are displaying at the moment.'

It was decided to raise troops not from the whole population indiscriminately but from ten tribes only, selected by lot; from these ten all men of military age were conscripted. Once active service had begun, the relationship between the two tribunes was by no means improved; on the contrary, the same passion in each of them for supremacy only intensified the quarrel: they agreed in nothing and neither would budge an inch from his own opinion: each, determined upon the sole validity of his own strategy and orders, regarded the other with contempt, until the very proper complaints of their junior officers forced them to adopt an arrangement by which they should exercise supreme command on alternate days. When the story of these goings-on reached Rome, the aged and experienced Quintus Servilius is said to have prayed solemnly that history might not repeat itself – that discord in the command might not prove even more disastrous than it had proved at Veii – and then, as if certain defeat were imminent, to have urged his son to enrol troops and make all preparations for the defence of the City. He was a true prophet: it was Sergius's day to command, and the enemy, by way of a feint, had withdrawn to the rampart of their camp. The ruse succeeded, and the Roman troops, following them up in the vain hope of taking the camp by storm, found themselves in an exceedingly awkward position. The Aequians attacked, caught them off their guard, and drove them in a headlong flight down a steep gully, where, falling over one another in their desperate attempt to get away, large numbers of them were overtaken and killed. The Roman camp was only just saved, and on the next day it was shamefully abandoned, the men slipping out through the gate in the rear after it had been nearly surrounded. The two commanders with their officers and such men as remained with the standards made for Tusculum, the rest scattering all over the countryside and finding their way somehow or other back to Rome, where they reported an even worse defeat than had actually been sustained.

The alarm at this news was less than it might have been, as it could hardly have been called a surprise; moreover, a reserve force which could be looked to in an emergency had already been mobilized by Gaius Servilius, who also, after restoring a semblance of order through the agency of his subordinate officials, had lost no time in sending scouts to ascertain the true position, and had received from them the report that the army and its commanders were in Tusculum and that the enemy had not moved from his original position. But what more than all this increased confidence in the City was a decree of the Senate appointing Quintus Servilius Priscus Dictator – a man whose clear-sightedness in public affairs had already on many occasions been proved to his countrymen, and had been proved yet again in the present instance as he was the one man to have anticipated disaster from the failure of the military tribunes to work together in harmony. As Master of Horse he nominated his son, who in his capacity of military tribune had named him dictator – though another tradition asserts that the Master of Horse that year was Servilius Ahala. Then, with fresh troops, he marched from Rome, sent orders to the force at Tusculum to join him, and took up a position two miles from the enemy.

Success had so far spoiled the Aequians that they were now no less careless and arrogant than the Roman commanders had been before their defeat. Nor was it long before they paid for their folly: in the very first clash the dictator completely disorganized their front line by a cavalry charge promptly followed by a massed infantry attack – a standard-bearer who hesitated to obey the order to advance being summarily executed. So high was the spirit of the Roman troops that the Aequians were unable to hold them; they broke and retreated in disorder to their camp, which was assaulted and taken in even less time and with even less effort. The camp was sacked and the soldiers permitted to keep whatever of value it contained, and immediately afterwards the cavalry returned from its pursuit of the fleeing enemy with the news that the whole force from Labici had been defeated and that many of the surviving Aequians had taken refuge there; on the next day, therefore, the Dictator ordered an advance to Labici which was promptly surrounded, entered by scaling-ladders, and sacked. Thus a week after his appointment the dictator brought his victorious army back to Rome, and resigned. The Senate, at a full meeting, passed a resolution to send settlers to Labici, and 1,500 people left Rome to settle there, with a grant of about one and a half acres of land each. The resolution was a timely one, as it forestalled any attempt on the part of the tribunes to propose a distribution of the territory belonging to Labici, and thus to start serious trouble over the whole question of land reform.

Next year opened with the election to the military tribuneship of Agrippa Menenius Lanatus, Lucius Servilius Structus, Publius Lucretius, Tricipitinus (all for the third time) and Spurius Veturius Cassius; they were succeeded the year after by Quintus Fabius Vibulanus, Aulus Sempronius Atratinus (for the third time), Marcus Papirius Mugilanus, and Spurius Nautius Rutulus – the two last both for the second time. Throughout these two years there was peace abroad, though domestic politics were embittered by the old struggle for land reform. The leaders of the popular agitation were the two tribunes Spurius Mecilius and Metilius (both elected in their absence, and the former serving his fourth term, the latter his third). These men proposed a measure for the distribution amongst the population of all land which had been acquired by force of arms, which measure, if passed by plebiscite, would have meant the confiscation of the fortunes of a great part of the nobility; for Rome having been originally founded upon alien soil had hardly any territory but what had been acquired in war, while the little which had been sold or assigned by the state was held only by plebeians. This being the position, it looked as if a desperate struggle between the two parties were imminent. Debates in the Senate and private discussions between the military tribunes and the leading senators led to no decision upon what policy to adopt; the government was at its wits' end, until the youngest member of the House, Appius Claudius – grandson of the *decemvir* – came forward with an ingenious solution. 'I have brought you a plan,' he said, 'which is a sort of heirloom in my family. My grandfather, as you know, pointed out to the Senate that there was one way, and one way only, of breaking the power of the tribunes: namely, by getting some of them to veto the proposals of their colleagues. Men who are enjoying their first taste of political power can easily be led to change their minds if someone from one of our great political families approaches them in the right way: all he need do is to forget for a moment the dignity of his position, and speak to the purpose. These fellows are all weathercocks and time-servers: let them see that some of their number, by taking a bold initiative, have stolen the favour of the mob, while they themselves are left out in the cold, and they will readily enough turn their coats and support the senatorial cause, in the hope of ingratiating themselves with our party as a whole and with its leaders in particular.'

Young Appius's suggestion met with universal approval, not least from Quintus Servilius Priscus, who warmly congratulated him on being a worthy scion of the Claudian stock, and it was acted upon without delay. The first step was to induce as many of the tribunes as possible to veto the bill; so as soon as the Senate adjourned, the leading members started operations: each button-holing his man, they succeeded, by mingled flattery and threats and the promise of the gratitude of the Senate, both individually and collectively, in getting six of them to undertake to use their veto. Next day, according to plan, a question was asked in the Senate about the attempt of the two tribunes Mecilius and Metilius to stir up sedition by their monstrous scheme of agrarian reform, and the leading members of the House, in their speeches on the subject, indicated their inability to see any way out of the danger except through the assistance of the tribunes. The beleaguered country, they declared, had now no resource but to do what individuals did in cases of distress, and turn for succour to the tribunate; the tribunes could be justly proud of their office, and of themselves as holders of it, in that they knew it possessed no less power to resist their colleagues' wicked attempts at subversion than to harry the senatorial party and stir up political strife.

Sentiments of this sort were met with cheers from every part of the House, while appeals to the tribunes made themselves heard through the hubbub. At last order was restored, and those of the tribunes who had been won over to the opposition declared their intention of vetoing their colleagues' bill, as they themselves, like the Senate, considered it subversive. The House then tendered them its formal thanks, and the proposers of the bill, having vented their rage by convening an assembly and calling the renegades betrayers of the people's welfare, toadies of the governing class, and any other abusive names they could think of, allowed the measure to drop.

Next year Publius Cornelius Cossus, Gaius Valerius Potitus, Quintus Quinctius Cincinnatus, and Marcus Fabius Vibulanus were appointed military tribunes with consular powers. There would have been two campaigns this year, had not operations against Veii been delayed by the superstitious fears of the Veientine nobility, whose estates had been flooded by the Tiber with serious damage to farm-buildings; at the same time the Aequians were deterred by the defeat they had suffered three years before from going to the assistance of their kinsmen of Bolae. These people in a raid on the territory of Labici had attacked the new settlers there, and hoped to save themselves from the consequences by the support of the Aequians generally; but they were disappointed: no support came, and after a campaign almost too trivial to mention, consisting as it did of a siege and one small battle, they lost both town and lands. An attempt was made by the plebeian tribune Lucius Sextius to pass a measure for sending settlers to Bolae, just as they had been sent to Labici; but the proposal was vetoed by his colleagues, who declared their unwillingness to allow any plebiscite to pass without the backing of the Senate.

Bolae was retaken in the following year and the Aequians sent fresh settlers to occupy it, so it was considerably stronger than it had been. At Rome this year the government was in the hands of four military tribunes – Cnaeus Cornelius Cossus, Lucius Velerius Potitus, Quintus Fabius Vibulanus (for the second time), and Marcus Postumius Regillensis. The last named – Postumius – was given the command against the Aequians. He was in some ways a bad man, though the defects in his character did not become apparent until the campaign had been brought to a successful end. In raising troops, and proceeding at once to Bolae, he showed great energy; a few minor engagements were enough to break the spirit of the enemy, and he soon forced an entrance into the town. That done, however, he turned against his own men and broke the promise, made at the time of the assault, that all plunder taken in the town should be the property of the troops. I, at least, am inclined to believe that that was the reason of the soldiers' anger, though it has been suggested that it was caused merely by the fact that, as the town had been sacked not long before and was now occupied by new settlers, fewer valuables were found in it than the men had been led by their commander to expect. But angry they were – and they were soon to be angrier still; for when Postumius had been recalled by his colleagues to Rome to help deal with certain anti-government proposals which were being brought forward by the people's tribunes, he made a remark, at a public assembly, which was surely unworthy of any reasonable or intelligent person. The tribune Sextius, introducing a proposal for land reform, declared that he would further propose that settlers be sent to Bolae, as it was only right, in his view, that the town and territory should belong to the men who took them by force of arms; whereupon Postumius was heard to say: 'Unless my men keep their mouths shut on *that* matter, they had better look out!' Everyone in the assembly was shocked, as indeed was the Senate when they came to hear of it soon after. Sextius, the tribune, who was an effective speaker and not the man to let an opportunity slip, was quick to see how he could make political capital out of an opponent like Postumius; for clearly such a man, haughty in temper and hasty in speech, could be irritated and provoked into saying things which would rouse resentment not only against himself but against the senatorial order as a whole and the cause for which it stood; accordingly he made a point of drawing Postumius into an argument as often as he could. On the present occasion, after the heartless and brutal remark I have mentioned, 'Men of Rome,' he cried, 'do you hear how he threatens his soldiers as if they were slaves? What, will you think a swine like him better deserves the high position he holds than the men who would settle you on brand-new farms of your own – men who are anxious to provide a home for your old age, and fight for your welfare against your cruel and haughty enemies? You may well begin to wonder why it is that so few are willing to shoulder the burden of your cause: for what can they expect of you? Not, assuredly, the honours which you hand out to your political adversaries instead of to your champions and protectors! What this fellow said just now drew from you, to be sure, a gasp of horror; but what of that? If at this moment you were asked for your votes, you would give them not to those friends whose one desire is to secure your fortunes and give you farms to live on, but to the man who swears he will take the whip to your backs!'

It was not long before Postumius's unfortunate remark was known in the army too, where it caused even greater indignation at the thought that the commander, not content with cheating his men out of their spoils, actually threatened them with punishment as well. There was no attempt to conceal the resentment which was universally felt, and the quaestor, Publius Sestius, thinking that the mutiny, started by trickery and the threat of violence, could best be quelled by similar methods, picked on a man who was bawling his head off and sent a lictor to arrest him. Yells and imprecations broke out, and a stone was thrown at Sestius, who withdrew from the scuffle, the soldier who had thrown it shouting after him that the quaestor had got what the general had threatened to give his men. Postumius was sent for and made everything worse by his remorseless inquiries and savage punishments, and at last, when a crowd had gathered at the cries of some wretched victims whom he had ordered to be crushed to death under a hurdle, he lost control of himself altogether, left the tribunal, and ran like a madman to where the attempt was being made to stop the executions. The lictors and centurions were doing what they could to disperse the mob of enraged soldiery, but to no effect: such was the fury of the troops that Postumius was stoned to death – a commander-in-chief murdered by his own men.

When the report of this dreadful crime reached Rome, the other military tribunes wished to institute a senatorial inquiry into the death of their colleague, but the proposal was vetoed by the people's tribunes. The conflict which thus arose was also connected with the Senate's anxiety lest the populace in its present mood, exacerbated as it was by fear of investigations, should elect men from its own class as military tribunes for the coming year, and with the consequent efforts of the senatorial party to procure the election of consuls. The upshot was that the people's tribunes blocked the Senate's decree ordering an investigation and also vetoed the election of consuls, so that the government reverted to an *interregnum*. After that the senatorial party got its way, consular elections were held under the presidency of the *interrex*, Quintus Fabius Vibulanus, and the successful candidates were Aulus Cornelius Cossus and Furius Medullinus.

The new year had hardly begun when the Senate passed a resolution that the tribunes should bring the inquiry into Postumius's death to the notice of the people at the earliest possible opportunity and that the people should themselves select whomever they thought a suitable person to conduct it. By a unanimous resolution the matter was referred to the consuls, who then proceeded to carry out their task with great leniency. Only a handful of the mutineers were condemned to death – and even those few were generally believed to have committed suicide. Nevertheless the consuls, for all their moderation, failed to satisfy the populace, who continued bitterly to resent the whole transaction and to complain that while nobody bothered for years about such reforms as would improve their lot, a law which involved their capital punishment was promptly and effectively carried out. It would have been an excellent opportunity, now that the mutiny had been dealt with, to bring up the question of distributing the territory of Bolae; this would have been an effective sop to the angry populace and would have made them less anxious for the agrarian reform which was intended to disappropriate the nobility from what was felt to be their illegal occupation of the public lands. As things were, however, the sense of anger and frustration continued, not only because the nobility persisted in hanging on to the domain lands, which they held by force, but also because they refused even to distribute such land as had been recently acquired by conquest – land which, they knew, would soon, like all the rest, go to enrich the few.

During this year the consul Furius led a force against the Volscians who were raiding the territory of the Hernici. Failing to make contact with the enemy, he took the town of Ferentinum to which considerable numbers of the Volscians had retired – though they had gone before he got there, for, having little hope of defending the place, they had slipped away under cover of darkness, taking their gear and valuables with them. So there was less plunder for Furius's men than they had hoped. The town was taken next day, almost empty. It and the land belonging to it were given to the Hernici.

After a year of comparative tranquillity owing to the restraint of the tribunes, Quintus Fabius Ambustus and Gaius Furius Pacilus entered upon the consulship. This year Lucius Icilius became tribune and proved true to his name by at once arousing strong anti-government feelings with various proposals for agrarian reform; but the occurrence of an epidemic, which threatened to be worse than it actually proved, diverted people's thoughts from politics and concentrated them upon the more intimate problem of how to keep alive. Probably the epidemic caused less damage to the country than would serious political troubles, had they arisen. As it happened, though a great many caught the disease, the number of deaths was very small, a piece of luck which was, however, counterbalanced by the usual result of a year of pestilence, namely a bad harvest, due to the inadequate cultivation of the land. The new consuls were Marcus Papirius Atratinus and Gaius Nautius Rutilus, and from the beginning of their term of office lack of supplies would have been more serious than the epidemic, if the situation had not been remedied by foreign purchases of grain, for which delegations were dispatched over a wide area along the Tiber and the Etruscan seaboard. The Samnites in Capua and Cumae insolently refused to trade, unlike the lords of the Sicilian communities, who gave generous assistance; but the largest supplies were brought down the Tiber, with the goodwill of the Etruscans. In these difficult circumstances there were so few people left in the city that the consuls could not find more than a single senator for each delegation, and were compelled in every case to make up the number by adding two knights.

Apart from the epidemic and the subsequent shortage of food there were no annoyances, domestic or foreign, during those two years; but no sooner were those difficulties overcome than the country was involved again in its old troubles – political strife and foreign war.

In the consulship of Marcus Aemilius and Gaius Valerius Potitus the Aequians mobilized for war with the unofficial support of the Volscians, who joined them as a volunteer mercenary force. News of their preparations reached Rome after they had already penetrated into Latin and Hernican territory, and promptly, to meet the threat, the consul Valerius proceeded to raise troops; Menenius, however, one of the tribunes and a staunch advocate of agrarian reform, blocked the levy, so that every man who wished to avoid service availed himself of the tribune's protection to refuse to take the oath. It was at this juncture that the alarming news suddenly arrived of the fall of Carventum. The humiliating defeat was a double blow at the machinations of Menenius, for it not only gave the Senate a handle for bringing him into disrepute, but also provided the other tribunes, who had already been induced to veto the proposed land reforms, with a better reason for opposing their colleague. The dispute was nevertheless a long one: the consuls swore by heaven and earth that Menenius, and Menenius alone, was responsible by his action in blocking the levy for any humiliation or defeat already sustained or likely to be sustained in the future, while Menenius, on his side, loudly protested that he was willing to withdraw his opposition provided that the patricians surrendered their illegal occupancy of the public domains. The end came when nine of the tribunes interposed a resolution, declaring in the name of their college that they would support the consul in the event of his fining or otherwise coercing all who refused to serve, in spite of Menenius's veto. On the strength of this resolution Valerius had the few who appealed hauled up before him, and the rest were scared into taking the oath.

The army then proceeded to Carventum, and though the relationship between the consul and his troops was about as bad as could be, there was no lack of vigour in the way operations were carried out; the fact that some of the garrison had been allowed to leave their posts in search of plunder opened the way to attack, and the Roman force easily drove out the remainder and liberated the stronghold. A considerable amount of plunder was taken, as the enemy had been engaged in constant raids and all the stuff he had collected had been stored in the stronghold for safe keeping; the consul ordered the quaestors to sell it by auction and pay the proceeds into the treasury, announcing that the troops would have their share only when they did not refuse service. This action exacerbated the ill feeling of the soldiers, and of the commons generally, towards Valerius, so that when he entered Rome in the ovation which the Senate had granted him in honour of his success, the substance of the somewhat indecorous songs which are expected from the rank and file on such occasions consisted in abuse of the consul and praise of Menenius, while at every mention of the tribune's name the crowds of spectators applauded and shouted their approbation with such enthusiasm that the soldiers' voices were almost drowned in the noise they made. This all too obvious support of Menenius was more disturbing to the senatorial party than the men's impertinence to their commander – for that, after all, was a more or less traditional licence – as it seemed to indicate that if Menenius stood for the military tribuneship, he would certainly be elected. However, consular elections were held, and Menenius was kept out.

The new consuls were Cnaeus Cornelius Cossus and Lucius Furius Medullinus (for the second time). Never had the popular party been so angry; they showed their anger at the subsequent election of quaestors – and also had their revenge, for plebeian candidates were returned for the first time in history. Amongst the four successful candidates room was found for only one patrician, Gaius Fabius Ambustus, the three plebeians – returned above the heads of men of the very best families – being Quintus Silius, Publius Aelius, and Publius Pupius. I have read that it was the influence of the Icilii which was responsible for this highly democratic voting; three members of that notoriously anti-patrician family were tribunes that year, a success which they owed to the extravagant promises of reform which they poured into the eager ears of the populace; they had declared, moreover, that unless the masses themselves at the coming quaestorial election – the only one which the Senate had left open to both parties – had enough spirit to get what they long had wanted and which was now legally open to them to acquire, they would not lift a finger in their behalf. It was a great victory for the popular party, or so they thought; that the office of quaestor carried only limited powers was, for the moment, of little consequence; the important thing was that a beginning had been made: new men could at last see their way clear to the highest office of state and the most splendid military honours. The patricians, on the

contrary, were as angry as if they had lost their right to office altogether, instead of merely being forced to share it with their opponents;
what, they asked, if the world were coming to such a pass, would be
the use of rearing children only to have them robbed of their proper
inheritance, seeing others in possession of their rightful honours, and
themselves, without position or power, left with nothing but the
humble duty of sacrificing on the people's behalf in the capacity of
Leaping Priests or Fire-kindlers at the altar? Feelings, in fact, ran high
in both parties; and since the commons were elated by their success
and had three extremely distinguished men to lead them, the patricians, who naturally felt that every election in which a candidate from
either party was allowed to stand would go the same way as the election for the quaestorship, did all they could to prevent an election for
military tribunes, and stood out for consular elections, which were not
yet open to plebeian candidates. The Icilii, equally of course, opposed
them, declaring that the time had come for the commons to have their
share of real power.

The popular leaders were, however, in a difficulty, as they had no
means of enforcing their demand. They might, indeed, have wrung a
concession from their opponents by blocking some consular bill, had
there been any, at the moment, before the Senate; but there was none,
so it was a stroke of luck for them when a report came in that Volscian
and Aequian forces were raiding Latin and Hernican territory. Promptly
they seized their chance and strained every nerve to stop the levy which
the Senate had authorized to meet the danger; fortune, they declared,
had played into their hands and into the hands of their party. All three
of them were men of great driving power, and men of family too, in
spite of their plebeian origin, and they went to work methodically,
two of them assuming the task of keeping continuous and careful watch
upon the consuls, while the third was given the role of propagandist
amongst the commons, holding meetings to rouse them to action or
keep them in check as circumstances dictated. For a time there was
deadlock: the consuls failed to hold their levy, the tribunes got no nearer
to the elections they desired; then, when the fortunes of the struggle
were beginning to favour the popular cause, news came that the Aequians had seized the fortress of Carventum: the garrison had left their
post to pick up what they could in the countryside, the few remaining
guards had been killed, and the rest of the garrison had been cut down
piecemeal either in the open or as they were trying to hurry back to

their posts. This reverse gave the tribunes a fresh weapon; every effort was made to induce them, in these circumstances, to withdraw their opposition to preparations for war, but in vain; they refused to yield either in consideration of the national danger or of their own reputation, and finally succeeded in forcing the Senate to issue a decree for the election of military tribunes, though the conditions were added that no one who had been people's tribune that year should be allowed to stand, and that no people's tribune should be re-elected for a further term. These conditions were obviously aimed at the Icilii, whom the Senate accused of seeking from the people the highest office of state as a reward for the violently anti-aristocratic measures which they had sponsored as tribunes.

Recruiting and general mobilization now began without opposition. Whether both consuls proceeded to Carventum, or whether one of them remained in Rome to preside at the elections is not determined, as our authorities differ; all, however, agree that the siege of Carventum was long and fruitless and that after it was abandoned the same troops as had been employed in it liberated Verrugo, a town in Volscian territory, and that raids on a large scale both there and in Aequian territory secured for the Romans a great mass of plunder of all kinds.

In Rome the popular party had scored a victory in forcing the election of military tribunes, but the result of the election was no less of a victory for their opponents, for contrary to everyone's expectation all three successful candidates were patricians – Gaius Julius Julus, Publius Cornelius Cossus, and Gaius Servilius Ahala. The rumour went round that the patricians had rigged the elections: the story was (the Icilii accused them of it at the time) that they had included in the list of genuine candidates a number of preposterously unsuitable plebeians, thereby causing the mass of voters to reject the plebeian candidates as a whole from their disgust at the notorious vices of a few.

An unconfirmed report then reached Rome that the Volscians and Aequians, encouraged, perhaps, by their successful defence of Carventum, or angered by the loss of their garrison at Verrugo, were preparing for war with all the resources at their command. The fountain-head of the rising was Antium: representatives from that town had visited the various communities of both peoples, upbraiding them for cowardice in having lurked behind their walls during the previous year while Roman troops devastated their farmlands with impunity and the garrison at Verrugo was surprised and overwhelmed. They went on to prophesy that worse was to come: soon not merely raiding-parties but settlers would come from Rome to establish themselves in their domains; and already the Romans, not content with dividing their possessions amongst themselves, had taken Ferentinum from them and made a present of it to their friends the Hernici. Inflammatory remarks of this kind had their effect, and in the various townships which the envoys visited recruiting began, and at last their whole military potential was concentrated at Antium, where they fortified a camp and awaited the approach of the enemy.

In Rome the news of these movements caused more excitement than the actual situation warranted, and the Senate lost no time in ordering the appointment of a Dictator, always the last resource in a crisis. The two military tribunes Julius and Cornelius are said to have resented this order, and a bitter argument ensued; in vain the leaders of the Senate complained that the military tribunes were not subject to the Senate's authority, and even appealed to the people's tribunes, reminding them that on a similar occasion they had brought pressure to bear on the consuls. The people's tribunes were, of course, delighted with this split in the ranks of their opponents, and said they had no intention of helping those who refused to treat them as free citizens – or even as human beings; but if ever office were thrown open to both parties and government fairly shared between them, they would only too gladly take steps to stop magistrates from getting above themselves and thwarting the Senate's decrees. All they could suggest meanwhile was that the patricians should continue their disregard for law and the constitution, while they, the people's tribunes, got on with their job as they saw fit.

This quarrel, coming at a moment when a major campaign was on hand, was a most unfortunate one; everyone's attention was absorbed by it; day after day Julius and Cornelius took turns in complaining that, as they were perfectly capable of taking command, it was unjustifiable to deprive them of the position with which the nation as a whole had entrusted them. And so the wrangle continued until at last the other military tribune, Servilius Ahala, intervened. The reason, he declared, why he had kept silent so long was not inability to make up his mind – for what good citizen ever separated his own from the national interest? – but his hope that his two colleagues would consent to submit to the Senate instead of allowing the authority of the people's tribunes to be invoked against them. 'Even now,' he went on, 'if circumstances permitted, I should have gladly given them time to modify the inconvenient obstinacy of their views; but since war is a harsh master and does not wait upon the deliberations of men, I shall put the good of the country above my colleagues' favour, and, if the Senate still adheres to its opinion, I shall name a Dictator tonight. Should anyone veto the Senate's resolution, I shall content myself with the expression of its wishes.'

Ahala's intervention was universally commended, as it deserved to be; Publius Cornelius was named Dictator, and Ahala himself appointed as his Master of Horse. Evidently there are occasions, as this story shows, when favour and promotion fall most readily into the lap of the man who does not seek them.

About the ensuing campaign there was nothing memorable. In a single engagement, and that an easy one, the enemy forces at Antium were destroyed; Roman troops laid waste the Volscian farmlands, and stormed a fortress at lake Fucinus, where 3,000 prisoners were taken. The rest of the Volscians were driven to take refuge within their walls, leaving their farms undefended. The Dictator had done what fortune demanded of him, little though that was; he returned to Rome successful, indeed, but hardly covered with glory, and resigned his office.

The military tribunes had not forgotten their resentment at the appointment of a Dictator, and it was for that reason, I fancy, that without saying anything about a consular election they announced that military tribunes should be elected again for the following year, a betrayal of the patrician cause which, coming as it did from within the party, caused greater concern than ever. The patricians reversed their tactics of the previous year; then, it will be remembered, they had succeeded in bringing all the plebeian candidates into contempt by including a number of scallawags in the list; this time they put up leading senators of the highest distinction and popularity and were thus able to secure all the places. No plebeian had a chance at all. Four men were elected, all of whom had held the office before: Lucius Furius Medullinus, Gaius Valerius Potitus, Cnaeus Fabius Vibulanus, and Gaius Servilius Ahala. Ahala obtained this second consecutive term by reason of the popularity he had won through his wise restraint in the recent crisis, though his other qualities as well undoubtedly entitled him to it.

This year the truce with Veii ended and steps were taken to obtain a settlement for previous damages. The representatives from Rome who, accompanied by the fetials, were dispatched for the purpose, were met on the frontier by a deputation from the town and asked not to proceed until they themselves had had an audience of the Senate. The request was granted, and the Senate agreed not to demand a settlement, as Veii was, at the moment, distracted by party strife and Rome had no desire to take advantage of other people's difficulties.

Shortly afterwards the garrison at Verrugo was lost. The cause of the disaster was the all-important factor of time: the besieged garrison asked for assistance, and might have been saved if it had been promptly given; but the force dispatched for the purpose found the enemy dispersed about the countryside in search of plunder – and every man in the garrison had already been killed. The military tribunes were as much responsible for the delay as the Senate; reports had come in that the garrison was making a strong resistance, but the tribunes failed to realize that there are limits to human strength and that no valour, however great, can go beyond them. But the brave soldiers, dead or alive, were not to be unavenged.

Next year the military tribunes were Publius and Cnaeus Cornelius Cossus, Cnaeus Fabius Ambustus, and Lucius Valerius Potitus. War was declared with Veii, and the occasion of it was an insulting remark made by the Veientine senate: representatives had been sent from Rome to demand reparations, and the answer they received was that unless they cleared out of the country instantly Veii would see that they got what Lars Tolumnius had given their predecessors. This was not to be tolerated and the Roman Senate instructed the military tribunes to ask the people's consent at the earliest possible moment to a declaration of war. The result was a spate of sullen protests: the Volscian war, it was said, was not yet over; two garrisons had recently been wiped out and the rest were being held only at great risk; never a year passed without a major engagement somewhere, and now, as if they had not troubles enough, a fresh campaign was on foot against an exceedingly powerful neighbour, who would probably raise all Etruria against them. The people's tribunes took care to fan the flames of the general discontent, taking the line that the real enemy which the Senate was fighting was not Veii or any other foreign state but the commons of Rome. The Senate, they declared, deliberately tormented the commons with military service and got their throats cut whenever they could, keeping them employed in foreign parts for fear lest, if they enjoyed a quiet life at home, they might begin to think of forbidden things – liberty, farms of their own to cultivate, the division of the public domains, the right of voting as their consciences dictated. They got hold of old campaigners, counted their years of service, their wounds and scars, and asked with pious indignation if there was still on their poor bodies a whole spot to receive another gash, or what blood they had left in their veins to shed for their country. By remarks of this sort – and similar arguments were repeated in public speeches – the tribunes succeeded in arousing strong popular opposition to the declaration of war with Veii, whereupon the matter was temporarily dropped, as it was clear that it stood no chance of getting through in face of the resentment it had caused.

Meanwhile the decision was taken to send a force under the military tribunes against the Volscians; one of them only, Cnaeus Cornelius, was left in Rome, and the other three, after finding no sign of organized resistance, split the force into three divisions and went off individually to do what damage they could. Valerius made for Antium, Cornelius for Ecetra, both of them destroying farmlands and farm buildings over a wide area with the object of preventing any concentration of the enemy's forces. Fabius marched direct to Anxur (the modern Tarracinae), which was his principal objective, and threatened an assault on the side of the town where it slopes down to the marshes; at the same time four cohorts under Servilius Ahala occupied a ridge of high ground behind the town, whence they made a sudden attack upon a sector of its walls which was undefended. The small force attacked with all the noise and racket it could possibly raise, which had the desired effect of distracting the enemy troops who were defending the lower part of the town against Fabius and enabling scaling-ladders to be brought into position. A moment later Roman soldiers were all over the town – to stand or to flee made no matter; soldiers and civilians alike were mercilessly butchered. The slaughter went on till at last the helpless townsmen, seeing they would get no quarter if they surrendered, were compelled to fight, when the Roman commander suddenly gave the order to hurt no one who was not carrying arms, with the result that every single soldier immediately laid down his sword. Some 2,500 prisoners were taken. Fabius did not allow his men to touch anything of value in the place until his colleagues arrived, on the ground that the troops under their command had contributed to the capture of Anxur by keeping other Volscian forces from coming to the defence of it. When they did arrive, the three contingents were allowed to sack the town; a long period of prosperity had made it rich, and this act of generosity on the part of the three commanders was a first step towards a better feeling between the commons and the patricians. It was followed by the most seasonable favour which has ever been conferred on the populace by the chiefs of state: the Senate, without any suggestion from the people or their tribunes, issued a decree for the payment of soldiers on service out of public funds. Hitherto every man had served at his own private expense.

The joy at this innovation was unprecedented. Men mobbed the Senate House, wrung the hands of members as they came out, called them Fathers indeed, in every sense of the word, and declared that thenceforward not a man, while any strength remained, would spare his body or blood in defence of so munificent a country. Indeed, the gift was doubly welcome: it was a good thing for the poor soldier to know that while he was bound in law to give his body in the national service his little property would at least grow no less; but better even than that was the fact that the offer was spontaneous and owed nothing to anything that had ever been said either by their tribunes or by themselves – it was that which added so much both to their satisfaction and their gratitude.

The only people who did not share the general pleasure and mutual good feeling were the plebeian tribunes, who prophesied that the new measure would prove less universally agreeable and less successful than was imagined. Admirable though it seemed at first sight, experience would soon reveal its deficiencies. Where, for instance, was the money to come from? If it came, as presumably it must, from a tax on the people, then the Senate would merely have been generous at others' expense. Moreover, however the rest might feel, veteran soldiers who had earned their discharge would never endure to see younger men enjoying better conditions of service than they themselves had been forced to accept, or submit to the injustice of contributing to other men's expenses when they had also, of necessity, defrayed their own.

Arguments of this sort were not without influence on a section of the commons; finally a tax was imposed and the tribunes publicly announced that they would protect anybody who refused to pay it. The patricians, however, would not let their promising innovation be so easily defeated; they were themselves the first to contribute and, as there was not yet a silver coinage, some of them made quite a spectacle by driving to the treasury with wagonsful of bronze bars. That started the ball rolling, and when the senators had all faithfully paid the amount at which they were assessed, the leading men of plebeian rank, who were friends of the nobility, began, as they had agreed to do, to pay up; then, when the riff-raff saw these men applauded by the patricians and honoured as good citizens by all who were liable to military service, they, too, rushed forward to pay and thought no more of the promised protection of the tribunes. After that, the proposal to declare war on Veii was passed and new military tribunes proceeded to the scene of action with an army composed mostly of volunteers.

The military tribunes were Titus Quinctius Capitolinus, Quintus Quinctius Cincinnatus, Gaius Julius Julus (for the second time), Aulus Manlius, Lucius Furius Medullinus (for the third time), and Manlius Aemilius Mamercus. They were the first commanders of a Roman army to besiege Veii. Soon after the siege began the Etruscan communities at a full council at the shrine of Voltumna failed to agree upon whether or not the whole nation should unite in defence of Veii.

The following year some of the Roman commanders were called away with a part of the army to carry on the Volscian campaign, so the siege of Veii was somewhat relaxed. The new military tribunes were Gaius Valerius Potitus (for the third time), Manlius Sergius Fidenas, Publius Cornelius Maluginensis, Cnaeus Cornelius Cossus, Gaius Fabius Ambustus, and Spurius Nautius Rutilus (for the third time). The Volscians were successfully engaged between Ferentinum and Ecetra, after which the siege of the Volscian town of Artena was begun. During an attempted break-out the enemy were driven back within the walls and Roman troops, in the confusion, were able to force an entrance. The town was taken, except for the central fortress, which was a natural stronghold; a few men managed to establish themselves within it, while in the town below a great many were either killed or captured. The stronghold itself was then surrounded. For its size it was adequately defended, and could not be taken by assault; nor was there hope of starving it into surrender, as all the publicly owned grain had been stored there before the town fell; indeed, the besieging force would have wearied of the hopeless task, had not a slave betrayed the place into their hands. The traitor guided some Roman soldiers up a precipitous ascent and admitted them to the fortress; they killed the sentries on duty, and the rest of the garrison, caught unawares, was terrified into surrender. The fortress and the town itself were demolished, Volscian territory was evacuated and the whole strength of Roman arms was concentrated against Veii. The traitor was rewarded with his liberty and with the gift of the property of two families, and was re-named Servius Romanus. Some suppose – wrongly – that Artena was not a Volscian town but belonged to Veii; the source of the error is the fact that there was another town of the same name between Caere and Veii, a place which was a dependency of the former and was destroyed in the time of the Roman kings. The Artena, the destruction of which I have just related, was in Volscian territory.

BOOK FIVE

The Capture of Rome

THE coming of peace elsewhere found Rome and Veii facing each other with such mutual hatred and ferocity that none could doubt but that defeat for either would mean extinction. Elections in the two towns revealed a wide difference in the policy of each: the Romans increased the number of their military tribunes to the unprecedented number of eight – Manlius Aemilius Mamercus (for the second time), Lucius Valerius Potitus (for the third time), Appius Claudius Crassus, Marcus Quinctilius Varus, Lucius Julius Julus, Marcus Postumius, Marcus Furius Camillus, Marcus Postumius Albinus; the Veientes on the contrary, in disgust at the annually recurring scramble for office which had not seldom given rise to bitter quarrels, had appointed a king. The other Etruscan communities had taken offence at this innovation, for personal reasons no less than for political, as the man who was given supreme power in Veii had been generally disliked owing to his wealth and, more particularly, because of the outrage he had committed on their religious feelings by breaking up a solemn national festival. The Twelve Peoples had failed to elect him as priest, and in rage at this rebuff he without warning, and while the show was still in progress, withdrew the performers, most of whom were his own slaves. The Etruscan communities, deeply learned as they were in sacred lore of all kinds, were more concerned than any other nation with religious matters, and for that reason they determined to refuse assistance to Veii while the king ruled there. In Veii itself this decision was kept dark, as people were afraid of the king who was always inclined to take the bearer of this sort of news as a likely leader of rebellion – never as a mere reporter of gossip. The Romans were well aware that the question of aid to Veii was being brought up at all the meetings of the Etruscan communities, so in spite of reports that all was at present quiet there, they took the precaution of constructing their field-works both for offence and defence – facing the town to prevent sorties, and also confronting the open country to block any assistance which might come from elsewhere in Etruria.

The Roman commanders, in the belief that a siege offered better prospects of success than a direct assault, took the hitherto unprecedented step of beginning the construction of winter quarters,

intending to continue hostilities throughout the year. For some time
now the tribunes in Rome had been without a pretext for stirring up
trouble, but the moment they got news of the commanders' intention
they jumped at their chance: hurriedly calling an assembly they did
all they could to inflame the mob. 'So that' (they exclaimed) 'is why
the soldiers have been granted pay! A gift indeed, but a poisoned one
– just as we knew it would be. The liberty of the people has been sold.
All who are fit for service have been got out of the way for ever –
banished from city life and politics – no longer allowed even during
the storms of winter to visit their homes or see to their affairs. What's
behind this new idea of winter campaigning? We'll tell you: it is
simply and solely to prevent the presence in Rome of large numbers
of those active men who constitute the whole strength of the popular
cause – if they are not here, then nothing will be done for you. Moreover, these soldiers of ours are being subjected to far worse suffering
than our enemies in Veii, who have their houses to live in during the
winter months and can look for protection to the natural strength and
excellent defences of their city, while our own men have to grind
their hearts out in frost and snow, living under canvas and not permitted to sheathe their swords even in those months which have
always brought a respite from all wars, whether by sea or land. To
campaign upon compulsion, summer and winter alike? Why, this is
slavery beyond any imposed by the kings, or by those haughty consuls in the old days before we tribunes existed; it is worse than anything done by the gloomy and remorseless power of the dictatorship,
or by the self-willed and arrogant *decemvirs*.

'These men who have acted with such savagery wield, as yet, only
the shadow of consular authority – what, then, do you think they will
do when they are consuls indeed – or Dictators?

'My friends, you deserve your fate. Eight military tribunes were
elected, and you did not find room amongst them for a single man of
your own class. Once patrician candidates used to fill three places a
year, and that only after a hard-fought election, but now they come
galloping up to the poll like an eight-horse team with us plebeians
absolutely nowhere – not a commoner in sight to remind his
colleagues, if nothing else, that the soldiers on service are not slaves
but free men and fellow-citizens, who ought in winter at least
to be allowed to return to the comfort of their homes, to see
their parents and wives and children at any rate for a part of the

year, and to use their privilege, as burgesses of Rome, of voting at elections.'

The tribunes were quickly confronted by a man thoroughly well qualified to answer their impassioned tirades; this was Appius Claudius, who had been left by his colleagues in Rome for the express purpose of dealing with any trouble which the tribunes might raise. For most of his adult life he had been deeply engaged in active opposition to the popular party, and it was he, as I have already recorded, who a few years previously had suggested that the power of the tribunate might be broken by getting some of the tribunes to veto the proposals of the others. He was a clever man and a practised speaker, and the speech he delivered on the present occasion was to the following effect. 'Men of Rome, if there has ever been any doubt whether it is for your sakes or for their own that the tribunes have always encouraged sedition, that doubt is surely now at an end. For years you have failed to see the true state of the case – but you see it now, and I am thankful. Moreover I congratulate you – as I congratulate the country on your behalf – that the mistake has been cleared up at a time when things are going well for you. Is it not as plain as daylight that by no injustice you ever suffered – as you may have done, possibly, from time to time – have your tribunes been roused to such a pitch of indignation as by the free gift which the Senate gave you when payment was granted for military service? What they were afraid of then, and what they are seeking to destroy today, is – obviously – concord between the orders – between nobility and commons – as they are convinced that it would contribute more than anything else to the collapse of the tribunate. They are like dishonest tradesmen looking for work – it suits them best if there is always something wrong in the body politic, so that you can call them in to put it right.

'Tell me, which side are you tribunes on? Are you defending or attacking the commons? Are you for or against our soldiers in the field? Personally I suspect your real position is mere contrariness – you object to anything and everything the Senate does, regardless of its political implications. Just as masters refuse to let anyone outside the family help or harm their slaves, or have anything to do with them, so you try to stop all intercourse between patricians and commons, for fear lest our kindliness and generosity have their due effect upon them, and they, in their turn, learn to listen to our counsel. If you loved your country – nay, if you had a spark of humanity in you – you ought rather to have welcomed and, so far as you could, to have fostered a proper relationship between patricians and populace – kindliness on the one hand, obedience on the other. Could the harmony between them but last for ever, who would hesitate to affirm that we should quickly become the dominant power amongst our neighbours?

'As to the decision of my colleagues not to withdraw the troops from Veii until their object is accomplished, I will explain presently why it is not merely a sound, but also a necessary decision. First, however, I should like to say a word about the actual condition of the soldiers on the spot. Now surely not only you but they too, if they could hear what I am saying and had every chance to criticize, would admit the fairness of arguments which I am perfectly willing to borrow from my opponents, should I fail to find enough of my own. The tribunes were saying just now that pay ought not to have been granted to the soldiers, because it had never been granted before. How then can they now object if men who are better off than they used to be are asked to do more for it – to contribute additional service in proportion to their gain? There is, to speak generally, no such thing as work without gain or gain without work: toil and pleasure, though apparent opposites, are indissolubly linked. Men on active service used to resent having to serve the country at their own expense, but they were glad, at least, to have a part of the year for working their farms and earning something for the support of their families even when they had to go abroad again. Now they are no less glad that the state is contributing to their incomes – they are by no means averse to drawing their pay. Let them, therefore, put up with being away a little longer from their homes and from that property of theirs which no longer has to bear heavy expenses during their absence. To put the matter on a strictly business footing, might not the state say: "You have a year's pay, so give a year's work. Or do you think that twelve months' pay for six months' service is a fair proposition?"

'I find it distasteful to labour this point, as it is the sort of argument which would be appropriate in the case of an army of mercenaries. We, on the contrary, wish to deal with our fellow-citizens, and claim to be similarly dealt with ourselves: what you discuss with us, you are discussing with your country.

'Men of Rome, either this war ought never to have been undertaken or it ought to be conducted worthily and ended as quickly as possible – and ended it will be, if we press the siege and withdraw only when the capture of Veii shall have crowned our hopes. God help us, my friends, shame itself, if nothing else, should keep us in the field: there was a time when for one woman's sake a city was besieged for ten years by the united armies of Greece – far from home, with many lands and the sundering seas between! How, remembering that, can we shrink from sticking it for a single year – barely twenty miles away, too; nay, almost within sight of home? Is our quarrel with Veii such a slight one? Have we no grievance against them sufficient to keep us at our task? Come, come: on seven separate occasions they have started hostilities against us; in the intervals of peace we could never trust them; a thousand times they have devastated our farm-lands; they have forced Fidenae to revolt, killed our settlers, prompted, in contravention of all human decency, the impious murder of our envoys, and attempted to raise all Etruria against us. They are still trying to do so now, and, when our envoys demanded redress, they were within an ace of laying violent hands upon them. Are those the sort of people we should fight with the gloves on – or dilatorily? Righteous indignation should be enough to move us, but there is more too, and I beg you in God's name to understand what it is: Veii is already surrounded by siege-works on a vast scale; all the inhabitants are shut up within their walls; their farms are neglected, and any cultivated land there was has been ruined. If, then, we raise the siege, can you doubt for an instant that they will invade us – not only in desire for revenge but from the sheer necessity of recouping their own losses by plundering somebody else? Raise the siege, and we shall not be postponing the war till next summer: no indeed – we shall be fighting it on our own territory.

'To come now to purely military considerations – to what personally touches our troops in the field – those troops whom the gallant tribunes, after trying to rob them of their pay, now suddenly wish to protect from hardship. Consider the position: they have completed the immensely laborious construction of a rampart and trench extending over miles of country; they have built forts in increasing numbers as their own strength grew, and defence-works of all sorts to guard against attack not only from the town but from the surrounding country, and in addition to these major works there has been the preparation of all the elaborate apparatus needed for a siege – towers, mantlets, tortoises, and goodness knows what. Can you really believe that now, when all this mass of work has been brought to a successful conclusion, it ought to be abandoned, only to be begun over again, with the same labour, the same sweat, next summer? Surely it is infinitely easier to keep what we've got, to press relentlessly on – in short, to finish the job. It will not take us long, if only we keep at it and do not deliberately postpone the fulfilment of our hopes by interruptions and delays. I speak of the waste of time and labour, but there is a worse danger we run by putting off our operations, and all these meetings of the Etruscan communities to discuss aid to Veii are not likely to let us forget it. As things are at the moment, there is no love lost between these communities and Veii – they are refusing to help, and for all they care we are at liberty to take the place; but who can guarantee that if our present operations are broken off they will not change their minds? Once we relax our efforts, there will be, in the first place, an increased diplomatic offensive on Veii's part, and, in the second, the cause of the other Etruscans' resentment, the monarchial government in Veii, may well be removed either in the natural course of things or by the will of the people who might hope thereby to get on terms again with the rest of Etruria – indeed the king himself, unwilling to endanger his people, might voluntarily abdicate. Only consider the train of consequences which are bound to follow this disastrous policy – the sheer waste of our laboriously constructed siege-works, the imminent devastation of our own countryside, war not with Veii only but with a united Etruria.

'That, then, is the policy the tribunes recommend. It reminds me of a doctor who, by indulging his patient's craving for food and drink, protracts his disease, and perhaps renders it permanently incurable, when strict treatment would have set him on his feet again within a week. Even apart from this particular campaign, it was of the utmost importance to military discipline that our troops should accustom themselves not merely to the enjoyment of victory but to a certain dogged endurance when things are moving slowly; they must learn to wait for the fulfilment of their hopes, maybe for years; if their work is not finished by the summer's end, they must learn to face the winter too, and not look around as soon as autumn comes for a comfortable shelter like our summer visitors, the birds. If a passion for hunting can draw a man, whatever the weather – frost or snow – into the woods and hills, surely in the stern stresses of war we can show the same power of physical endurance which is ordinarily elicited by the pleasure of sport? Or are we to think that our soldiers have gone so soft in mind and body that a single winter on active service is intolerable to them? Have they turned sailors – to wage war with an eye on the weather and incapable of bearing heat or cold? Such a charge would fill them with shame and indignation: they would stoutly maintain that they are tough and determined fellows, perfectly capable of fighting a winter campaign as well as a summer one, that they never expected the tribunes to provide a featherbed for effeminate idlers, and remembered, moreover, that the men who long ago created the tribunate, had themselves fought their battle in the open, courageously, not without dust and heat. To be worthy of the Roman name and of the valour of your soldiers, you must look beyond the present campaign against Veii, and seek a reputation in the eyes of the world which will stand you in good stead in other wars hereafter; what you do now will – believe me – make a considerable difference to our future reputation: either our neighbours will think that no town which has succeeded in defending itself against us for five minutes need have anything else to fear, or the terror of the Roman name will be such that the world shall know that, once a Roman army has laid a siege to a city, nothing will move it – not the rigours of winter nor the weariness of months and years – that it knows no end but victory and is ready, if a swift and sudden stroke will not serve, to persevere till that victory is achieved. Perseverance is necessary in all kinds of warfare, but most of all in sieges. Few towns can be taken by assault; most are too strongly defended, or built upon impregnable sites; it is time, with its accompanying thirst and hunger, which makes the final breach in the stubborn walls – as it will do at Veii, unless the tribunes turn traitor and the Veientes find in Rome the help which in Etruria they are seeking in vain.

'The most welcome gift we could give to Veii would be to involve ourselves here in Rome in political dissensions, and then to let the poison of sedition spread to our army in the field. Our enemies – alas – are very different from ourselves: such is the force of control in Veii that neither the prospect of a long and weary siege nor even of the continuance of the monarchy has caused any sort of revolt; Etruria has refused its aid, yet the Veientes have remained calm. And why? Because any rebel will be summarily executed, and no one in that town will be allowed to say the kind of things which here are said with impunity.

'With us, a deserter or runaway is clubbed to death, but the instigators of desertion and cowardice get a hearing not from an odd traitor or two but from whole armies openly assembled for the purpose. The truth is that the tribunes have poisoned your minds: you have grown accustomed to listen to whatever they say, no matter how treasonable or destructive of the common weal; the tribunate is like a drug and you have found it so sweet that you are willing to ignore any and every crime which lies concealed beneath it. It remains only for these tribunes to repeat their howls of rage before the soldiers in the field, to corrupt the army and urge it to mutiny – and why not, for does not Roman liberty consist in the glorious privilege of snapping our fingers at the Senate and magistrates, and looking with contempt upon law, tradition established ordinance, and military discipline?'

Appius both in the Senate and at mass meetings outside was already proving himself a match for the tribunes, when a reverse at Veii, whence bad news of that sort was least expected, gave, in a moment, the preponderating weight to his cause, and at the same time drew the contending parties closer together and increased the general determination to press the siege with greater vigour than before. The earthen rampart round the town had already been carried well forward and the mantlets were nearly in contact with the walls, as work on them had been going on almost without intermission during the hours of daylight; unfortunately however they were inadequately guarded at night, with the result that hundreds of men with burning flares made an unexpected sortie and set the whole thing in a blaze. Within an hour weeks of hard work were reduced to ashes, and many who tried in vain to cope with the situation perished either by fire or sword. In Rome the news of the disaster caused universal distress, and in the Senate there was acute anxiety lest, in consequence of it, it should no longer be possible to stop a rising both in the city and in the army – to the great delight of the tribunes who would, no doubt, congratulate themselves on their victory over the government. Happily however the anxiety was rendered needless by a most unexpected offer: all the men who were rated as 'knights' but had not been equipped with horses at the state's expense, determined at a private meeting to present themselves before the Senate, and then, when leave to put their case had been granted, volunteered to serve with their own horses. They received the thanks of the Senate, expressed in highly honourable terms, and as soon as the news of their offer spread through the city, the populace caught the patriotic fervour and mobbed the Senate House, declaring that, as the order of knights had done their duty, it was now up to the 'order of footsloggers', too, to offer themselves for voluntary and special service, at Veii or elsewhere. Should it be at Veii, they vowed never to return until the town was taken.

The satisfaction of the Senate knew no bounds: in the case of the knights their gratitude had been expressed officially, through the magistrates; this time the response was wholly spontaneous. No one was summoned to the House to receive an official answer to the offer; the senators did not even remain within the House themselves, but came hurrying out on to the steps, from which they all, individually and personally, conveyed by voice and gesture to the crowds in the square below the national joy at this act of generosity, calling out that by reason of this unlooked-for collaboration Rome was blessed indeed and would for ever remain invincible. Not one of them but was loud in his praises for knights and populace alike; the very day was a red-letter day for the country, since even the generosity and goodwill of the Senate had been surpassed. Tears of joy and mutual congratulation flowed freely, until at last the Senate reassembled and a motion was adopted to convey through the military tribunes at a mass meeting the formal thanks of the country to the new divisions of infantry and cavalry, with the added assurance that the government would not forget their patriotism. They were to be told, moreover, that every man who had volunteered for service would receive pay, including the cavalrymen. This was the first occasion on which cavalrymen served on their own horses.

The army of volunteers then proceeded to Veii, where it repaired the damage done by the fire and put in hand new works as well. In Rome increased care was taken to ensure adequate supplies, in order that troops who had shown such a magnificent spirit should lack for nothing.

The military tribunes for the following year were Gaius Servilius Ahala (for the third time), Quintus Servilius, Lucius Verginius, Quintus Suplicius, Aulus Manlius (for the second time), and Manlius Sergius (for the second time). This year, while everyone's attention was concentrated upon the operations at Veii, the garrison at Anxur was overwhelmed and the town taken. The disaster was due to neglect: troops were away on leave, Volscians were being indiscriminately admitted for trading purposes, with the result that the sentries at the gates were suddenly and treacherously attacked. Casualties were not heavy, simply because most of the men who were not on the sick list were scattered around the neighbouring towns and villages, doing business like sutlers.

Nor was it much better with the infinitely more important operations at Veii. For one thing, the Roman commanding officers were showing more energy in quarrelling with one another than in pressing forward the siege, and, for another, the strength of the opposition was increased by the unexpected arrival of contingents from Capenae and Falerii, two Etruscan communities which, by reason of their proximity, naturally supposed that if Veii fell they would themselves be the next object of attack. Falerii had, moreover, already incurred the hostility of Rome by her part in the war with Fidenae, so with that additional reason for her present course of action she had engaged in diplomatic exchanges with Veii and bound herself to render assistance. The troops from Falerii appeared on the scene quite suddenly and attacked the Roman position at the point where Manlius Sergius was in command; the effect was alarm and confusion on the grand scale, as the Romans imagined that all Etruria had risen and was about to crush them with a vast and irresistible army. The same erroneous belief roused the troops in Veii to action, with the result that the Romans found themselves caught between two simultaneous thrusts, front and rear. Rapid manoeuvring was of little avail, and they were unable either to contain the Veientes or to repel the assault upon their own defence-lines on the side away from the town. Their only hope was to get reinforcements from the larger camp, for it would then be possible to fight on both fronts simultaneously with some chance of success. It so happened, however, that the man in command of the larger camp was Verginius, and between Sergius and Verginius there was a private feud of great bitterness; Verginius accordingly, on receiving a report that most of his colleagues' strong points had been stormed and his defences scaled, took no action whatever: if Sergius, he declared, wanted help, he would no doubt ask for it himself. But Sergius was as pigheaded as Verginius was arrogant, and, rather than appear to have asked help from a man he hated, preferred defeat by the enemy to victory gained through the intervention of a compatriot. His force, surrounded as it was, suffered heavy losses, until finally the position was abandoned; a handful of men made their way to Verginius's camp, the majority of the survivors, with Sergius himself, going on to Rome.

Arrived in Rome, Sergius threw all the blame for his defeat upon his colleague, who was ordered to return to the city for questioning, leaving his subordinate officers in charge. The affair was then debated in the Senate and in the course of the hearing each man abused the other to the top of his bent, the members of the House taking one side or the other as personal considerations prompted them, and few, if any, concerning themselves with the real issue – the national welfare. The leaders of the House finally proposed that, whether the ignominious defeat were due to ill-luck or to incompetence, all the military tribunes should be immediately superseded, without waiting for the normal date of the elections. The new men should take up their duties on 1 October. During the voting on this proposal none of the military tribunes except the two who were primarily concerned raised any objection; those, two, however – Sergius and Verginius, the very men on whose account the Senate wanted a clean sweep – first asked to be spared the humiliation and then, when their request was ignored, vetoed the proposal and flatly refused to resign before 13 December, the usual date. At this the people's tribunes, who had unwillingly kept silent so long as harmony prevailed and everything was going well, promptly returned to the attack and threatened to order the arrest of the military tribunes unless they submitted to the Senate's authority. Gaius Servilius Ahala intervened: 'As for you,' he said, addressing himself to the people's tribunes, 'I should much like to prove that your menaces are as illegal as you yourselves are dastardly. To resist the authority of the Senate is a serious crime: very well then; stop trying to find in our disputes an occasion for raising trouble, and my colleagues shall either do as the Senate proposes or I will myself, if they prove obstinate, immediately name a Dictator, to force their resignation.'

These sentiments won universal approval; the Senate was greatly relieved to have found another, and more powerful, instrument for coercing the military tribunes than the people's tribunes' miserable threats. Opposition was at an end, and the military tribunes yielding to the unanimous feeling of the House, held the election for their successors, who were to enter upon office on 13 October. They themselves resigned before that date.

The men elected for the succeeding year were Lucius Valerius Potitus (for the fourth time), Marcus Furius Camillus (for the second time), Manlius Aemilius Mamercus (for the third time), Cnaeus Cornelius Cossus (for the second time), Caeso Fabius Ambustus, and Lucius Julius Julus. It was to be in all respects an eventful year. In the first place, a number of campaigns were simultaneously on hand – at Veii, at Capena, at Falerii, and the operations for the recovery of Anxur. In Rome neither recruitment nor the collection of the war-tax was going altogether smoothly; there was trouble over the co-opting of people's tribunes, and no little excitement over the trial of Sergius and Verginius. The new military tribunes' first concern was the raising of troops, and, circumstances being what they were, they did not stop at the enrolment of the younger men but compelled others who were past the age for active service to enlist for home defence. The increase in the number of troops meant a corresponding increase in the money needed to pay them; an attempt was made to collect it from taxation, but this was resented by the older men who were not detailed for service abroad, on the ground that their own task of home defence was just as much military and national service as any other. The tax was, in fact, a serious burden, but the tribunes jumped at the chance to make it appear worse than it was, making violent anti-government speeches in which they asserted that the Senate's object in paying the troops was simply to ruin by taxation those of the commons whom they failed to get butchered in the field. One campaign was already in its third year, and it was being deliberately misconducted in order to prolong it still further; then troops were being raised for four more, and boys and old men were being dragged from their homes to go on service; summer and winter, nowadays, were all alike – there was no rest left for the wretched commons, and, as the last straw, they were now to be taxed. Poor creatures! – crawling home exhausted, mutilated, decrepit with age, they would find everything gone in their long absence to wrack and ruin, only to be faced with the necessity of raising money out of their dwindling resources in order to return to the treasury three times as much as they received in service pay, as if it had been a loan on interest!

What with recruiting and the new tax and other weighty preoccupations, the candidates at the election of people's tribunes fell short of the required number, whereupon an effort was made to get patricians co-opted into the vacant places. The effort failed, but – as the next best way of invalidating the law – two plebeians, Lacerius and Acutius, were co-opted, undoubtedly through patrician influence. Now it so happened that one of the tribunes for the year was Cnaeus Trebonius, and a man of that name and family was clearly in duty bound to defend the Trebonian law, which forbade co-optation to the tribunate. Accordingly he declared that the military tribunes had illegally forced through a measure which the Senate – unsuccessfully at the time – had once attempted to carry; the Trebonian law had been made nonsense of, in that tribunes, instead of being elected by popular vote, had been co-opted at the dictation of the patricians – in fact, the intolerable position had been reached that the tribunes must now be either patricians themselves or the patricians' toadies. Bitterly he complained that the tribunate was being torn from their grasp, their sacred laws annulled – and all by the dishonesty of the governing class and the criminal treachery of his colleagues.

In consequence of this outburst feeling was running high not only against the patricians but equally against the tribunes they had co-opted when three other members of the college, Publius Curatius, Marcus Metilius, and Marcus Minucius, in alarm for the security of their own positions, created a diversion by turning upon Sergius and Verginius, the military tribunes of the preceding year, whom they summoned to stand their trial and by that means provided a fresh object for popular rage to vent itself upon; the line they took was that anyone who resented the levy or the tax or the long duration of foreign service, all who grieved over the defeat at Veii or whose homes were in mourning for sons, brothers, or kinsmen, could now, thanks to them, enjoy both the right and the power of avenging their private sorrows, and the sorrows of the country, upon the two guilty men. 'Sergius and Verginius,' they said, 'are responsible for all your troubles. They are as ready to confess their guilt as their accuser is to prove it, as their behaviour shows: each blames the other, who is as great a scoundrel as himself, Verginius taxing Sergius with running away in face of the enemy, and Sergius retorting with an accusation of betrayal. Indeed the conduct of both men has been so near lunacy that it appears more than likely that the whole wretched affair was a put-up job, engineered by the patricians, who first allowed the Veientes to set fire to the siege-works in order to prolong the war, and have now betrayed the army and treacherously surrendered a Roman camp to the men of Falerii. They are doing all they can to ruin us; they want our soldiers to grow old at Veii; they want to prevent the tribunes from bringing proposals before the people for land-distribution, or for anything else that might alleviate their lot, and from getting on with their programme of reform, and obstructing the government's conspiracy against us, at packed meetings here in Rome.

'The two accused men have already been condemned in advance by the Senate, by the people, and by their own colleagues – the Senate cashiered them, their colleagues scared them into resigning by the threat of appointing a Dictator, and the people elected successors to take up their duties two months before the normal date, because they knew that it would be all up with the country if these two scoundrels remained in office a day longer. Yet what do they do? Condemned in advance and cut to pieces as they are, they present themselves before you for trial apparently supposing that they have sufficiently paid for their errors simply by taking off their uniforms a couple of months too soon; it does not seem to occur to them that their forced resignation was not a punishment at all – it was merely a precaution to stop them doing further mischief, as is obvious from the fact that their colleagues, too, were forced to resign, though undoubtedly innocent.

'We ask you, men of Rome, to remember what you felt on the day of the defeat at Veii, when you watched our battered troops stagger in fear and disorder through the City gates – and not a man of them laid the blame on ill luck or angry gods, but only upon their commanding officers. Is there anyone here present who did not on that day damn both of them to hell – head, house, and fortune? And if you then prayed heaven to punish them, it is surely unreasonable not to use your own power against them now. The law allows it and your duty urges it; the gods, remember, never lay hands upon guilty men – they are content to arm the injured with an opportunity for revenge.'

The people, far from deaf to appeals of this sort, condemned both men to pay a fine of 10,000 *asses* (old currency), ignoring Sergius's attempt to lay the blame on his luck and the common chances of war, and Verginius's pathetic appeal not to be made even more unfortunate at home then he had been on the battlefield. Amidst the passions aroused by this trial the question of co-opting tribunes and the evasion of the Trebonian law were almost forgotten.

The tribunes, full of their triumph, immediately rewarded the commons for their condemnation of the two commanders by bringing forward their customary proposal for the distribution of the public domains, and at the same time forbade the collection of the war-tax, in spite of the fact that there were so many armies needing to be paid and that the military situation, though not wholly adverse, was none the less such that in none of the various theatres was there any prospect of rapid success. At Veii the lost position had been retaken and strengthened, under the command of Manlius Aemilius and Caeso Fabius. Marcus Furius at Falerii and Cnaeus Cornelius at Capena had made no contact with the enemy in open country; they had plundered and burnt crops and farms unopposed, but made no attempt against the towns. The Volscian campaign directed by Valerius Potitus looked less promising: after devastating the countryside Potitus had made an unsuccessful assault on the hill-town of Anxur, and, having found the place impregnable, had started to invest it. In short, the conduct of the various campaigns evinced only a very moderate sort of vigour on the part of the men in command; the same, however, cannot be said of the internal conflict in Rome, which was both serious and violent. The action of the tribunes had stopped the collection of the tax: the troops were loudly demanding their pay, but no money was being sent to the commanding officers, and it began to look as if the army too, would catch the disease of mutiny against authority. Popular resentment against the patricians being thoroughly aroused, the tribunes seized the opportunity of declaring that now was the time to make liberty secure by excluding from the highest office of state men like Sergius and Verginius and transferring it to the honest and capable hands of picked plebeians; but in spite of their protestations they succeeded in procuring the election of only a single plebeian candidate for the military tribuneship, Publius Licinius Calvus. It was a bare assertion of the rights, and all the others were patricians – Publius Manlius, Lucius Titinius, Publius Maelius, Lucius Furius Medullinus, and Lucius Publilius Vulscus.

As for the mass of the people, they were astonished at their success – but not more so than the successful candidate himself who, though an elderly member of the Senate, had never previously held office. Nobody really knows why it was he, rather than anybody else, who was first called to taste the delights of this unprecedented honour; some think he was dug out of his comfortable obscurity through the influence of his relative Cnaeus Cornelius, who as military tribune in the previous year had arranged for the cavalry to be paid three times as much as the infantry; or his success may possibly have been due to a well-timed speech he made, in which, to the great satisfaction of both parties, he urged the burying of the political hatchet. In their triumph at this electoral victory the people's tribunes withdrew their opposition to the tax, which was thereupon duly collected and the money dispatched to the army. The government's most serious difficulty was thus removed.

In the Volscian campaign Anxur was soon retaken – a festival was in progress, and the sentries on guard had neglected their duties.

This year was memorable for a winter of great severity with much snow. Roads were blocked and the river closed to traffic. Fortunately there were good supplies of grain in the City, so prices did not rise.

The election of Licinius had been accompanied by no disorders; so quietly had it gone through that the satisfaction of the commons was much more marked than any resentment on the part of the Senate; accordingly, as he showed a similar tact in the conduct of his office, popular ambition was aroused of getting plebeian candidates, at the forthcoming elections too, into the military tribuneship. The ambition was fulfilled, and the only patrician to secure a place was Marcus Veturius; the others – Marcus Pomponius, Cnaeus Duilius, Publilius Volero, Cnaeus Genucius, and Lucius Atilius – were all plebeians and were elected by an almost unanimous vote of the centuries.

For some reason or other – perhaps because of the sudden change from excessive cold to excessive heat – the hard winter was followed by an unhealthy summer. Plague was rife, and neither human beings nor animals were immune. The disease was incurable, its ravages appalling, and in despair of understanding its cause or of foreseeing its end the Senate ordered a consultation of the Sybilline Books. The two officials in charge of such matters performed, for the first time in Rome, the ceremony of the *lectisternium* or Draping of Couches: to win the favour of Apollo, Latona, and Diana, of Hercules, Mercury and Neptune, for eight successive days three couches, as richly furnished as the times could afford, were left standing out of doors for the divine company to recline on. A similar ceremony was celebrated in private houses: in every street doors were left open and viands of all sorts displayed for the promiscuous use of anyone and everyone; friends and strangers alike were, we are told, invited in and hospitably entertained; men talked with kindliness and courtesy to their bitterest enemies; quarrels were forgotten, no process was served, and even the prisoners in gaol were relieved of their chains – indeed, when the week was over, it seemed a sin to send back to prison the unfortunates whom the gods had thus helped in their distress.

At Veii meanwhile, where Roman troops had to face the united strength of three enemies, the situation was a most dangerous one. Again, as before, contingents from Capena and Falerii arrived without warning to assist in the defence of the town, thus subjecting the Romans in the smaller camps to pressure from three armies simultaneously from three different directions. Their greatest support in this critical position was the knowledge that Sergius and Verginius had been condemned. This time the mistake was not repeated: from the larger camp, where on the previous occasion the fatal delay had occurred, a force was sent round by the shortest route to take the Capenates in the rear as they threatened an assault on the Roman rampart. The ensuing engagement also shook the contingent from Falerii, which was already in some confusion when a well-timed sortie from the camp put it to flight. The victorious Romans pursued the fugitives with great slaughter, and soon afterwards a raiding-party happened to fall in with them and destroyed the few stragglers who still survived. The Veientes, too, suffered heavily, for the gates of the town had been shut to prevent an irruption of the Romans, and many of them were killed outside before they could get through.

It had certainly been an eventful year, and now the elections were approaching. The patricians were almost more anxious about the result of them than they were about the progress of the war, being painfully conscious that they had not merely been forced to share the supreme office of state with their opponents, but had come near to losing it altogether. They agreed, therefore, to put up their most distinguished men as candidates, men whom they felt the people could hardly have the face to reject, and at the same time launched a great campaign of canvassing – almost as if they were all seeking election themselves. Leaving no stone unturned, they rallied heaven and earth to their support – particularly heaven, as they blamed the result of the election of the year before last upon the anger of the gods; in that year, they said, there had been a winter so unbearable that it looked like a divine warning to guilty men; last year warnings had been succeeded by events; the city and countryside had been smitten with plague – obviously by the wrath of heaven which, as the Books of Prophecy indicated, had to be appeased before any relief could be obtained. The conclusion was clear: the presiding deities of Rome were insulted because at an election held under their auspices, the high offices of state were vulgarized and family distinctions ignored.

This policy proved a success, for even apart from the dignity of the candidates people in general were touched in their religious susceptibilities, and the candidates elected were all patricians and mainly the most illustrious amongst them. They were Lucius Valerius Potitus (for the fifth time), Marcus Valerius Maximus, Marcus Furius Camillus (for the third time), Lucius Furius Medullinus (for the third time), Quintus Servilius Fidenas (for the second time), and Quintus Sulpicius Camerinus (for the second time).

The new military tribunes did nothing of any note at Veii, but concentrated their strength on the devastation of the countryside. The two
chief commanders, Potitus at Falerii and Camillus at Capena plundered
on a great scale and left untouched nothing that fire or sword could
destroy.

Stories meanwhile were coming in of a number of inexplicable and
ominous occurrences. Most of the stories, being vouched for only by
individuals, were received with incredulity and contempt – moreover,
Rome always employed Etruscan soothsayers and because of the war
with Etruria there were none, at the time, in the city. One occurrence,
however, caused universal anxiety: the lake in the Alban Wood, without any unusual rainfall or other natural cause, rose much above its
normal height. The thing was a prodigy, and a mission was dispatched
to the Delphic oracle to inquire what the gods might mean by it. Meanwhile, however, an interpreter of the Fates presented himself nearer
home in the person of an old man of Veii, who while Roman and
Etruscan soldiers were exchanging chaff as they faced each other on
their respective guard-posts, suddenly burst into prophecy and declared that Rome would never take Veii until the water in the Alban
lake was drained off. The soldiers at first merely laughed, taking what
the old fellow said as meaningless gibe; but after a minute or two they
began to talk it over, and finally one of them asked a man belonging to
the town (the war had gone on so long that Romans and their enemies
frequently talked to each other) who the old fellow was who had made
the mysterious remark about the Alban lake. The answer was that he
was a soothsayer. Now the Roman sentry who had asked the question
was of a superstitious turn of mind, so pretending a wish to consult the
soothsayer, should he be able to spare the time, about some private
puzzle of his own, got him to come out and talk to him. Neither was
armed, and they had walked off together some distance in apparently
perfect mutual confidence, when the sentry, who was young and
strong, suddenly seized his aged companion and carried him bodily to
the Roman lines. The Etruscans who saw the act – indeed, it was obvious to everyone – raised a tremendous outcry but could do nothing to
stop it.

The soothsayer was taken to headquarters and then sent on to the
Senate in Rome, where he was asked to explain what he had meant. In
reply he said that the gods must indeed have been angry with Veii on
the day when they put it into his mind to reveal the doom which was

destined to fall upon his country, and for that reason what he had then been inspired to speak he could not now recall as if it had never been spoken; for it might well be that it was as great a sin to conceal what the gods wished to be known as to speak what should remain concealed. He went on to say that it was known to Etruscan lore and written in the books of fate that if the Romans drained the water from the Alban lake after it had risen high, then they would be granted victory over Veii; till then, the gods of Veii would never desert her city walls. He then began to explain in detail the proper method of drawing off the water. The Senate felt that the old man's authority was hardly adequate in a matter of such importance, so they decided to await the return of their mission to Delphi with the answer of the Pythian oracle.

Before its return with instructions how the prodigy at Alba should be met, the new military tribunes began their year of office. They were as follows: Lucius Julius Julus (for the second time), Lucius Furius Medullinus (for the fourth time), Lucius Sergius Fidenas, Aulus Postumius Regillensis, Publius Cornelius Maluginensis, and Aulus Manlius. This year the men of Tarquinii joined the ranks of Rome's enemies; they knew that the Romans were already engaged on many fronts, against the Volscians at Anxur, where the garrison was under siege, against the Aequians at Labici where the Roman settlement was being subjected to pressure, not to mention the major struggle with Veii, Capena, and Falerii. They were also well aware that what with political dissensions things were hardly quieter in the City itself. In these circumstances, as the chance of inflicting some damage seemed a good one, light forces from Tarquinii were sent to raid Roman territory in the belief that Rome would either take no counter-measures, to avoid involving herself in further hostilities, or attempt to deal with the raid only with small and inadequate forces. The Romans felt the raid less as a cause for anxiety than as an insult to their pride, and the measures they took to deal with it were not long delayed and cost little effort: Postumius and Julius raised a contingent – not by the normal process of enlistment, which the tribunes refused to allow – but by appealing to men, as good patriots, to volunteer – and marching by cross-country tracks through the territory of Caere surprised and crushed the raiders as they were on their way home with their loot. Many were killed, and all were relieved of their luggage. The Roman party returned to Rome with the lost property recovered. The owners of the property were given two days to identify and claim it, then all that remained unidentified – a great deal of it belonged to the enemy – was sold by auction and the proceeds distributed amongst the soldiers.

Operations in the other theatres of war, especially at Veii, were dragging inconclusively on and the Romans, in despair at success by their own unaided efforts, were beginning to turn their thoughts towards help from destiny or heaven, when the mission arrived back from Delphi. The oracle they brought with them agreed with the prophecy of the old soothsayer who had been carried off from Veii. 'Let not, O Roman' (it ran) 'the Alban water be contained within its lake; let it not flow with its own stream to the sea. Thou shalt draw it out and water thy fields with it; thou shalt disperse it in rivulets and put out its power. Then mayst thou take courage and thrust against the enemy's walls, remembering that over the city, which for so long thou hast besieged, victory has been granted thee by the fates which are now revealed. When the war is done and thou hast conquered, bring to my temple a rich gift, and restore and celebrate in the fashion of thy fathers the sacred rites thou hast neglected.'

From that moment the captured soothsayer was held in the highest esteem, and the military tribunes Cornelius and Postumius employed him to direct the ritual expiation of the prodigy and the ceremonies for appeasing the angry gods. It was finally discovered that the 'neglect of sacred rites' – or, rather, the improper celebration of a festival – of which the gods accused them consisted simply in the fact that the magistrates who had announced the date for the Latin Festival and the solemn sacrifice on the Alban Mount had done so improperly and had not been elected with due observance of the formalities. There was one way, and one way only, to put this right, namely to procure the resignation of the military tribunes, who were the magistrates concerned, to take the auspices afresh and to enter, for the time being, upon an *interregnum*. This was done by a resolution of the Senate, and the office of *interrex* was held by three men in succession: Lucius Valerius, Quintus Servilius Fidenas, and Marcus Furius Camillus. The whole period was marked by continuous disturbances, the tribunes refusing to allow any election to go through until it had been agreed that a majority of the new military tribunes should be plebeians.

About this time the Etruscan communities held a conference at the shrine of Voltumna. Envoys from Capena and Falerii pressed for the union of all Etruria in a common effort to raise the siege of Veii, but the council replied that a similar request had been refused on a previous occasion because it was not felt that a people who had omitted to ask advice in a matter of such importance had the right to demand assistance. Now, however, the situation had changed, and it was their own difficulties which precluded them from sending aid; for in the greater part of Etruria there were now new settlers of strange nationality with whom their relations were ambivalent and far from comfortable. Nevertheless they were willing, out of regard for the pressing dangers of men of their own name and blood, to offer no objection if any of their fighting men should volunteer for that service. It was said in Rome that the number of such volunteers was very large, and for that reason, naturally enough, domestic quarrels began to lose their intensity in face of a common peril.

It caused the Senate but little annoyance when the centuries of the Knights, whose privilege it was to lead the voting at elections, returned as military tribune Publius Licinius Calvus – a man of proved moderation but now too old for active work – though he had not presented himself as a candidate. It was clear that all who had been his colleagues during his year of office would also be re-elected – namely Lucius Titinius, Publius Manlius, Publius Maelius, Cnaeus Genucius, and Lucius Atilius. But before their election was formally declared at an assembly of the tribes, Calvus obtained the permission of the *interrex* to make a public statement. 'Fellow citizens,' he said, 'you have not forgotten our former tenure of office, and I know therefore that in this election you are looking for what our country most needs in the coming year – an omen of concord. Now my colleagues are the same men as they always were, though the better by experience; but I am not the same – in me you see but the name and shadow of Publius Licinius. My strength is gone; I am hard of hearing and half blind; the edge of my mind is blunted. See then' – here he laid his hand upon his son – 'the true copy and reflection of the man who was the first plebeian to be raised by your suffrages to the military tribuneship. Take him in my stead; my own principles governed his upbringing, and I dedicate him now to the country's service as my representative. I did not seek the honour you have offered me – my son does seek it; I ask you therefore to grant it to him, and to my prayers.'

The old man's request was not refused, and his son – Publius Licinius like his father – was declared military tribune with consular powers together with the others I have already mentioned.

Titinius and Genucius took command of the operations against the forces of Falerii and Capena; unfortunately, however, they showed more dash than tactical ability and fell plump into a trap. Genucius atoned for his reckless incompetence by an honourable death, fighting in the van; his colleague Titinius withdrew his badly shaken troops to some high ground where he was able to reorganize, but refused to risk a full-scale engagement on the flat country below. The incident was only a minor defeat, but it might have been very serious indeed, and the moral effect of it was tremendous; in Rome, where exaggerated reports were current, there was something like panic; the army at Veii was in not much better case, and when the rumour ran round that the two commanding officers and their whole force had perished, while the victorious troops of Capena and Falerii together with the combined might of all Etruria were already close at hand, the men could with difficulty be restrained from taking to their heels. The rumours in Rome were more alarming still: people believed that the camp at Veii was being stormed and that another enemy army was marching on the City; the walls were hastily manned, and women, called from their houses by the noise and excitement in the streets, flocked to the temples to pray that, if the sacred rites had been duly renewed and the signs from heaven answered as piety demanded, destruction might be averted from their homes and holy places, that the walls of Rome might be suffered to stand and the horrors of war turned against Veii.

And now the Games having been held, the Latin Festival duly celebrated, and the water drained from the Alban Lake, the doom of Veii was at hand. Marcus Furius Camillus, the man destined to destroy that city and to save his country, was appointed Dictator and named Publius Cornelius Scipio his Master of Horse. Immediately the whole aspect of things changed with the change of command: courage and hope were renewed, the fortune of the City seemed to take on a new lease of life. Camillus's first act was to punish in accordance with martial law the men who had deserted during the panic at Veii – an act which taught troops to know something worse than the enemy to fear; he then fixed a date for enrolling new recruits and after a hurried visit to Veii to strengthen the army's morale returned to Rome to superintend the enlistment. There was no attempt to avoid service; even the Latins and Hernici promised to send contingents to the support of Rome, and were formally thanked in the Senate by Camillus, who then, when all was ready for the coming campaign, vowed in accordance with the Senate's decree that if he captured Veii he would celebrate the Votive

Games and restore and rededicate the temple of Mater Matuta which
was first consecrated many years before by King Servius Tullius.

There was more hope than confidence in the City when Camillus
and his troops left for the front. The first clash occurred in the neighbourhood of Nepete, against the forces of Falerii and Capena. It was
brilliantly successful, and good generalship was followed, as it usually
is, by good fortune. Defeat of the enemy in the field was crowned by
the capture of his camp; a mass of valuable material was taken, most of
which was given for disposal to the quaestor, only a small proportion
being distributed amongst the men. The army then proceeded to Veii,
where Camillus increased the number of redoubts and by giving out
that no one was to fight without orders put a stop to the frequent and
somewhat pointless skirmishes which took place between the town
walls and the Roman stockade. The men who had been employing
themselves in this way were turned on to digging. Of the digging
operations, by far the most important and laborious was the construction of a tunnel to lead up into the central fortress of the town; this work
was now begun, and to keep it going without intermission the men
engaged upon it were divided into six parties, working six hours each in
rotation – as continuous labour underground would soon have broken
them up. The orders were that digging should go on day and night
until the tunnel was complete and a way opened into the enemy citadel.

In course of time Camillus began to realize that victory was within
his grasp and that a town of great wealth was about to fall into his
hands. He knew that it would yield more in plunder than all the previous campaigns put together, and he was anxious neither, on the one
hand, to alienate his troops by giving them an insufficiently generous
share, nor, on the other, by an over-lavish distribution to get on the
wrong side of the Senate. Accordingly he wrote to the Senate to ask
what they wished him to do, now that, as he expressed it, by the
favour of God, the stout-heartedness of his men, and his own skilful
tactics Veii would soon be in the power of Rome. The Senate was
divided on the question: the aged Licinius, who, we are told, was first
called upon by his son to speak, proposed a public announcement to
the effect that whoever wanted a share in the plunder should go to
Veii and get it; but Appius Claudius strongly objected to such a suggestion: in his view a free gift on that scale would be not only unprecedented but unfair and ill-advised, and he accordingly urged that, if
people had suddenly found something evil in the established custom

of paying captured enemy assets into the treasury (which was in any case depleted by the expenses of war), the money should be used for paying the troops, thereby relieving the commons of some of their burden. Every family would feel the benefit, and city idlers would be prevented from laying greedy fingers on a prize that should go by rights to men who had fought bravely for their country; for it was only human nature that the quicker a man was to seek the lion's share of danger and hard work, the slower he would be to snatch what he could find for his own enrichment.

Licinius countered by arguing that this money would be a constant cause of suspicion and hatred and would inevitably give rise to public prosecutions, and so to sedition and the seeds of revolution; it would be better, in his view, to make a gift of it, as he had suggested, and thus conciliate the commons, who were already bled white by many years of taxation; it would be a real relief to them, and they would feel that they had got something at long last from a war which had taken the best years of their life. After all, there was more pleasure and satisfaction in what a man took with his own hand and carried home than in ten times the value of it doled out to him at the whim of another. Even the Dictator wanted to avoid the invidious task of making a decision in this affair and applied to the Senate for instructions; so now the Senate should refer the question to the commons and let every man keep whatever the fortune of war gave him.

Licinius's proposal seemed the safer of the two, as it would range the Senate on the side of the commons, and a proclamation was accordingly issued, that anyone who pleased might go to Camillus and the army at Veii to claim his share in the plunder. Thousands took advantage of it, and swarmed into the camp.

The crisis in the long campaign had now come. Camillus left his headquarters and took the auspices; then he ordered all troops to stand to. 'Pythian Apollo,' he prayed, 'led by you and inspired by your holy breath, I go forward to the destruction of Veii, and I vow to you a tenth part of the spoils. Queen Juno, to you too I pray, that you may leave this town where now you dwell and follow our victorious arms into our City of Rome, your future home, which will receive you in a temple worthy of your greatness.'

From every direction and with overwhelming numbers Roman troops moved forward to the assault, to distract attention from the more imminent danger from the tunnel. No one in the town was yet aware that foreign oracles, and even their own soothsayers, had already foretold their doom; none knew that gods had been invited to a share in their spoils and in answer to prayer were even then turning their divine eyes towards new homes in the temples of their enemies; ignorant as yet that their last day had come, without the least suspicion of the dreadful truth that their defences were already undermined and that at any moment enemy troops would be in the citadel, the doomed citizens seized their swords and ran to defend the walls, puzzled at what might be the significance of this sudden, wild, and apparently reckless assault, when for weeks past not a single Roman soldier had moved from his post.

There is an old story that while the king of Veii was offering sacrifice, a priest declared that he who carved up the victim's entrails would be victorious in the war; the priest's words were overheard by some of the Roman soldiers in the tunnel, who thereupon opened it, snatched the entrails, and took them to Camillus. Personally I am content, as a historian, if in things which happened so many centuries ago probabilities are accepted as truth; this tale, which is too much like a romantic stage-play to be taken seriously, I feel is hardly worth attention either for affirmation or denial.

In readiness for the decisive stroke the tunnel had been filled with picked men, and now, without warning, it discharged them into the temple of Juno on the citadel. The enemy, who were manning the walls against the threat from outside, were attacked from behind; bolts were wrenched off the gates; buildings were set on fire as women and slaves on the roofs flung stones and tiles at the assailants. A fearful din arose: yells of triumph, shrieks of terror, wailing of women, and the pitiful crying of children; in an instant of time the defenders were flung from the walls and the town gates opened; Roman troops came pouring through, or climbed the now defenceless walls; everything was overrun, in every street the battle raged. After terrible slaughter resistance began to slacken, and Camillus gave the order to spare all who were not carrying arms. No more blood was shed, the unarmed began to give themselves up and the Roman troops with Camillus's leave, dispersed to sack the town. The story goes that when the plunder was brought to him and he saw that it was more in quantity and greater in value than he had either hoped or expected, he raised his hands and prayed that, if any god or man thought his luck, and the luck of Rome, to be excessive, he might be allowed to appease the envy it aroused with the least possible inconvenience to himself or hurt to the general welfare of Rome. Tradition goes on to say that while he was uttering this prayer he turned round and happened to trip – which was taken, by those who were wise after the event, as an omen of his subsequent condemnation and of the capture of Rome, a disaster which occurred a few years later. So ended that famous day, of which every hour was spent in the killing of Rome's enemies and the sacking of a wealthy city.

Next day, all the free-born townsfolk were sold, by Camillus's orders, into slavery. The proceeds of the sale was the only money which went to the treasury, but the commons were aggrieved about it none the less; for the loot which they brought home individually they gave the credit not to the commander-in-chief who had referred to the Senate a matter he ought to have decided independently, in order, as they felt, to get support for his own meanness, nor yet to the Senate itself, but to the two Licinii – to the elder for his generous proposal on their behalf, and to the younger for procuring a vote upon it.

When all property of value belonging to men had been taken from Veii, work began on the removal of what belonged to the gods – the temple treasures and the divine images themselves. It was done with the deepest reverence; young soldiers were specially chosen for the task of conveying Queen Juno to Rome; having washed their bodies and dressed themselves in white, they entered her temple in awe, and shrank at first from what seemed the sacrilege of laying hands upon an image, which the Etruscan religion forbade anyone except the holder of a certain hereditary priesthood to touch. Suddenly one of them said: 'Juno, do you want to go to Rome?' Whether the question was divinely inspired or merely a young man's joke, who knows? but his companions all declared that the statue nodded its head in reply. We are told, too, that words were uttered, signifying assent. In any case – fables apart – she was moved from her place with only the slightest application of mechanical power, and was light and easy to transport – almost as if she came of her own free will – and was taken undamaged to her eternal dwelling-place on the Aventine, whither the Dictator had called her in his prayer. And there Camillus afterwards dedicated to her the temple he had vowed.

Such was the fall of Veii, the wealthiest city of Etruria. Even her final destruction witnessed to her greatness, for after a siege of ten summers and ten winters, during which she inflicted worse losses than she suffered, even when her destined hour had come she fell by a stratagem and not by direct assault.

The scenes in Rome when the great news arrived beggar description. Not that the City was unprepared for it – the evil omens had been averted, the soothsayers' prophecies and the oracle from Delphi were common knowledge; all that human wisdom could do had been done in the appointment to the supreme command of Camillus, the world's greatest general: nevertheless, simply because of the length of the war with its constantly varying fortune and many defeats, victory, when it came, seemed like a gift from heaven, and the joy it caused was beyond belief. Women, without waiting for a word from the government, flocked to the temples and thanked the gods for their mercies; the Senate decreed a public thanksgiving to last four days – longer than ever before. The return of Camillus drew greater crowds than had ever been seen on such an occasion in the past, people of all ranks in society pouring through the city gates to meet him; and the official celebration of his Triumph left in its splendour all previous ones in the shade. Riding into Rome in a chariot drawn by white horses he was the cynosure of every eye – and indeed in doing so he was felt to be guilty of a certain anti-republican arrogance, and even of impiety. Might there not be sin, people wondered, in giving a man those dazzling steeds and thus making him equal with Jupiter or the God of the Sun? It was this disquieting thought that rendered the celebration, for all its magnificence, not wholly acceptable.

The ceremony over, Camillus contracted for the building of Juno's temple on the Aventine, consecrated a shrine to Mater Matuta, and resigned his office – his duties to religion and to the State being all accomplished.

The question of the gift to Apollo now came up for discussion. Camillus recalled the fact that he had vowed to Apollo a tenth part of the plunder taken from Veii, and the priests gave it as their opinion that the people were in duty bound to discharge this obligation; but it was not easy to find a way of getting individuals to produce the various articles of value they had taken so that they could be assessed for the due contribution. Recourse was finally had to what seemed least likely to cause hard feelings: everyone, namely, who wished to discharge the obligation on himself and his family, was asked to value personally his own bit of the plunder and to pay into the treasury a tenth of the sum.

The money thus received was to cover the cost of a golden gift to Apollo, worthy of his godhead and of the splendour of his temple – such a gift, in fact, as the People of Rome need not be ashamed of. But even this failed to satisfy the commons and increased their hostility towards Camillus.

It was at this juncture that Volscian and Aequian envoys arrived in Rome to negotiate a peace. Peace was granted them – less because of the justice of their request than because Rome was weary of the long war and would be glad to see an end to it.

For the year that followed the fall of Veii six military tribunes were elected; they were the two Cornelii, Cossus and Scipio, Marcus Valerius Maximus (for the second time), Caeso Fabius Ambustus (for the third time), Lucius Furius Medullinus (for the fifth time), and Quintus Servilius (for the third time). Lots were drawn and the direction of the war with Falerii fell to the Cornelii, and of the war with Capena to Valerius and Servilius. No attempt was made against the two towns either by siege or direct attack, the Roman armies confining themselves to depredations on the countryside, where they stripped every acre of land bare of its produce, fruit or grain. This brought the people of Capena to their knees; they asked for peace and it was granted them, so that the campaign at Falerii was now the only one that remained on hand.

In Rome meanwhile anti-government agitation reached a new intensity. The government in an attempt to appease it had proposed to send three thousand settlers into Volscian territory, and the special commissioners had assigned about two acres of land to each family; the people concerned, however, felt this to be totally inadequate, and a mere sop to their expectation of much greater things. To them it seemed both absurd and unfair that commoners should be sent into exile amongst the Volscians when the beautiful town of Veii with its cultivated lands, richer and more extensive than those of Rome, was only a few miles away. Simply as a town they preferred it to Rome: it had better amenities of all kinds – a better situation, finer houses, and more splendid temples. This was, in fact, the first stirrings of the movement for the migration to Veii – a movement which gathered many more supporters after the capture of Rome by the Gauls. On the present occasion the idea was that Veii should be taken over by half the commons together with half the Senate, in the belief that both towns could become Roman and form, as it were, a single polity; but this suggestion was violently opposed by the aristocratic party – they would sooner die, they declared, than see any such thing brought to the vote. If in one city the opposing parties were perpetually at each other's throats, what would it be like in two? How could anyone possibly prefer the vanquished to the victor, or bear to see captured Veii rise to a greatness she never achieved in her years of security and independence? 'We may be abandoned by our fellow-citizens,' they bitterly exclaimed, 'but no force in the world will ever drive us to leave our homes and friends – never shall we follow Sicinius, the author of this monstrous proposal, to see him found the City of Veii, or abandon God's son, the divine Romulus, father and founder of Rome.'

The quarrel led to ugly scenes: the patricians had induced some of the tribunes to support them, and the only thing which restrained the mob from actual violence was the action of the leading senators, who, every time the savage yells which signalled a riot arose, were the first to confront the surging mass and to inform them calmly that, if they wanted victims, they were ready to their hands. The age and rank of these men had due effect, and the mob, shrinking from doing violence to those who had held positions of such consequence, were shamed into controlling their rage against others as well.

Camillus meanwhile was constantly addressing the people at mass meetings all over the city. 'No wonder,' he said, 'the country has gone raving mad. Under a solemn obligation, as you all are, to discharge your vow, you think of anything rather than of your duty to make your peace with God. I say nothing of your twopenny-halfpenny contribution – that is your own personal affair and does not involve the State; but I cannot, for very shame, pass over in silence the fact that the tenth part owed to Apollo should be supposed to consist only of moveable property, while no mention is made of the town itself and of the lands belonging to it, all of which should of course be included.'

Camillus's point was a nice one, and the Senate, unable to reach an agreement, referred it to the priests, who after further consultation with Camillus pronounced the opinion that all property which before the vow was made had belonged to the Veientes and had subsequently come into the possession of Rome, was liable to the charge of a tenth of its value for the purpose of the gift to Apollo. This, of course, included the town and its lands. Money accordingly was drawn from the treasury and the military tribunes were instructed to buy gold; and when it proved that there was not enough gold to be had, the women of Rome met to discuss the situation, and agreeing unanimously to promise the military tribunes the gold they wanted, proceeded to bring all their personal ornaments to the treasury. Nothing had ever given the Senate greater satisfaction, and we are told that in recognition of this munificent gift it gave the women the privilege of driving to games and festivals in four-wheeled carriages and of using ordinary carriages at all times – working days or holidays. When all the gold objects had been received and their value assessed for payment, it was decided that Apollo's gift should take the form of a gold mixing-bowl, to be carried to his temple in Delphi.

No sooner were men's minds at rest on the score of their religious obligations than the people's tribunes began to stir up trouble again, doing all they could to incite the mob against the government leaders, and particularly against Camillus, who, they declared, by devoting all the assets of Veii either to the State or to religious purposes had frittered them away to nothing. Their attacks, to be sure, were confined to the absent, as they lacked the impudence to abuse any who faced them squarely. As soon as it became clear that the dispute would not be settled that year, they began to work for the re-election of the tribunes who supported the migration to Veii, while the patricians exerted themselves in the interest of those who opposed it. The result, on balance, was that most of the same men were returned.

At the elections for the military tribuneship the senatorial party made every effort to procure the return of Camillus, ostensibly as a tried soldier to meet the military needs of the moment, but in reality because they wanted a man capable of resisting the anti-government measure to distribute the territory of Veii. Their efforts were successful. With Camillus were elected Lucius Furius Medullinus (for the sixth time), Gaius Aemilius, Lucius Valerius Publicola, Spurius Postuminus, and Publius Cornelius (for the second time).

At the beginning of the year the people's tribunes waited for Camillus to leave Rome for Falerii – where he had been given charge of operations – before they made any fresh move. But they were slow to get to work and people began to lose interest, while Camillus, their doughtiest antagonist, increased his reputation at Falerii by a series of successes. At the outset of the campaign the enemy were unwilling to leave their defences, but Camillus by burning their farmhouses and devastating their crops forced them to come out into the open. Not liking to advance too far, they took up a position about a mile from the town where they fancied they would be safe from attack simply because the place was awkward to get at, all the tracks in the vicinity being rough and broken and either very narrow or very steep. Camillus, however, used as a guide a prisoner he had picked up in the neighbourhood, and breaking camp round about midnight presented himself at dawn in a commanding position. He then started to dig in, a third of his men working while the rest stood to arms; an attempt by the enemy to stop the work was easily repulsed – indeed they were completely shattered and took to their heels in panic, running straight past their camp, which lay between them and Falerii in a wild scramble to reach the safety of the town. Many were killed or wounded before they could get through the gates. Camillus took over the abandoned camp and turned over to the quaestors everything of value found in it: this the troops violently resented, but discipline was good and they could not but admire the strict honesty of their commander however much they might disapprove of it.

Siege operations then began, diversified by occasional sorties against the Roman strong-points and a few skirmishes. Time went on, and there seemed little chance of a decision either way; the besieged had laid in grain and other necessaries before the campaign began and were better supplied than the besiegers, so it appeared not unlikely to be as protracted a business as the siege of Veii had not a stroke of luck brought unexpected victory and at the same time an opportunity for Camillus to prove once again his nobler qualities as a soldier.

Schoolmasters in Falerii used to have charge of their pupils both in and out of school hours, and, as in Greece today, one man was entrusted with the care of a number of boys. The children of the leading families were, naturally enough, taught by the best available scholar. Now this man had been in the habit during peacetime of taking his boys outside the town walls for play and exercise, and had continued to do so in spite of the fact that his country was at war, going sometimes a shorter, sometimes a longer distance and distracting the boys' attention by talk on various subjects. One day he saw his chance for a longer stroll than usual, and took his young charges right through the enemy outposts to the Roman camp and, finally, to Camillus's headquarters. Such treachery was bad enough, but what he said was even more revolting: 'These boys' parents', he coolly observed, 'control our affairs. I have delivered them into your hands. So Falerii is now yours.'

'Neither my people,' Camillus replied, 'nor I, who command their army, happen to share your tastes. You are a scoundrel and your offer is worthy of you. As political entities, there is no bond of union between Rome and Falerii, but we are bound together none the less, and always shall be, by the bonds of a common humanity. War has its laws as peace has, and we have learned to wage war with decency no less than with courage. We have drawn the sword not against children, who even in the sack of cities are spared, but against men, armed like ourselves, who without injury or provocation attacked us at Veii. Those men, your countrymen, you have done your best to humble by this vile and unprecedented act; but I shall bring them low, as I brought Veii low, by the Roman arts of courage, persistence, and arms.'

Camillus had the traitor stripped and his hands tied behind his back; then, telling the boys to escort him home, gave each of them a stick with which to beat him back into the town. A crowd gathered to see the sight, and later, when the magistrates had called a meeting of the council to discuss this odd turn of events, the feelings of the whole population were completely changed: where once fierce hatred and savage rage had made even the destruction of Veii seem a better fate than the tame capitulation of Capena, there was now a unanimous demand for peace. In street and council chamber people talked of nothing but of Roman honour and the justice of Camillus; by universal consent representatives were sent to him, and were allowed to proceed to Rome to lay the submission of Falerii before the Senate. We read that they addressed the Senate in the following terms: 'Gentlemen, the victory over us which you and your general have won neither God nor man could grudge you. We admit our defeat, and surrender to you in the belief – than which nothing can do more honour to the victor – that we shall live better lives under your government than under our own. From this war two things have emerged which humanity would do well to lay to heart: you preferred honour to an easy victory; we respond to that noble choice by an unforced submission. We now recognize your sway. Our gates are open: arms, hostages, the town itself are at your disposal. You will have no cause to regret your trust in us, nor we to repent of accepting your dominion.'

Camillus received the formal thanks both of Falerii and of Rome. Falerii was laid under tribute for a sum to cover the cost of the army's pay for the year, thus relieving the Roman people of the war-tax. The war was over, and the Roman troops returned to the City.

Camillus's fame now rested upon a finer achievement than when the team of white horses had drawn his triumphal chariot through the streets of Rome, for this time he entered the City in all the glory of a victory won by justice and honour. The Senate was uneasy about the obligation he had incurred by his vow, and though he did not mention the matter himself, such was their respect for him that they could not rest till it was cleared up; accordingly they entrusted three men, Lucius Valerius, Lucius Sergius, and Aulus Manlius, with the duty of carrying the gift – a golden bowl – to Apollo's temple at Delphi. Sailing in a warship, unescorted, they were captured by pirates near the Sicilian narrows and taken to their stronghold at Liparae. The people of Liparae lived by a sort of communal piracy, sharing out any prizes they took, but it so happened that their chieftain that year, a man named Timasitheus, had, unlike his countrymen, something of the Roman in his character. The men he had captured were envoys and he respected that title, just as he respected the reason for their mission and the god to whom the gift was being conveyed; he succeeded moreover in inspiring his people (for more often than not the masses will take their cue from their leader) with a proper sense of the solemnity of the occasion, so that he was able to entertain the three envoys as guests of the State, convoy them to Delphi, and ensure their safe return to Rome.

In recognition of this act he was made, by decree of the Senate, an Honorary Guest of the Roman People – not to mention other and more tangible rewards.

In the course of this year a campaign was fought against the Aequians, but so indecisively that no one in Rome, or even in the opposing armies, could say who had won and who had lost. The Roman commanders were two of the military tribunes, Gaius Aemilius and Spurius Postumius; at first they acted jointly, but after a successful engagement they decided to take separate spheres of action. Aemilius accordingly garrisoned Verrugo and Postumius undertook to do what damage he could to the countryside in general. The recent success had made him careless, and his men were straggling along more or less as they pleased when they were suddenly attacked by the Aequians and forced to take refuge in considerable confusion among the neighbouring hills, whence the alarm was communicated to the other army in Verrugo. Postumius told his men, who at the moment were safe enough, in no uncertain terms what he thought of their conduct – of their disgraceful panic and precipitate retreat from a contemptible enemy who trusted his heels more than his sword – and was answered by a spontaneous and universal admission of guilt. Every word, the men declared, was justified – but they would soon put things right and see to it that the enemy's triumph was short-lived. The Aequian camp was in full view below them, and they demanded, as one man, to be allowed to attack it immediately, professing their willingness to suffer any punishment their commander could inflict if they failed to take it before dark. Postumius commended their change of heart and ordered them after eating and resting to be ready at the fourth watch.

But the Aequians were not to be caught unawares. They were already watching the track to Verrugo, to prevent the Romans making their escape that way under cover of darkness; thus they encountered Postumius on his way down from the hill before dawn broke. The moon was still up, giving adequate light, and when the fight began the noise of it carried to Verrugo, where it caused the utmost consternation. The men all supposed that Postumius's camp was being overwhelmed, and neither orders nor appeals from Aemilius could do anything to stop them from taking to their heels and making, each man for himself, for Tusculum, whence the rumour soon reached Rome that Postumius and his army had been destroyed.

Postumius, however, as soon as daylight had convinced him that there was no fear of falling into a trap if he followed up the advantage he had already gained, rode down his lines and reminded his troops of their protestations of the previous night. The men's response was magnificent, and they returned to the attack with such vigour that all resistance was broken; the Aequians fled, and the slaughter which ensued was more like the rage of vengeance, than the customary valour of soldiers in action. The whole force was wiped out. Thus Rome had been frighted with false fire; the depressing news from Tusculum was followed by a laurelled dispatch from Postumius announcing his victory and the destruction of the Aequian army.

The People's tribunes having failed as yet to carry their proposals, the commons worked hard to procure the re-election of the supporters of the measure to migrate to Veii, while the patricians were no less active in their efforts to thwart them. But in spite of senatorial opposition the commons got the tribunes they wanted. The Senate avenged this set-back by decreeing the election of consuls, a move they knew the commons would bitterly resent. For fifteen years military tribunes had been at the head of government; the succession was broken, and

Lucius Lucretius Flavus was elected to the consulship with Servius
Sulpicius Camerinus as his colleague.

The beginning of the year saw an all-out effort on the part of the
tribunes to push through their bill, as the college was now unanimous
in support of it. Precisely for that reason the consuls offered an equally
vigorous resistance, and while public attention was all focussed upon
the struggle, Vitellia, a Roman settlement in Aequian territory, was
attacked and taken. A gate had been treacherously opened one night,
but as the opposite quarter of the town was unwatched most of the
settlers made their escape through, so to speak, the back door, and got
safely to Rome. The consul Lucretius, to whose lot it fell to deal with
the situation, marched from Rome, successfully engaged the enemy,
and returned to the City only to find a more serious conflict awaiting
him. Aulus Verginius and Quintus Pomponius, who had been tribunes
two years previously, had been summoned for trial. All the patricians
agreed that the Senate was bound in honour to defend them, as the sole
ground on which the prosecution rested was the fact that they had
vetoed the proposed measure of the other tribunes to curry favour
with the Senate; there was not a word about maladministration or any
complaint of their personal conduct. But the Senate's support proved
less strong than popular resentment, with the disgraceful result that
the two innocent men were found guilty and ordered to pay a fine of
10,000 *asses* each. The Senate was indignant; Camillus openly denounced the criminal lunacy of the commons not only in turning
against their own representative magistrates but in failing to see that
their dishonest verdict had virtually robbed the tribunate of the veto,
and that, the veto gone, the tribunate itself was undermined. They
were deceived, he said, if they imagined that the Senate would tolerate
the unbridled excesses of that magistracy, and if the lawless behaviour
of some tribunes could no longer be held in check by their more level-
headed colleagues, the Senate would find another weapon to deal with
it. He also attacked the consuls for letting down the two tribunes who
had supported the Senate and had relied, naturally enough, upon
government protection.

These frank expressions of opinion, delivered in public speeches,
fanned the ever-increasing flame of popular anger, but Camillus, undeterred, continued to press the Senate to make a stand against the
proposed migration to Veii. 'When it comes to a vote,' he said, 'I beg
you to enter the Forum in the spirit of men who know they will be

fighting for their hearths and altars, for their native soil and the temples of their gods. As for myself – if I may without offence remember my own reputation when Rome's life is at stake – it would be an honour to see a town I captured thronged with people, to have a constant reminder of what I once achieved, to feast my eyes from hour to hour upon the city which adorned my triumph, to have all men following in the footsteps of my fame; nevertheless religion forbids that a town which God has abandoned should be inhabited by men: it is a sin to think that our people should ever live on captive soil or exchange victorious Rome for vanquished Veii.'

The Senate was deeply moved. On the day the proposal was put to the vote all members, old and young alike, went in a body to the Forum, where they scattered in search of their fellow-tribesmen and besought them with tears in their eyes not to desert their native city, for which they and their fathers had fought with such courage and success; pointing to the Capitol and the Temple of Vesta and the other holy places, they begged that no one should let the people of Rome be hounded from its native soil and household gods and driven like a wandering exile into a city of its enemies, a tragedy indeed to make one wish that Veii had never fallen – if only to prevent the abandonment of Rome. This was canvassing with a difference: no force was brought to bear – only entreaties; and for this reason, added to the fact that the gods were frequently mentioned, it proved successful. The consciences of most people were touched, and the proposed measure was defeated by a majority of one tribe. The Senate was so delighted by the victory, that on the following day it issued a decree, on the consul's motion, granting some three and a half acres of land from the estates of Veii to every plebeian – not heads of families only, but including in the number of recipients all free-born members of each household. Such a prospect would, it was hoped, encourage them to rear children.

This generosity put the Commons into a sufficiently amiable frame of mind not to object to another consular election. It was accordingly held and Lucius Valerius Potitus and Marcus Manlius, later surnamed Capitolinus, were elected. The new consuls proceeded to celebrate the Great Games which had been vowed by Camillus during the war with Veii, and the same year saw the consecration of the temple to Juno, which had also been vowed by Camillus on the same occasion. It is said that the women of Rome, in particular, attended the ceremony with deep devotion.

A campaign was fought on Algidus with the Aequians: it was of little importance, the enemy running away almost before they could be got at. Of the two consuls Valerius, who showed the greater perseverance in pursuing – and killing – the fugitives, was awarded a Triumph, Manlius an Ovation only. A fresh quarrel arose this year – this time with Volsinii. A dry and excessively hot season had caused famine and disease in the neighbourhood of Rome, and it was in consequence not possible to send out an expeditionary force, a fact which, not unnaturally, acted as a tonic on Volsinii. The people of the place joined forces with Sappinum and, full of confidence, invaded Roman territory. War was then declared on both towns.

The censor Gaius Julius died about this time and Marcus Cornelius was appointed to fill the vacant place. There was felt later to have been a sort of impiety in this, as it was during that five-year period that Rome was captured. In any case it has never happened since that a new censor has been appointed in the place of one who has died. The consuls, too, fell ill, and it was decided to carry on the government through an *interrex*. The Senate accordingly instructed the consuls to hand in their resignations, and Camillus was made *interrex*. As his successor Camillus appointed Publius Cornelius Scipio, who, in his turn, appointed Lucius Valerius Potitus. Potitus presided at the election of six military tribunes, to ensure having enough magistrates to carry things on even if some of their number fell sick. On 1 July the new military tribunes took up their duties; they were Lucius Lucretius, Servius Sulpicius, Marcus Aemilius, Lucius Furius Medullinus (for the seventh time), Furius Agrippa, and Gaius Aemilius (for the second time).

The campaign against Volsinii fell to the command of Lucretius and Aemilius; that against Sappinum to Agrippa and Sulpicius. Fighting started at Volsinii, where there was little real opposition in spite of the enemy's immense numbers; a single thrust sufficed to break them up, and 8,000 men, cut off by Roman cavalry, laid down their arms. News of the defeat deterred the men of Sappinum from risking a battle, and they withdrew for protection within the defences of the town. Roman troops roamed unmolested over the territories of both Sappinum and Volsinii, taking what they pleased, until the people of the latter place got sick of it and asked for terms. They were granted a twenty-years' armistice on condition of restoring Roman property and meeting the cost of the army's pay for the year's service.

About this time a plebeian named Caedicius told the tribunes that in the New Road where the shrine now stands above the temple of Vesta, he had heard, in the silence of the night, a voice. The voice was something more than human, and 'Tell the magistrates,' it said, 'that the Gauls are coming.' The tale was more or less laughed off, partly because Caedicius, who told it, was a person of no consequence, and partly because the Gauls lived a long way off and were therefore little known. Nevertheless the Voice was a warning from heaven – doom was drawing near, but the warning was ignored. As if this were not enough, a further folly deprived Rome of Camillus, the one man who might have saved her. While still in mourning for the death of his young son, he had been indicted by the tribune Apuleius on a charge of mishandling the plunder taken in Veii; following the summons, he called to his house his fellow-tribesmen and dependants (who formed no small part of the commons) and after sounding them on their attitude towards his case received the reply that though they were prepared to contribute between them the amount of any fine which might be imposed, they could not admit his innocence. He accordingly went into exile, with the prayer that if he were innocent and wrongfully accused, the gods might speedily cause his ungrateful country bitterly to regret that he had gone. He was fined – in absence – 15,000 *asses.*

The man whose presence would certainly – if anything in life is certain – have made the capture of Rome impossible, was gone, and calamity was drawing nearer and nearer to the doomed city. It was at this juncture that a mission from Clusium arrived to ask for assistance against the Gauls.

There is a tradition that it was the lure of Italian fruits and especially of wine, a pleasure then new to them, that drew the Gauls to cross the Alps and settle in regions previously cultivated by the Etruscans. Arruns of Clusium, the story goes, had sent wine into their country deliberately to entice them over, as he wanted his revenge for the seduction of his wife by his ward Lucumo, a man in too powerful a position to be punished except by the help of foreigners called in for the purpose. It was he who guided the Gallic hordes over the Alps and suggested the attack on Clusium. Now I have no wish to deny that Gauls were brought to Clusium by Arruns, or some other citizen of that town, but it is, none the less, generally agreed that these were by no means the first Gauls to cross the Alps. Two hundred years before the attack on

Clusium and the capture of Rome, men of this race came over into Italy, and long before the clash with Clusium Gallic armies had frequently fought with the peoples between the Alps and the Apennines. Before the days of Roman domination Etruscan influence, both by land and sea, stretched over a wide area: how great their power was on the upper and lower seas (which make Italy a peninsula) is proved by the names of those seas, one being known by all Italian peoples as the Tuscan – the inclusive designation of the race – and the other as the Hadriatic, from the Etruscan settlement of Hatria. The Greeks know them as the Tyrrhenian and Adriatic seas.

On each side of the Apennines they built twelve towns, the first twelve on the southern side towards the Lower Sea, and later the second twelve north of the range, thus possessing themselves of all the country beyond the Po as far as the Alps with the exception of the little corner where the Venetians live around the shores of their gulf. The Alpine tribes have pretty certainly the same origin, especially the Raetians, though the latter have been so barbarized by their wild surroundings that they have retained nothing of their original character except their speech, and even that has become debased.

The following account has come down to us of the Gallic migration. During the reign of Tarquinius Priscus in Rome the Celts, one of the three Gallic peoples, were dominated by the Bituriges, and their king was consequently a member of that tribe. At the time we are concerned with the king was one Ambitgatus, who by his personal qualities, aided by the good luck which blessed both himself and his subjects, had attained to very considerable power; indeed under his rule Gaul became so rich and populous that the effective control of such large numbers was a matter of serious difficulty. The king therefore, being now an old man and wishing to relieve his kingdom of the burdensome excess of the population, announced his intention of sending his two nephews, Bellovesus and Segovesus, both of them adventurous young men, out into the world to find such new homes as the gods by signs from heaven might point the way to; he was willing to give them as many followers as they thought would ensure their ability to overcome any opposition they might encounter. The gods were duly consulted, with the result that to Segovesus were assigned the Hercynian uplands in South Germany while Bellovesus was granted the much pleasanter road into Italy; whereupon collecting the surplus population – Bituriges, Arverni, Senones, Aedui, Ambarri, Carnutes, Aulerci

– he set out with a vast host, some mounted, some on foot, and reached the territory of the Tricastini at the foot of the Alps.

There in front of him stood the mountains. I am not surprised that they seemed an insuperable barrier, for as yet no track had led a traveller over them – at any rate within recorded time, unless one likes to believe the fabled exploits of Hercules. There, then, stood the Gallic host, brought to a halt by the towering wall, and looking for a way over those skiey peaks into another world. Another consideration also delayed them, for they had heard that a strange people – actually the Massilienses, who had sailed from Phocaea – were seeking for somewhere to settle and were in conflict with the Salui. The superstitious Gauls took this as an omen of their own success and helped the strangers to such effect that they were enabled to establish themselves, without serious opposition, at the spot where they had disembarked; they then themselves crossed the Alps by the Taurine passes and the pass of Duria, defeated the Etruscans near the river Ticinus, and, having learnt that they were in what was known as the territory of the Insubres, the same name as one of the cantons of the Aedui, took it as another favourable omen and founded the town of Mediolanium.[1]

Later another wave, this time of the Cenomanni, followed in their footsteps, and crossing, under the leadership of Etitovius, by the same pass and without opposition from Bellovesus, settled near where the towns of Brixia and Verona are today. After them came the Libui, then the Salluvii who settled on the Ticinus, near the ancient tribe of the Laevi Ligures. Then the Boii and Lingones came over by the Poenine pass, and finding all the country between the Alps and the Po already occupied, crossed the river on rafts and expelled not the Etruscans only but the Umbrians as well; they did not, however, pass south of the Apennines.

At the time of which we are speaking the Senones, who had been the last tribe to migrate, held all the country from the Utens to the Aesis, and I understand that it was this tribe which came to Clusium and later to Rome – though it is not certain whether they came alone or with the support of the other Gallic tribes on the Italian side of the Alps.

The plight of Clusium was a most alarming one: strange men in thousands were at the gates, men the like of whom the townsfolk had never seen, outlandish warriors armed with strange weapons, who

1. Milan.

were rumoured already to have scattered the Etruscan legions on both sides of the Po; it was a terrible situation, and in spite of the fact that the people of Clusium had no official ties with Rome or reason to expect her friendship, except perhaps that they had refused assistance to their kinsmen of Veii, they sent a mission to ask help from the Senate. Military aid was not granted, but the three sons of Marcus Fabius Ambustus were sent to remonstrate with the Gauls in the Senate's name and to ask them not to molest a people who had done them no wrong and were, moreover, friends and allies of Rome. Rome, they added, would be bound to protect them, even by force, should the need arise, though it would be better, if possible, to avoid recourse to arms and to become acquainted with the new immigrants in a peaceful manner.

The object of the mission was wholly conciliatory; unhappily, however, the envoys themselves behaved more like savage Gauls than civilized Romans. To their statement in the Council the Gauls gave the following answer: 'This is the first time we have heard of Rome, but we can believe none the less that you Romans are men of worth, for Clusium would never otherwise have sought your help in time of trouble. You say you prefer to help your friends by negotiation rather than by force, and you offer us peace. We, for our part, need land, but we are prepared to accept your offer on condition that the people of Clusium cede to us a portion of their territory – for they have more than they can manage. You can have peace on no other terms. We wish to receive our answer in your presence; should it be a refusal, then you will see us fight, and thus be in a position to tell your compatriots by how much the Gauls exceed all other men in valour.'

When the three envoys asked by what sort of justice they demanded land, under threat of violence, from its rightful owners, and what business Gauls had to be in Etruria anyway, they received the haughty reply that all things belonged to the brave who carried justice on the point of their swords. Passions were aroused and a fight began – and then it was that the envoys took their fatal step. Urged by the evil star which even then had risen over Rome, they broke the law of nations and took up arms. To conceal the crime was impossible; strangers as they were, their Roman valour was all too obvious – the valour of three of Rome's finest and most blue-blooded fighting men, laying about them in the Etruscan van. Quintus Fabius riding ahead of the line straight for the Gallic chieftain as he was making for the Etruscan standards, killed him with a spear-thrust through the side and began to strip him of his armour. It was then that the Gauls realized who he was, and word was passed through their ranks that he was the envoy from Rome. At once the trumpets sounded the retreat; the quarrel with Clusium was forgotten and the anger of the barbarian army was turned upon Rome. Some urged an immediate march upon the City, but more cautious counsels prevailed and envoys were sent to lodge a complaint against the breach of international law and to demand the surrender of the Fabii. The Senate, having listened to what the Gallic envoys had to say, by no means approved the conduct of their own envoys; but though they admitted to themselves that the demand was a fair one, they refused, where three men of such rank were concerned, to take what they really knew to be the proper action: their own interests as the governing elders, prevented them. Accordingly, to avoid the responsibility for any losses which might result from a clash with the Gauls they referred the envoys' demands to the people for decision, with the result that the three guilty men, whose punishment was supposed to be under discussion, were elected as military tribunes with consular powers for the following year: such was the influence on the mind of the populace of wealth and position. The Gallic envoys were naturally – and rightly – indignant, and before leaving the City openly threatened war. In addition to the three Fabii, Quintus Sulpicius Lagus, Quintus Servilius (for the fourth time), and Publius Cornelius Maluginensis were elected military tribunes.

Calamity of unprecedented magnitude was drawing near, but no adequate steps were taken to meet it. The nation which so often before, – against Fidenae or Veii or other familiar enemies – had as a final resource in its hour of danger appointed a Dictator to save it, now that a strange foe, of whose power it knew nothing either directly or by hearsay, was on the march from the Atlantic Ocean and the furthest shores of the world, instituted no extraordinary command and looked for no special means of self-preservation. How true it is that destiny blinds men's eyes, when she is determined that her gathering might shall meet no check! The military tribunes, whose reckless conduct had been responsible for the war, were in supreme command; recruiting they carried out coolly and casually, with no more care than for any other campaign, even going so far as to play down the gravity of the danger. The Gauls, for their part, wasted no time; the instant they knew of the insult to their embassy and the promotion to command of the men who had violated the unwritten law of all mankind, they flamed into the uncontrollable anger which is characteristic of their race, and set forward, with terrible speed, on the path to Rome. Terrified townships rushed to arms as the avengers went roaring by; men fled from the fields for their lives; and from all the immense host, covering miles of ground with its straggling masses of horse and foot, the cry went up 'To Rome!'

Rumour had preceded them and messages from Clusium and elsewhere had already reached the City, but in spite of warnings the sheer speed of the Gallic advance was a frightful thing. The Roman army moving with all the haste of a mass emergency levy had covered hardly eleven miles before it met the invaders at the spot where the river Allia descends in a deep gully from the hills of Crustumerium and joins the Tiber not far south of the road. The ground in front and on both sides was already swarming with enemy soldiers, and the air was loud with the dreadful din of the fierce war-songs and discordant shouts of a people whose very life is wild adventure.

The Roman commanders had taken no precautions – no regular defensive position had been chosen, no fortifications prepared to give shelter in case of need; without sign from the flight of birds or the entrails of beasts – the very gods, to say nothing of men, forgotten – they drew up their line on as broad a front as they could, hoping not to be outflanked by the enemy's superior numbers; but the hope was vain, even though they stretched it so thin that the centre was weakened and hardly held. The reserves were ordered to a position on some high ground a little to the right, and the fact that they were there, and the subsequent attack upon them, though it started the panic in the main body of the Roman army, also enabled some of them to escape with their lives; for Brennus, the Gallic chieftain, suspected a trap when he saw the numbers opposed to him so much smaller than he had expected, and supposing the high ground to have been occupied with the purpose of delivering an attack, by the reserves posted there, upon the flank and rear while he was engaged in a straight fight with the legionaries, changed his tactics and made his first move against the reserves, confident that, should he succeed in dislodging them, his immensely superior numbers would give him an easy victory elsewhere. Alas, not good fortune only, but good generalship was on the barbarian side.

In the lines of the legionaries – officers and men alike – there was no trace of the old Roman manhood. They fled in panic, so blinded to everything but saving their skins that, in spite of the fact that the Tiber lay in their way, most of them tried to get to Veii, once an enemy town, instead of making for their own homes in Rome. As for the reserves, they found safety, though not for long, in their stronger position; but the main body of the army, at the first sound of the Gallic war-cry on their flank and in their rear, hardly waited even to see their strange enemy from the ends of the earth; they made no attempt at resistance; they had not courage even to answer his shouted challenge, but fled before they had lost a single man. None fell fighting; they were cut down from behind as they struggled to force a way to safety through the heaving mass of their fellow-fugitives. Near the bank of the river there was a dreadful slaughter; the whole left wing of the army had gone that way and had flung away their arms in the desperate hope of getting over. Many could not swim and many others in their exhausted state were dragged under water by the weight of their equipment and drowned. More than half reached Veii alive, but sent no message to Rome of their defeat – far less any assistance to her in her peril. The men on the right wing, who had been further from the river and closer to the hills, all made for Rome, where without even closing the gates behind them they took refuge in the Citadel.

The Gauls could hardly believe their eyes, so easy, so miraculously swift their victory had been. For a while they stood rooted to the spot, hardly realizing what had happened; then after a moment of fear lest the whole thing were a trap, they began to collect the arms and equipment of the dead and to pile them, as their manner is, in heaps. Finally, when no sign of an enemy was anywhere to be seen, they marched, and shortly before sunset reached the vicinity of Rome. Mounted men were sent forward to reconnoitre: the gates stood open, not a sentry was on guard; no soldiers manned the walls. Once more the astonishing truth held them spellbound. Yet still the night might have hidden terrors – and the city was totally unknown; so after a further reconnaissance of the walls and the other gates to discover, if it were possible, their enemy's intention in his desperate plight, they encamped somewhere between the city and the Anio.

As more than half the Roman army had taken refuge in Veii, it was universally believed in Rome itself that the rest, who had made their way home, were the only survivors. Rome was indeed a city of lamentation – of mourning for the living and the dead alike. Then news came that the Gauls were at the gates; the anguish of personal bereavement was forgotten in a wave of panic, and all too soon cries like the howling of wolves and barbaric songs could be heard, as the Gallic squadrons rode hither and thither close outside the walls. All the time between then and the following dawn was filled with unbearable suspense. When would the assault come? Again and again they believed it to be imminent: they expected it on the first appearance of the Gauls – for why had they marched on the city, and not stayed at the Allia, unless this had been their intention? They expected it at sunset – because there was little daylight left, and surely it would come before dark. Then, when darkness had fallen, they thought it had been deliberately postponed in order to multiply its terrors. But the night passed, and dawn, when it drew near, made them almost desperate; and then at last, hard upon this long-drawn-out and insupportable anxiety, came the thing itself, and the enemy entered the gates.

During that night and the following day Rome showed little resemblance to her fugitive army on the Allia. As there was no hope of defending the city with the handful of available troops, the decision was taken to withdraw all men capable of bearing arms together with the women and children and able-bodied senators into the fortress on the Capitol; from that stronghold, properly armed and provisioned, it was their intention to make a last stand for themselves, for their gods and for the Roman name. The priest and priestesses of Vesta were ordered to remove their sacred emblems to some spot far away from bloodshed and burning, and their cult was not to be abandoned till there were none left alive to observe its rites. It was felt that if the Citadel, home of the city's tutelary gods, could survive the impending ruin – if the few men still able to fight, if the Senate, fountain-head of true government, could escape the general disaster, it would be tolerable to leave in the city below the aged and useless, who had not, in any case, much longer to live. It was a stern decision, and to make it easier for the commons to bear, the old aristocrats who long before had served as consuls or celebrated their Triumphs said that they would die side by side with their humble compatriots, and never consent to burden the inadequate stores of the fighting few with bodies which could no longer bear arms in the country's defence. To tell each other of this noble resolve was the only consolation of the doomed men, who then turned to address words of encouragement to the young and vigorous whom they were seeing on their way to the Capitol, and to commend to the valour of their youth whatever good fortune might yet remain for a city which for three hundred and sixty years had never been defeated.

The time came to part – these to the Capitol with the future in their hands, those to the death to which their own resolve not to survive the city's fall had condemned them. It was a cruel separation, but even more heart-rending was the plight of the women, who weeping and torn by love and loyalty did not know which way to go, but followed now husbands, now sons, in grief and bewilderment at the terrible choice they had had imposed upon them. Most, in the end, went with their sons to the Citadel – they were not encouraged to do so, but no one tried to stop them, as it would have been inhuman to reduce deliberately the number of non-combatants in the Citadel, as purely military considerations required. Thousands more – mostly plebeians – who could neither have been lodged nor fed on the small and inadequately provisioned hill, streamed in an unbroken line from the city towards the Janiculum, whence some scattered over the countryside while others made for neighbouring towns – a rabble without leader or common aim. For them, Rome was already dead; each was his own counsellor and followed where his hopes led him. Meanwhile the priest of Quirinus and the Vestal Virgins, careless of their personal belongings, were discussing the fate of the sacred objects in their care – what to take and what to leave, as they had not the means to carry all away, and where what they could not take might be safely deposited. The best course, they thought, would be to store them in jars and bury them in the shrine near the priest's house (at the spot where spitting is now considered sacrilegious); the rest they managed between them to carry along the road which leads over the pile-bridge to the Janiculum. On the slope of the hill they were noticed by a man of humble birth named Albinius, who was driving his wife and family in a cart, amongst the rabble of other non-combatants escaping from the city. Even at such a moment Albinius could remember the difference between what was due to God and what to man, and feeling it to be an impious thing that he and his family should be seen driving while priestesses of the state toiled along on foot carrying the nation's sacred emblems, he told his wife to get out of the cart with her little boys, took up the Vestals and their burdens instead, and drove them to their destination in Caere.

In Rome everything possible in the circumstances had now been done to prepare for the defence of the Citadel, and the grey-haired senators had gone home to await, unflinching, the coming of the enemy. It was the wish of those who had held the highest offices of state to dress for death in the outward signs of such rank as they had enjoyed or service they had rendered in the days of their former fortunes; so putting on the ceremonial robes of the dignitaries who at the Circensian Games escort the chariots of the gods, or of generals who enter the City in triumph, they took their seats, each in the courtyard of his house, on the ivory-inlaid chairs of the curule magistrates, having first – we are told – repeated after Marcus Folius the Pontifex Maximus a solemn vow to offer themselves as a sacrifice for their country and the Roman people.

A night having passed without action, the Gauls found their lust for fighting much abated. At no time had they met with any serious resistance, and there was no need now to take the city by assault. When therefore they entered on the following day, it was coolly and calmly enough. The Colline Gate was open, and they made their way to the Forum, looking with curiosity at the temples and at the Citadel, the only place to give the impression of a city at war. They left a reasonably strong guard in case of attack from the fortified heights and then dispersed in search of plunder; finding the streets empty, crowds of them broke into the first houses they came to; others went further afield, presumably supposing that buildings more remote from the Forum would offer richer prizes, but there the very silence and solitude made them uneasy, separated as they were from their companions, and suggested the possibility of a trap, so that they soon returned, keeping close together, to the neighbourhood of the Forum. Here they found the humbler houses locked and barred but the mansions of the nobility open; the former they were ready enough to break into, but it was a long time before they could bring themselves to enter the latter: something akin to awe held them back at what met their gaze – those figures seated in the open courtyards, the robes and decorations august beyond reckoning, the majesty expressed in those grave, calm eyes like the majesty of gods. They might have been statues in some holy place, and for a while the Gallic warriors stood entranced; then, on an impulse, one of them touched the beard of a certain Marcus Papirius – it was long, as was the fashion of those days – and the Roman struck him on the head with his ivory staff. That was the beginning: the barbarian flamed into anger and killed him, and the others were butchered where they sat. From that moment no mercy was shown; houses were ransacked and the empty shells set on fire.

The extent of the conflagration was, however, unexpectedly limited. Some of the Gauls may have been against the indiscriminate destruction of the city; or possibly it was their leaders' policy, first, to start a few fires in the hope that the besieged in the Citadel might be driven to surrender by the fear of losing their beloved homes, and, secondly, to leave a portion of the city intact and to use it as a sort of pledge or security – or lever – to induce the Romans to accept their terms. In any case the havoc wrought by the fire was on the first day by no means universal – or even widespread – and much less than might have been expected in the circumstances.

For the Romans beleaguered in the Citadel the full horror was almost too great to realize; they could hardly believe their eyes or ears as they looked down on the barbaric foe roaming in hordes through the familiar streets, while every moment, everywhere and anywhere, some new terror was enacted: fear gripped them in a thousand shapes; now here, now there, the yells of triumph, women's screams or the crying of children, the roar of flames or the long rumbling crash of falling masonry forced them to turn unwilling eyes upon some fresh calamity, as if fate had made them spectators of the nightmare stage-scene of their country's ruin, helpless to save anything they possessed but their own useless bodies. Never before had beleaguered men been in a plight so pitiful – not shut within their city, but excluded from it, they saw all that they loved in the power of their enemies.

The night which followed was as bad as the day. Another dawn came, and brought with each succeeding moment the sight of some new disaster; yet nothing could break the determination of the little garrison, under its almost intolerable weight of anguish, to hold out to the end: even if the whole city were burnt to dust before their eyes, they were resolved to play the man and defend the one spot which still was free – the hill where they stood, however small, however ill-provided. Thus day after day the tale of disaster went on, until sheer familiarity with suffering dulled the sense of what they had lost. Their one remaining hope was in their shields and swords.

The Gauls by this time had become aware that a final effort was necessary if they were to achieve their object. For several days they had been directing their fury only against bricks and mortar. Rome was a heap of smouldering ruins, but something remained – the armed men in the Citadel; and when the Gauls saw that, in spite of everything, they remained unshaken and would never yield to anything but force, they resolved to attempt an assault. At dawn, therefore, on a given signal the whole vast horde assembled in the Forum; then, roaring out their challenge they locked shields and moved up the slope of the Capitol.

The Romans remained calm. Guards were strengthened at every possible point of approach; where the thrust seemed to be coming, the best troops were stationed to meet it. Then they waited, letting the enemy climb, and confident that the steeper the slope he reached the more easily they could hurl him back. About half-way up the attackers paused, and the Romans, from the heights above them, charged; the steepness of the descent itself made the weight of their impact irresistible, and the Gallic masses were flung back and down with such severe losses that a similar attempt, with either a part or the whole of their forces, was never made again. Disappointed, therefore, of their hopes of a direct assault, they prepared for a siege. For them the decision was an unfortunate one, for, not having thought of it before, they had destroyed in the fires all the city's store of grain, while what had not yet been brought in had been smuggled during the past few days into Veii; their solution of the difficulty was to employ a part of their force to invest the Citadel, while the remainder supplied it by raiding the territory of neighbouring peoples.

Destiny had decreed that the Gauls were still to feel the true meaning of Roman valour, for when the raiders started on their mission Rome's lucky star led them to Ardea, where Camillus was living in exile, more grieved by the misfortunes of his country than by his own. Growing, as he felt, old and useless, filled with resentment against gods and men, he was asking in the bitterness of his heart where now were the men who had stormed Veii and Falerii – the men whose courage in every fight had been greater even than their success, when suddenly he heard the news that a Gallic army was near. The men of Ardea, he knew, were in anxious consultation, and it had not been his custom to assist at their deliberations; but now, like a man inspired, he burst into the Council chamber. 'Men of Ardea,' he cried, 'old friends – fellow-citizens as now you are, for your kindness and my misfortunes would have it so – I beg you not to think I have forgotten my station in thus thrusting myself upon you. We are all of us in peril, and every man must contribute what he can to get us out of it. When shall I prove my gratitude for all you have done for me, if I hang back now? When will you need me, if not on the battlefield? At home it was by war I won my place; unbeaten in the field, I was hounded out in time of peace by my ungrateful countrymen. My friends, your chance has come: you can show your gratitude to Rome for all the services she did you long ago – how great you yourselves remember – nay, you do, and I would not reproach you – and this town of yours can win glory from our common enemy. That enemy is near – his disordered columns are close upon us. They are big men – brave men too – at a pinch – but unsteady. Always they bring more smoke than fire – much terror but little strength. See what happened at Rome: the city lay wide open, and they walked in – but now a handful of men in the Citadel are holding them. Already they are sick of the siege, and are off – anywhere, everywhere – roaming the countryside; crammed with food and soused in drink they lie at night like animals on the bank of some stream – unprotected, unguarded, no watches set – and a taste of success has now made them more reckless than ever. Do you wish to save your city – to prevent this country from being overrun? Very well, then: arm yourselves early tonight, every man of you, and follow me – you shall slit their throats as they lie! If I don't give them to you to slaughter in their sleep like cattle, let me be scorned in Ardea as once I was scorned in Rome.'

Whatever their personal feelings for Camillus, everyone in Ardea knew well enough that as a soldier he had no living equal, so when the council had been adjourned they dined and rested, and then waited for his signal. It was given, and in the early hours of darkness they marched through the silent town to the gates, where Camillus awaited them. All went as Camillus had foretold: not far beyond the walls they came upon the Gallic encampment – completely unguarded – and flung themselves upon it with a yell of triumph. There was no resistance; unarmed men were killed in their sleep, and in a few minutes the whole place resembled a slaughterhouse. Some at the far side awoke in time, sprang up and ran for it, not knowing who or what had hit them; blind panic carried not a few straight into the arms of the enemy. Most, however, got to the neighbourhood of Antium, where they roamed about till the Antiates came out and rounded them up.

Similar punishment was inflicted upon the Etruscans near Veii. Nor was it less deserved, for these men had shown so little sympathy with a city which for nearly four hundred years had been their neighbour and was now under the heel of a strange and barbarous enemy, that they had actually chosen that moment to raid Roman territory and, enriched at Rome's expense, were even meditating an attack on the garrison in Veii, the last hope of the Roman name. The Roman soldiers had noticed a certain amount of activity in the neighbourhood; then they had seen Etruscan columns driving off the cattle they had stolen – and the Etruscan camp, too, was in sight, not far from the town. Their first reaction was to be sorry for themselves, but self-pity soon gave way to indignation, and finally to rage at the thought that Etruscans, whom Rome had saved at her own expense from a Gallic invasion, should gaily take advantage of their misfortunes. It was all they could do not to rush immediately to the attack, but the centurion Caedicius, whom they had made their commander, managed to check them, and operations were postponed till after nightfall. They were a complete success: all that was lacking was a general like Camillus; in everything else things followed the same plan, and with the same result. Further, on the following night they got some prisoners who had survived the general massacre to guide them to another Etruscan contingent near the Saltworks, and a second surprise attack was equally successful and even more bloody.

In Rome meanwhile the siege operations were more or less at a standstill; neither side showed any activity, and the Gaul's only anxiety seemed to be to prevent any of the Romans from slipping through their lines. It was in these circumstances that a young Roman soldier performed a feat which won the admiration of friend and foe alike. There used to be an annual sacrifice on the Quirinal, and the duty of celebrating it belonged to the family of the Fabii. Determined not to allow the ceremony to lapse, Gaius Fabius Dorsuo risked his life to perform it: wearing a toga girt up in ceremonial fashion and carrying the sacred vessels, he made his way down the slope of the Capitol and through the enemy pickets, ignoring challenges and threats, to the Quirinal, where with due solemnity, omitting nothing, he performed the rite, and with the same firm step, the same resolute face, returned by the same way to his companions on the Capitol, sure that the gods would favour one who had not neglected to serve them even for the fear of death. The Gauls did nothing to stop him; perhaps they were too much astonished by his incredible audacity, perhaps even touched (for the religious sentiment is strong in them) by a sort of awe.

The situation in Veii was now rapidly improving; the strength of the garrison as well as its confidence was increased by the accession not only of Romans who had been rendered homeless by the defeat and capture of the City, but also of numbers of volunteers from Latium who saw a chance of a share in the plunder; it was felt, therefore, that the time was ripe for an attempt to recover Rome. But who was to lead them? They had the body, but not, so to speak, the brains. Now no one could be in Veii without thinking of Camillus, and many of the troops there had already fought, and won, under Camillus's command; Caedicius, moreover, presented no obstacle, for though nothing on earth would make him resign his authority against his will, he was prepared on his own initiative to remember his rank and demand the appointment of a general. It was therefore unanimously resolved to send to Ardea and invite Camillus to undertake the command, but not before the Senate in Rome had been consulted – for even in their almost desperate plight they still preserved a proper respect for form and were unwilling to overstep their constitutional rights.

To get a message to the Senate meant passing at great risk through the Gallic outposts, and an enterprising young soldier named Pontius Cominus volunteered for the task. Floating on a life-buoy down the river to Rome, he took the shortest way to the Capitol up and over a bluff so steep that the Gauls had never thought of watching it; he was then taken to the magistrates, to whom he delivered the army's message. The Senate passed its resolution: 'that Camillus' (it ran) 'by vote of the curiate assembly, in accordance with the people's will, be forthwith named Dictator, and the soldiers have the commander whom they desire.' Cominus hurried back to Veii by the same route, and a mission was at once dispatched to fetch Camillus from Ardea. It may be, however – and I myself prefer to believe – that Camillus did not leave Ardea until he knew that the Senate's resolution had been passed, as he could not change his place of residence without the people's authorization, and could not assume command of the army until he had been appointed Dictator. That would mean that the resolution was passed in the curiate assembly and that he was named Dictator in his absence.

During these transactions in Veii the Citadel in Rome passed through a brief period of extreme danger from an attempted surprise. It may be that the messenger from Veii had left footprints, and the Gauls had noticed them, or possibly they had observed, in the ordinary course of their duties, that the rocky ascent near the shrine of Carmenta was easily practicable. In any case, one starlit night, they made the attempt. Having first sent an unarmed man to reconnoitre the route, they began the climb. It was something of a scramble: at the awkward spots a man would get a purchase for his feet on a comrade below him, then haul him up in his turn – weapons were passed up from hand to hand as the lie of the rocks allowed – until by pushing and pulling one another they reached the top. What is more, they accomplished the climb so quietly that the Romans on guard never heard a sound, and even the dogs – who are normally aroused by the least noise in the night – noticed nothing. It was the geese that saved them – Juno's sacred geese, which in spite of the dearth of provisions had not been killed. The cackling of the birds and the clapping of their wings awoke Marcus Manlius – a distinguished officer who had been consul three years before – and he, seizing his sword and giving the alarm, hurried, without waiting for the support of his bewildered comrades, straight to the point of danger. One Gaul was already up, but Manlius with a blow from the boss of his shield toppled him headlong down the cliff. The falling body carried others with it; panic spread; many more who dropped their weapons to get a better grip of the rocks were killed by Manlius, and soon more Roman troops were on the scene, tumbling the climbers down with javelins and stones, until every man of them was dislodged and sent hurtling to the bottom of the cliff.

When the excitement had died down, the garrison was undisturbed for the remainder of the night – so far as the phrase can be used of men in such a situation, unable, as they were, to think even of the past peril without a shudder. At dawn next morning the bugle summoned all ranks to parade before the military tribunes, to be rewarded – or punished – for the events of the night before. Manlius, having been commended for his brave conduct, was given presents not only by the commanding officers but by the troops as well, every one of them agreeing to take to his house in the Citadel half a pound of flour and a gill of wine. That may sound a small thing, but in the light of the general scarcity the fact that the men in order to show their appreciation of a comrade were willing to go short of necessary supplies, was a signal proof of their affectionate regard. The sentries who had been on guard and had failed to observe the enemy's ascent were then called. It was the intention of Sulpicius, one of the officers in command, to punish all of them with death, in the 'military manner'; but he was induced to change his mind by the unanimous protest of the troops, who insisted that one man only had been to blame. The rest were accordingly spared, and the single culprit, whose guilt was beyond doubt, was flung from the rock. Both verdict and punishment were universally approved. The memory of that night of peril led the Romans to keep a stricter watch; the Gauls, too, began to tighten their precautions, as it was common knowledge that messages were passing between Veii and Rome.

In both armies it was hunger that now caused more distress than anything else. The Gauls had disease as well to contend with, as the position they occupied on low ground between hills was an unhealthy one, and rendered more so by the parched conditions of the earth after the conflagrations, and the heat, and the choking clouds of ashes and dust whenever the wind blew. Such conditions were intolerable to a people accustomed to a wet, cold climate; the heat stifled them, infection spread, and they were soon dying like cattle. Before long the survivors had not the energy to bury the dead separately, but piled the corpses in heaps and burnt them. The spot where they burnt them came afterwards to be known as the Gallic Pyres.

About this time an armistice was agreed to and the commanders allowed the troops to communicate with each other. Gallic soldiers used frequently in talking to tell the Romans that they knew they were starving and ought therefore to surrender, and the story goes that the Romans, to make them believe that they were not, threw loaves of bread from various points in their lines down into the Gallic outposts. None the less the time soon came when hunger could no longer be either concealed or endured. Camillus was raising troops at Ardea, where after instructing his Master of Horse, Lucius Valerius, to bring up his men from Veii, he was busy training a force fit to deal with the Gauls on equal terms – while the beleaguered army on the Capitol waited and hoped. It was a terrible time: ordinary military duties were by now almost beyond their strength; they had survived all other ills that flesh is heir to, but one enemy – famine – which nature herself has made invincible, remained. Day after day they looked to see if help from Camillus was near; but at last when hope as well as food began to fail, and they were too weak to carry the weight of their equipment when they went on duty, they admitted that they must either surrender, or buy the enemy off on the best terms they could get – for the Gauls were already letting it be known pretty clearly that they would accept no very great sum to abandon the siege. The Senate accordingly met, and the military tribunes were authorized to arrange the terms; Quintus Sulpicius conferred with the Gallic chieftain Brennus and together they agreed upon the price, one thousand pounds' weight of gold – the price of a nation soon to rule the world. Insult was added to what was already sufficiently disgraceful, for the weights which the Gauls brought for weighing the metal were heavier than standard, and when the Roman commander objected the insolent barbarian flung his sword into the scale, saying 'Woe to the vanquished!' – words intolerable to Roman ears.

Nevertheless it was neither God's purpose nor man's that the Romans – of all people – should owe their lives to a cash payment. The argument about the weights had unduly protracted the weighing-out of the gold, and it so happened that before it was finished and the infamous bargain completed, Camillus himself appeared upon the scene.

He ordered the gold to be removed and the Gauls to leave, and answered their indignant remonstrances by denying the existence of any valid agreement; such agreement as there was had, he pointed out, been entered into after his appointment as Dictator and by an inferior magistrate acting without his instructions. The Gauls, therefore, must prepare to fight. He then ordered his troops to pile their baggage and get ready for action. 'It is your duty,' he said, 'to recover your country not by gold but by the sword. You will be fighting with all you love before your eyes: the temples of the gods, your wives and children, the soil of your native land scarred with the ravages of war, and everything which honour and truth call upon you to defend, or recover, or avenge.'

It was no place for military manoeuvre: the city was half in ruins and the ground, in any case, uneven and rough; but Camillus in his dispositions made the best of his opportunities, such as they were, and used all his experience to give the initial advantage to his own men. The Gauls were taken by surprise; arming themselves hurriedly, they attacked, but with more fire than judgement. Luck had turned at last; human skill, aided by the powers of heaven, was fighting on the side of Rome, and the invaders were scattered at the first encounter with as little effort as had gone to their victory on the Allia. A second, and more regular, engagement was fought later eight miles out on the road to Gabbi, where the Gauls had reorganized, and resulted in another victory for Camillus. This time it was bloody and complete: the

Gallic camp was taken, and the army annihilated. Camillus returned in triumph to Rome, his victorious troops roaring out their bawdy songs and saluting their commander by the well-merited titles of another Romulus, father of his country and second founder of Rome.

For Camillus it was not enough to have saved Rome from her enemies; for beyond doubt he saved her a second time now that the war was won by preventing the migration to Veii in spite of powerful opposition, both from the tribunes who, since the havoc wrought by the fires, had been more urgently pressing it, and of the people themselves who were increasingly inclined to favour it, even without the tribunes' lead. It was that reason combined with strong pressure from the Senate to stand by his country at this moment of anxious indecision that determined Camillus not to resign the Dictatorship after the celebration of his triumph. His first act in accordance with his character as a man with the strictest sense of his religious duties, was to procure a decree of the Senate authorizing first, that all sacred buildings having been in possession of the enemy, should be restored and purified – together with a re-definition of their boundaries – and that the formula of purification should be sought in the Sybilline Books by two officials appointed for the purpose; secondly, that a Treaty of Friendship and Hospitality should be made with the people of Caere in recognition of the fact that they had given asylum to Roman priests and the sacred objects of Roman religion, thereby ensuring the continuity of religious observance and worship; thirdly, that the Capitoline Games should be held, to celebrate the preservation in a time of peril, by Jupiter Greatest and Best, of his own temple and of the Citadel of Rome, the directors of the Games to be chosen by the Dictator Camillus from those who lived on the Capitol. Mention was also made of the need to expiate the guilt of ignoring the mysterious Voice which had been heard in the night prophesying disaster before the war, and for that purpose a shrine was to be built on the New Road, dedicated to the God of Utterance; the gold which had been saved from the Gauls, together with what had been taken, during the alarm, from various temples and deposited in the shrine of Jupiter, as no one could now remember precisely where it belonged, was all to be considered sacred to Jupiter and placed underneath his throne. The public sense of what was fitting in this connection had already been notably exemplified; for when it was found that there was not enough gold in the treasury to pay the Gauls the agreed sum, contributions from the women had been accepted, to avoid touching what was consecrated. The women who had contributed were formally thanked and were further granted the privilege, hitherto confined to men, of having laudatory orations pronounced at their funerals.

Camillus felt that the demands of religion were now satisfied and that he had done all that could be done through the agency of the Senate. Only then, as the tribunes were still holding continual mass meetings at which they urged the abandonment of the ruins of Rome and the migration to Veii which stood, as it were, all ready to receive them, did he make his final appeal. Escorted by the whole body of senators, he came before the people, mounted the speaker's platform and delivered the following address:

'Men of Rome, these contentions with the tribunes are so little to my taste that all the time I was in Ardea the sole comfort of my bitter exile was the fact that I was well away from the scene of them, and because of these same wretched disputes I had intended never to return – no, not though Senate and people invited me home again a thousand times. What now has forced me to come back to you is the change not in my own feelings but in your situation: the question was no longer whether or not I personally should live in my native city, but whether the city should herself remain on the spot of earth which is her own. Even now I should gladly stand aloof and hold my tongue, were not the issue at stake a national issue, to shirk which, while life remains, is for any man a crime but for me worse than a crime – a sin. Why did we save Rome from the hands of our enemies, if we are to desert her now? When the victorious Gauls had the city in their power, the gods of Rome and the men of Rome still clung to the Capitol and the Citadel – and shall we now, in the hour of victory, voluntarily abandon even those strongholds which we held through the days of peril? Shall victory make Rome more desolate than defeat? Even were there no sacred cults coeval with Rome and handed down from generation to generation, so manifest at this time has been the power of God working for our deliverance that I, for one cannot believe that any man could slack his duties of worship and thanksgiving. Only consider the course of our history during these latter years: you will find that when we followed God's guidance all was well; when we scorned it, all was ill. Remember the war with Veii – so long, so hard – and how it ended only when we obeyed the divine injunction and drained the Alban Lake. And what of this unprecedented calamity which has just befallen us? It never showed its ugly head till we disregarded the Voice from heaven warning us that the Gauls were coming – till our envoys violated the law of nations and we, who should have punished that crime, were again so careless of our duty to God as to let it pass. That is why we suffered defeat; that is why Rome was captured, and offered us again for gold; that is why we have been so punished by gods and men as to be an example to the world.

‘Evil times came – and then we remembered our religion: we sought the protection of our gods on the Capitol, by the seat of Jupiter Greatest and Best; having lost all we possessed, we buried our holy things, or took them away to other towns, where no enemy would see them; though abandoned by gods and men, we never ceased to worship. Therefore it is that heaven has given us back our city and restored to us victory and the old martial glory we had forfeited, turning the horror of defeat and death upon the enemy who, in his blind avarice for more gold, was disloyal to his compact and his plighted word. As you consider these manifest instances of the effect upon human destiny of obedience or of disobedience to the divine, can you not understand the heinousness of the sin which, though we have barely as yet won to shore from the shipwreck brought on us by our former guilt, we are preparing to commit? We have a city founded with all due rites of auspice and augury; not a stone of her streets but is permeated by our sense of the divine; for our annual sacrifices not the days only are fixed, but the places too, where they may be performed: men of Rome, would you desert your gods – the tutelary spirits which guard your families, and those the nation prays to as its saviours? Would you leave them all? Contrast this wicked thought with what Fabius did, that noble young soldier, only the other day during the siege – a deed which won the admiration of the enemy no less than your own – when braving the Gallic spears he made his way from the Citadel to the Quirinal, to celebrate there the annual sacrifice of his clan! Can you wish to abandon in time of peace our national ceremonies and our country’s gods, when you allowed no interruption of family rites even in war? Are the pontiffs and flamens to care less for the religion of our country than one man has shown himself to care for the tutelary deity of his clan?

‘It may be said perhaps that we shall perform these duties in Veii – or send our priests to perform them here. But in neither case could the proper sanctities be preserved. I cannot now make mention of all our gods, or of all our rites – but think, for instance, of Jupiter's Feast: how could his couch be decked anywhere but on the Capitol? What of Vesta's eternal fires, or of the image preserved in her shrine as a pledge of Rome's dominion? What of the sacred shields of Mars and of Quirinus, our Father? All these things you would leave behind on unconsecrated ground – sanctities as old as Rome, or older. How different we are from the men of long ago! Our fathers entrusted to us the celebration of certain sacrifices on the Alban Mount and in Lavinium: to transfer them – from enemy towns, as they were then – to Rome was felt to be impious – yet now you would take others of our own *into* an enemy town. How is that possible without sin? Remember, I beg you, how often some rite has to be performed afresh because by negligence or chance some portion of the ancient ritual has been omitted; why, only the other day, after the prodigy of the Alban Lake, it was the renewed, and perfect, performance of the holy ritual – that and nothing else – which saved our country in the struggle with Veii. Moreover, as if we still had some sense of the ancient pieties, we have given other men's deities a home amongst us, and instituted new cults of our own: Queen Juno was brought from Veii and given her temple on the Aventine – and what a day that was! Who can forget the crowds and the passionate joy of our women? We have agreed to build a shrine to the God of Utterance because of the celestial Voice which was heard in the New Road; to our other annual festivals we have added the Capitoline Games, and by the Senate's authority a new board has been set up to administer them: but what was the need of all these undertakings if we meant to leave Rome when the Gauls did – or if our remaining on the Capitol all those months of the siege was no wish of our own, but due simply to fear of the enemy?

'I speak of holy rites and holy places, but what of the priests? Surely it has occurred to you what sacrilege you are proposing to commit. The Vestal Virgins have their place – their *own* place, from which nothing but the capture of the City has ever moved them; the Flamen of Jupiter is forbidden by our religion to spend even one night outside the City walls – yet you would make them, one and all, go and live for ever in Veii. Ah, Vesta! Shall thy Virgins desert thee? Shall the Flamen of Jupiter live abroad night after night and stain himself and our country with so deep a sin?

'Remember, too, our public functions nearly all of which we transact, after due ceremony, within the pomerium, and to what oblivion and neglect we are condemning them. The Meeting of the Curies, to deal with questions of war, the Meeting of the Centuries for the election of consuls or military tribunes – where with the proper rites can these be held but in the places tradition has made sacred? Either, I suppose, we shall transfer them to Veii, or else the people will come here, to a city deserted by gods and men, just to vote at elections – a convenient alternative indeed!

'Perhaps you will reply that, in spite of all I have said, to go is still a necessity: circumstances compel it – Rome is rubble and ashes, Veii stands unharmed: we cannot lay the burden of rebuilding upon our helpless and impoverished people. But I think you know even without my telling you that such an argument is only an attempt to justify yourselves, aware, as you are, that this question of migrating to Veii was discussed before the invasion, while every house, every temple and public building of Rome was still as perfect as on the day it was built. But oh! what a gulf there is, in this whole business, between the tribunes and me! As for them, they believe that even if the migration was inadvisable then, it is inescapable now; I, on the contrary – and do not be surprised till you understand my meaning – am convinced that even if it was right to consider going while Rome still stood, to abandon her ruins now would be grievously wrong. And why? Because then the reason for our going to live in a captured city would have been our victory – something for ourselves and our posterity to be proud of; but now such a removal is for us a wretched and shameful thing – the Gauls, not we, will glory in it, for it will be only too clear that we have not left our native city as conquerors, but lost it by defeat. The world will think that the rout on the Allia, the capture of Rome, and the siege of the Capitol have forced upon us the bitter necessity of deserting our beloved homes and of condemning ourselves to flee as exiles from a spot we had not the strength to defend. Must it be seen that Gauls could tumble Rome to the ground, while Romans are too weak to lift her up again? And suppose they come back, with a second army – for everyone knows that their numbers are almost beyond belief: suppose they want to settle here, in this city they captured and which you deserted – what could you do but let them? Or maybe your old enemies the Aequians or Volscians might take it into their heads to do the same – and how would you like to change nationalities with *them*? Surely you would rather Rome were your own wilderness than built again to house your enemies – a thing which in my view, at least would be an outrage to the deepest feelings upon which patriotism rests. I cannot believe that you would commit so shameful a crime simply because you shrink from the labour of restoring these ruins; even if it were impossible to build here anything better or bigger than Romulus's Hut, surely it would be nobler to live like country shepherds amongst everything we hold sacred than to go into universal exile, deserting the gods of our hearths and homes. Those herdsmen long ago and that rabble of refugees, when there was nothing here but forest and swamp, made short work enough of building a new town – but we today, when the temples are still standing and the Capitol and Citadel intact, cannot bring ourselves to rebuild what the fires have destroyed! Shall we refuse as a nation to do what any one of us would have done if his own house had been burned down?

'Suppose some fool, or some knave, should set Veii on fire – suppose the wind spread the flames and half the town were destroyed – what should we do then? Move on to Fidenae, or Gabii, or anywhere else we could find? So it seems – if indeed the soil of our native city and the earth we call our mother have so weak a hold upon us that our love of country is co-extensive with timber and stone. Men of Rome, I do not like to recall the wrong you did me, but I confess to you that whenever, in my absence, I thought of my country, what I saw in my mind's eye were these hills and plains, the Tiber and this beloved countryside, and the familiar sky under which I was born and bred. I can but hope that the love of these things will move you now to stay, and that the loss of them will not, in after years, tear your hearts with vain regret. Not without reason did gods and men choose this spot for the site of our City – the salubrious hills, the river to bring us produce from the inland regions and sea-borne commerce from abroad, the sea itself, near enough for convenience yet not so near as to bring danger from foreign fleets, our situation in the very heart of Italy – all these advantages make it of all places in the world the best for a city destined to grow great. The proof is the actual greatness – now – of a city which is still comparatively young; Rome, my friends, is 365 years old, and throughout those years you have been at war with many ancient peoples, yet – not to speak of single enemies – not the united strength of the powerful townships of the Aequians and Volscians, not the combined might of the armies and navies of Etruria, whose vast domains occupy the breadth of Italy from sea to sea, has ever been a match for you in war. What then in the devil's name makes you want to try elsewhere, when such has been your fortune here? Should you go, I grant you may take your brave hearts with you, but never the Luck of Rome. Here is the Capitol, where, in the days of old, the human head was found and men were told that on that spot would be the world's head and the seat of empire; here, when the Capitol was to be cleared of other shrines for the sake of Jupiter's temple, the two deities Juventas and Terminus refused, to the great joy of the men of those days, to be moved; here are the fires of Vesta, the sacred shields which fell from heaven, and all our gods who, if you stay, will assuredly bless your staying.'

Camillus's oration is said to have moved his hearers, especially those parts of it which touched upon religion, but it was not decisive; what finally settled the matter was the chance remark of a centurion on duty. Soon after Camillus had ended, the Senate was holding a debate in the Curia Hostilia, and some soldiers returning from guard-duty happened to pass through the Forum; as they reached the Comitium, their centurion gave the order to halt, adding, 'we might as well stop here'. The words were heard in the Senate House; the senators hurried out exclaiming that they accepted the omen, and the crowd in the street signified its approval. The proposal for the migration was rejected, and the rebuilding of the city began.

The work of reconstruction was ill-planned. Tiles were supplied at the state's expense; permission to cut timber and quarry stone was granted without any restrictions except a guarantee that the particular structure should be completed within the year. All work was hurried and nobody bothered to see that the streets were straight; individual property rights were ignored, and buildings went up wherever there was room for them. This explains why the ancient sewers, which originally followed the line of the streets, now run in many places under private houses, and why the general lay-out of Rome is more like a squatters' settlement than a properly planned city.

Maps of Latium
and Rome

LATIUM

and the surrounding
country

Miles

0   20

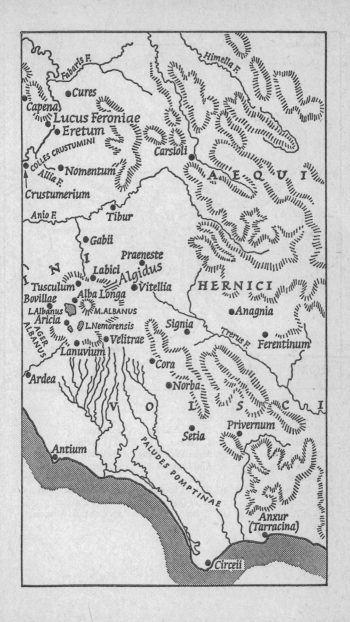

ROME

SUGGESTIONS FOR FURTHER READING

LIVY

P. G. Walsh, *Livy: His Historical Aims and Methods*, Cambridge University Press, 1961

Sir Ronald Syme, *Harvard Studies in Classical Philology*, 1959

Gordon Williams, *Tradition and Originality in Roman Poetry*, Oxford, 1969

THE EVIDENCE

E. Badian in *Latin Historians* (ed. T. A. Dorey), Routledge & Kegan Paul, 1966, pp. 1–38

A. Alföldi, *Early Rome and the Latins*, Ann Arbor, 1965

THE HISTORY

A. Alföldi, *Early Rome and the Latins*, Ann Arbor, 1965

R. Bloch, *The Origins of Rome*, Thames & Hudson, 1960

A. H. McDonald, *Republican Rome*, Thames & Hudson, 1967

M. Pallottino, *The Etruscans*, Penguin Books, 1955

A. Momigliano, 'An Interim Report on Early Rome', *Journal of Roman Studies*, 1963

E. Gjerstad, *Early Rome I–IV*, Lund.

J. B. Ward-Perkins and others, *Papers of the British School at Rome*, 1961

R. M. Ogilvie, *A Commentary on Livy 1–5*, Clarendon Press, 1965 (second revised edition 1970)

R. Bloch, *Tite-Live et les premiers siècles de Rome*, Paris, 1965

INDEX

Actium, battle of, 8, 54
Acutius, tribune, 352
Adriatic Sea, 35, 379
Aebutius Cornicen, Postumus, consul, 282
Aebutius Helva, Marcus, commissioner, 282
Aebutius Helva, Postumus, Master of the Horse, 293
Aebutius, Lucius, consul, 189, 190
Aebutius, Titus, consul, 125–6, 127
Aedui, Gallic tribe, 379, 380
Aelius, Publius, quaestor, 329
Aelius Tubero, Quintus, Roman historian, 12, 294
Aemilius, Gaius, military tribune, 370, 373, 374, 377
Aemilius, Lucius, consul, 153, 163, 164, 168
Aemilius Mamercus, Manlius, military tribune and dictator, 288–91, 294–6, 302, 303–7, 314, 337, 341, 351, 354
Aemilius, Marcus, military tribune and consul, 328, 377
Aemilius, Titus, consul, 176, 177, 183
Aeneas, 34, 35; and Antenor, 18; and Anchises, 18; travels, 35; fights Latinus, 35; builds Lavinium. 36; has son, 36; fights Rutuli and Etruscans, 36; death, 36, 37
Aequians, hill-people, 24–5, 93–4, 138–40, 151, 153–4, 158, 161–3, 168, 173, 175, 177, 179, 183–9, 192–5, 200–201, 203, 206, 208–12, 215, 217–18, 225, 230, 247, 250, 257–8, 262–4, 269, 271, 277, 296–7, 301, 308, 316, 317, 319–21, 323, 324, 328, 330–31, 359, 368, 373–4, 375, 377, 400, 401
Aequicolae, pre-Roman tribe, 69

Aequimaelium, site of Spurius Maelius's house, 287
Aesis, river, 380
Agrippa, king of Alba, 37
Alba, king of Alba Longa, 37
Alba Longa, 17, 40, 55, 57, 62, 63, 66, 68, 359; founded, 37; control passed to Numitor, 39; excess of population, 40; fall of, 67; Albans, 40, 57–61, 64–6, 91, 274; Alban hills, 17, 18, 37, 68, 360, 399; Alban knights, 67; Alban Lake, 358, 359, 360, 362, 397, 399; valley of Alba, 190; Alban Wood, 358
Albinius, pious plebeian, 386
Albinus, Lucius, tribune, 142
Albula, river (later the Tiber), 37
Alienus, an aedile, 218
Algidus, town, 184, 185, 210, 212, 214, 216–18, 225, 230, 231, 250, 252, 254, 260, 297, 298, 302, 319, 377
Allia, river, 383, 385, 395, 400
Alps, the, 35, 378–9, 380
Ambarri, Gallic tribe, 379
Ambitgatus, king of the Bituriges, 379
Ameriola, Latin town, 77
Amulius, king of Alba, 37, 39, 40
Anchises, father of Aeneas, 35
Ancient Latins, see Priscus Latinus
Ancus Marcius, fourth king of Rome, 19, 69, 71, 72, 73, 78; sons of, 79–80
Anio, river, 24, 63, 74, 76, 123, 132, 141, 178, 289, 293
Antemnae, neighbouring settlement to Rome, 44–6
Antenor, 18, 34–5
Antiates, inhabitants of Antium, 195, 208, 390

Index

Index